The Industrialisation of Soviet Russia Volume 7: The Soviet Economy and the Approach of War, 1937–1939

R. W. Davies · Mark Harrison
Oleg Khlevniuk · Stephen G. Wheatcroft

The Industrialisation of Soviet Russia Volume 7: The Soviet Economy and the Approach of War, 1937–1939

palgrave
macmillan

R. W. Davies
Centre for Russian, European, and Eurasian Studies
University of Birmingham
Birmingham, UK

Mark Harrison
Department of Economics
University of Warwick
Coventry, UK

Oleg Khlevniuk
National Research University Higher School of Economics
Moscow, Russia

Stephen G. Wheatcroft
School of Historical and Philosophical Studies
University of Melbourne
Melbourne, Australia

ISBN 978-1-137-36237-7 ISBN 978-1-137-36238-4 (eBook)
https://doi.org/10.1057/978-1-137-36238-4

Library of Congress Control Number: 2018939734

Cover illustration: Victor Koretsky, 'If there's war tomorrow…' (1938). Image courtesy of Stephen White, used with permission.

Printed on acid-free paper

This Palgrave Macmillan imprint is published by the registered company Macmillan Publishers Ltd. part of Springer Nature
The registered company address is: The Campus, 4 Crinan Street, London, N1 9XW, United Kingdom

To Michael and Lucia

Preface

This volume concludes *The Industrialisation of Soviet Russia*. The series aims to provide an authoritative history of the Soviet Union's industrial transformation between 1929 and 1939 in seven volumes. R. W. Davies has been the author or co-author of every volume from the first, which appeared in 1980. When he envisaged the series, the world looked very different from today. The Soviet Union was a global superpower, the Cold War was in full swing, and the leaders of many countries emerging from poverty looked to the Soviet Union for military and economic assistance and advice. The writing of Russian history was also different from today, for the Soviet archives of the period were entirely closed to independent researchers. The world has changed and the writing of Russian history has also changed. In concluding our series, we are able to look back on the Soviet economy as a more passing phenomenon than appeared at the time, although one that has left indelible traces in the modern world. Today we can also look back with far more complete knowledge than we dreamed about in the 1970s, based on millions of pages of formerly secret official reports, investigations, and memoranda, including the private letters of Stalin, Molotov, Kaganovich, and other Soviet leaders.

Volumes 1–3 of our series narrated the sweeping transformations that Stalin set in motion in 1929 and 1930: the collectivisation of 25 million peasant farms, and the centralisation of the entire economy under a hierarchy of plans and quantitative controls. These changes were aimed at securing the basis of an immense national effort to industrialise the country and modernise its economic and military power. While great steps were now taken towards these goals, the immediate result was a great crisis that spread across both town and countryside. In the context of unexpected harvest shortfalls in 1931 and 1932, Stalin's policies brought about a famine that carried away up to six million lives. The evolution of that crisis was recounted in Volume 4 and 5.

In the middle years of the decade, that is, from 1934 to 1936, the crisis receded. The harvest returned to a more normal level in 1933, and this was followed by a more general recovery. The recovery was promoted by a turn away from the extremes of 1929 and 1930. The more moderate policies of the mid-1930s included greater toleration of private farming and food markets, the limitation of repression and violence directed at managers and industrial specialists, and a more stable, predictable policy framework. This allowed not only the recovery of agriculture and food distribution but also the belated completion of many projects begun in earlier years. There was an upsurge of industrial production and productivity. The progress of this period, described in Volume 6, was remarkable.

The present and final Volume 7 covers the years 1937–1939. In contrast to the progress of the economy in the mid-1930s, the events we describe are darker in tone. Our period is dominated by war preparations. It begins with the Great Terror and concludes with the German-Soviet pact of 1939 and the outbreak of the Second World War in Europe. In this context, many chapters display common themes: the Soviet leaders' growing sense of war threats, the mobilisation of the society and economy against both internal and external enemies, the forced expansion of industrial production and particularly of war production, and the resources poured into capital projects to increase the country's industrial and defence capacities. In the absence of significant further growth of the economy's aggregate production, there was increased compulsion of labour of detainees held in camps under grim conditions, employees in factories and offices and of peasants in collective farms were increasingly regimented, and living standards were placed under severe pressure.

Surprisingly, perhaps, this is not the entire story of our book. Its chapters also describe factors at work in the economy that fell outside the party leaders' sphere of control. Among these uncontrolled influences were ordinary people. At work they were often recalcitrant or pushed back against the heavy hand of regulation; they also persisted in being born, reproducing, and dying at rates that fell outside government projections. Foreign governments and international markets behaved unpredictably, sometimes to the frustration of party plans and directives, sometimes bringing unexpected opportunities for gain. One of the greatest forces that resisted Soviet rule was nature, which continued to exert more influence over the Soviet harvest than the planners.

Our book is organised chronologically and thematically. Chapter 1 sets out the extent of the mass repressions of 1937 and 1938, their possible causes, and their economic consequences. Chapter 2 describes the changes in the Soviet political and ideological order that accompanied the repressions, from the growing sense of war threat to the increasingly extreme centralisation of Stalin's authority. Chapter 3 traces the economic impact of repression in the sudden slowdown of the planned economy during 1937. Chapter 4 then examines the various branches and activities making up the economy in 1937. While the year was largely dominated by the struggle against internal and external enemies, there was also an unexpected bonus: good weather and a record harvest.

Chapter 5 turns to a different aspect of 1937, the population census held that year, the disappointing results of which led to a collision between demographic expertise and political authority. As the chapter recounts, a second census was held in 1939 with a quite different outcome.

Chapter 6 reviews developments through 1938. The narrative starts from the collapse of the state's capacity to plan the economy under the pressure of purges and continues through the subsequent rebuilding of the planning process. The economy's main branches and activities are considered, apart from agriculture. Chapter 7 is devoted to agricultural developments through 1939. The common thread of this story is the state's struggle to regain control over grain surpluses, temporarily lost after the 1937 harvest, paving the way to increased restriction of private farming activities.

Chapter 8 considers the state of the economy in early 1939 as the Soviet leaders prepared for and then held the eighteenth party congress. At the congress, Soviet leaders thought aloud about the third five-year plan, the requirements of economic modernisation, the threat of war, and the need for increased regimentation of the workforce in both state industry and collective agriculture. Chapter 9 summarises the further developments of the economy in 1939 under the impact of the additional measures for war mobilisation taken at the time. The second half of 1939 was dominated by the sudden warming of Soviet-German relations and the opening of the Soviet economy to German trade as the Second World War began.

Chapter 10 concludes the book, and the series, with a retrospective view on the industrialisation of the Soviet economy in the 1930s. It considers the pattern of forced industrialisation, the measures of its progress that were made available at the time, the extraordinary militarisation of a mobilised society and economy, the emergence of the Soviet Union as a global military power, and the scope for reforms within the system that Stalin created and ruled over. To finish, we ask what kind of economic development this was.

***

Many people and organisations have contributed to the research for this volume, and we owe thanks to all of them. Various institutions have provided financial and other support. Professor Davies thanks the Centre for Russian, European, and Eurasian Studies of the University of Birmingham; he remains grateful to the Economic and Social Research Council of the UK for its past support of the Soviet Industrialisation Project, the foundation of the present series. Professor Harrison thanks the Department of Economics of the University of Warwick and its ESRC Centre for Competitive Advantage in the Global Economy. Professor Khlevniuk thanks the Basic Research Program at the National Research University Higher School of Economics of the Russian Federation and the Russian Academic Excellence Project '5-100' for research funding. Professor Wheatcroft thanks the University of Melbourne, Nazarbayev University, Hokkaido University, and Deakin University, and the Australian Research Council for funding under Discovery Project 120104384.

Our work would have been impossible without access to the wonderful resources of the Russian state archives. We thank the directors and staff of the Archive of the President of the Russian Federation (APRF), the State Archive of the Russian Federation (GARF), the Russian State Economic Archive (RGAE), and the Russian State Archive of Social and Political History (RGASPI), for their sincere cooperation and unmatched expertise. We extend the same gratitude to the British National Archives and their director and staff.

We have been blessed in our colleagues and friends, who have freely given their time and experience to help us. We are deeply grateful to

Mike Berry, who at the last minute dropped everything to assist with the final preparation of the text; and to Leonid Borodkin, Mikhail Denissenko, Jane Gatrell, Ian Gazeley, Yoram Gorlizki, Amanda Gregg, Saulius Grybkauskas, Paul Gregory, Melanie Ilič, Viktor Kondrashin, Debin Ma, Joe Maiolo, Andrei Markevich, Mikhail Nakonechnyi, Steven Nafziger, Evgeny Rebrov, Arfon Rees, Ivan Rodionov, and Filip Slaveski. We thank Nicky Vinti for permission to use her photograph in the Afterword. We have tried the patience and valued the assistance of our editors, Molly Beck and Oliver Dyer, and of our production manager, Subasree Sairam, and we are grateful to them too. Finally, we thank those nearest to us for their love and support through our project: Anne, Dasha, Maurice, Nicky, and Ragini.

Birmingham, UK	R. W. Davies
Coventry, UK	Mark Harrison
Moscow, Russia	Oleg Khlevniuk
Melbourne, Australia	Stephen G. Wheatcroft

Contents

About the Authors

R. W. Davies is Emeritus Professor of Russian Economic Studies at the University of Birmingham. He is the author of *The Development of the Soviet Budgetary System*; *Foundations of a Planned Economy, 1926–1929*, vol. 1 (with E. H. Carr); *Soviet History in the Gorbachev Revolution*; *Soviet History in the Yeltsin Era*; *Soviet Economic Eevelopment from Lenin to Khrushchev*; and the six preceding volumes of *The Industrialisation of Soviet Russia*: vol. 1, *The Socialist Offensive: The Collectivisation of Soviet Agriculture, 1929–1930*; vol. 2, *The Soviet Collective Farm, 1929–1930*; vol. 3, *The Soviet Economy in Turmoil, 1929–1930*; vol. 4, *Crisis and Progress in the Soviet Economy, 1931–1933*; vol. 5, *The Years of Hunger: Soviet Agriculture, 1931–1933* (with Stephen G. Wheatcroft); and vol. 6, *The Years of Progress: The Soviet Economy, 1934–1936* (with Oleg Khlevniuk and Stephen G. Wheatcroft).

Mark Harrison is Professor of Economics at the University of Warwick, a research associate of Warwick's ESRC Centre on Competitive Advantage in the Global Economy, and a senior research fellow of the Centre for European, Russian, Eurasian Studies, University of Birmingham. He is the author of *Soviet Planning in Peace and War 1938–1945*; *The Soviet Home Front, 1941–1945: A Social and Economic History of the USSR in World War II* (with John Barber); *Accounting for War: Soviet Production, Employment, and the Defence Burden, 1940–1945*; *The Economics of World War II: Six Great Powers in International Comparison* (editor); *The Soviet Defence Industry Complex from Stalin *to Khrushchev* (editor with John Barber); *The Economics of World War I* (editor with Stephen Broadberry); *Guns and Rubles: The Defense Industry in the Stalinist State* (editor); *The Economics of Coercion and Conflict*; and *One Day We Will Live Without Fear: Everyday Lives Under the Soviet Police State.*

Oleg Khlevniuk is Professor of History at the National Research University Higher School of Economics, Russian Federation, and leading research fellow of its International Centre for the History and Sociology of World War II and its Consequences. He is author of *The Stalin–Kaganovich Correspondence, 1931–1936* (with R. W. Davies, E. A. Rees and others); *The History of the Gulag from Collectivization to the Great Terror*; *Master of the House: Stalin and His Inner Circle*; and co-author of vol. 6, *The Years of Progress: the Soviet Economy, 1934–1936* (with R. W. Davies and S. G. Wheatcroft) of the present series.

Stephen G. Wheatcroft is Professor of History at Deakin University and a Professorial Fellow and Associate of the University of Melbourne. He is editor and co-author of *Challenging Traditional Views of Russian History*; *Materials for a Balance of the Soviet National Economy, 1928–1930* (with R. W. Davies); and *The Economic Transformation of the Soviet Union, 1913–1945* (with R. W. Davies and Mark Harrison); and co-author of vol. 5, *The Years of Hunger: Soviet Agriculture, 1931–1933* (with R. W. Davies) and vol. 6, *The Years of Progress: The Soviet Economy, 1934–1936* (with R. W. Davies and Oleg Khlevniuk) of the present series.

List of Tables

Chapter 4

Chapter 5

CHAPTER 1

The Repressions of 1937–1938 and the Soviet Economy

The opening of the Soviet archives has enabled us to obtain a much more accurate understanding of the character and scope of the terror, its various phases and their interconnection. From the beginning of 1936, on Stalin's initiative, the treatment of the former members of the party oppositions changed for the worse (Vol. 6: 281–283). In previous years many of them were expelled from the party, and some were confined to prison or exiled. But many others were given posts in the party or in government departments. In 1936, however, measures were prepared and enforced which indicated that the whole group was to be eliminated. The visible manifestations of these repressions were the public trials of August 1936 and January 1937. Early in 1937 a general purge of senior economic officials was launched, extending well beyond the former oppositionists, and this was accompanied by an attack on the middle ranks of the official strata more generally, including leading personnel in the regions. This continued during 1937 and 1938 and, on a reduced scale, in the last two and a half years before the war.

These developments may be categorised as the *nomenklatura purge*. The *nomenklatura* was a list (or rather a set of lists) of posts, appointments to which were approved by the party. Such lists existed at many levels of the hierarchy and in every region. By extension, Soviet officialdom has often been called 'the nomenklatura.' We had a general understanding of the nomenklatura purge of the late 1930s before the opening of the archives, because many of its actions were reported in the press at

R. W. Davies et al., *The Industrialisation of Soviet Russia Volume 7: The Soviet Economy and the Approach of War, 1937–1939*,
https://doi.org/10.1057/978-1-137-36238-4_1

the time or were publicised after Stalin's death.[1] But almost nothing was known about the *mass purges* of the same period which, including the 'mass operations' against 'anti-Soviet elements' and 'counter-revolutionary nationalist groups' undertaken between August 1937 and November 1938, involved the execution, imprisonment, or deportation to remote areas of over a million Soviet citizens.

The nomenklatura purge and the mass purges were linked. These were not chaotic events. Initiated and planned by the top leadership, they were carried out on the basis of decrees issued in Moscow. These circumstances are crucial to an attempt to ascertain the causes and impact of the terror. Purges and terror were utilised to a greater or lesser extent throughout the Stalin era. Within the interwar period, markedly different phases of repressions can be distinguished. Intensive repression took place during the Civil War, in the years of 'the great breakthrough' from 1928 to 1933, and during the terror of 1936–1938. In 1928–1933 and 1936–1938 political repression involved the concoction on a large scale of plots and conspiracies against the regime attributed to those arrested. On the other hand, during 1922–1927 and 1933–1935 a much more calculated and moderate policy was pursued. In these periods the political leadership placed less emphasis on the use of extra-judicial violence to solve problems, and switched to a relatively more sophisticated policy.[2] But the terror of 1936–1938 was far more intensive and violent than previous repressive measures, and requires a special explanation.

1 The Nomenklatura Purge

There are little or no grounds for the view that economic difficulties impelled the leadership to launch the nomenklatura purge in 1936.[3] This was a year of unparalleled industrial development, and grain stocks were sufficient to enable the state to overcome the consequences of the bad harvest of 1936 without large-scale famine. However, Stalin and the

[1] Conquest (1968).

[2] See *Australian Journal of Politics and History*, 53(1) (2007): 20–43 (S. G. Wheatcroft). This article shows that during the periods of intensive repression Ye. G. Yevdokimov (a central figure in the Shakhty trial of Soviet and foreign engineers and managers in 1928) and his associates played a major role.

[3] See Ilič, ed. (2006): 11–37 (R. W. Davies). For a contrasting viewpoint see Getty and Manning (1993): 116–117 (R. T. Manning).

other leaders had unrealistic hopes that the economy might expand even more rapidly, and Stalin was evidently convinced that young, more vigorous and Soviet-educated staff could give the economy a new impulse. The older generation of economic managers and politicians had been through the extreme tensions of rapid industrialisation and agricultural disaster; the belief among this élite that Stalin had a large share of the responsibility for the economic crisis and famine of 1932–3 may have been widespread. Stalin himself certainly believed that hostility from the established economic and political leaders was threatening his dictatorship in conditions where the danger of aggression by Germany and Japan was growing rapidly more acute. He warned early in 1937 that the capitalist countries 'are encircling the Soviet Union and awaiting the opportunity to attack it, to destroy it, or at the very least to disrupt its strength and weaken it.'[4]

While the nomenklatura purge had its own grim logic, it was by no means an inexorable consequence of previous developments. There is no evidence that a major purge of economic and political officials was being prepared before the autumn of 1936. At the June 1936 council of the Commissariat of Heavy Industry, People's Commissar Ordzhonikidze explicitly praised the loyalty and hard work of his officials, and Kaganovich took the same attitude to the staff of the Transport Commissariat. In the Commissariat of Heavy Industry only a handful of enterprise directors were dismissed in 1935 and the first seven months of 1936, and only nine of these were arrested.[5] At the February–March 1937 plenum which launched the nomenklatura purge, Yezhov complained, 'I do not know a single fact when on their own initiative they rang me up and said "cde. Yezhov, something is suspicious about this person".' Molotov, the prime minister, noted that the Commissariats of Light Industry and Water Transport had failed to expose a single wrecker.[6] Similar remarks were made by participants in the plenum. Gurevich, deputy Commissar of Heavy Industry responsible for the metal industries, summed up the general view:

[4] Speech at the February–March plenum of the Central Committee, March 3, 1937 (*Voprosy istorii* (1995), no. 3: 5).

[5] Ilič, ed. (2006): 40 (Khlevniuk).

[6] *Voprosy istorii* (1994), no. 2: 21; *Voprosy istorii* (1994), no. 8: 2.

> Among managers there are attitudes that wrecking is on a relatively small scale and affects only a few industries, and that therefore it is not necessary to give too much attention to wrecking.[7]

Even Mikoyan acknowledged that the idea that a Communist could blow up his own power stations 'did not enter my head'.[8] Voroshilov took the same attitude to the military. At the meeting of the Military Council in October 1936 almost nothing had been said about wrecking, and even at the February–March 1937 plenum Voroshilov reported with some pride 'our great delight' that in the armed forces 'so far not many enemies have been exposed'.[9]

All the evidence shows that cases against wreckers were initiated by the NKVD, with support and pressure from Stalin. The repressions greatly increased after Yezhov took over the commissariat in September 1936. The number of 'members of anti-Soviet and Trotskyite organisations and groups' in the state administration who were condemned between October 1, 1936, and March 1, 1937, amounted to 2020 persons out of a Central Committee nomenklatura covering approximately 30,000 government officials across the various people's commissariats and other central agencies[10]:

- Heavy Industry and Defence Industry: 585 persons
- Education: 228
- Light Industry: 141
- Transport (mainly railways): 137
- Agriculture (mainly collective farms and machine-tractor stations): 102
- Food Industry: 100
- Water Transport: 88
- Internal Trade: 82
- Academy of Sciences and higher education establishments: 77
- Editorial boards and publishing houses: 68
- Local Industry: 60
- Health: 64

[7] *Voprosy istorii* (1994), no. 1: 21.

[8] *Voprosy istorii* (1994), no. 6: 16.

[9] *Voprosy istorii* (1994), no. 8: 5–6. No army engineers had been found to be wreckers by this date, and 'only' six generals.

[10] *Voprosy istorii* (1994), no. 8: 18.

- Timber Industry: 62
- Communications: 54
- State Farms: 35
- Finance: 35
- Courts and procuracy: 17
- Staff of the Soviets: 65.

Staff of the Commissariat of Heavy Industry accounted for 29% of the arrests listed above. These followed the arrest of the former Trotskyite Pyatakov, who was Ordzhonikidze's first deputy. The public trial of the 'anti-Soviet Trotskyite centre,' arraigning Pyatakov and his associates, took place between January 23 and 30, 1937, and was very widely publicised in the Soviet press and abroad (the English translation of the verbatim report of the trial is a huge volume of 585 pages).[11] Eleven of the 17 officials who were put on trial worked in the Commissariat of Heavy Industry. They included Rataichak, who until his arrest had been head of the chemical industry, and also the Kuzbass officials allegedly responsible for the Kemerovo explosion in September 1936 and for arranging delays in the construction of the chemical combine in Kemerovo. Kaganovich's second-in-command in the Commissariat of Transport, Lifshits, was another prominent person accused, and three other leading officials of Transport were also put on trial.

Ordzhonikidze accepted these developments at first. In September 1936, he joined in the condemnation of Pyatakov, and he did not criticise the public trial of the 'anti-Soviet Trotskyite centre' in January 1937. But he was increasingly unenthusiastic, and in the last two weeks before his death he made a valiant attempt to halt the mounting repression of economic officials. He sent out three commissions instructed 'to distinguish intentional sabotage from inadvertent mistakes'.[12] One, headed by Gal'perin, went to Kemerovo, and presented a detailed report which made no mention of sabotage or wrecking. A second, headed by Osipov-Shmidt, one of Ordzhonikidze's deputies, was sent to investigate the coking-chemical industry in the Donbass, and reported back in similar terms. The third, headed by Ginzburg and Pavlunovskii, went to Uralvagonstroi, a major engineering plant in Nizhnyi Tagil. According to

[11] *Report of Court Proceedings* (1937).

[12] *Za industrializatsiyu*, September 21, 1937 (Professor N. Gal'perin).

Ginzburg's memoirs, his commission reported to Ordzhonikidze by telephone that the factory had been 'well built, without shoddiness'.[13] These reports constituted a counter-indictment of the NKVD campaign against alleged wreckers. Ordzhonikidze reported these findings to Stalin. But matters were taken no further. On February 18, Ordzhonikidze committed suicide (or may have been murdered).[14]

In public, Ordzhonikidze's death, supposedly from 'heart failure', was appropriately commemorated, and the Central Committee's plenum was delayed for his funeral. The plenum assembled from February 23 to March 5. Its major topics were the Bukharin-Rykov case, which moved further towards their trial and execution; preparations for the elections to the Supreme Soviet established by the constitution of December 1936; and 'Lessons from wrecking, diversion and espionage by Japanese, German and Trotskyite agents'. Under separate items the plenum dealt with wrecking in the Commissariats of Heavy Industry and Transport, introduced by lengthy reports from Molotov and Kaganovich, and wrecking in the NKVD itself, introduced by Yezhov. All these reports were directed at showing that, contrary to the prevailing view, wrecking was very widespread. Molotov emphasised the wide range of wrecking activities in the Commissariat of Heavy Industry which, he asserted, were taking place in the chemical and coal industries, 'a number of branches of the engineering industry, including a number of branches of the defence industry', and the construction of power stations. He did not confine himself to heavy industry. 'Wrecking acts' had also taken place in light industry, 'although we have not yet gone into this matter properly', in the Commissariats of Communications and of State Farms, and in the banks. He politely described the commission to Uralvagonstroi as headed by 'our respected comrades and major managers' Ginzburg and Pavlunovskii, but strongly criticised its findings. He emphasised that the construction manager Mar'yasin and party secretary Okudzhava had already been exposed as wreckers:[15]

> The commission travelled out to Uralvagonstroi as recently as February to check what had been happening there and concluded 'wrecking activity at the site did not develop greatly.' (*Voices from the floor*: Did not develop?

[13] *Voprosy istorii KPSS* (1991), no. 3: 91–92.

[14] For further details of these events, see Khlevniuk (2009): 157–165.

[15] This Mar'yasin is not the former head of Gosbank named in Table 1.

Table 1 The nomenklatura purge by dates: turnover of heads of economic departments of the central government, 1936–39

Date	*Agency*	*Name*	*Circumstances of departure*
1936			
July 24	Gosbank	Mar'yasin	Arrested later
Oct.1	Timber Industry	Lobov	Arrested later
Summary for 1936: 2 removals			
1937			
Feb. 18	Heavy Industry	Ordzhonikidze	Suicide
Apr. 11	State Farms	Kalmanovich	Arrested
May 23	TsUNKhU (statistics)	Kraval'	Arrested
June 14	Foreign Trade	Rozengol'ts	Arrested later, Oct. 1937
June 25	Health	Kaminskii	Arrested
July 22	State Farms (second occasion)	Demchenko	Arrested
Aug. 4	Agricultural Procurements	Kleiner	Arrested
Aug. 16	Finance	Grin'ko	Arrested
Aug. 16	Communications	Khalepskii	Arrested later, Nov. 1937
Aug. 21	Commission for Soviet Control	Antipov	Arrested
Sept. 9	Light Industry	Lyubimov	Arrested later, Sept. 24, 1937
Sept. 15	Gosbank (second occasion)	Kruglikov	Already arrested, Sept. 11, 1937
Oct. 15	Defence Industry	Rukhimovich	Arrested
Oct. 17	Gosplan	Smirnov, G. I.	Arrested
Oct. 17	Foreign Trade	Veitser	Arrested
Oct. 29	Agriculture	Chernov	Arrested
Oct. 31	Timber Industry (second occasion)	Ivanov, V. I.	Arrested
Nov. 19	State Committee for the Higher School	Mezhlauk, I. I.	Arrested
Dec. 1	Gosplan (second occasion)	Mezhlauk, V. I.	Arrested
Dec. 4	TsUNKhU (second occasion)	Vermenichev	Arrested
Summary for 1937: 20 removals. In addition, Yakovlev, former commissar of agriculture and chief of the Central Committee's Agricultural Department, was arrested on October 12			
1938			
Jan. 15	Justice	Krylenko	Arrested
Jan. 19	Finance (second occasion)	Chubar'	Arrested later, July 4, 1938

(continued)

Table 1 (continued)

Date	*Agency*	*Name*	*Circumstances of departure*
Apr. 5	Transport	Bakulin	Arrested later, July 23, 1938
Apr. 8	Water Transport	Pakhomov	Arrested
Apr. 29	Agriculture (second occasion)	Eikhe	Arrested
May 3	Commission for Soviet Control (second occasion)	Kosior, S. V.	Arrested
May 5	Agricultural Procurements (second occasion)	Popov, M. V.	Arrested
June 24	Food Industry	Gilinskii	Arrested
June 29	Machine Building	Bruskin	Arrested
July 16	Trade (second occasion)	Smirnov, P. A.	Arrested
July 16	Gosbank (third occasion)	Grichmanov	Arrested
July 16	Health (second occasion)	Boldyrev	Arrested
July 29	Timber Industry (third occasion)	Ryzhov	Arrested
Nov. 22	State Farms (third occasion)	Yurkin	Dismissed, not arrested
Nov. 29	Foreign Trade (second occasion)	Chvyalev	Arrested later, April 1939
Dec. 24	Communications (second occasion)	Berman	Arrested
Summary for 1938: 16 removals. In addition, Rozengol'ts, Chernov, and Grin'ko were sentenced to death at the Bukharin trial on March 13, 1938			
1939			
Jan. 11	Defence Industry (second occasion)	Kaganovich, M. M.	Removed, suicide July 1, 1941
Apr. 23	Commission for Soviet Control (third occasion)	Belen'kii (acting)	Arrested later, Aug. 16, 1938
May 3	Foreign Affairs	Litvinov	Dismissed, not arrested
Summary for 1939: 3 removals			

Source Terms of appointment and biographical data from *Soviet Government Officials* (1989); *Gosudarstvennaya vlast'* (1999); *Sovet narodnykh komissarov* (1999).

> Nonsense. Did not develop?) … Comrades from Narkomtyazhprom [the Commissariat of Heavy Industry], shouldn't you check again both Mar'yasin and the commission which travelled out there? (*Voices from the floor*: Hear! Hear!)

In his reply to the discussion, Molotov also strongly criticised the Gal'perin commission to Kemerovo, which had produced a 54-page report that did not even use the words 'wrecker' and 'wrecking,' and the Osipov-Shmidt commission to the Donbass, which suffered from the same defect. He concluded that 'very many of our officials are politically backward.' Molotov's contributions to the plenum made a very strong call for further vigilance: 'It is our duty to meet blow with blow, to destroy everywhere the detachments of infiltrators and demolition men from the fascist camp who get in our way.' Contradicting Voroshilov, he insisted that it was 'complacency' to think that there were no wreckers in military industry, and he forebodingly remarked of the military generally that 'we will not check its work now, but somewhat later its work will be checked very strongly.'[16]

Kaganovich, who had obediently abandoned his conciliation of the specialists, took the same harsh attitude.[17] Mikoyan also repudiated his own previous views, insisting:

> It is necessary to deliver a most decisive blow, and to cleanse so that this cleansing should guarantee us for many years from any possibility of repeating these outrages.[18]

Stalin, in his speech of March 3, predicted disaster in the event of war if potential saboteurs were not dealt with:

> To mess things up and do harm does not need a large number of people. To construct Dneprostroi, tens of thousands of workers had to be involved. To blow it up needs perhaps several dozen people, no more. To win a battle in wartime may need several corps of Red Army men. To prevent this success on the front, a few spies somewhere in the army staff or

[16] *Voprosy istorii* (1993), no. 8: 3–26 (Molotov's report); (1994), no. 8: 17–28 (reply to the discussion).

[17] *Voprosy istorii* (1993), no. 9: 3–32.

[18] *Voprosy istorii* (1994), no. 6: 20.

> even in the divisional staff would be sufficient, they could steal the plan of operations and hand it over to the enemy. To build a large railway bridge needs thousands of people. But to blow it up only a few people are needed. Dozens and hundreds of such examples could be given.
>
> Therefore one should not console oneself by thinking that we are many and the Trotskyite wreckers are few.
>
> We must make sure that there are no Trotskyite wreckers in our ranks.[19]

Stalin and Molotov were careful to provide some hope to those previous oppositionists who knew themselves to be innocent of wrecking. Stalin rejected the notion of condemning 'anyone who on some occasion walked down the road with some Trotskyite, or who on some occasion somewhere had a meal in a canteen next to a Trotskyite', and assured the plenum that some former Trotskyites were now 'good workers' and 'real Bolsheviks'. Molotov cited positively the example of the successful aero-engine factory in Perm which was headed by a former Trotskyite who had recruited other former Trotskyites to work with him.[20]

But the main thrust of the plenum was to launch the very widespread and far-reaching nomenklatura purge, which continued to the end of 1938 and beyond.[21] Most of the arrests took place without publicity, but between March 5 and 12, 1938, the trial of Bukharin, Rykov, Yagoda and 18 others was reported in great detail and caused an international sensation. The trial reflected the deep inroads into the existing economic structure which had been made in the course of 1937. Those arraigned included Grin'ko, Chernov and Rozengol'ts, the experienced economic administrators who had headed the Commissariats of Finance, Agriculture and Foreign Trade. But those arraigned in public were a small minority of the high-level economic leaders removed and executed. Of the twenty people's commissars and their equivalent concerned with the economy in the summer of 1936, only two remained at the beginning of 1939: Mikoyan and Kaganovich. Ordzhonikidze committed suicide, and the remaining 17 were arrested and executed. As Table 1 shows, two commissars or their equivalent were removed in 1936, 21 in

[19] *Voprosy istorii* (1995), no. 3: 13–14. This passage appears in the version of Stalin's speech published in *Pravda*, March 29, 1937.

[20] *Voprosy istorii* (1993), no. 8: 18–19; (1995), no. 11–12: 12.

[21] For a more detailed account of the purges of economic officials, see Ilič, ed. (2006): 38–67 (Khlevniuk).

1937, 16 in 1938, and three in 1939 (in 1940 there were none). These figures include some posts which were rotated two or three times.

The carnage was equally widespread at the level immediately below the commissars. In Heavy Industry, all the heads of chief administrations but one, Ginzburg, were removed during 1937 and 1938, and nearly all of those removed were arrested and executed.[22] Similar sweeping changes took place in most of the other commissariats. In the Commissariat of Foreign Trade, according to Mikoyan, 'not a single person remained of the 46 who were deputy commissars or members of the collegium in the period from 1930.'[23] Of the 73 Central Committee members who spoke at the February–March plenum, 50 were executed in the Stalin years, nearly all of them by 1940, two more after Stalin's death, and two committed suicide.[24]

The repression of directors of trusts, factories and major construction sites whose posts were listed in the Central Committee nomenklatura was somewhat more restrained, but the numbers were still remarkably high. Precise figures are not available, but the extent of the purge is indicated by the number of new appointments made during 1937 and 1938. Table 2 shows that, of the 32,899 posts on the nomenklatura of state officials at the beginning of 1939, 15,485, or 47%, were appointed within the previous two years, including 45% of directors of industrial enterprises. On the railways, by November 1938 as many as 2245 out of 2968 senior posts (76%) were occupied by persons appointed since November 1, 1937.[25] By the end of the purge, the nomenklatura was a mixture of long-established cadres who had survived the purge and younger people who had been rapidly promoted to fill the positions left by alleged wreckers.

[22] Ilič, ed. (2006): 55 (Khlevniuk). Ginzburg was expelled from the party in October 1938, but reinstated in January 1939.

[23] Mikoyan (1999): 337.

[24] Zavenyagin was one of the few to be dismissed and survive. Head of the Magnitogorsk combine from 1933 to 1937, then promoted to deputy Commissar of Heavy Industry, he was dismissed from this post on March 17, 1938. On March 22 he wrote to Molotov, 'I would work with interest in the Far North or Siberia for many years.' On April 4, 1939, he was appointed head of construction for the Noril'sk nickel combine of the NKVD, and in 1941 became a Deputy People's Commissar in the NKVD; see *Sovetskoe rukovodstvo* (1999): 392.

[25] *Zheleznodorozhnyi transport (1926–1941)* (1970): 309 (report dated November 17, 1938).

Table 2 The nomenklatura purge by numbers: Soviet and economic agency employees included in the Central Committee nomenklatura at the beginning of 1939, by date of appointment

	Total number	*Of which, newly appointed, 1937–1938* *Number*	*Per cent of total*
People's commissars of the USSR and RSFSR, heads of chief administrations, and chairmen of committees of Sovnarkom (USSR and RSFSR)	70	29	41.4
Deputies of the above	125	77	61.6
Heads of chief administrations and associations of People's Commissariats of USSR and RSFSR	548	366	66.8
Deputies of the above	617	355	57.5
Directors of trusts	1,130	637	56.4
Deputies of the above	971	477	49.1
Directors of industrial enterprises	6,394	2,895	45.3
Deputies of the above, heads of technical departments, and chief engineers	3,637	1,704	46.9
Directors of machine-tractor stations and state farms	3,369	1,204	35.7
Chiefs of construction projects	278	117	42.1
Deputies of the above and chief engineers	188	66	35.1
Chiefs of railways, shipping companies, and water basin managements	101	56	55.4
Deputies of the above and service chiefs	394	191	48.5
Managers of provincial branches of the State Bank	2,656	1,036	39.0
Total	32,899	15,485	47.0

Note The exact date to which the table refers is not given, but was probably January 1, 1939. For comparison with the 15,485 (41.5% of the total) appointed over the two years 1937 and 1938, just 5693 persons (17.3%), were appointed over the three years from 1934 to 1936. The categorisation of the nomenklatura in this table is not exhaustive. In all, approximately 40,000 people were sentenced by the military tribunal of the USSR Supreme Court in 1937 and 1938 (Ilič, ed. (2006): 45 (Khlevniuk)).
Source RGASPI, 477/1/41: 82–84; see also Ilič, ed. (2006), 57 (Khlevniuk).

2 The Mass Purge

Historians differ on whether the mass purges were, to a greater extent than the nomenklatura purge, an inevitable consequence of previous developments. The two principal Western investigators of the background to the mass purges, Paul Hagenloh and David Shearer, differ in their conclusions. Both agree that the decision to launch the purges was taken by Stalin personally. Hagenloh maintains that 'the mass purges were not an abrupt change in policy on Stalin's part but rather the culmination of years of regime policies towards population groups deemed to be "dangerous" to the security of the state.'[26] Shearer at first assessed the repressions 'as a response to an ongoing crisis of social order', but later revised this view, and concluded that they were 'a prophylactic response' to the threat of a 'potential uprising in case of invasion'. He draws attention to Yagoda's report to Sovnarkom in March 1936, which concluded that, with some significant exceptions, the problem of social disorder had been resolved.[27]

Statistical trends are not conclusive. Some indicators suggest that repression was diminishing. The 131,168 arrests carried out by the NKVD in 1936 were not only fewer than in 1935 (193,083 arrests) but the smallest number since 1930. The same was true of the 1118 death sentences in 1936 (compared with 1229 in 1935). All these figures were the lowest since 1930. On the other hand, the numbers sentenced to imprisonment in camps and exile increased in 1936 from 219,447 to 243,137, the latter figure being a record high. This increase resulted from the decision to accelerate the sentencing of those arrested but not put on trial in previous years, and from a decline in the use of lighter sentences.[28]

Were the mass purges an inevitable result of the nature of the repressive system which had emerged in the USSR by the mid-1930s? Whatever we conclude, Hagenloh and Shearer are obviously correct in one respect: it was Stalin who took the decision to launch the mass purge in July 1937 (though he was of course able to take this decision because historical and systemic prerequisites in the USSR made this possible), and to wind down the purges in the autumn of 1938. In embarking on the mass purge, he was influenced by considerations similar to those which guided the launch of the nomenklatura purge a few months earlier. The presence in the Soviet Union of large numbers of former kulaks and other disgruntled peasants, and of many other secret opponents

[26] Hagenloh (2009): 283–284.

[27] *Cahiers du Monde russe*, 39(1–2) (1998): 119–148 (D. Shearer); 42(2–4) (2001): 506 (Shearer); Shearer (2009): especially 240–242. For Yagoda's report see GARF, 5446/18a/904. For the Great Terror as Stalin's preventive war against the 'fifth column', see Cooper et al. eds. (1995): 158–176 (O. V. Khlevniuk).

[28] *Istoriya Stalinskogo Gulaga*, 1 (2004): 609.

of the regime, was seen as a threat to its stability. The preamble to the top-secret NKVD Order no. 00447 'On the operation to repress former kulaks, criminals and other anti-Soviet elements', which launched the mass purge, and was submitted to the Politburo by the NKVD on July 30, 1937, listed with some precision the groups seen as a potential danger to the regime. These included various categories of former kulaks, former members of anti-Soviet parties, Whites, former tsarist policemen, priests and sectarians, and various categories of criminals. The preamble to the order grimly concluded that 'this whole gang of anti-Soviet elements' must be 'destroyed in the most merciless fashion'. 'At last, once and for all time finish with their base disruptive work against the foundations of the Soviet state.' The order stated specifically that people in these categories should be exiled or executed if they engaged in anti-Soviet activity, but this restriction was greatly modified by a final blanket category which gave very wide powers to the security services:

> 9. All the categories listed above shall be subject to repression if they are at present in the countryside—in kolkhozy, sovkhozy and agricultural enterprises—or in the towns—in industrial and trading enterprises, in transport, in Soviet establishments and in construction.[29]

A particular feature of Order no. 00447 was the speedy investigation and determination of individual cases. The typical investigation was concluded in a few weeks. In most cases the prisoner had to fill in a questionnaire, and witnesses were called to testify to anti-Soviet behaviour. But the witnesses were under great pressure to provide the required evidence. As for outcomes, the order established a *troika* (a committee of three named officials) for each of the 64 main provinces of the USSR, responsible for adjudicating cases 'with expedition and in a simplified manner'. This provision allowed cases to be considered in the absence of the accused, without the presumption of innocence, and without the rights of defence or appeal. This resembled the procedures in the nomenklatura purge, but was greatly abbreviated. At the end of the

[29] For the text of the order, see *Lubyanka* (2004): 274–281. The order was approved by the Politburo on the following day (ibid., 281–282). For a translation of Order no. 00447, see Getty and Naumov (1999): 471–478.

investigation a troika would sentence several hundred people in a single sitting.[30] Nearly all those arrested were condemned.

The necessity of a simplified process is readily understood in the context of the initial targets of the order.[31] These envisaged that within four months 75,950 persons would be executed, and a further 195,000 sent to camps and prisons. In an average week, therefore, the typical troika (each of whose members already had a full-time job), while meeting for a few hours at most, was expected to consider 250 cases, issue 70 death sentences, and fix the terms of detention of the rest.

During the next months, the mass operations were extended and the quotas were greatly increased. Under Order no. 00447 alone, up to November 1938, 386,798 persons were eventually executed, and a further 380,599 sentenced to incarceration in camps.[32] Meanwhile, further operations were undertaken by the NKVD on Politburo authority against suspected persons belonging to national minorities, especially Poles and Germans. The 'national operations' were carried out by a particularly simplified procedure. Whereas arrests under Order no. 00447 were subject to quotas (*limity*) decided centrally for each province, no quotas were fixed for the national operations. Lists of names were compiled in the localities and sent to the centre for approval (this procedure was modified, however, in the last two months of the purge). In the national operations a particularly high proportion of those arrested was executed (64% on average, compared with 50% for Order no. 00447).

The total number of sentences in all the purges in 1937 and 1938, reported in Table 3, was approximately 1.3 million, half of them executed and most of the remainder imprisoned in labour camps. The total number executed amounted to 0.4% of the total population, or 0.67% of the population aged over sixteen years, and was equal to two-thirds of the number of citizens of the Russian Empire directly killed in military action during the First World War. Both in the First World War and in the purges the overwhelming majority of those killed were men.

The study of records of victims of the purges is at an early stage. The records are plentiful but require caution. Grounds for arrest were based on information that the NKVD assembled from its own records

[30] For full documentation of the case of a single individual who worked in a kolkhoz as a smith, see Yunge et al. (2008): 352–401.

[31] On the logic of 'simplified methods', see Gregory (2009): 202–218.

[32] Yunge et al. (2008): 598.

Table 3 The mass purges, 1937–1938: numbers arrested and sentenced

	Executed	*Detained in camps and exile*	*Total*
Total arrested by NKVD	–	–	1,575,259
Total sentenced	681,692	653,028	1,334,720
Of which			
—Under Order no. 00447	386,798	380,599	767,397
—Under 'national' operations	247,157	88,356	335,513
Subtotal	633,955	468,955	1,102,910
—Other (including nomenklatura purge)	47,737	184,073	231,810

Note The first two rows of the table show that the number of those arrested exceeded the number sentenced by more than 240,000. The fate of those arrested but not sentenced is not certain. Not more than 30,000 were released; others were sentenced later or died or were killed before they could be sentenced.
Source Totals arrested and sentenced from *Istoriya Stalinskogo Gulaga*, 1 (2004): 609. Arrested under Order no. 00447, from Jansen and Petrov (2002): 103. Under national operations, from *Repressii protiv polyakov* (1997): 33 (N. V. Petrov and A. B. Roginskii). The subtotal is the sum of the two preceding rows. Other (sentenced by judicial and non-judicial bodies other than troiki): this is a residual category, subtracting the subtotal from the total number sentenced.

and from other local agencies. In three provinces of Ukraine (Donetsk, Stalinsk and Voroshilovgrad), for example, 16,204 of the 18,018 condemned were recorded as having a 'colouring' (*okraska*—a taint from their past activity or social position): 49.5% had been kulaks, traders or their children, 23.2% had been White Guards or had committed counter-revolutionary crimes, 13.4% criminals or recidivists, and 4.3% members of counter-revolutionary parties.[33] This corresponds very broadly to the categories specified in Order no. 00447. The remaining 1814 had no record of a 'doubtful' past.

The aggregate data shown in Table 4 show the reported social composition of nearly 1.4 million people arrested in cases that went through some form of investigation in 1937 and the first half of 1938, alongside data for 1936 for comparison.[34] Care is required to understand the numbers, for the classification allowed a person's current employment status (e.g. 'manual worker'), which would have been relatively straightforward, to be overridden by judgements of family background or social

[33] Yunge et al. (2009): 827–828 (Nikol'skii).

[34] The origin and exact meaning of these figures is discussed in Harris, ed. (2013) (S. G. Wheatcroft).

Table 4 The mass purges, 1936–July 1938: persons under NKVD arrest and investigation by former social status and current occupation (numbers and per cent)

	Numbers			*Per cent*		
	1936	*1937*	*1938 (Jan.–July)*	*1936*	*1937*	*1938 (Jan.–July)*
Persons under arrest and investigation, total	131,168	914,542	473,637	100.0	100.0	100.0
Of which						
Classified by former social status						
'Former kulaks'	–	367,530	151,894	–	40.2	32.1
Other 'former people'	–	113,739	74,519	–	12.4	15.7
All 'former' elements, subtotal	35,229	481,269	226,413	26.9	52.6	47.8
Classified by current occupation						
Office workers	41,009	129,250	90,440	31.3	14.1	19.1
Manual workers	22,973	42,563	39,464	17.5	4.7	8.3
Collective farmers	12,869	40,142	28,383	9.8	4.4	6
Military personnel	2,840	11,406	6,300	2.2	1.2	1.3
Security personnel	1,945	3,679	3,113	1.5	0.4	0.7
All state employees and collective farmers, subtotal	81,636	227,040	167,700	62.2	24.8	35.4
Individual peasants	8,425	25,731	13,443	6.4	2.8	2.8
Artisans	0	7,221	8,543	0.0	0.8	1.8
Religious servitors	–	33,191	11,186	–	3.6	2.4
Persons without identified employment and déclassé elements	–	127,047	38,011	–	13.9	8
Other and unspecified	5,878	13,043	8,341	4.5	1.4	1.8
All self-employed, unemployed, and priests, subtotal	14,303	206,233	79,524	10.9	22.6	16.8

Note Other 'former people' are 'former landowners, gentry, traders, gendarmes, etc.' Manual workers are workers in industry and transport, and seasonal agricultural and other workers. Office workers are engineering and technical staff; scientists; teachers; doctors; workers in literature and the arts; agricultural technicians; other office workers. Military personnel are senior Red Army commanders and political commissars; Red Army soldiers, junior officers, and trainees; Red Army administrative staff. Security personnel are NKVD operative workers; operative workers of the militia. 'Other and unspecified' includes housewives and pensioners.

Source Tables B.1 and B.2, somewhat rearranged. Figures for 1937 and the first half of 1938 are those labelled (B) in the source.

status that were formed in previous waves of political mobilisation and social strife (former kulak). Many of those classed as 'former kulaks', for example, were now employed in the socialist economy as members of collective farms or, having fled the countryside, as manual or office workers in state-owned enterprises.[35]

In 1936, the last year before the Great Terror, Table 4 suggests, an absolute majority of those investigated was made up of people working in the socialist economy in various capacities: industrial and transport workers, office workers, and collective farmers. In 1937/38 the numbers arrested in all categories increased absolutely, and in some categories much more than others. But during the mass and national operations the emphasis shifted, apparently, to 'socially alien elements' such as former kulaks, traders, and landowners, and the unemployed. Despite the pejorative label, however, most 'socially alien elements' were actually employed in the socialist economy at the time of their arrests. If we look instead at the numbers categorised as 'without gainful employment and déclassé elements' (which might correspond roughly with the unemployed and unemployable), we find relatively small numbers (although still a large number absolutely), no more than 14% of all cases in 1937, for example. A wider concept of those outside the socialist sector, adding independent farmers, artisans, and priests to the unemployed and 'déclassé elements' still yields less than one-quarter (22.6%) of cases in 1937.

This pattern is confirmed in local reports, which tended to show that large majorities of those arrested were engaged in collective farms or state organisations and enterprises at the time of arrest.[36]

[35]This is made clear by data on the social origins and current occupations of the 14,876 persons sentenced by the troika in the mainly agricultural Altai region between October 30, 1937, and March 15, 1938. On a 5% sample, 80.3% of those sentenced were classed by origin as 'former kulaks'. When reclassified by current occupation, however, an even larger majority, 85%, was now employed in the socialist sector as collective farm and state farm workers, or as manual and office workers, teachers, doctors, and paramedics. Yunge, Bordyugov, and Binner (2009): 719–745 (G. D. Zhdanova).

[36]This applied to 57.7% of the 79,000 persons arrested in Ukraine in 1937 for whom records are available (Yunge, Bordyugov, and Binner (2009): 832–833 (V. N. Nikol'skii)). In the Krasnoozero district of Western Siberia, an agricultural area, 79% of the 178 people arrested in 1937–8 were collective or state farm workers, and 6% were office workers employed by the state. In the Prikam'e region, which was highly industrialised, 61% of the 8000 people arrested were manual or office workers; among the farm workers (26%), individual peasants were not distinguished from collective and state farm workers. Yunge, Bordyugov, and Binner (2009): 610 (O. L. Leibovich). For Mordoviya, see Ilič, ed., 178–179, 182–183 (M. Ilič and C. Joyce).

Given that most victims were snatched from regular employment, it is natural to ask whether they were in fact hostile agents, as the regime suspected, who had wormed their way into the Soviet collective farm and factory with the purpose of disrupting production and politics, or were they, rather, in the process of adjusting themselves to the new order? On the assumption typically applied by Soviet historians, an arrival from the countryside would have assimilated to the factory within a few years. How far those arrested would have settled into kolkhoz or factory life if they had not been arrested requires further investigation. A Russian historian who studied industrial workers arrested in the Prikam'e (now Perm) region concluded:

> Whoever the repressed persons may have been before they arrived at the factory, in 1937 they were already real workers with five or six years' service. In the factory brigades and sections they worked together with skilled and free workers. Even those who were formerly in special settlements had become part of the working class in their way of life and in their social circle, and in their social and economic situation.[37]

The mass purges caused great human suffering, affecting not only the victims but also their families and friends. Their 'effectiveness' in producing an orderly society is very doubtful. David Shearer concludes that 'legal, judicial, and social-order institutions of Soviet society were in nearly complete disarray' at the end of the purges and that 'disruption caused by the purges recreated the conditions of social chaos that mass social cleansing was supposed to remedy.'[38] And there is no evidence that the sudden removal of part of the labour force in a factory or kolkhoz led to an improvement in labour discipline or in industrial efficiency generally.

3 The Effect of the Repressions on the Economy

While the effect of the mass purges on the economy as a whole has not yet been clearly established, it is certain that the nomenklatura purges were an important factor in the deterioration of economic performance

[37] Yunge et al. (2009): 183 (A. N. Kabatskov).

[38] Shearer (2009): 369–370.

in industry, transport, and construction.[39] A significant slowdown in the economy began in the last quarter of 1936 (Vol. 6: 313). It is tempting to conclude that this was due to the removal of key figures: Pyatakov in heavy industry, Lifshits on the railways, and Mar'yasin at Gosbank. In each case the arrest of the key figure was accompanied by a wave of arrests of their officials.[40] The less successful performance of the economy continued in the following years.

The waves of arrests led to a pronounced shortage of qualified and experienced personnel and were closely accompanied and followed by a deterioration in economic performance.[41] In the coal industry, arrests of senior personnel were so extensive in the first few months of 1937 that in March the deputy head of the Commissariat of Heavy Industry's Chief Coal Administration complained to his superiors of the 'complete collapse of work' in the mine construction trust Shakhtostroi. Two months later he complained that no work had been done in the trust for five months because the whole board of the trust had been arrested.[42] Arrests were widespread throughout the industry. Coal output per day declined steadily in the months January–May 1937, and did not recover to the level of December 1936 until November 1937.[43]

According to David Hoffmann, who has made an extensive study of Moscow in this period, 'labor discipline deteriorated rapidly with the onset of the purges (as shown by a marked increase in worker absenteeism and tardiness), and resulted in a substantial fall in factory production.'[44]

A study of the work of Lenenergo, the Leningrad electric power trust, in 1937–38, made by A. P. Vorob'ev, deputy director of the trust from 1937 to 1968, reaches similar conclusions. According to Vorob'ev,

[39] For a previous attempt to establish the point, see the *Journal of Economic History*, 35(3) (1975): 567–590 (B. G. Katz). This paper, which was pioneering for its time, but necessarily relied on a handful of annual observations of low-quality data, concluded that the industrial slowdown that became marked in 1938 was better explained by the incidence of repression than by the pattern of rearmament.

[40] For the railways, see Rees (1995): 154–156; for heavy industry, see Vol. 6: 294.

[41] On the shortage of qualified personnel, see Ilič, ed. (2006): 58–61 (Khlevniuk).

[42] RGAE, 7566/1/2753: 115 (Kagan to Gurevich, letter dated March 7, 1937) and 55–53 (Kagan to Zavenyagin, letter in two versions, one undated, the other dated May 21, 1937).

[43] *Osnovnye pokazateli* (November 1937): vi.

[44] Getty and Manning, eds. (1993): 166 (D. Hoffman).

Lenenergo over-fulfilled its plan in 1936, and so had fulfilled the second five-year plan in four years. But at the end of May 1937 the chief engineer shot himself, and in mid-June the director of the trust was arrested, followed by the heads of power stations and trust departments. By the end of 1937 all directors and chief engineers in the power stations, and the heads of the Lenenergo departments, had been replaced. This resulted in 'complete lack of preparedness for the autumn-winter load of 1937–8'. In October–December 1937 the production of electric power declined, and the number of accidents increased.[45]

In March 1939, a few months after the end of the Great Purge, a certain M. Pakhomov claimed in an outspoken letter to Stalin:

> If last year and now the majority of industries has not fulfilled their plan, the cause of this is our weak cadres, who were promoted to leading work during the past year ... The atmosphere of lack of confidence and over-suspiciousness in the relations between people and at work is not at all justified ... Such an atmosphere and the over-suspiciousness blunts the initiative and energy of the personnel, and has an extremely harmful effect on all the work.[46]

Evidently the removal of very large numbers of experienced economic officials and engineers was a major factor in this deterioration.[47]

The impact of the purges on agriculture is less clear. On one hand, as we will see, the agricultural officials were purged with the same murderous enthusiasm as elsewhere in the machinery of state. On the other hand, it is not possible to identify any immediate effect on agricultural production, which improved sharply in 1937 under favourable weather conditions. This does not mean that agriculture was unaffected by repression. The story that we will tell below (in Chapters 4 and 7) shows how repressive policies affected the composition of activities and the distribution of the produce, rather than the volume of production.

[45] *Leningradskii martirolog*, 5 (2002): 549–555.

[46] RGASPI, 17/120/336: 9–16; this letter to Stalin was forwarded to Zhdanov by Stalin's assistant Poskrebyshev.

[47] There are counter-examples. In the Belomor combine, where purges of the officials were particularly intense in 1937, the amount of timber felled more than doubled, while the labour force increased at a slower pace. For data see Baron (2007): 177, 285.

CHAPTER 2

The Political Context of Economic Change: 1937 to the Spring of 1939

1 The Advance of German and Japanese Aggression

These years saw the relentless advance in Europe of Nazi Germany, increasingly supported by fascist Italy, and of militarist Japan in China. Their advances were countered by the considerable efforts of the Soviet Union, supported by anti-fascists in the democracies, to establish 'collective security', in alliance with Britain and France, against Nazi aggression in Europe, and to stem the Japanese advance by supporting an uneasy alliance between the Guomindang (nationalists) and the communists in China. Led by Stalin's foreign minister, Litvinov, and broadly supported by Stalin himself, the struggle for collective security secured popular support in Europe and achieved some notable successes both in Europe and the Far East. But it was undermined by Stalin's own repressions, which reached beyond the Soviet Union itself into the Comintern and the heart of the Spanish Republic. Eventually the Soviet Union utterly failed to secure the support of the French and British governments against Hitler, and their support, together with the United States, against Japan. The Munich agreement in October 1938, by which Britain and France acquiesced in the dismemberment of Czechoslovakia, was followed within six months by the collapse of the Spanish Republic and the seizure of the whole of Czechoslovakia by Nazi Germany. The dismissal of Litvinov on May 3, 1939, foreshadowed a turn in Soviet foreign policy towards

R. W. Davies et al., *The Industrialisation of Soviet Russia Volume 7: The Soviet Economy and the Approach of War, 1937–1939*,
https://doi.org/10.1057/978-1-137-36238-4_2

accommodation with Nazi Germany and led to the conclusion of the Molotov Ribbentrop agreement in August.

In fact, the Soviet search for collective security was marked by periodic efforts to improve relations with Germany. One such attempt took place at the beginning of 1937. The efforts were made by David Kandelaki, Stalin's personal emissary, appointed as the Soviet Union's commercial attaché in Berlin, meeting with Hjalmar Schacht, Hitler's minister of economics. Following one such meeting, a draft document prepared by Litvinov, and endorsed by Stalin, declared on January 8 that the Soviet government had nothing against 'political negotiations with the German government ... in the interests of improving mutual relations and general peace'. But following a further meeting between Kandelaki and Schacht, on February 11, the German foreign minister instructed Schacht that Hitler considered that such negotiations 'will not lead to any result'. In the course of the next few weeks further attempts by the Soviet side to improve relations came to nothing: on March 21 the Soviet ambassador in Germany reported that Schacht 'whispered to me (literally whispered) that he does not at present see any prospect for a change in our relations'.[1] Two weeks later Kandelaki was removed from his post as trade attaché in Germany.[2]

In Spain during 1937 the insurgent forces, while failing to capture Madrid, seized Malaga, Bilbao and Guernica. By November their advance compelled the Republican government to move from Valencia to Barcelona. Throughout 1937 Litvinov continued his efforts to win over the Western powers to collective security. On May 28 and September 21, in powerful addresses to the General Assembly of the League of Nations, he warned about the growing threat to peace of the aggressive powers.[3] On November 27, addressing his electors in Leningrad, he denounced the 'three states which show no restraint in publicly, loudly, day in and day out proclaiming their resolve to accept no international laws ... their resolve to annex other people's territory,

[1] *Voprosy istorii* (1991), no. 4–5: 150–152; this account, based on Soviet foreign policy archives, is chronologically confused but what happened emerges clearly.

[2] *Izvestiya*, April 2, 1937. The ambassador was transferred to France (*Voprosy istorii* (1991), no. 4–5: 152). Schacht also lost his influence: in November 1937 he was removed from the post of minister of economics and in January 1939 from the presidency of the Reichsbank.

[3] Litvinov (1939).

wherever they can'.[4] He secured the active support of an increasing number of people in Western Europe, and on October 5 Roosevelt called, in what became a famous speech, for 'an end to acts of international aggression', and a 'quarantine' against world lawlessness, which he compared to a disease.[5]

But Roosevelt's hands were tied by the prevailing American mood of isolationism. And in Europe the prospect for collective security was increasingly unpromising. Action in support of Spain by the Popular Front coalition in France was restricted by the caution of the Radical Party, and in June the Popular Front lost power for a time. In Britain the chances of action against Hitler were even less favourable. At a meeting of the Cabinet on January 8, the Home Secretary Sir Samuel Hoare, who had distinguished himself as foreign secretary in 1935 by his appeasement of the Italian invasion of Abyssinia, complained that 'we appeared to be getting near a situation where, as a nation, we were trying to stop General Franco from winning. That was the desire of the Parliamentary Parties of the Left; but there were others, including perhaps some members of the Cabinet, who were very anxious that the Soviet should not win in Spain. It was very important to hold the scales fairly.'[6] Two months later at the Cabinet there were complaints that a daily BBC bulletin about Spain 'resulted in pressure being put by constituents on members of parliament'; if the BBC could be induced to drop these nightly statements this 'would have a quietening effect'. The Cabinet also agreed that 'the raising of the Abyssinian massacres in the House of Commons' should be avoided in the foreign affairs debate on the following day.[7] The course towards appeasement was strengthened by the appointment of Neville Chamberlain as prime minister in May.

Towards the end of 1937 the fascist powers took further steps towards war. On November 5, Hitler met military and political leaders in secret; he stated his determination to 'solve the German problem of space at the latest by 1943–45', after which time the situation would otherwise turn against Germany; and that the first step must be to take over Austria

[4]Haslam (1984): 151–152 (citing *Pravda*, November 28, 1937).

[5]Haslam (1992): 96.

[6]National Archives, CAB/23/87 (January 8, 1937).

[7]National Archives, CAB/23/88 (March 24, 1937).

and Czechoslovakia.[8] On November 6, Italy joined the Anti-Comintern Pact, and left the League of Nations a month later. The British government was complacent. The British ambassador to Germany, Sir Neville Henderson, after attending the Nuremberg rally (September 6–13), reported that 'Germany does not want adventure,' and that he had been told by von Neurath, the Foreign Minister, 'Austria is the first and last of our aims,' and the question of the German minority in the Sudetenland could be amicably settled 'if Czechoslovakia left the Russian orbit'.[9] Shortly afterwards, Lord Halifax, who was to be appointed secretary of state for foreign affairs after Eden resigned in February 1938, met Hitler and reported to the British Cabinet that Hitler had said of Czechoslovakia that 'she only needed to treat the Germans living within her borders well and they would be entirely happy.' Halifax concluded that 'the Germans had no policy of immediate adventure.'[10]

While the civil war in Spain was at its fiercest, full-scale war broke out between China and Japan following a clash on July 7, 1937, between Chinese and Japanese forces on the Marco Polo Bridge near Beijing. Japanese troops were located there on the basis of the treaties signed by the Chinese early in the century, following the Boxer rebellion. The Soviet Union soon offered its support to the Guomindang against the Japanese aggression. On August 21 a non-aggression pact was signed between China and the Soviet Union, and on September 14 the Soviet Union supplied a loan to China for the purchase of Soviet arms, later supplemented by further substantial loans.[11] An uneasy truce was secured between the Guomindang and the Communists in September; the Communist troops were at least nominally incorporated into the Chinese forces as the Eighth Route Army.[12] Some of the Soviet arms supplied to China were allocated to the communists. On November 11 Stalin met Dimitrov and three Chinese Communist leaders in the Kremlin, and Stalin strongly supported the idea of a unified Chinese national front against the Japanese:

[8] *Documents on German Foreign Policy*, D-1 (1949): 29–39 (minutes of conference in the Reich chancellery, Berlin, November 5, 1937: the Hossbach memorandum).

[9] National Archives, CAB 24/271 (September 12, 1937).

[10] National Archives, CAB 23/90a (November 24, 1937).

[11] *VKP(b), Komintern, i Kitai* (2007): 22–23; Safronov (2001): 180–181.

[12] *VKP(b), Komintern, i Kitai* (2007): 22–24.

(1) Now the main thing for the Chinese Communist party is to join the war of the whole nation and take a leading part.
(2) Now the most important thing is the war—not the agrarian revolution or the confisc[ation] of land.

He insisted that China must develop its own defence industry, including the production of aircraft and tanks, for which the Soviet Union could supply materials: 'If China has its own war industry, no one will be able to defeat it.'[13]

The Soviet Union was not much more successful in the Far East than in Europe in establishing collective security against aggression. No practical support for China was forthcoming from the other powers. The USA and other countries were constrained by business interests in Japan. Between November 3 and 24, 1937, a lengthy international conference in Brussels got nowhere. During the conference Shanghai was captured by the Japanese and Nanking was under threat; its seizure in December was accompanied by a massacre of the civilian population.[14]

In 1938 the Nazi drive to war accelerated. On March 12 Germany invaded Austria and incorporated it as a province of the Third Reich. Five days later, at a press conference, Litvinov described the German action as 'force carried out in the centre of Europe, creating an indubitable danger for ... all European states, and not merely for European states', and reiterated that the Soviet government was willing 'to enter immediately into discussions with other powers, within the League of Nations or outside it'.[15] But any possibility of joint action was blocked by the Chamberlain government, still intent on compromise with Hitler. In the next few months Britain, with France at her tail, moved towards putting pressure on Czechoslovakia to relinquish the Sudetenland. At a meeting of the British cabinet following Chamberlain's meeting with Hitler at Berchtesgaden, Lord Runciman, who had been negotiating informally on behalf of the government, reported that 'the transfer of the [Sudeten] area to Germany would almost certainly be a good thing,' and that 'the Czechs were, in fact, themselves responsible for most of the trouble.' Chamberlain stated that he 'had formed the opinion that

[13] *VKP(b), Komintern, i Kitai* (2007): 74–75, as recorded by Dimitrov. Stalin added: 'When (the war) finishes, the question will arise of how to fight among themselves!'.

[14] Haslam (1992): 96–102; Safronov (2001): 193.

[15] *Dokumenty vneshnei politiki*, 21 (1977): 128–129; also Haslam (1984): 165.

Table 1 Soviet armaments supplied to Spain, 1937–1939 (units)

	October 1, 1936, to August 1, 1937	*December 14, 1937, to August 11, 1938*	*December 26, 1938, to January 28, 1939*	*Total*
Aircraft (all types)	496	152	0	648
Tanks	322	25	0	347
Armoured cars	60	0	0	60
Artillery pieces	714	469	3	1,186
Machine guns	12,804	4,910	2,772	20,486
Rifles (thousands)	338	125	35	498

Source Rybalkin (2000): 45.

Herr Hitler's objectives were strictly limited'; Hitler had declared that 'he regarded his boundary with Poland as being definitely fixed.'[16] On September 29 the Munich Agreement transferring the Sudetenland to Germany was signed by Germany, Britain, France and Italy; Czechoslovakia and the Soviet Union were not invited to the meeting.[17]

In the meantime the insurgents advanced in Spain against stubborn resistance by the Republicans. The Republican defence was hindered by internal dissension which was intensified by the active intervention of the NKVD, and by the diminution and temporary cessation of Soviet arms supplies (see Table 1).[18] In April the Republic was split in two by the insurgents. The insurgents were temporarily halted by resistance on the river Ebro near Madrid, but eventually broke through in November. The end came rapidly. The insurgents seized Barcelona on January 26, 1939, and Madrid on March 28. But even before the surrender of Madrid the British government recognised the Franco regime as legitimate.

In China the Guomindang, supported by substantial military supplies from the Soviet Union, resisted further Japanese advances in 1938. After months of battle, however, at the end of October the Japanese seized Wuhan, the second largest town in China. In the meantime, Japanese

[16] National Archive, CAB 23/95 (September 17, 1938).

[17] *Documents on German Foreign Policy*, D-2 (1950): 1014–1016 (agreement signed at Munich between Germany, the United Kingdom, France, and Italy, September 19, 1938).

[18] The delay in supplies has been variously attributed to the closure of the French frontier with Spain, or to Stalin's reluctance to supply arms to what he regarded as an unstable Spanish government, or to the necessity of supplying arms to China.

Table 2 Soviet and Axis military equipment delivered to Spain, 1936–9 (units)

	From the USSR to the Republicans	*From Germany and Italy to the nationalists*
Aircraft (all types)	648	1,593
Tanks and armoured vehicles	407	1,200
Artillery units	1,186	2,630
Machine guns	20,486	34,436
Rifles (thousands)	498	397
Cartridges (millions)	862	575
Shells (millions)	3.4	8.8
Aviation bombs (thousands)	110	17
Submarines and torpedo boats	4	8

Source Rybalkin (2000): 44. Rybalkin also presents alternative estimates that are somewhat higher. These figures do not include 1008 aircraft manufactured in Spain on Soviet licences.

and Soviet forces had clashed when the Japanese attempted to seize a contested hilltop near Lake Khasan, which Soviet units had occupied on July 9. The Japanese eventually retreated, and a ceasefire was signed on August 10.[19] This was the first battle directly involving military action between the Soviet Union and an Axis power.

Overall, the Soviet Union allocated substantial military resources to support the anti-fascist forces in Spain and China. In Spain, both the Soviet Union and the fascist countries made great efforts to supply military equipment to their allies. In 1936–8 the Soviet Union supplied aircraft, tanks, artillery pieces, machine guns and rifles to Spain, together with ammunition, mainly in the first year of the war.[20] As Table 2 shows, Germany and Italy, less hindered by transport difficulties, were able to supply Franco's forces in much larger quantities.[21] The supply of Soviet military equipment to China, meanwhile, accelerated in the spring of 1938, and continued until the German invasion of the Soviet Union in June 1941.

[19] Haslam (1992): 114–118.

[20] *Rossiskaya istoriya* (2009), no. 5 (Novikov): 58.

[21] *Rossiskaya istoriya* (2009), no. 5 (Novikov): 62–63. Both sides also provided military advisers and some troops.

Table 3 Soviet military equipment delivered to Spain and China, compared with Soviet domestic production (units and per cent)

	Deliveries to Spain		*Deliveries to China*	
	Units delivered, 1936–39	*Per cent of Soviet production, 1937–38*	*Units delivered, 1937–41*	*Per cent of Soviet production, 1938–40*
Aircraft (all types)	648	4.7	904	3.3
Tanks	347	8.7	82	1.0
Artillery units	1,186	6.5	1,140	2.7
Machine guns	20.5	11.0	9.7	4.7
Rifles (thousands)	498	28.7	50	1.2
Aviation bombs (thousands)	110	4.4	32	0.5
Shells (thousands)	3,400	19.6	1,900	4.2
Cartridges (millions)	862	30.1	180	2.6
Motor vehicles (all types)	–	–	1,516	0.3

Source Deliveries to Spain, as Table 2. Deliveries to China, from Sladkovskii (1977): 138, noting that (a) figures for cartridges and shells are 'approximate', and (b) other figures are available, usually but not always of comparable magnitude to those given here, for example, in Grechko et al., eds., *Istoriya*, 2 (1974): 72; we have preferred Sladkovskii on the grounds of greater transparency, despite minor discrepancies and uncertainties that are apparent. The bulk of deliveries to Spain was made in 1937–1938, and to China in 1938–1940; Soviet domestic production in these years has therefore been taken for comparison, from figures in Table B.14.

Soviet deliveries to Spain and China were a substantial burden on the Soviet defence industry. An estimate is made in Table 3. In 1937 and 1938, supplies to Spain alone absorbed 5–10% of Soviet domestic production of aircraft, tanks, and guns, and around one-third of the rifles and cartridges produced. The rate of deliveries to China between 1937 and 1941 was generally lower; the aggregate numbers of aircraft and guns were of the same order as supplies to Spain, but were spread over a somewhat longer period in which the Soviet military-industrial build-up was somewhat more advanced, so their burden was generally less. These deliveries also involved large transport costs. Most of the arms to Spain were transported on elaborately disguised ships. Arms for China had to be transported over vast distances from factories located in European Russia to China's central provinces. In addition, the Soviet Union sent thousands of technicians and servicemen (particularly airmen) to assist in the manning and maintenance of aircraft and other equipment, and in developing the manufacture of weapons in both Spain and China. In return, Spain sent its 510-ton gold reserve to the USSR.[22] The cost of Soviet arms exports to China was met by substantial Soviet loans.

The failure of the attempt to establish collective security against fascism led Stalin to announce a substantial shift in Soviet foreign policy. At the eighteenth party congress on March 10, 1939, he denounced in strong terms the three aggressive states, Germany, Italy, and Japan, which had 'begun a new imperialist war' and had already dragged into war a territory inhabited by 500 million people. But he also criticised the non-aggressive states who had 'retreated, granting concession after concession to the aggressors', and condemned 'some politicians and people from the press' who had expressed their regret that the Germans had failed to move further into the East and attack the Soviet Union. In presenting the main tasks of the party in foreign policy, he included a significant item:

> To be cautious and not allow our country to be drawn into conflicts by provocateurs of war, who are accustomed to have others pull the chestnuts out of the fire for them.[23]

Stalin's remarks were followed within days by the German occupation of Czechoslovakia, in violation of Hitler's Munich agreement with Britain, France, and Italy. His policies having failed, Litvinov was dismissed as foreign minister on May 3, 1939, and most of his close associates were arrested. He was replaced by Molotov, who immediately made an unnecessary attack on British proposals for cooperation, perhaps a signal to Berlin that the Soviet orientation was now changeable.[24] Henceforth Soviet foreign policy was managed in detail by Molotov under Stalin's close control, a development to which we will return in Chapter 9.

[22] Rybalkin (2000): 90–101.

[23] *XVIII s"ezd* (1939): 11–15.

[24] Weinberg (1980): 572.

2 The Revised Political Ideology

For Stalin, as we saw in Chapter 1, the removal from the population of enemies and potential enemies was essential if the Soviet Union was to be secure in the forthcoming war. At a dinner in Voroshilov's apartment on November 7, 1937 Stalin expressed this alleged necessity in frank and brutal words[25]:

> Whoever attempts to destroy that unity of the socialist state, whoever seeks the separation of any of its parts or nationalities—that man is an enemy, a sworn enemy of the state and of the peoples of the USSR. And we will destroy each and every such enemy, even if he was an old Bolshevik; we will destroy all his kin, his family. We will mercilessly destroy anyone who, by his deed or his thoughts—yes, his thoughts—threatens the unity of the socialist state. To the complete destruction of all enemies, themselves and their kin! (*Approving exclamations*: To the great Stalin!)

As Stalin saw it, the repressions were only a prerequisite for the great constructive work of moulding a united Soviet people which would face the external enemy with greater determination and work more enthusiastically and efficiently. In Stalin's view, by 1936 the Soviet Union had been transformed into a socialist society in which the exploitation of one class by another had been eliminated, and the working class, the peasantry and the 'working intelligentsia' were cooperating, and class distinctions were being steadily eliminated. The new constitution, adopted on December 5, 1936, provided the legal framework for the 'socialist state of workers and peasants'.[26] In 1936 Stalin devoted much time and effort to the preparation of the constitution and spreading the word about it, and throughout 1936–9 he used his influence to encourage the formation of a revised Soviet ideology and culture.

This was not a smooth process. The historian David Brandenberger has argued that the effect of the Great Terror was to precipitate a crisis in the sphere of ideology.[27] Stalin's response was to launch the preparation of what became known as the *History of the CPSU(b): Short Course*, which became the political core of the struggle for a new ideology.

[25] Dimitrov (2003): 65.

[26] For example, Stalin, *Sochineniya*, 14 (1997): 121–125 (report to the eighth congress of Soviets, November 25, 1936).

[27] Brandenberger (2011).

Several years earlier, on January 7, 1932, the Politburo had established a commission to prepare a new party history as the foundation of an appropriate party ideology, but no history emerged in the next five years to which Stalin was willing to give his approval.[28] In the spring of 1937, following the completion by Yaroslavskii of the latest of many versions of a party history, Stalin carefully prepared a short draft (sometimes known as his 'instructions') as the basis for a new textbook (the draft went through five revisions). He complained that existing textbooks were 'unsatisfactory' for three reasons: they were written 'without being connected to the history of the country', or 'they were restricted to a narrative, a simple description of the events and facts of the struggle between tendencies', without the necessary Marxist explanation, or 'they were incorrectly designed, with an incorrect periodisation of events.' The new textbook should correct these deficiencies, and in particular should show that the contradictions and disagreements within the party reflected the existence of antagonistic classes, the petty-bourgeois nature of the country and the heterogeneous structure of the working class. Above all, it must show that the party would degenerate without the defeat of anti-Leninist tendencies and groups. This statement was approved by the Politburo on April 16, 1937 and published in *Pravda* on May 9.[29]

The Politburo resolution stated that the textbook was intended for provincial party secretaries, but eventually the audience was much wider. In his speech at Voroshilov's dacha in November 1937 Stalin strongly emphasised the importance of the 'middle cadres' as the main prerequisite for success—and not only the middle cadres of party officials, but also those who worked in the economy and the armed forces. In another speech a year later he explained that in the 1920s the party had to administer the Soviet people through a state machinery which included 'many alien people who backed us before collectivisation but went away from us during collectivisation'. He acknowledged that the party leaders had missed out on training new cadres and 'lost a good number of cadres who were capable people'. In particular, he maintained, there were

[28] For the Politburo resolution, see RGASPI, 17/3/867: 11; for Stalin's preceding letter of October 26, 1931, criticising previous party histories, including Yaroslavskii's, which 'contain a number of mistakes both in principle and in history', see Vol. 4: 81, and Stalin, *Sochineniya*, 13 (1951): 84–102.

[29] For the various drafts of Stalin's statement, see *Kratkii kurs istorii VKP(b)*, 1 (2014): 221–227.

ten to twenty thousand or more followers of Bukharin, and the same number of Trotskyites: 'politically naked (*ne podkovannyi*), theoretically uneducated, people who did not know the laws of political development and therefore did not succeed in assimilating the abrupt turn … to the collective farm'.[30] This deficiency in the education of cadres, he declared, must be corrected.

Stalin worked assiduously between the spring of 1937 and the autumn of 1938 on revisions of the drafts of the textbook. He undertook this work simultaneously with his management of the repressions. In August 1937, while the mass purge was being launched, he circulated Yaroslavskii's new draft to the Politburo, with comments by Stetskii.[31] A substantially new draft by Yaroslavskii was submitted to Stalin at the end of February 1938, and in March and April, during and after the Bukharin trial, Stalin inserted new passages in the text justifying collectivisation, and instructed the authors of the textbook that the conclusion must state that 'all opposition trends within the party' (he specifically mentioned among others the Trotskyites and the Bukharin-Rykov group) 'became enemies of the people and agents (spies) of foreign intelligence services'.[32]

Stalin made numerous changes, large and small, to the textbook.[33] To achieve this thorough revision he made very few appointments in his Kremlin office throughout May to August 1938.[34] He then circulated the revised texts to the Politburo for comment, chapter by chapter.

Stalin's most important and substantial change was to delete from Chapter IV, which covered the years 1908–12, the whole of Section 2, 'The activity of the Bolsheviks in the years of reaction,' and replace it with a much longer section, 'Dialectical and historical materialism'.[35]

[30] *Stenogrammy zasedanii Politbyuro*, 3 (2007): 690–697 (at an extended Politburo meeting, October 11, 1938).

[31] *Kratkii kurs istorii VKP(b)*, 1 (2014): 249–263.

[32] *Kratkii kurs istorii VKP(b)*, 1 (2014): 297–313.

[33] For these changes see *Kratkii kurs istorii VKP(b)*, 1 (2014): 347–354, 372–381.

[34] He met visitors on just nine days in May, nine in June, five in July and eight in August, whereas in every other month in 1938 (except December) he met visitors on at least 15 days, and much more frequently.

[35] The omitted section contained frequent references to the crucial role of Stalin in this period. Stalin later criticised an earlier version of the textbook as 'based on individuals', and commented, 'Individuals must be spoken about, but only to the extent that this is needed';

The inclusion of this section was fundamental to Stalin's version of Bolshevik history. Addressing the Politburo after the publication of the history, he explained that, previously, party history, dialectical materialism and historical materialism had been taught as three separate subjects, and Marxism had been taught separately from Leninism. This 'functional separation clouded people's consciousness.'[36] But the new party history 'unifies all this':

> The short course is a completely different type of party history. Basically, party history is treated as illustrative material in order to set out the main ideas of Marxism-Leninism. This course is skewed towards theoretical questions.

Hence 'the emergence of chapter IV of the short course is not at all accidental. We wanted to unify these divided parts.' 'Here dialectical materialism is tied in with historical materialism, and historical materialism is tied in with politics and economics, all this together is what constitutes Marxism-Leninism.'[37] And the task was to 'prepare a person who has the required general knowledge of the theory and practice of Marxism ... an integrated human being, not a specialist'.[38]

Following these months of detailed work, in September 1938, coincident with the series of decisions to wind down the mass repressions, the Politburo authorised the publication of *The History of the CPSU(b): Short Course* in six million copies in Russian, and also in the other languages of the Soviet Union, and in 15 foreign languages.[39] It was also printed in full in *Pravda* in the issues from September 9 to 19. By the time of Stalin's death in 1953, 42 million copies had been published in 67 languages. The *Short Course*, taught in vast numbers of classes in the Soviet

see Stalin's speech at a conference of propagandists, September 27, 1938, in *Kratkii kurs istorii VKP(b)*, 1 (2014): 429. The final version of the history rarely mentioned individuals other than Lenin or Stalin. This enabled the book to omit the names of the numerous Bolshevik leaders who had later been executed.

[36] 'Functionalism' in the economy was the separation of line management by function, such as labour and finance, rather than by the type of product; it was roundly condemned in 1931–1932 (Vol. 4: 384, 388).

[37] *Stenogrammy zasedanii Politbyuro*, 3 (2007): 690–693 (October 11, 1938).

[38] *Stenogrammy zasedanii Politbyuro*, 3 (2007): 728 (October 12, 1938).

[39] RGASPI, 17/3/1002: 12 (September 19); 25 (September 23); 28 (September 27).

Union and in foreign Communist parties, was correctly excoriated for its oversimplifications and falsifications by critics abroad and concealed critics in the Soviet Union. But it undoubtedly exercised the influence that Stalin hoped for as a unifying text for the new generations of minor and major officials. The section on 'Dialectical and Historical Materialism', reprinted in large editions as a separate pamphlet, was a careful and straightforward account of Marxist doctrine which strongly influenced Soviet thinking. Its influence was summed up in Dudintsev's novel *Not by Bread Alone* in 1956 by the story of the factory manager who kept the pamphlet at his bedside and cited it to justify his actions.[40] But in Stalin's lifetime the trouble was that the political system which reached an apogee in the repressions of 1937–8 had made it utterly impossible to criticise any statement at all in the *Short Course* or in the pamphlet. The resources of the state had been mobilised in the huge effort to unify Soviet society in preparation for war, combining brutal force with an attempted ideological transformation. One of the prices paid was the ossification of Communist thought. Dudintsev's factory manager, once a dynamic force in his factory, had become a conservative brake on progress.

Together with the preparation of the *Short Course*, a basic textbook for the third and fourth school years, covering both the pre-revolutionary and post-revolutionary history of the Soviet Union, was prepared under the editorship of Shestakov, with Stalin's participation, and published in 1937.[41] In October 1938 Stalin announced that it was also necessary to prepare authoritative textbooks on world history and political economy.[42] The textbook on world history was duly prepared, but the effort to prepare a political economy of socialism did not succeed. At the end of his life Stalin convened a major conference on this theme, and his last writings were devoted to it, but no textbook emerged until after his death.[43] This whole intellectual effort reflected the inability of the Soviet state under Stalin to modernise.

[40] Dudintsev (1957) (serialised in 1956 in the columns of the literary magazine *Novy mir*).

[41] Shestakov (1937).

[42] *Stenogrammy zasedanii Politbyuro*, 3 (2007): 736.

[43] The reports of these debates are translated from the archives by Pollock (2001), working paper.

3 Politics and Society in 1937 and 1938

During 1937 and 1938, the continuing repressions in the economy were accompanied by changes in economic administration which were partly a response to the increasing complexity of the economy, and which also embodied the increasing autocratic control of which the repressions were a dramatic part.

From the early 1930s, responsibility for supply was delegated to a few commissariats, each divided into a few chief administrations (*glavki*). These were now replaced by a multiplicity of more specialised commissariats and glavki (the detail of these and other reorganisations is set out for easy reference in Appendix A). Glavki or groups of glavki were elevated into commissariats, and the number of glavki greatly increased. The first step towards the subdivision of the commissariats was taken at the beginning of 1932 with the breakup of Vesenkha, the original Soviet Ministry of Industry, into separate commissariats for the heavy, light, and timber industries (Vol. 4: 203–204). The process was resumed at the end of 1936 when the Commissariat of Heavy Industry (Narkomtyazhprom) lost most of its armaments capacity to a new Commissariat of Defence Industry (Narkomoboronprom). On August 22, 1937, a new Commissariat of Machine Building (Narkommash) was also separated from Narkomtyazhprom. Then at the beginning of 1939 further dramatic changes took place. On January 11 the Commissariat of Defence Industry was replaced by four separate commissariats. On January 24 the Commissariat of Heavy Industry was itself broken up into seven further commissariats. On February 5 the Commissariat of Machine Building was divided into three new commissariats. At the end of this process the single commissariat for heavy industry had become 13 commissariats, the leaders of which were all members of Sovnarkom.

Similar but less dramatic changes took place in other sectors of the economy. On January 2, 1939, a new Commissariat of the Textile Industry was separated from the Commissariat of Light Industry (Narkomlegprom). On January 19 new Commissariats of Food Industry and the Meat and Dairy Industry were also split away from the Commissariat of Light Industry. On April 9 the Commissariat of Water Transport was divided into separate commissariats for river and sea transport. In addition, over this period, two already-powerful state committees attached to Sovnarkom were also elevated to the status of commissariats: the Committee for Agricultural Procurements on January 15, 1938, and the Committee for

Construction on May 29, 1939. In total, by the summer of 1939, in place of the eight 'economic' commissariats which existed in the autumn of 1936, there were now 19. Within each commissariat additional glavki were instituted. For example, ten new glavki were established in 1937 alone in the Comissariat of Defence Industry. This process of fragmentation continued, but more slowly, until 1953 when it was briefly reversed.[44]

The new subdivisions had a clear purpose. Narkomtyazhprom had become an unwieldy empire, with too many subdivisions and too many layers between the minister and the multitude of enterprises. The horizontal boundaries between layers impeded the upward flow of information and the downward cascade of orders. Smaller commissariats with shorter chains of command offered improved ministerial oversight and accountability. But this came at a price, because the process of fission multiplied and strengthened the vertical barriers between specialised industries, increasing the costs of coordination among them.

Previously, coordination had been fostered by STO, the Council for Labour and Defence, which had acted as an economic sub-committee of Sovnarkom. But the new constitution abolished STO. On November 23, 1937, STO was replaced by an Economic Council (Ekonomsovet), attached to Sovnarkom and supported by its own administrative machinery. Like STO, the Council was presided over by the chair of Sovnarkom. Its members were the vice chairs of Sovnarkom and a representative of the trade unions. Its responsibilities included the examination of quarterly and annual plans before they were referred to Sovnarkom; approving the plans for supplies, railways and agricultural procurements; questions of prices, labour and wages; and taking decisions about the formation and abolition of economic agencies (this included the commissariats).[45] How far the Council was effective in managing economic affairs would emerge in subsequent years. Gosplan, which had been through many vicissitudes in 1937, was re-established as an effective planning agency with the appointment of Voznesenskii as vice chair on November 23, 1937, the day on which the Ekonomsovet was established, and as chair of Gosplan on January 19, 1938.[46]

[44] On the Soviet economics of supply chain planning under more and less specialsed ministries, see *Soviet Studies*, 42(1) (1990): 41–60 (J. R. Crowfoot and M. Harrison).

[45] SZ (1937), no. 75: art. 365 (November 23, 1937).

[46] Harrison (1985): 11–13.

As control of the economy became more centralised, the NKVD played a larger role. Thus, on April 29, 1937, the committee of reserves was transformed into an Administration of State Reserves attached to Sovnarkom, with its own local agencies, and Sovnarkom ruled that 'in view of the importance and secrecy of this question' all officials without exception were to be selected jointly with the NKVD.[47]

In the same month far-reaching changes were launched in the planning and management of defence. On April 27, 1937, the Politburo-Sovnarkom Commission on Defence, established in 1930, was abolished and replaced by a Committee of Defence attached to Sovnarkom, consisting largely of members of the Politburo, and with a more extensive administrative machinery than the former Commission.[48] For the time being the defence sector of Gosplan, which had played an important advisory role under various names since the 1920s, continued to exist. On September 17 it was reorganised into a Department of Defence (*otdel oborony*), divided into three sectors responsible for the plans of the defence industry, for the mobilisation preparedness of the economy as a whole, and for the plans of the Defence Commissariat (i.e. the army and navy) and of the NKVD.[49] This arrangement was short-lived, however. On December 7 the Politburo approved a decision of the Committee of Defence to remove the Department of Defence from Gosplan and the military supervision groups from the Commissions of State and Party Control and 'transfer all their functions to the machinery of the Committee of Defence and its chief inspectorate'.[50] The division of functions between Ekonomsovet and the Committee of Defence was not formalised until September 1939, and a few weeks before the German invasion their functions were taken over by a new Bureau of Sovnarkom which, like Sovnarkom itself, was headed by Stalin.[51]

A further development in 1938 was the establishment on March 13 of the Chief Military Council (GVS) of the defence commissariat. Unlike the Military Council which preceded it, GVS was a much smaller body and at first met more regularly. Both the Military Council and GVS were

[47] GARF, 5446/1/495: 35 (art. 1488).

[48] Khlevniuk (1996): 251.

[49] SZ (1937), no. 62: art. 270 (September 17, 1937).

[50] RGASPI, 17/162/22: 70 (art. 406).

[51] Khlevniuk (1996): 251–255.

chaired by Voroshilov, but unlike the Military Council the GVS was almost always attended by Stalin. These confusing changes all consolidated the authority of Stalin as it was reflected in his personal position in the supreme agencies of state.

The endeavours of these years were sometimes heroic, but heroism too was inextricably intertwined with savage repression and increasing central control. Thus in 1937 the Soviet Union achieved its long-cherished aim of becoming the first nation to establish a scientific expedition on the Polar ice floes. The four members of the team, headed by Ivan Papanin, were landed on the ice by a modified heavy four-engine bomber ANT-6 (TB-3), and began work on May 21, 1937. They remained on the ice for 274 days. When the ice began to break up they were rescued by ship and reached Leningrad on March 15, 1938 (their arrival was delayed by two days, presumably so that it did not coincide with the sentencing and execution of the accused in the Bukharin trial). Their triumphant return was enthusiastically publicised. Behind the scenes, however, the fate of Glavsevmorput', the Northern Sea Route Administration, was being decided. In 1937, following successful navigation of the Northern Sea Route in 1934–6, none of the vessels succeeded in breaking through before winter set in, partly because of extremely bad weather. The management of Glavsevmorput' was blamed for this failure. Many of its staff were arrested and executed.[52] On March 28, 1938 a Sovnarkom decree strongly criticised its work. Later in 1938 it was stripped of its economic functions, and these were largely transferred to the NKVD. This brought an end to the bold attempt to integrate the social and economic development of the Soviet Arctic. On March 4, 1939, the veteran scientist Otto Shmidt was dismissed from the directorship of Glavsevmorput' and replaced by Papanin. Papanin lacked scientific education, and his function as the head of the residual apparatus of Glavsevmorput' was limited to securing the successful navigation of the Northern Sea Route, a task at which he proved competent. The successful rescue of Papanin and his colleagues was accompanied by a further failure of the airship industry, however: On February 8, 1938, SSSR V-6, the largest Soviet airship, despatched to assist in the rescue of the Papanin group, crashed into a mountain and caught fire.[53]

[52] Lar'kov and Romanenko (2010): 345–346.

[53] Lar'kov and Romanenko (2010): 343.

The triumphs of Soviet aviators continued to be publicised in the Soviet press. The achievement by three women aviators of the world women's record for a non-stop flight (see Sect. 4 in Chapter 6) provided a further opportunity to balance the limitations imposed on women in 1936 (by the legislation against abortion, and by the campaign to strengthen the family) with a celebration of the role of women in Soviet society. At a reception held on October 27, 1937, in honour of the crews of the aircraft *Rodina*, soon after the women's record, Stalin praised the 'brilliant achievements of Soviet women in all branches of production, culture and science and in such an extremely difficult activity as aviation, which seemed inaccessible to women'; 'in all these walks of life Soviet women ... are now standing side-by-side with men and in many cases are ahead of them.'[54] In unpublished remarks Stalin placed this event in the context of world history:

> He recalled that very long ago there was a period in history when women dominated men, the period of the matriarchate. He said that 20,000 and perhaps 40,000 years ago was a period on our planet in which the means of production were very weak, among primitive people men engaged in hunting and women tended the food, the poultry and the animals. A man was honoured in the family only if he brought in animals or birds; if there was no catch, his position was difficult ...
>
> On the contrary, the period of more recent history shows the age-old repression of women in almost all countries in the world. But in 1938 women had turned the tables and taken their revenge for all the offences against them.[55]

These were years of great difficulty for Soviet science. At the time, Soviet scientists were making great strides forward in nuclear physics. But in 1937 many scientists were arrested in the Ukrainian Physical-Technical Institute in Khar'kov and in the physics department of Leningrad University. Some of the most prominent, including V. Fock and L. Landau, were released only because Kapitsa, a Soviet citizen who had been retained forcibly in the USSR in 1935 when he was visiting the country from Cambridge, interceded with Stalin on their behalf.

[54] *Pravda*, October 28, 1938.

[55] *Zastol'nye rechi Stalina* (2003): 214–215.

The turmoil was increased by the proliferation of commissariats. Covering most of industry, the unified commissariat of heavy industry had been able to provide finance for inter-disciplinary research but, after its fragmentation, nuclear physics fell outside the interests and beyond the means of any of the more specialised commissariats. The building of a cyclotron, well advanced by 1937, was temporarily halted in 1938. The problem was eventually solved by transferring such projects to the Academy of Sciences. At least research in physics did not cease in the years of repression. By the beginning of 1937 Kapitsa's Cambridge laboratory had been installed in a new building in Moscow, and he soon succeeded in liquefying hydrogen and constructing apparatus for the rapid production of oxygen, but he was then confronted with the difficulty, particularly acute in the Soviet Union, of the development and industrial application of his inventions.[56]

On the cultural front, throughout the purge years, the repression of major and minor writers and other cultural figures continued. In the spring of 1937 nearly all the foreign correspondents of Soviet newspapers—both foreign and Soviet citizens—were dismissed, and many were arrested. The purge of journalists reached its climax on December 12, 1938, with the arrest of the immensely popular anti-fascist journalist Mikhail Kol'tsov.[57] Meanwhile, on March 5, 1937, in spite of its praise of Pavel Morozov, Eisenstein's film *Bezhin Lug* was rejected during the second attempt to complete it, and Shumyatskii, then in charge of Soviet cinema, proposed that Eisenstein should no longer be used as a film director. Then at the beginning of 1938 the prestigious and innovative Meyerhold Theatre was closed on the grounds that it was unable to cope with the successful production of Soviet plays.

In these years the major shift continued towards traditional and patriotic values which were already becoming dominant in 1936. This was marked by events through the year. February 10, 1937, the hundredth anniversary of Pushkin's death, marked the climax of the vast celebrations of his life and work; the *Pravda* editorial on that day described him as 'the glory and pride of the Russian people', and huge editions of his writings were published in all the languages of the Soviet republics. Pushkin's name was conferred on the State Art Museum, and Bol'shaya

[56] Kojevnikov (2004): 97–98, 128–131.

[57] *Bol'shaya tsenzura* (2005): 472–475, 487.

Dmitrovka was renamed Pushkin Street.[58] On May 22 Academician Shmidt established the Soviet Polar Station, and its difficulties and triumphs were a major preoccupation of the media in the following months. The First All-Union Congress of Architects, held from June 16 to 26, was celebrated by the opening of a permanent building exhibition on the Frunze Embankment.[59] July was a particularly busy month. On July 12 as many as 40,000 athletes took part in the annual Physical Culture Parade; on July 15 the Moscow-Volga Canal was opened, accompanied by an amnesty for 56,000 of the prisoners who took part in its construction; and on July 22 the Seventeenth International Geology Congress was held in Moscow. In the summer months a series of record-making flights was accompanied by great publicity. They were followed in early September 1937 by the showing of Part One of Aleksei Tolstoy's film of Peter the Great, now transformed in Bolshevik eyes from a brutal despot to the progressive great reformer of the Russian nation. In November the twentieth anniversary of the Bolshevik revolution was celebrated with great ceremony. Offices were closed for three days. On the eve of the anniversary, November 6, Molotov addressed a meeting in the Bol'shoi theatre, and his speech was at the centre of press and radio attention. On that day Romm's *Lenin in October*, a firmly Stalinist version of the events of the Bolshevik revolution, also appeared. The next day, a huge parade passed through Red Square. The year ended on a more sombre note. The twentieth anniversary of the establishment of the Cheka was celebrated on December 12 with a well-publicised meeting in the Bol'shoi, addressed by an enthusiastic speech by Mikoyan, in spite of, or because of, his reputation as a moderate and amiable leader.

Behind the scenes, during 1937, established views of Russian history began to be modified in a nationalist direction. The view that Ivan the Terrible was a mad megalomaniac began to transmute into the revised assessment of him as eccentric unifier of the Russian lands. Early in 1937 Stalin began to clear the way for this change when he checked the proofs of Shestakov's textbook and crossed out Repin's famous portrait of Ivan holding the body of his son, whom he had murdered.[60]

[58] Schlögel (2012): 144–159.

[59] Schlögel (2012): 231–235.

[60] Platt and Brandenberger, eds. (2006): 158.

In 1937 other changes in a nationalist spirit were also initiated. In May, after Eisenstein had written to Stalin, pleading to work on a new film about the revolution, the Politburo decided, in spite of Shumyatskii's hostility to Eisenstein, that Shumyatskii should use him, supplying a theme and checking the screen play in advance.[61] Prokofiev, who had returned to the Soviet Union in 1936, wrote the music, and the resulting film was *Alexander Nevsky*, glorifying the thirteenth-century prince's struggle against the Teutonic invaders. On May 8, 1938, Stalin wrote to Dukel'skii about the film script: 'It seems not to have come out badly.'[62] It was first shown on November 7, the twenty-first anniversary of the Bolshevik revolution, to considerable popular approval.[63]

Throughout these years the production of popular musicals with a political message continued, one of the most successful being *Volga-Volga* (1938). The historian Richard Stites wrote that 'the sound of execution trenches being dug and bullets crashing into the skulls of NKVD victims were inaudible beneath the soaring and joyful songs of enthusiasm.'[64]

On April 2, 1938, the Politburo provided a further impetus to the film industry by passing a lengthy resolution calling for a speeding up of the production of three films. *Professor Mamlok* showed the travails of a German Jewish anti-fascist professor under the Nazis. *Chest'* (*Honour*) depicted an engine-driver's struggle against an official who proved to be a wrecker. *Pobeda* (*Victory*) told the story of three aviators' successful round-the-world flight. These films were all produced in 1938.[65] In general, these films of the purge years were of high quality and some have proved to be outstanding classics of the cinema. The resolution of April 2 also called for the production of more films: on defence subjects; on life in the Red Army and Navy and among the frontier troops; on the struggle with the agents of internal fascism; on Stakhanovism; science;

[61] Maksimenkov (1997): 241–249.

[62] *I. V. Stalin*, 1 (2006): 443–444.

[63] Platt and Brandenberger, eds. (2006): 233–258.

[64] Stites (1992): 95.

[65] *Professor Mamlok* was banned in Britain until February 1940, five months after the outbreak of war. Author R. W. Davies saw the film in an English seaside town in 1940. All subtitles referring to Marxism, Communism and the Soviet Union had been blanked out. Like other anti-Nazi films, it was also banned in the Soviet Union from August 1939 to June 1941.

the friendship of the peoples; women and the family; and sports and comedy films, as well as films on past Bolshevik leaders including Kirov, Kuibyshev and Ordzhonikidze.

Meanwhile significant changes took place in the agencies administering Soviet culture. In January 1938 Shumyatskii himself fell a victim to the purges: he was removed from the headship of Soviet cinema and later executed. His replacement was the old OGPU hand S. S. Dukel'skii, who, on March 23, 1938, was placed in charge of a Committee on Cinematography attached to Sovnarkom. The new committee thus had higher status than its predecessor, which had been subordinate to the Committee on the Arts. The priority attached to the cinema in these years is indicated by the fact that 92 million rubles were assigned to the Committee on Cinematography in 1938 and 87 million rubles in 1939, while the amount given to the Committee on the Arts for all the other arts was only 86 million and 55 million rubles in the same years.[66]

Kerzhentsev was removed from the chair of the Committee on the Arts on January 15, 1938, the immediate pretext being that he had permitted Stalin to be presented as a character on the stage without permission, but he may also have been removed because he exercised too much autonomy generally. He was demoted to work as an editor, holding fairly senior posts until his death in 1940. He was replaced on January 19 by A. I. Nazarov, a party official who had been trained as a journalist. Dukel'skii and Nazarov were much weaker figures than their predecessors, and these moves meant that control of the cinema and the arts was henceforth much more firmly in the hands of Stalin and his associates in the Politburo, notably Zhdanov.

[66]GARF, 1562/10/710a: 2–3 (not dated but 1939 or 1940); 1562/10/991a: 4–5 (not dated but 1940).

CHAPTER 3

The Economic Slowdown of 1937

1 The 1937 Plan: The Shift Back to More Balanced Growth

In 1936, alongside a shift to more moderate treatment of grumbling workers and awkward managers, the Politburo returned to policies of more balanced growth. Stakhanovite methods continued to be advocated, but the revised economic policy tacitly renounced the extravagant hopes which only recently had been placed on Stakhanovism. The reasons for this shift in policy have not yet been fully ascertained. One important factor was anxiety about financial stability. On April 29, 1936, the Politburo decided to reduce the interest on mass 'loans' from the population and to extend the length of the loans (Vol. 6: 301). Moreover, both Gosplan and the Commissariat of Finance, with Molotov's general support, were long committed to stabilising the currency and, if possible, to improving the purchasing power of the ruble by lower retail prices. Except on those occasions when Stalin actively supported the rapid expansion of state expenditure, the policy of balanced growth tended to prevail.

A renewed desire for more balanced growth emerged clearly during the preparation of the 1937 economic plan. In July 1936 Gosplan despatched to Stalin and Molotov the draft plan directives for 1937. In an accompanying letter, Mezhlauk paid due respect to the successes of Stakhanovism and the prospects for exceeding the second five-year

R. W. Davies et al., *The Industrialisation of Soviet Russia Volume 7: The Soviet Economy and the Approach of War, 1937–1939*,
https://doi.org/10.1057/978-1-137-36238-4_3

plan, but the practical proposals were different in tone and content. The main tasks of heavy industry in 1937 were to pull up the lagging industries, considerably improve the quality of production, ensure that products were complete with all their component parts, reduce the amount of unfinished production, reduce losses and considerably reduce costs. Against this background Gosplan proposed that the rate of growth of industrial production in 1937 should be only 20.1% in comparison with the 34.4% planned for 1936, while the productivity of labour would increase by 20%, as rapidly as production. Capital investment policy followed similar lines: the volume of investment should be planned at 28.6 billion rubles in 1937 as compared with the planned 35.1 billion in 1936.[1] This substantial reduction corresponded to the similar reduction which Gosplan, supported by Molotov, had unsuccessfully proposed for the 1936 plan in July 1935, against Stalin's opposition (Vol. 6: 264–268).

In July 1936, in sharp contrast to the decisions about the 1936 plan a year earlier, the Politburo accepted the Gosplan proposal for capital investment in 1937 with little change (see Table 1). On July 5, according to Stalin's appointments diary, Mezhlauk met Stalin, Molotov, Mikoyan and Kosior for nearly two hours, evidently to discuss the draft proposals.[2] Twelve days later, on July 17, an enlarged Politburo meeting lasting less than half an hour was attended by 28 people, including all the people's commissars concerned with the economy; and the Politburo and Sovnarkom approved the 'Directives for the control figures of the 1937 plan' on July 19.[3]

Mezhlauk's proposals to reduce the capital investment plan for 1937 varied considerably between the different government departments. The Commissariat of Heavy Industry allocation was as much as 28% lower than in 1936, even though planned investment in the defence industries,

[1] RGAE, 4372/92/63: 210–225.

[2] The meeting lasted from 17:15 to 19:00. For part of the time it was also attended by Chernov and Kalmanovich. Stalin's daily calendar of meetings has been published in *Na prieme u Stalina* (2008). For the present work we have consulted the Melbourne Gateway to Research on Soviet History (Stalin's meetings day by day) at http://www.melgrosh.unimelb.edu.au/.

[3] RGASPI, 17/3/979: 56–59; and the joint Central Committee and Sovnarkom decree: GARF, 5446/1/487: 114–122 (art. 1282/236s). See also Rees, ed. (1997): 57–58 (Davies and Khlevniuk).

Table 1 Capital investment: the evolution of plans during 1936 (million rubles and per cent)

	Plan for 1936 (May 29, 1936)	*Plans for 1937*			
		July 19, 1936	*Change, per cent*	*Dec. 7, 1936*	*Dec. 27, 1936*
Heavy industry	10,005	7,200	−28.0	8,440	8,667
Timber industry	899	800	−11.0	900	1,010
Light industry	1,372	1,250	−8.9	1,400	1,406
Food industry	1,178	770	−34.6	970	970
Local industry	1,078	770	−38.6	770	770
Agriculture (collective farms)	2,192	2,300	+4.9	2,300	2,301
Railways	5,487	4,200	−24.5	4,200	5,541
Education	1,100	1,100	0.0	1,100	1,100
Health	–	1,000	–	1,000	1,000
Defence	2,400	2,250	−6.2	2,450	2,450
NKVD	–	1,805	–	1,971	2,031
Other items	–	5,155	–	5,169	5,291
Total	35,053	28,600	−18.4	30,670	32,537

Note The four columns up to and including the plan for 1937 of December 7, 1936, are in estimate prices of 1935. The plan of December 27, 1936 is in prices of Dec. 1, 1936.
Source Table B.5; changes in the plan for 1937 of July 19, 1936, are calculated over the 1936 plan. Figures for 'Other items' are differences between the total below and the rows above.

which still formed part of that Commissariat, was increasing rapidly, and had reached a quarter of all investment in heavy industry. The allocation to the Commissariat of Transport (responsible mainly for railways), which had increased rapidly in 1935 and 1936, was reduced by a similar amount. Even more drastic reductions were made for the food and local industries (the reason for this has not been established, but it was probably due to the bad harvest of 1936). The smallest reductions were made for the light and timber industries, and, not surprisingly, in the investment planned for the Commissariat of Defence. The relatively modest plan for industrial production also stipulated that light, food, timber and local industries would grow more rapidly than heavy industry.

The directives of July 19 also proposed a significant departure in planning procedures:

> The established practice of recording the fulfilment of the plan of gross production is incorrect ...; the fulfilment of the plan of every industrial

> enterprise must be valued first of all by its production of finished and complete output which precisely corresponds to the fixed standards of quality and technical conditions, and to the product-mix fixed for the particular enterprise.

Ordzhonikidze had already foreshadowed one aspect of this change in his speech to the Commissariat of Heavy Industry council on June 29, 1936, in which he announced that Stalin had proposed a shift from measurement in gross production to measurement in commodity production. This indicates that Stalin was still paying attention to problems of industrial policy in spite of his increasing preoccupation with the preparation of the Kamenev-Zinoviev trial.

During the next few months the commissariats prepared their plans on the basis of these directives. It emerged later in the year that the counter-demands of the All-Union commissariats alone asked for an additional investment of 12,863 million rubles above the 28,600 million rubles in the July directives.[4] The strongest pressure for an increase came from Narkomtyazhprom, the Commissariat of Heavy Industry, which had been squeezed most. As early as July 23 Ordzhonikidze requested an extra 1257 million rubles in a long memorandum to Stalin and Molotov, without success.[5] In its plan for 1937 Narkomtyazhprom requested 12,744 instead of 7200 million rubles, claiming that the increase was made necessary by the new defence plans approved by the government.[6] The Narkomtyazhprom plan was signed in Ordzhonikidze's absence by his deputy Rukhimovich. At the beginning of October 1936 Ordzhonikidze wrote to Stalin from Kislovodsk with a further plea for support, insisting that he could not manage with only 7200 million rubles.[7]

The Politburo now began to retreat from the moderate investment policy. On December 7, 1936, the investment plan was increased by 2070 million rubles or 7.2%. Of the increase, 1240 million (or 60%) went to Narkomtyazhprom (see Table 1); this included 400 million rubles for the

[4] GARF, 5446/20/1916: 51–52.

[5] GARF, 5446/20a/371: 108–117.

[6] GARF, 5446/20a/371: 84–107.

[7] RGASPI, 558/11/778: 118.

defence industry.[8] The Politburo also decided on December 7 that the original allocation to Narkomput', the Commissariat of Transport, which, like the allocation to Narkomtyazhprom, was considerably lower than in 1936, should be reconsidered by Mezhlauk and Kaganovich. Kaganovich was the more senior and more forceful figure. Not surprisingly, when the 1937 plan was approved by a full meeting of the Politburo on December 27, the investment plan for Narkomput' had been increased from 4200 to 5541 million rubles, restoring the plan to the very high level of the previous year.[9]

The decision of December 7 also established a broader commission of Ordzhonikidze, Mezhlauk, Khrushchev (the Moscow party secretary) and Bulganin (chair of the Moscow city soviet) to consider the allocations to the Moscow Metro and the new vehicle factories. The allocation to the Metro was not increased, but the allocation to Narkomtyazhprom grew by a further 227 million rubles. As a result of these and some minor changes, the investment plan for 1937 was now only 9.3% less than in the 1936 plan, rather than 18.4% less.[10] But in spite of these

[8]For this decision (dated December 6; approved by Sovnarkom on the following day), see RGASPI, 17/3/982: 67–69. On January 17, 1937, the Politburo approved a proposal of Gosplan that the total investment plan for the defence industries should amount to 3390 million rubles, shared between the newly-formed Commissariat of the Defence Industry (2527 million rubles) and the residual defence production of the truncated Commissariat of Heavy Industry (853 million) (RGASPI, 17/162/20: 162–163, 192–193 (art. 137)). This amounted to 39.1% of the total investment plan for the two commissariats which had been approved on December 27.

[9]The decision 'On the national-economic plan for 1937' was item one on the agenda; the meeting was attended by the heads of the main commissariats concerned with the economy. RGASPI, 17/3/982: 1–2, 99–100.

[10]A further complication was a price change carried out by Gosplan between December 7 and 27. The investment plan of December 7 was stated to be measured in estimate prices of 1935, and the December 27 plan in actual prices of December 1, 1936. According to Gosplan, the large increases in the wholesale prices of fuel and materials in 1936 had been offset by the decline in building costs and overheads for most commissariats, but costs had increased in the transport commissariats because of the large increases in the cost of rolling stock and ships. As a result, the 1937 investment plan had increased from 31,517 million to 32,079 million rubles (by 562 million rubles, or 1.8%) (RGAE, 4372/92/63: 150–153 (December 20, 1936)). Most of this increase was presumably incorporated in the increased allocation to the Transport Commissariat; the allocation to the Commissariat of Water Transport was increased in the December 27 plan from 650 to 718 million rubles, evidently partly as a result of the price change.

increases in December, Narkomtyazhprom, as in previous years, suffered the largest reduction.

The Politburo maintained the relatively modest plan for industrial production. The December 7 decision even instructed Chubar' and Mezhlauk to determine the plan 'on the basis of the possibility of some reduction of industrial production as compared with the Gosplan proposals'.[11] On December 27 the increase in production for the whole of industry in 1937 was planned at 20%, a figure almost exactly the same as that proposed by Gosplan in the previous July (20.1%).

On December 27 the Politburo also approved the state budget for 1937.[12] In its original memorandum on the budget, dated July 16, Narkomfin, the Commissariat of Finance, had accepted the proposal to reduce capital investment and had argued that a sum of 4.0 billion rubles should be set aside for price reduction, and that there should be no net currency issue in 1937. It also argued that the Gosplan proposal to increase retail trade from the 103 billion rubles expected for 1936 to 130 billion in 1937 was unrealistic, and would require a higher rate of increase in the production of consumer goods than Gosplan anticipated.[13] By December, Narkomfin had modified its proposals: it now suggested that the net currency issue in 1937 would have to amount to one billion rubles, and that the budget should set aside the sum of 2.5 rather than 4.0 billion rubles to enable prices to be reduced.[14]

Similar provisions for price reductions in previous years had been unsuccessful. Gosplan rejected the Narkomfin proposals, arguing that the amounts of turnover tax and loans proposed by Narkomfin should be increased, and in consequence there should be no net currency issue in 1937.[15] The budget approved by the Politburo in December 27 was closer to the Gosplan than to the Narkomfin proposals. The draft before the Politburo still included a surplus of 2.5 billion rubles to enable price reductions to take place, but the Politburo decided that 'the reserve for reducing retail prices shall be excluded, and the revenue of the budget of the USSR shall be increased by a corresponding amount.' After further

[11] GARF, 5446/1/488: 198–204 and 5446/57/43: 198–201 (art. 2075/403s).

[12] RGASPI, 17/3/983: 2–3 (item II).

[13] RGASPI, 82/2/772: 46–55; the memorandum was sent to Stalin and Molotov with copies to Mezhlauk and Chubar'.

[14] RGAE, 4372/92/67: 36ff (memorandum by Grin'ko, December 23, 1936).

[15] RGAE, 4372/92/67: 62–68, 83 (memorandum by Mezhlauk, December 26).

Table 2 The state budget for 1937: preliminary and final variants (million rubles)

	Date	*Revenue*	*Expenditure*	*Surplus*
Narkomfin	July 16, 1936	95,000	92,000	3,000
Narkomfin	Dec. 23, 1936	96,187	93,687	2,500
Politburo	Dec. 27, 1936	96,595	94,095	2,500
Politburo	Jan. 10, 1937	97,782	96,832	950
TsIK	Jan. 13, 1937	98,069	97,120	949

Source July 16, 1936, from RGASPI, 82/2/772: 55. The expenditure total included 2500 million for price reductions; the surplus was designated 'to strengthen the credit resources of Gosbank'. December 23, 1936, from RGAE, 4372/92/67: 36ff (memorandum by Grin'ko). December 27, 1936, from RGAE, 4372/92/67: 62–68, 83 (memorandum by Mezhlauk, December 26). January 10, 1937, from RGASPI, 17/3/982: 25 (art. 102). January 13, 1937, from *Industrializatsiya 1933–1937* (1970): 133–137.

changes, increasing both revenue and expenditure, the budget was approved by a full session of TsIK, the Central Executive Committee of the USSR, on January 13 (Table 2). The annual plan for net currency issue was fixed at the compromise figure of 700 million rubles.[16]

In some previous years, including 1936, the national economic plan was approved on the same occasion as the state budget by a full session of TsIK. But in 1937 the final economic plan was not approved until March 29, 1937, evidently because normal decision making was interrupted by the Pyatakov trial, the February–March plenum of the party's Central Committee, and the arrests of economic officials which accompanied and followed these events. Between December 27, 1936, and March 29, 1937, further substantial allocations were authorised for capital investment, including an additional 260 million rubles for the Moscow Metro and an additional 110 million rubles for ZiS, the Stalin motor vehicle factory in Moscow.[17] But in the final plan investment was planned at 32,593 million rubles, only 56 million rubles greater than on December 27. In the final plan the increase of production for all industry was again fixed at only 20%, as in the plan approved on December 27. Its targets for the increase in labour productivity and the reduction in industrial costs were somewhat more modest than those in the original

[16] RGAE, 4372/92/63: 435 (report by G. Smirnov, September 16, 1937: we have not found any earlier reference to this figure).

[17] RGASPI, 17/3/983: 20–21 (art. 87, January 7) and 24–25 (art. 100, January 8).

Table 3 Planned productivity and costs of the industrial commissariats, 1937 (change over 1936, per cent)

	Change in productivity		*Change in costs*	
Date of plan	*July 19, 1936*	*Mar. 29, 1937*	*July 19, 1936*	*Mar. 29, 1937*
People's Commissariats				
Heavy Industry	23	19.8	−9	−4.5
Light Industry	23	18.3	−6	−1.6
Food Industry	20	19.2	−1	−0.6
Timber Industry				
—Factory production	21	23.5	−5.5	−4.5
—Timber procurement	28	28.0	–	−7.5

Source RGASPI, 17/3/979: 56–59 (July 19, 1936) and *Narodno-khozyaistvennyi plan Soyuza SSSR na 1937 g.* (Moscow, 1937). Within the Commissariat of Light Industry as planned in July 1936, costs exclusive of bread baking were to decline by 7%.

directives of July 19, 1936 (Table 3).[18] The plan still insisted that the managers of economic agencies and enterprises must pay proper attention 'to securing favourable conditions for the development of the Stakhanov movement and for the determined dissemination of the experience of individual Stakhanovites among the workers'.[19] But the production plans for 1937 demonstrated that even the more modest hopes attached to Stakhanovism would not be realised, let alone the doubling, trebling or quadrupling of productivity about which the leaders had earlier held forth.

Meanwhile the VK (*valyuta* or Foreign-Currency Commission) and the Commissariat of Foreign Trade had already embarked on the preparation of the foreign trade and balance of payments plans for 1937. As usual, the supply commissariats and their principal chief administrations sought to maximise their own imports and minimise their exports. In the preparation of the 1937 plan, the conflict was particularly fierce.

[18]See *Narodno-khozyaistvennyi plan Soyuza SSSR na 1937 g.* (1937): 7–40 (decree of TsIK and Sovnarkom); the production figures are on pp. 42–45, and the investment figures on pp. 142–143. The March 29 decree did not give figures for cost reduction, but they are included here.

[19] *Narodno-khozyaistvennyi plan Soyuza SSSR na 1937 g.* (1937): 11.

Owing to the poor 1936 harvest, grain was not available for export. But the defence industries imperatively demanded increased imports of the most modern armaments and equipment to produce them, and also of non-ferrous and rare metals which the USSR produced in insufficient quantities. On November 21, 1936, the VK considered the disagreements between the commissariats about the imports and exports of raw materials, and agreed on quotas which reduced the import of iron and steel and increased the import of non-ferrous and rare metals.[20] But disagreements continued, and on January19 a high-level commission under Molotov increased the import plan by 17.5%, including an increase of 30% in the planned value of the imports of non-ferrous metals. But it was able to increase the export plan by less than half of the proposed increase in imports, even though the proposed increase in exports included scarce commodities needed at home such as petrol and manganese ore.[21] When the balance of payments plan came before the Politburo on February 14, it showed a small deficit, unlike the plans for previous years, and the Politburo promptly resolved that the foreign trade part of the plan should be revised so as to have 'a certain positive balance'.[22] The very detailed plan, occupying 100 folios in the archives, adopted by Sovnarkom three days later, showed a small surplus of 6.5 million foreign-trade rubles, out of a 1483-million total.[23]

Following the adoption of the 1937 plan, as in previous years, further ad hoc additional allocations to capital investment were approved, including 175 million rubles for railway construction in the Far East and 74 million rubles to the Donbass coal industry.[24]

2 Plans and Purges

Although the annual plan was not publicly promulgated until the end of March 1937, the execution of the plan proceeded without interruption. The full session of the Politburo on December 27, 1936, had approved

[20] GARF, 8422/3/9: 309–312.

[21] GARF, 8422/3/9: 6–10. The commission included Ordzhonikidze, Voroshilov, and Mezhlauk, and the principal people's commissars concerned with the economy.

[22] RGASPI, 17/162/20: 179 (art. 347).

[23] GARF, 5446/1/490: 179–279 (art. 272/59, February 17, 1937).

[24] GARF, 5446/1/492: 169–170 (art. 651/149, April 22, 1937) and art. 693 (April 29, 1937).

both the 1937 plan and the plan and state budget for the first quarter of the year. The quarterly plan was relatively moderate. For instance, investment was planned at 20.4% of the annual total, the plan for railway transport was 87,000 wagons per day as compared with the annual target of 95,000, and cost reduction in the Commissariat of Heavy Industry was planned at 2.7% as compared with the planned reduction of annual costs of 4.5% in 1936.[25]

Planning decisions in Narkomtyazhprom (the People's Commissariat of Heavy Industry) and Gosplan were disturbed in the early weeks of 1937, first, by the separation of defence industry from heavy industry, and secondly, by the death of Ordzhonikidze and the subsequent transfer of Mezhlauk from Gosplan to take Ordzhonikidze's place as commissar of Heavy Industry.[26]

Sovnarkom resolved to establish a People's Commissariat of Defence Industry and to appoint Rukhimovich as its first head on December 8, 1936.[27] On December 21, Sovnarkom approved a list of 275 establishments, including over 200 factories and construction projects, to be transferred from Heavy Industry to the new commissariat. These included not only armaments factories but also some factories producing special steels, engineering factories with a strong military component such as the Khar'kov locomotive works, and specialised machine-tool factories still under construction.[28] As Table 4 reports, nearly one-quarter (23.4%) of the staff of the old Heavy Industry Commissariat was scheduled for transfer to Defence Industry, including nearly 30% (28.7%) of the engineering and technical staff. Those employed under Defence Industry earned, on average, 13% more than those remaining in Heavy Industry.[29] In the 1937 plan, Defence Industry was allocated as much as

[25] For the quarterly budget and plan, see RGASPI, 17/3/962: 3 (items II and III of the Politburo session of December 27, 1936); 103–106 (appendix).

[26] SZ (1937), section 2, no. 10: art. 48 (February 25, 1937).

[27] SZ (1936), no. 63: art. 461 (establishment of the new commissariat, December 8, 1936) and SZ (1936), section 2, no. 42: art. 346 (appointment of the new commissar on the same day).

[28] GARF, 5446/1/488: 216–226.

[29] GARF, 5446/1/491: 191–192 (March 31, 1937).

Table 4 The heavy and defence industries: employment plans, April–June 1937 (thousands)

	Commissariat of Heavy Industry	*Commissariat of Defence Industry*	*Combined total*
Industrial employees			
—Manual workers	2,258	650	2,908
—Engineering and technical staff	236	95	331
—Clerical staff	138	51	189
—Other	254	77	331
Industrial employees, subtotal	2,886	873	3,759
Building, research, administration etc.	701	222	923
Employees, total	3,587	1,095	4,682

Source GARF, 5446/1/491: 191–192 (March 31, 1937).

29.2% of the total investment in the two commissariats.[30] A considerable amount of military work was still undertaken in Heavy Industry, which was allocated an additional separate sum for its own defence production, equal to one-third of the investment in the Commissariat of Defence Industry. In all, 39% of investment in the two commissariats was allocated to the defence industries, broadly defined.

The changes in personnel in Gosplan and the Commissariat of Heavy Industry at the beginning of 1937 did not form part of the repressions; they were more administrative than political. These key sectors of the economy continued to be managed by very experienced people. Rukhimovich had had charge of both the coal industry and the railways at various times; Mezhlauk had been head of the Commissariat of Heavy Industry's Chief Administration of Metallurgy from 1921 to 1929; and G. I. Smirnov, who replaced Mezhlauk as head of Gosplan, had worked in Gosplan since 1930, first as head of capital construction planning and then as Mezhlauk's deputy.

[30]This was 2527 million rubles out of an 8667-million total (RGASPI, 17/162/20: 191–192 (January 17, 1937)). For the two commissariats' combined total before their divorce, see Table 1).

A further development in 1937, which does not seem to have been part of the repressions, was the separation of civilian machine building from the Commissariat of Heavy Industry; this involved Narkommash, a new People's Commissariat of Machine Building, established on August 22. Mezhlauk was transferred from Heavy Industry to Machine Building, and Kaganovich was appointed to Heavy Industry in his place. Kaganovich temporarily relinquished his post as commissar of transport; his place was taken by Bakulin, one of his deputies and head of the Commissariat's Political Administration.

While these changes were evidently not part of the repressions, during the first quarter of 1937 the repressions were already disrupting the progress of industry. By March 1, 1937, nearly one thousand officials had already been arrested in the various industrial commissariats, 47% of all officials arrested. They included many factory managers and senior officials. Pyatakov and the head of the chemical industry, Rataichak, were arraigned in the public trial of January 1937 and subsequently executed (see Sect. 1 in Chapter 1). A wave of arrests spread throughout industry, culminating in the autumn of 1937 with the arrest of the three people's commissars appointed at the beginning of the year: Rukhimovich, Mezhlauk and G. I. Smirnov (see Table 1 in Chapter 1). In the course of 1937 all the heads of the many chief administrations responsible for particular industries were also deposed; and nearly all were arrested (see Table 2 in Chapter 1).

The repressions also affected all other aspects of the economy. During 1937, the heads of nearly all the economic government departments were removed and arrested: in April Kalmanovich (the Commissar of State Farms); in May Kraval' (the chief of TsUNKhU, the Statistical Administration); in June Rozengol'ts (Commissar of Foreign Trade); in August Grin'ko (Commissar of Finance) and Kleiner (chief of the Committee for Agricultural Procurements); in September Lyubimov (Commissar of Light Industry), and Kruglikov (director of Gosbank, the second to be arrested); in October Chernov (Commissar of Agriculture), Veitser (Commissar of Internal Trade) and V. I. Ivanov (Commissar of the Timber Industry, the second to be arrested). Many of these men had been conspicuously successful, notably Rozengol'ts, who had brought about a positive balance of payments, Kleiner, who had established the grain stocks which enabled the USSR to negotiate the bad harvest of 1936 without famine, and Veitser, who had begun the modernisation of internal trade. In all these cases the new persons appointed were inferior in experience and competence to those they replaced.

The campaigns against the activities of key economic institutions and their most prominent leaders continued throughout 1937, frequently initiated by articles in *Pravda* written by previously little-known authors. The Gosplan journal *Planovoe khozyaistvo* (Planned economy) was strongly criticised in an article headed 'Impossible backwardness'. Two major statistical handbooks were lambasted, *Trud v SSSR* (*Labour in the USSR*) as 'an unsuitable handbook', and the annual statistical survey *Sotsialisticheskoe stroitel'stvo SSSR* (*Socialist construction in the USSR*) as 'Statistical cretinism'.[31]

A characteristic of such assassinations by printed word was that some of the specific criticisms seemed or even were reasonable. The labour handbook failed to include a complete coverage of the wage bill, data on vacations were inadequate, and data on Stakhanovism completely absent. The statistical handbook failed to compare plans with results, used two different definitions of 'large-scale industry', and its tables on labour prepared in the industrial department of TsUNKhU were not consistent with the data from its labour department; its data on capital investment were confused and incomplete, and showed expenditure on investment but not its output. These are defects in the statistics with which Western economic historians have struggled for many decades; they were often the fault not of the statisticians but of those who controlled their activities. But the *Pravda* authors attributed many of these weaknesses to wrecking. Thus N. Tumanov, in charge of the Industrial Bank, who wrote the article on investment in the planning journal, had been 'exposed as an enemy of the people', and other articles had been written by 'the Polish spy Dombal', the 'double-dealing Trotskyist Petrovskii', and G. Abezgauz, 'now exposed as an enemy of the people'. The labour handbook had allegedly excluded the data on vacations 'for the benefit of the Mensheviks'. The critic of the statistical annual was not so crude, but nevertheless claimed that this volume, like most TsUNKhU publications, was 'characterised by an abundance of figures not needed by anyone', as if it 'specifically intended to confuse things'. The authors of these attacks were sometimes pursuing vendettas of their own or of their associates, but were often responding to signals from the NKVD, claiming that a particular person or group had been exposed by its investigations.

[31] *Pravda*, May 14, 1937 (A. Karavakhov); August 3 (A. Vinnikov); August 14 (A. Semenov).

These attacks did not lead to the publication of better information, but they provided a pretext for greatly reducing what was reported to the public. *Planovoe khozyaistvo* continued to be published but was greatly restricted in its scope. Statistical publications were reduced in number and after the end of 1937 they contained little data. Handbooks such as *Trud* and *Sotsialisticheskoe stroitel'stvo* did not resume publication until 1956 and 1957, years after Stalin's death.

Another favourite mode of criticism followed by repression was the launching of an attack on a prominent individual by a signal from an official source. Thus on July 6, 1937, a certain A. Kukhtin, in an article in *Pravda*, 'Put the system of price formation in order', strongly criticised the Commissariat of Internal Trade for the complexity and confusion of prices which its officials had allegedly made worse. The article was accompanied by a note from the editors of *Pravda* agreeing that 'these questions require the most serious attention' and naming Veitser, the responsible people's commissar, as the person who should 'explain the situation with price formation on the pages of this newspaper'. A month later Veitser published a long reply; he conceded that many of the criticisms were justified but also defended some aspects of price policy.[32] He explained that some of the complexity arose because prices were 'increased or reduced ... in order to increase demand, to bring the commodity to the consumer'. As an example, he gave a reduction of the prices of perfumes on June 1. But he could not acknowledge that industrial goods were generally in short supply because the state had fixed their prices too low, because that would have amounted to a criticism of official policy.

In a normal year this incident would have been without serious consequences. But in 1937 a cloud hung over Veitser. On October 17, he was removed from his post and arrested on the same day.

The purge of many leading agricultural officials, including Chernov, the people's commissar of Agriculture, and Kleiner, the head of the Committee for Agricultural Procurements, is particularly well documented. On April 7, 1937, a full meeting of the Politburo decided to remove seed testing from the institute led by the world-famous plant scientist Vavilov. Instead, high-quality seeds would be produced and tested by local organisations under a ministerial board that included Vavilov

[32] *Pravda*, August 7, 1937.

but would be dominated by politicians (such as Molotov) and ideologues (such as the notorious pseudo-scientist Lysenko). The Politburo also received a proposal from Chernov about the state high-quality seed fund and referred it to the commission.[33] The decisions gave no hint of criticism of Chernov, still less of wrecking. On the same day the Politburo solicitously (or sinisterly) resolved that Chernov's working day should be reduced to six hours, with two days off every six days.[34]

It was against this background that the Politburo met on June 19, 1937. Reviewing the forthcoming plenum of the Central Committee, the Politburo approved the agenda. The first and second items were reserved for Yezhov and for discussion of the new electoral law. After that, there would be items on seed improvement (introduced by Yakovlev), on crop rotation (Chernov), and on improving the work of the 'machine-tractor stations' or MTS (Chernov again). The session also approved draft plenum resolutions on crop rotation and on the improvement of seeds.[35]

The Central Committee then met from June 23 to 29. The first days were taken up with Yezhov's report on conspiracies within the party and state. Then, the meeting turned to other matters, especially agriculture. On June 27, Yakovlev spoke on wrecking in seed selection. Chernov was due to speak about improved rotation systems the following day. But before the day came, his former deputy Muralov was arrested. Among Muralov's alleged crimes was that he had conspired with other Agricultural Commissariat officials to resist collectivisation, waste high-quality seed, and undermine the health of livestock.[36] When Chernov spoke, on June 28, he noted, as if in the spirit of an apology: 'It seems that my deputy was a wrecker.'[37] On the subject of his speech,

[33] RGASPI, 17/3/985: 2–3 (agenda item III).

[34] RGASPI, 17/3/985: 42 (art. 171).

[35] RGASPI, 17/3/988: 1–2.

[36] The NKVD report, reproduced in *Tragediya*, 5(1) (2004): 254–255, gives details of a 70-strong 'counter-revolutionary organisation' in the Agriculture Commissariat, all now arrested. The editors date the report 'not earlier than 11 June,' the day on which the first of the arrests took place. But the arrests were apparently spread over more than two weeks. According to his daughter's first-hand testimony, Muralov was arrested on June 28 (Muralova, 1990, at http://scepsis.net).

[37] Chernov's speech and discussion: RGASPI, 17/2/618: 112–130.

he suffered a setback; on Molotov's recommendation, his proposals were returned for further consideration.[38] Chernov's second speech, on the development of the MTS, was also badly received; it precipitated a dispute with Eikhe, a candidate member of the Politburo. Chernov sought tighter central control of MTS funding. Eikhe objected. Chernov responded that it was people like Eikhe who were the problem.[39]

As for the improvement of seeds, the resolution was prepared by Yakovlev, and presumably was close to the text approved by the plenum. The plenum resolution (included in the unpublished minutes) uncompromisingly declared:

> As a result of wrecking, organised by right-wing counter-revolutionaries and fascist Trotskyists, and of the carelessness and short-sightedness of the land agencies, particularly the chief grain administration of Narkomzem [the People's Commissariat of Agriculture] of the USSR and the grain administrations of the People's Commissariat for State Farms, fulfilment of the task set by the second five-year plan was disrupted: the achievement of sowing by selected seed on 75 per cent of the whole grain area.

The resolution also complained that the poor organisation of the assessment of seeds had enabled enemies of the state and of the peasants to conceal good seed and introduce poor seed. It called for the establishment of a new system along the lines of the resolution of April 7 and the establishment of a state fund of improved seed amounting to one-half million tons.[40]

Yakovlev's report to the plenum, a version of which was published in *Pravda*, specifically claimed that valuable Russian peasant seeds, almost eliminated in Russia, were widely used in the United States: almost half of the winter wheat sown in the USA consisted of varieties of the Russian seed *krymka*. Simultaneously, poor-quality seeds had been widely disseminated in the USSR. According to Yakovlev, some of these actions were undoubtedly due to wrecking, while others were due to incompetence:

[38] RGASPI, 17/2/620: 47, 95.

[39] RGASPI, 17/2/620: 50–78 (Chernov's speech) and 79–82 (the dispute with Eikhe).

[40] RGASPI, 17/2/618: 66–69.

> Where bureaucratic negligence ends and wrecking, bringing immense harm to the economy, begins—the agencies of the NKVD and the courts will of course be able to establish this.[41]

Matters now moved rapidly towards the condemnation of the top officials in the agricultural agencies. On August 7 a resolution of Sovnarkom and the party's Central Committee condemned an order of July 3 signed by Chernov as people's commissar of Agriculture and Kleiner as chairman of Komzag: according to the resolution the order had sanctioned the mixing together of different seeds by categorising this mixture as 'commodity-improved seed' (*tovarno-sortovoe zerno*). This was described as a 'crude violation' of the plenum decisions and the subsequent decisions of Sovnarkom.[42] Kleiner had already been arrested on August 4, and on August 11 a directive from Stalin and Molotov to provincial party and executive committees and local officials of Komzag and Zagotzerno stated (without public announcement) that Kleiner 'has been exposed and arrested as an enemy of the people, organising wrecking in grain collections, the construction of grain elevators and the collection and storing of selected seeds'.[43]

For the moment, Chernov continued at liberty, fully engaged in his work as commissar of Agriculture. Later in the month a further resolution of Sovnarkom and the Central Committee rejected the commissariat's plan to allocate improved seed to different regions; it condemned the plan as leading to the loss of a 'considerable quantity of improved seed', and adopted an alternative plan. The resolution also ruled that 'in future the plan allocating improved seed should be approved by Sovnarkom (and not by Narkomzem)'.[44] This was the prelude to a Politburo decision of September 10 which reproved Chernov for violating state and party discipline by failing to cancel a 'wrecking order' of the commissariat dated March 27, 1936, which had allegedly removed from production a number of valuable seeds.[45] On the following day,

[41] Yakovlev's speech, which appeared in *Pravda* on July 5, 1937, was the only leading address on agriculture to be authorised for publication in full. Its transcript was not preserved, however.

[42] RGASPI, 17/3/990: 118–119 (art. 530).

[43] *Tragediya*, 5(1) (2004): 296. Kleiner was executed on November 26.

[44] RGASPI, 17/3/990: 65 (art. 770, August 25, 1937).

[45] RGASPI, 17/3/990: 5 (art. 25).

September 11, the Politburo approved a decree of Sovnarkom, which cancelled the 'standards for high-grade and ordinary seed' which had been adopted by the Commissariat of Agriculture on November 13, 1935. These standards, now described as 'wrecking', had allegedly increased the percentage of weeds permitted to exist in stocks of seed. The decree of September 11 also denounced as 'completely impermissible the rejection by Narkomzem on formal bureaucratic grounds of a proposal by rank-and-file officials of the commissariat to correct the wrecking standards'.[46]

In the following weeks, more savage action followed. Yakovlev, head of the Agricultural Department of the Central Committee, who had led the campaign against the alleged disruption of selected seeds at the June 1937 plenum, was arrested on October 12 (he was eventually tried in secret and executed on July 29, 1938). On October 20, 35 members of the Commissariat of Agriculture council were removed as 'enemies of the people', 14 were 'transferred to other work,' and six were expelled from the party and the land agencies.[47] Nine days later Chernov was removed from the commissariat, and he was arrested on November 7. Afterwards he appeared in the Bukharin trial of March 1938. The more prosaic charges on which he was sentenced to die involved spreading plant diseases, undermining the quality of seeds and crop rotations, disrupting the MTS, and destroying livestock.[48]

Even towards the end of 1937, at a reception on October 29 for Stakhanovites and leading officials of the iron and steel and coal industry, Stalin made clear that the repressions of economic officials had not come to an end:

> The nub of the matter is not fulfilling or overfulfilling the plan ...That's important, but it's not everything ... The main thing is that economic managers should understand that history has given them a great honour—to be leaders in the Soviet system, where leaders are surrounded not by the hatred of the people, but quite the reverse—by the love of the people ... I am not even convinced that there are not among you—I apologise again—people who are working under the Soviet system and are nevertheless

[46] RGASPI, 17/3/991: 5 (art. 14).

[47] RGASPI, 17/3/992: 76 (art. 357).

[48] 'Proekt obvinitel'nogo zaklyucheniya' (1938) at http://istmat.info.

> protecting themselves with some intelligence service—Japanese, German or Polish. I am not yet convinced of this.[49]

Historians of Stalin's nomenklatura purge have long searched for patterns in the destruction of some officials and the survival of others. Several factors appear to have been at work, especially personal history, career and record of achievement or failure, and past associations with other leaders.[50] Past personal connections with non-Bolshevik parties or with Bolshevik oppositionists of the 1920s were a particular danger, but age itself could be a risk, because Stalin had lost confidence in the skills and allegiances of much of the revolutionary generation and wished to promote younger officials who would owe loyalty to him personally.[51] It was a problem to be close to mishaps or shortfalls, where suspicion of sabotage could turn any mistake into a crime, because responsibility was often shared and everyone concerned had a clear incentive to shift the blame onto others.[52] Perhaps those with fewer moral scruples had an advantage over others at first, but some of them were eventually seen as liabilities, and the purges caught up with them later.[53]

Was the arrest of particular leaders connected in any systematic way with the policies and practices that they promoted? This idea is suggested by the observation that periods of heightened repression often coincided with more radical economic policies, and this prompted some observers to look for emergent radical and moderate factions that prospered at each others' expense as the political cycle went around. While organised factions certainly existed in the 1920s, the Stalin-era archives have turned up no evidence that they persisted beyond the early 1930s. This does not rule out the existence of personal networks based on some moral or professional affinity. It is evident that the nomenklatura purge was at first resisted by many economic officials, as Yezhov complained (see Sect. 1 in Chapter 1), and in particular by those linked to the industry commissar

[49] RGASPI, 81/3/96: 144–149 (uncorrected transcript).

[50] Khaustov and Samuel'son (2009): 152.

[51] Ilič, ed. (2006): 38–41 (O. Khlevniuk).

[52] Ilič, ed. (2006): 40 (Khlevniuk); Gregory (2009): 121–124; Khaustov and Samuelson (2009): 158–166.

[53] Viola (2017).

Ordzhonikidze. The latter's suicide, a vain response to Stalin's pressure, opened the way to a widening of the purge.[54] In the same way that some industrial officials resisted grandiose targets for their industries when they could, and declined to hunt for scapegoats when the targets failed, some agricultural officials apparently wanted the same for agriculture, and some statisticians tried to uphold statistical integrity when the party demanded inflated results. In that context we will return below to the turnover of agricultural officials (Chapter 4) and of statisticians associated with the population census (Chapter 5).

3 The First Half of 1937

The very poor harvest of 1936 resulted in a serious food crisis, the results of which began to appear in the last weeks of the year. As early as November 25, 1936, the provincial party secretary and the head of the executive committee in Chelyabinsk province wrote to Stalin and Molotov stating that 'as a result of the low harvest, due to the drought, many kolkhozy are already without grain'; only 1000 kolkhozy in the province would have sufficient grain. They requested a food loan amounting to five million puds to take them through to the next harvest.[55] By the beginning of 1937, serious food shortages and signs of famine had begun to appear in many villages in various regions. In consequence, hungry peasants made their way into the towns in large numbers, and in towns in Ivanovo, Leningrad, Sverdlovsk and other provinces huge queues appeared, and informal rationing was introduced.[56] Simultaneously other peasants made their way to factories and building sites in search of temporary work. At first the authorities displayed their usual reluctance to provide food assistance to the villages. On February 20 the Politburo noted that, in spite of the increase in the supply of flour in provinces such as Ivanovo, the bread supply had been interrupted and queues for bread had formed, particularly in workers' settlements. It resolved that bread and flour should be supplied in factory shops and canteens, and it called for action against 'speculators'.[57] The Politburo

[54] Khlevniuk (2009): 157–165.

[55] GARF, 5446/26/59: 9.

[56] Osokina (1998): 203–204; Garros, ed. (1995): 111–165 (diary of A. S. Arzhilovskii); Hessler (2004): 231–234.

[57] RGASPI, 17/3/984: 6, 40 (art. 23).

was particularly anxious about food supplies to Ivanovo because of the major food disturbances in the textile factories of the province in 1932 (Vol. 4: 188–191) In March it imposed restrictions on the amount of grain which could be sold in the villages per day. But by mid-March food loans to the countryside began to be authorised more generally, and by the time the new harvest began to appear in July 1937, food and fodder loans amounting to 1.1 million tons of grain had been issued to the countryside (Vol. 6: 282, 283).

Throughout 1937 the shattering blows against the leaders and staff of commissariats and enterprises increasingly dominated economic life. In the first quarter of 1937 their effect was already apparent. At this time, failures in industry were still reported fairly frankly in the press. On March 30 a *Pravda* editorial entitled 'The plan of the second Stakhanovite year', published shortly after the delayed public promulgation of the 1937 plan, complained:

> The third month of 1937 is coming to an end, and it must be recognised that the results are not comforting. They give rise to alarm. The plan targets have not been fulfilled in January, February and March. … It is time to put a stop to seasonal declines in production.

The editorial blamed the failures on 'weak everyday economic leadership'.[58]

Three days later, a more detailed survey by the son of the long-established Gosplan statistician A. Mendel reviewed 'The First Quarter of 1937'.[59] Noting that 'the successes of the fourth year of the second five-year plan [1936] have led to dizziness in the heads of many people,' he reported that not only was there a lag in the fulfilment of the state plan in January–March 1937 but 'in several branches of the economy there has been a retreat from the positions conquered last year.' In the coal industry, production had been lower than in January–March 1936 as a result of the 'extremely low level of economic and technical leadership'. The results in the oil industry were similar, and capital investment in January and February had also been lower than in the same months of 1936. In spite of poor results, the number of industrial workers was 9.5%

[58] *Pravda*, March 30, 1937.

[59] *Pravda*, April 2, 1937.

greater and the average wage 6.3% greater than in January and February 1936, so the wage bill had risen by 16.4%. A few days later, an article in the economic newspaper presented similar results, and pointed out that, as a result of the poor performance, freight carried on the railways in January and February amounted to only 78,000–79,000 wagons per day as compared with the 87,000 planned, and that this was only slightly higher than in the same months of 1936.[60] A further article noted that, as a result of the underperformance of the economy, the issue of bank loans was 100 million rubles less than planned.[61]

Behind the scenes the assessment was even bleaker. In a speech to a meeting of the heads of chief administrations of the Commissariat of Heavy Industry on February 5, two weeks before his death, Ordzhonikidze bluntly stated that it was 'really shameful' that production in all industries in January was lower than in January 1936. He acknowledged that this was partly due to the particularly bad weather at this time—'It is difficult now with transport, with snowstorms and blizzards, all that is true'—but he insisted that this should not be treated as an act of God: 'Immediately get to work and overcome these difficulties':

> If it goes on like this in February there will be a real scandal. ... If we leave things to take their own course in February as is happening at present then we shall have a defeat in February, there will be two months of failure, and, God knows, the programme is not so easy that we can recover from these two months and complete the programme in (the remaining) 10 months. ... I think we must today decide to send round to the factories all the heads of chief administrations and their deputies, and the best officials who are capable of doing things efficiently, so as to inspire the directors.[62]

Ordzhonikidze frankly attributed part of the trouble to the demoralisation of factory directors and workers consequent to the Pyatakov trial:

> Cde. Vasil'kovskii let me know that Al'perovich [head of the machine-tool industry] told him the story that now at some factories, in connection

[60] *Ekonomicheskaya zhizn'*, April 10, 1937 (I. Bolshakov). To deal with the transport situation, a full meeting of the Politburo held on March 17 established a commission to plan and control freight (RGASPI, 17/3/985: 3).

[61] *Ekonomicheskaya zhizn'*, April 24, 1937 (N. Leonov).

[62] RGASPI, 85/29/156: 55–56.

> with the trial of those scoundrels, people feel they are being attacked as if they were criminals, that they must all answer for Pyatakov and the others. Nothing of the kind, it must be said to them straight that they are not criminals but our cadres ... And we should not ignore the fact that there is gossip among the workers at the factories.[63]

Unpublished reports subsequently submitted by Gosplan to Stalin and Molotov continued to make harsh assessments of economic performance. On March 17 Smirnov criticised developments in the first weeks of 1937 in particularly severe terms. Industrial production in January had been 14.3% less than in December 1936, and the data for February 'show no improvement, and a worsening of the situation in a number of industries'. The production of coal and oil had fallen even below the level of the same months of 1936, and 'as a result the supply of the main fuels to industry and transport had been sharply reduced.' The results for iron and steel, chemicals and timber, for some engineering industries, and for transport had all been poor. Iron and steel production had been hindered by interruptions in the supply of ore and coke; in the southern factories the stock of coke amounted to only 36 hours. And currency in circulation, which was planned to decline by 500 million rubles in January–March, had declined by only 78 million rubles in the first two months of the year.[64]

Three months later, on June 7, a further report from Smirnov to Stalin and Molotov noted in almost equally harsh terms that the performance of most industries continued to be poor in the second quarter: 'As a result of the failure of the coal production plan, stocks held by users have fallen to extremely low levels: 4.5 days' stock in Narkomput' [the Commissariat of Transport], two days in the coke industry and 10 days in Narkomvod [the Commissariat of Water Transport].' Moreover, industrial costs had risen instead of declining. Capital investment continued to be far less than planned, largely because of the poor supply of metals, timber and cement. Building costs, planned to fall substantially, were considerably higher than in 1936, primarily because labour productivity was far less than planned.[65]

[63] RGASPI, 85/29/156: 56.

[64] RGAE, 4372/92/63: 258–272.

[65] RGAE, 4372/82/63: 302–306.

On July 31, a revised report on the results of the first six months stated that, in the upshot, industrial production as a whole was 12.9% greater than in January–June 1936. This increase, the report stated, was much smaller than planned, and also much smaller than the increase in the same period in all the previous three years. Unusually, the production of consumer goods (Group B) had increased more rapidly than the production of producer goods (Group A): this 'was not a result of the particularly successful performance of the industries producing consumer goods, but of the particularly unsuccessful performance of the industries producing producer goods'. The low level of timber production, described as 'a sharp and shameful lag', had resulted in a 'timber famine'. And although the cotton harvest had been good, the cotton textile industry had been unable to cope with the increased supply of cotton. The report complained of the 'serious weakening of economic leadership in a whole number of industries and economic units'; this hinted at the deleterious effect of the purges. The leadership of the Stakhanov movement was also weaker, and this had led to only a very small increase in labour productivity and a decline in labour discipline: unjustified absenteeism had increased. Costs of industrial production, instead of falling, had continued to rise and, in January–June as a whole, were 3% higher than in 1936. The report acknowledged two improvements. The decline in railway freight in the first quarter had been overcome in the second quarter by 'Bolshevik mobilisation', and a large grain harvest was now expected, amounting to five thousand million puds (98.2 million tons).[66]

In public, the press assessment of industrial development also continued to be particularly critical. A survey in *Pravda*—'Heavy industry in the first six months'—for example, listed 22 major industrial products. The production of only ten of these had increased by more than 10% as compared with the first six months of 1936, and in another ten cases, production had actually declined, including coal and coke, oil, pig iron and machine tools. In the iron and steel industry the efficiency with which open-hearth furnaces were utilised had declined. The shortage of metal had been harmful to the machine-building industry and transport, and the shortage of coal and oil had resulted in the depletion of fuel stocks.[67]

[66] RGAE, 4372/92/88: 8–12 (the report is not signed).

[67] *Pravda*, July 28, 1937 (G. Senin).

Table 5 Industrial production in the first halves of 1936 and 1937, change over the first half of the previous year (per cent) by branch and product group

	Number of product groups	*Per cent change over previous year at* *First quartile*	*Second quartile (median)*	*Third quartile*
1937, first half				
Fuels (inc. mining) and power	16	−0.6	0.4	3.0
Metals (inc. mining)	11	−2.2	6.1	15.5
Machinery and equipment	50	−10.0	6.7	38.2
Building materials and chemicals	12	−3.9	3.9	14.6
Timber and paper products	17	−21.9	−11.8	1.8
Light industry products	15	1.6	5.1	14.2
Food, drink and tobacco	25	−14.5	−0.8	16.3
All civilian industry	146	−8.6	1.7	16.5
1936, first half				
All civilian industry	134	3.9	20.7	40.1

Note The original reporting of the production series that are counted separately in each year (146 in 1937, and 134 in 1936) gives rise to some double-counting, which is of two kinds. A few series were subsidiary elements of other series, which are also counted separately and represented in the table. And many products were intermediate inputs into the production of other products. If anything is measured precisely in this table, it is the impression conveyed by the printed page of the statistical report to the original reader, the Soviet economic policy maker.
Source Calculated from data in *Osnovnye pokazateli* (June 1936): 10–17; ibid. (June 1937): 12–19.

The results for the first six months printed in the small-circulation confidential Gosplan bulletin showed in detail that the performance of industry had been extremely poor. Table 5 summarises the results for nearly 150 civilian product groups in the first six months of 1937. The contrast with the same period of 1936 is startling. In the first half of 1937 the growth rate at the median of the product distribution was barely positive (1.6%). Nearly half of all product groups had declined, and a quarter of them had declined at least 8%. The sudden turn to stagnation in 1937 is emphasised in the lower part of the table, which shows the distribution of performance in the first half of 1936 over the same period of 1935. One year previously, the growth of civilian industry had been buoyant. Nearly all product groups were expanding, and the growth rate over 1935 at the median of the product distribution had been more than 20%.

The pattern of performance reported in the summer of 1937 was best for machinery and equipment; these products were particularly liable to hidden inflation.[68] As the Gosplan reports had indicated, performance was relatively poor in the fuel and power sector, where almost half of all product groups declined. The monthly figures show that coal production was lower than in the same month of 1936 in every month except June, and pig-iron production followed the same course (see Tables B.3 and B.4). Even the production of electric power, the best-performing industry in this group, increased by only 10.6% above the same period of 1937 in the first six months of 1936. The performance of the food industry was also poor. And disaster struck the timber industry, where more than three-quarters of product groups declined. Industry had not experienced such a poor performance since the crisis year of 1933.

Unlike the situation in previous years, the increase in production depended on the increase in the labour force rather than the increase in labour productivity.[69] In Union and local industry as a whole, the number of workers increased by 7.3% in January–May 1937 over the same period of 1936, and output per worker (measured in plan prices of 1926/27) increased by 5.9%. The contrast with the first five months of 1936 is stark. While the increase in productivity in these months of 1937 over 1936 was responsible for less than half of the increase in production, in the first months of 1936 the increase in productivity over the previous year accounted for more than three-quarters.[70] Within industry, this pattern was broadly followed by both heavy industry and the food industry. In light industry the position was even worse: the number of workers increased by as much as 11%, but output per worker fell slightly.

After the rapid increase in capital investment in 1936, its performance in the first months of 1937 was extremely unsatisfactory. In the first five months of the year, just 22.8% of the annual investment plan was completed, compared with 32.7% of a much more ambitious plan in the first

[68] *Journal of Comparative Economics*, 28(1) (2000): 134–155 (M. Harrison).

[69] For the data in this paragraph, see *Osnovnye pokazateli* (June 1937): 20.

[70] Less than half: 5.9% (productivity growth) compared with 5.9 plus 7.3% (production growth). More than three-quarters: 25.9% compared with 25.9 plus 7.3%, these figures being given in Vol. 6: 297.

six months of 1936.[71] This decline was accompanied by a fall in the production of building materials, following a rapid increase in 1936.[72]

The authorities were particularly alarmed by the coal shortage, already a problem in 1936, which had serious effects throughout the economy. On April 28, a decree in the name of both Sovnarkom and the party's Central Committee condemned the work of the Donbass coal mines as 'unsatisfactory'.[73] It pointed out that the decrees issued during the coal crisis of 1933 (Vol. 4: 381–388) had led to a rapid increase in production in 1933 to 1935, but they had not been carried out consistently. Underground workers, and engineers and technicians who worked at the coal face, had not been provided with pay and conditions which sufficiently differentiated them from those who worked above ground. Not enough attention had been given to preparatory work in the mines, and the exploitation of some coal seams had been halted prematurely owing to the 'harmful bureaucratic "theory of concentration"'. On the question of wrecking, the decree faced both ways. It condemned the practice of 'wholesale accusations against managers, engineers and technicians' but called at the same time for 'specific measures to eliminate the damage to industry caused by the wreckers'. On the following day, April 29, an unpublished decree of Sovnarkom, 'Assistance to the Donbass coal industry', increased the planned investment in the industry in 1937 by 74 million rubles (including 25 million for housing), and provided a subsidy of 174 million rubles to cover the gap between production costs and the price charged for coal.[74] The wage bill was increased, and additional consumer goods, work clothes and food were allocated to the region. A substantial universal department store was to be built in Stalino in 1937, and three more were to be built in other provinces in 1938 to improve consumer supplies. The prices charged for meals in canteens were to be

[71] *Osnovnye pokazateli* (June 1937): 64. The best achievement was for the school-building programme, where 43.7% of the annual plan had been fulfilled by July 1 (ibid., 66).

[72] Production in January–June 1937 as compared with January–June 1936: cement, −7.7%; silica brick, −0.2%; window glass, −3.5% (*Osnovnye pokazateli* (June 1937): 16–7).

[73] SZ (1937), no. 28: art. 114 (April 28, 1937).

[74] This gap persisted despite the price reform of 1936 (Vol. 6: 355–359). The authors of the decree had second thoughts about the further reform of coal prices: a clause which envisaged price increases, especially for higher grades, by January 1, 1938, was crossed out.

kept down by subsidies.[75] But all these measures failed to bring about immediate improvement.

4 The Second Half of 1937

On June 11, 1937, the Politburo adopted the national-economic plan for the July–September quarter submitted by Gosplan. The only substantial change was an increase of the capital investment plan (this was very optimistic in view of the results so far that year). The Politburo decided that investment in the quarter would amount not to the 9413 million rubles proposed by Gosplan but to 10,348 million rubles, thus increasing the Gosplan proposal by 10%. Nearly half the increase was allocated to the heavy and defence industries, and to the People's Commissariat for Defence.[76]

No substantial improvement in performance took place in the third quarter, except in agriculture, where an outstanding harvest was achieved during these months (see Sect. 6 in Chapter 4). On September 16 Smirnov submitted a 16-page memorandum on the national economic plan for the fourth quarter of 1937 to Stalin and Molotov, which, like his memoranda for the previous two quarters, described the current situation quite frankly.[77] Its first paragraph pointed out that in the first eight months of 1937 industrial production had increased by only 13% in comparison with the same period of 1936; the 1937 plan, 'which envisaged a growth of output by 20.8%, has been considerably underfulfilled'. The figure of 20.8% had been exceeded only by the defence industry, where production had increased by 27.1%, and by local industry and the flour industry. The most important lags were in fuel, metal and timber, the shortage of which had damaged the general development of both production and construction. Only three days' supply of coal remained at the power stations, and on the railways. As in the second quarter, the third-quarter progress of the investment plan remained unsatisfactory. Only 12 of the 55 key projects scheduled for completion in Sovnarkom decisions of March 31 and June 28 had in fact been achieved. In contrast to this bleak picture, the railways and the food industry were achieving their plans; and the good harvest had resulted in a sharp decline in

[75] GARF, 5446/1/492: art. 693.

[76] RGASPI, 17/3/987: 134–136 (art. 517).

[77] RGAE, 4372/92/63: 421–436.

kolkhoz market prices. Retail trade turnover had lagged behind the plan so far, because the production of mass consumer goods in heavy and light industry was considerably less than planned. But the good harvest meant that the production of food and industrial consumer goods in the remainder of the year should enable the annual plan for retail turnover to be fulfilled.

Smirnov stressed that in the third quarter, as in the first six months of the year, the financial plans had been disrupted:

> During the first three quarters, as a result of the failure to achieve the plans for costs and wages, the overexpenditure of resources to cover the debt on the state loans, the underfulfilment of the trade plan, and faults in the work of the bank itself, the annual plan for currency issue has been considerably disrupted.

While net emission was planned at 700 million rubles for the whole of 1937, it was now expected to reach 1650 million rubles by the end of the third quarter.[78] On September 3 Kruglikov, now head of Gosbank, explained in a note to Molotov and Chubar' that the additional 300 million currency issue authorised on August 19 for return at the end of the month could not be returned because 'the receipts from retail trade were 600 million rubles less than the planned average level for the quarter.'[79]

In Smirnov's memorandum of September 16, Gosplan proposed that the production of industry as a whole in the fourth quarter should be 20.2% higher than in the same quarter of 1936, and that the plan for coal, oil and iron and steel in the fourth quarter should approximately equal the *planned* figure for the third quarter. This was more modest than the previous quarterly plans, but still proved to be too optimistic. Smirnov acknowledged that even if the quarterly plan was fully achieved the annual target for 1937 would be missed. Only the Commissariat of Food Industry and the Committee for Agricultural Procurements would exceed the annual plan (as a result of the bumper harvest of grain and sugar). He anticipated that the Commissariats of Heavy Industry and

[78]According to the original draft of the document, monetary issue was expected to increase by 800 million rubles in the third quarter and to reach 1500 million rubles over January–September as a whole. In the final version, 800 was replaced by 950 and 1500 by 1650.

[79]GARF, *fond* Mikoyana, *delo* 966: 99–100.

Machine Building would fall short of the plan by 5.8%, the Commissariat of Light Industry by 4.8, and the commissariats of local industry by 3.4%. The production of the Commissariat of the Timber Industry would be 6.8% lower than in 1936, which meant that it would fall short of the plan by as much as 18.7%. Because of the shortfall, the consumption of fuel would have to be controlled very strictly.

Smirnov's memorandum also made ambitious proposals to improve the financial situation in the fourth quarter. As a result of these measures, net currency issue could be restricted to 200 million rubles, a much smaller figure for the quarter than in the equivalent periods in 1935 and 1936. Even so, the currency issue which had already taken place meant that net issue through the year would reach 1805 million rubles, not the 700 million rubles stipulated in the 1937 annual plan.

A further memorandum submitted by Smirnov in September in connection with the preparation of the 1938 plan stressed the same points about developments in 1937 as the memorandum of September 16, but also emphasised the lag in civilian machine building, which had resulted in a lower level of production than in 1936 of such important items as locomotives, goods wagons and combine harvesters.[80]

Four days after the memorandum of September 16, on September 21, a full meeting of the Politburo approved the quarterly plan submitted by Gosplan.[81] It made two substantial changes: it increased capital investment in the quarter from 7839 to 7994 million rubles and it raised the nominal state budget surplus from 900 to 1500 million rubles. It also ruled that investment allocations for the period up to September 1 which had not been used should be withdrawn, and used only with the agreement of Sovnarkom.[82] It did not, however, make any ruling about currency issue. In fact, large currency issues took place in excess of the modest amount proposed by Gosplan. On November 21 the Politburo noted that the net

[80] RGAE, 4372/92/88: 136–143. For the later history of this memorandum, see Sect. 1 in Chapter 4.

[81] RGASPI, 17/3/991: 1–2; 17/162/22: 1. The meeting was attended by 16 people in all, including five full members and one candidate member of the Politburo. This was the only item on the agenda.

[82] Later in the quarter the Politburo approved an increase in investment by the Commissariat of Defence Industry by 198 million rubles (RGASPI/17/162/22: 35 (art. 405)). Exceptionally, the increase was to be funded from the unused part of the allocation left over from the first three quarters.

Table 6 Industrial production in 1937, third and fourth quarters (physical units)

	Third quarter		*Fourth quarter*	
	Target	*Outcome*	*Target*	*Outcome (estimate)*
Coal (thou. tons)	36,685	30,012	36,148	35,573
Of which, from Donbass	21,344	18,432	20,650	19,522
Oil and gas (thou. tons)	9,500	8,225	9,080	7,991
Oil drilling (thou. metres)	741	528	787	450
Iron ore (thou. tons)	8,550	7,309	8,400	6,666
Manganese ore (thou. tons)	933	718	880	717
Pig iron (thou. tons)	4,201	3,734	4,100	3,696
Crude steel (thou. tons)	5,327	4,292	5,348	4,787
Rolled steel (thou. tons)	3,948	3,081	3,836	3,511
Copper (thou. tons)	40.7	23.8	35.5	22.1
Water turbines (thou. kW)	24.2	16.8	57.5	20.2
Diesel engines (thou. HP)	1,25.0	54.0	125.0	100.5
Beshche hammers (units)	100	114		87
Locomotives E and SU (standard units)	564	451	564	421
Goods vehicles (thou.)	50.8	45.7	50.3	53.0
Motor cars (thou.)	7.5	5.5	6.7	6.8
Tractors (thou.)	12.5	5.2	12.7	14.3
Tractors (thou. HP)	412	120.7	448.8	366
Cement (thou. tons)	1,950	1,481	2,065	1,733
Paper (thou. tons)	218	195	220	264
Cotton fabrics (mn. metres)	999	781	972	1,050
Wool fabrics (mn. metres)	28	26	28	35
Linen fabrics (mn. metres)	67	59	85	77

Source July–September 1937, from *Osnovnye pokazateli* (September 1937); October–December 1937, from *Osnovnye pokazateli* (December 1937).

issues in the quarter amounted to 1300 million rubles, and ruled that 450 million rubles should be returned by the end of the quarter. Even so, the net issue in the quarter would amount to 850 million rubles as compared with the 200 million rubles in the quarterly plan.[83]

For a series of commodities for which figures are available, Table 6 shows that the October–December plan was in most cases close to

[83]RGASPI, 17/162/22: 61 (art. 289).

the July–September plan, though in a few cases it was somewhat more modest. In practice, however, while production usually increased in the fourth quarter, the July–September plan was reached or exceeded in the fourth quarter only in the case of goods vehicles, paper and the three groups of textiles. For six of the 21 products listed (oil, iron and manganese ore, pig iron, copper and locomotives), production actually declined in October–December. The quarterly plan had failed to bring about a substantial improvement in industrial production.

CHAPTER 4

1937 in Retrospect

1 Capital Investment

Throughout the planning process, capital investment had always been intended to decline in 1937, following the huge increase in 1936. In the event, investment in the economy as a whole declined by 9.3% measured in current prices (see Table 1), and investment costs, planned as usual to decline substantially, in fact increased, according to Gosplan estimates, by about 3%.[1] The only substantial increases in investment in the civilian sector were in health and light industry, both of which had been relatively neglected in previous years.

The investment plan for 1937 was less ambitious than that of the previous year. Despite this, realised investment fell substantially short of the plan (Table 2). In addition, a larger proportion of investment projects than in previous years was not completed as scheduled.[2] At a meeting of the Chief Administration for Supplies in the Commissariat of Heavy Industry on December 9, 1937, its head complained that 'we have a huge number of every kind of unfinished building projects,

[1]The cost of equipment declined by about 2%, but the cost of 'pure construction', which comprised about two-thirds of all investment costs, increased by over 4% (Vol. 6: 410); RGAE, 4372/92/101: 73–91 (May 11, 1938).

[2]According to RGAE, 1562/10/531a: 70–71, investment in 1937 amounted to 33,223 million rubles, and only 28,513 million were brought into operation.

R. W. Davies et al., *The Industrialisation of Soviet Russia Volume 7: The Soviet Economy and the Approach of War, 1937–1939*,
https://doi.org/10.1057/978-1-137-36238-4_4

Table 1 Capital investment, 1936–1937: outcomes (million rubles and per cent)

	1936	*1937*	*Per cent change*
Heavy industry	10,099	9,266	−8.2
Timber industry	790	786	−0.5
Light industry	1,133	1,233	+8.8
Food industry	1,546	1,368	−11.5
Local industries	830	552	−33.5
Agriculture (collective farms)	3,050	2,209	−27.6
Railways	4,602	4,217	−8.4
Education	896	746	−16.7
Health	525	805	+53.3
Other items	11,840	10,847	−8.4
Total	35,311	32,029	−9.3

Note As reported in Table B.7, there are several estimates for capital investments in 1937. The figures shown here are most comparable; in both years, they cover all state capital outlays, and are not limited to those falling under the main state plan for investment. Other outlays, which did not form part of the main state plan, were described as 'earmarked' (*tselevye*), 'above-the-limit' (*vnelimitnye*), and 'extra-plan' (*vneplanovye*). Such expenditure increased sharply in 1936 and 1937 (see Vol. 6: 269). In 1937, extra-plan investment amounted to 684 million rubles, and above-the-limit investment to 3826 million rubles. For this reason, however, the figures in this table cannot be compared with the plan figures shown in Table 1 in Chapter 3 without adjustment.
Source Table B.7; changes are calculated by us. Figures for 'Other items' are differences between the total below and the rows above.

which have been carried over to 1938; a huge amount of the nation's capital is tied up on these sites because of inadequate supplies.'[3] The decline in the production of building materials affected all capital construction. According to the 1937 report on the building department of the Chelyabinsk tractor factory, 'the basic cause of the failure to fulfil the plan was the shortage of materials.' Timber, cement and other materials were supplied in insufficient quantities, and 'the material comes by fits and starts, and is of a poor quality' and the metal supplied was inappropriate.[4]

[3] RGAE, 7297/5/2: 6. However, one report claimed that the low figure for completions of capital projects was because 1937 was the first year in which projects were counted as completed only when their acquisition was authorised by a deed of transfer (*akt priemki*) (RGAE, 1562/10/531a: 218–220). On the failure to control unfinished investment in the late 1930s, see further Davies, Harrison, and Wheatcroft, eds. (1996): 48–51 (Harrison).

[4] RGAE, 7297/2/100: 9–10 (early 1938).

Table 2 Capital investment, 1937: plans and outcomes (million rubles and per cent)

	Plan	*Outcome*	*Per cent of plan*
Heavy industry	8,667	8,609	99
Timber industry	1,010	680	67
Light industry	1,406	1,003	71
Food industry	970	789	81
Local industries	770	419	54
Agriculture (collective farms)	2,301	1,964	85
Railways	5,541	3,957	71
Education	1,100	649	59
Other items	10,772	9,449	88
Total	32,537	27,519	85

Note The plan figures shown here are those adopted on December 27, 1936. These were substantially more ambitious than the previous version of July 19, 1936. Small further revisions were agreed on March 29, 1937; see further Table B.5. The outcome figures are those listed in Table B.7 under 1937 (B). The coverage of these figures is limited to those capital outlays that were authorised by the plan. For their reconciliation with the figures shown in Table 1, see the note to that table.
Source Tables B.5 and B.7. Percentages of the plan are calculated (as are figures for 'Other items,' as differences between the total below and the rows above).

Many high-priority capital projects were associated with supplies for defence and the armament industries, and many of these were assigned to the forced labourers of the NKVD. Developments in the defence sector were complicated during 1937 by the administrative separation of most (but not all) of the defence industry from heavy industry, as well as by claims for additional projects that arose during the year. On March 16, 1937, for example, additional investment was allocated to the Commissariats of Defence Industry and Heavy Industry to the value of 132 million rubles for the production of armour steel for shipbuilding, and as with other investment decisions this was accompanied by an allocation for additional imports.[5] As late as October 22, a further 125 million rubles was allocated to increase armour-plating capacity.[6] By October 25 the total investment allocated to the Commissariat of Defence Industry alone for 1937 amounted to 3062 million rubles, as compared with the allocation of 2527 million rubles in the original 1937

[5] RGASPI, 17/162/20: 216–217 (art. 167).
[6] RGASPI, 17/162/21: 34–35 (art. 397).

Table 3 Capital investment in defence and the NKVD, 1936–1937 (million rubles and per cent)

	1936	*1937*	
	Outcome	*Target*	*Outcome*
By commissariat			
Defence industry	1,467	3,380	2,200
Defence (army and navy)	2,518	2,450	1,936
NKVD	2,694	2,047	2,643
Defence, subtotal	6,679	7,877	6,779
All capital investment	35,311	32,593	32,029
Defence, % of total	18.9	24.2	21.2

Note In Tables 1 and 2, capital investment in the defence industry would have been counted within the total for heavy industry; capital investment of the Defence Commissariat and the NKVD would have been counted under 'other investment'.
Source Table B.8.

plan.[7] But these allocations far outran the capacity of the economy to supply construction goods and labour, and eventually, investment in the defence industries was estimated variously at 2200 or 2473 million rubles (see the note to Table B.8). This was far below the 3380 million rubles originally planned for the defence industries under the Commissariats of Defence Industry and Heavy Industry combined, but still 50% greater than investment in 1936. While the total of investment in heavy industry as a whole declined by 8.2%, the share that went to the defence industries increased from 14.5 to 24–28%.

Investment by the NKVD, mainly in large projects in remote regions, many of them defence-related, was originally planned to decline by 24%. We will see that additional allocations during 1937, particularly to Dal'stroi and other projects in the Far East, had the result that the investment realised by the NKVD almost reached the level of 1936. In contrast, capital construction by the Defence Commissariat, which more than doubled in 1936, was planned to decline slightly in 1937, and in fact was 21% less than planned.

Investment in the defence industry and the NKVD as a whole thus increased slightly as compared with 1936, and as a share of all investment outlays (Table 3), while investment in the civilian sector of the

[7] GARF, 5446/1/496: 71–72 (art. 1919/427ss).

Commissariat of Heavy Industry declined by about 18%, continuing the trend which prevailed throughout the second five-year plan.

The greatest cutback fell on the Commissariat of Agriculture, responsible for collective farms and the MTS (machine-tractor stations) that supplied the collectives with machinery services. Its investment fell by more than a quarter (Table 1). This particularly affected farm construction, including storage facilities which, we will see, proved to be particularly important in the 1937 harvest. It was generally harder for the commissariat to lay hands on building materials than on the quotas of equipment assigned to agriculture, because such machinery was produced by powerful departments that were given preferential treatment by suppliers. Chernov, the commissar of Agriculture, was aware of the bias and tried to push against it but failed. Asking for 4.7 billion rubles for capital works in agriculture in 1937, he sought to allocate 30% of this very large sum to construction.[8] But the national plan that was adopted gave him a much smaller sum, 2.3 billion, and only 20% of that was assigned to construction.[9] And the plan, in turn, was substantially underfulfilled (Table 2).

2 The GULAG Economy

In 1937 the economy of the GULAG was at the focus of several powerful pressures. The NKVD was given charge of more than 6% of the country's programme of capital investment, according to the plan, and more than 8% in the outcome.[10] NKVD projects already included a number that were seen as particularly critical to the building of the country's political and economic potential, and more projects were piled onto to the NKVD agenda during the year. As for the capacity to meet these requirements, the size of the GULAG workforce was enlarged during the year by an inrush of detainees caught up in the mass operations of the terror. But the unplanned expansion was chaotic, and the chaos was accentuated by another factor: terror was at work inside the GULAG, as well as in the wider society beyond the barbed wire.

[8] RGAE, 7486/4/465: 70.

[9] RGAE, 7486/4/571: 266.

[10] For the 1937 plan, 2043 million rubles (Table 3) are compared with 32,537 million (Table 2) and, for the outcome, 2643 million (Table 3) with 32,029 million (Table 1).

The initial plans for the NKVD economy were lower than those for 1936, following the general trend in capital investment. A Sovnarkom decree of March 10, 1937, set the NKVD investment plan of 1937 in December 1, 1936 prices at 2.06 billion rubles, below the level of 1936, then expected to be 2.49 billion rubles at current prices (Table B.8). But on March 14, 1937, Sovnarkom increased investment in Dal'stroi by 100 million rubles; and on March 22 it increased the allocation to investment in the railways by GULAG in the Far East by 174.5 million rubles.[11] So the investment plans for the NKVD approved in the spring of 1936 were already heading towards the maximum level achieved in 1936. This took place against the background of a slight reduction in the number of prisoners in camps and colonies from 1,196,000 on January 1 to 1,038,000 on July 1.[12]

The situation changed fundamentally with the struggle against 'anti-Soviet elements,' launched on July 31 by Politburo approval of NKVD Order no. 00447 (see Sect. 2 in Chapter 1). It soon emerged that there were not enough camps to cope with the numbers being detained, and a Politburo resolution of July 31 proposed to establish additional camps in the remote parts of Kazakhstan and in the forest regions of the Far North, Siberia and the Urals. The plans for Kazakhstan proved impractical, so efforts were concentrated on the forest regions. The GULAG was instructed to establish seven camps for 103,000 detainees by January 1, 1938.[13] The choice of the timber industry was apparently motivated by two factors. Logging was labour-intensive, with few setup costs. And, half way through the plan year, the slow progress of timber procurement was already a cause for concern.[14]

The influx of prisoners arising from the mass operations may also have prompted a rush of decisions to transfer various large-scale projects to the NKVD in August and September 1937: hydroelectric power projects on the Volga and Kama Rivers; two new Siberian railway lines; the dredging of the Amur River; and a new naval base in the Gulf of

[11] Dalstroi, from GARF, 5446/1v/491: 195; railways in the Far East, from GARF, 5446/1v/492: 169.

[12] GARF, 9401/1/4479: 137; 9414/1/1138: 30; see also Table B.3.

[13] GARF, 5446/22a/139: 21.

[14] GARF, 5446/20a/376: 105–106; 5446/377: 200.

Finland.[15] In October 1937, moreover, the Sovnarkom confirmed an enormous project to link the coal mines of the NKVD's Ukhta-Pechora trust with the existing railway network.[16] But work did not begin on any of these projects until 1938.

Meanwhile, the initial flood of detentions was followed by fresh waves, one after another. A mechanism for escalation was built into Order no. 00447, which envisaged that local NKVD administrations would be able to exceed their initial quotas for arrests and executions, as long as they sought permission for Moscow. Alongside the operation against 'anti-Soviet elements' under Order no. 00447, moreover, further mass operations were launched against the relatives of 'enemies of the people', 'national counter-revolutionary elements', and others. The inflow of detainees rose again. By February 1, 1938, the camps and colonies held 1,467,000 detainees (including those in transit), an increase of more than 40% over the previous July. At the same time, a further 545,000 were held in prisons, many of whom would soon be despatched to the camps.[17]

In the later months of 1937, the condition of the unfortunate detainees deteriorated markedly. In principle, prisoners assigned to camps were required to be in reasonable health and fit for work. In fact, most new recruits had been held for months in appalling conditions, and many had suffered torture. They arrived in a weakened state, often ill or disabled, lice-ridden, sometimes lacking outer clothing. On arrival they were settled in overcrowded quarters, or in tents, lacking basic sanitation.[18] The churning and overcrowding of tens of thousands of people in poor health spread infectious diseases such as typhus through the North East and Siberia to the Far East.[19] Successive decrees of the NKVD

[15] Hydro power stations, from RGASPI, 17/3/990: 26, 126–128; GARF, 5446/1/494: 152–154 (August 10, 1937). New railways, from RGASPI, 17/3/990: 51, 140–142; GARF, 5446/1/494: 192–194 (August 17, 1937); RGASPI, 17/162/21: 173–174; GARF, 5446/1/495: 48–49 (September 5, 1937). Dredging the Amur, from *Glavnoe upravlenie lagerei* (2000): 721–722, 771–772 (Sovnarkom and Central Committee resolution of August 3, 1937). A new naval base, from RGASPI, 17/162/22, 19 (September 29, 1937); *Glavnoe upravlenie lagerei* (2000): 721, 773–774.

[16] GARF, 5446/1v/496: 103; 9414/1/2947: 52–53.

[17] GARF, 9414/1/1138: 21.

[18] GARF, 8131/37/111: 7–9; 9414/4/11: 133–149; Khlevniuk (2004): 173–177.

[19] As reported by USSR state prosecutor Vyshinskii to Stalin and Molotov on February 27, 1938. GARF, 8131/37/111: 34; Khlevniuk (2004): 173.

threatened officials with penalties for violating the rules on assignment of prisoners, but failed to improve the situation.[20]

The worst conditions were to be found in the seven new timber camps, set up without preparation in the uninhabited forests of the North and Siberia in the autumn of 1937. Of the 91,500 prisoners held there on January 1, 1938, only 41,200, or less than half, were classified as fit for heavy labour. That left 20,700 fit for work involving intermediate effort, 22,700 classed as fit only for light work (including 4900 disabled prisoners), and 6900 that were unclassified, but more likely unfit than otherwise. Their prospects were dismal: more than 12,000, or one in eight, would die in the winter months from December 1937 through March of the following year.[21] This grim total made up almost half of the 26,000 prisoner deaths in the entire Soviet labour camp system over the same period. Such patterns were not sustainable. In the outcome, four of the new camps were soon dissolved, one was relocated, and only two remained in place for a longer period.[22]

To complicate matters further, the GULAG was not just a passive receptacle for the human waste arising from the mass operations. The terror was also escalated within the GULAG itself, being directed against both prisoners and NKVD personnel. Order no. 00447 authorised the execution of 10,000 prisoners classed as especially dangerous. NKVD officials also became victims: Arrests in 1937 included the chiefs or deputy chiefs of GUSHOSDOR; the Dmitrovsk camp (first S. G. Firin, who was also a deputy chief of GULAG, and then Z. B. Katsnel'son, who replaced Firin in both capacities); Volzhlag; the NKVD 'special' (i.e. especially secret) construction unit; and Dal'stroi. With each superior officer's arrest, many subordinates were also swept away.[23]

Yezhov's leadership of the NKVD shifted its priority away from economic tasks to stricter controls and tougher measures against the 'counter-revolutionary underground' in the camps and colonies. In May 1937 the NKVD issued new instructions.[24] For all prisoners, regular searches

[20] GARF, 9401/12/94: 113–114 (NKVD decree, December 19, 1937); 9401/12/316: 353 (NKVD decree, April 17, 1938).

[21] GARF, 9414/1/2740: 53.

[22] Smirnov (1998): 69.

[23] For data on GULAG camp leaders, see *Glavnoe upravlenie lagerei* (2000): 798–857.

[24] GARF, 5446/20a/178: 67–68 ('On measures to reinforce the regime in prisons and colonies'); 77–78 ('On the isolation and reinforcement of the regime in camps for especially dangerous prisoners').

were instituted and punishments increased for the most minor infractions. Prisoners convicted of political crimes were put under special restrictions. They were to be removed from all positions of administrative or business responsibility. They could undertake skilled duties as supervisors, foremen, and technicians only under continual guard, both at work and going to and from work. Political detainees were no longer allowed unescorted movement within the camp perimeter. Any prisoners that the GULAG had contracted out to other production organisations, not held in compliance with these rules, were to be 'immediately withdrawn and transferred back to the camps'.

The new policies, introduced in advance of the mass operations, were reinforced when the latter began. During 1937, as a result, they eliminated the relatively progressive aspects of economic organisation of the GULAG that had begun to appear in previous years (Vol. 6: 343–346). Previously, many prisoners had been allowed unescorted movement so that their working time could be used more effectively. This came to an end. To hold and transport prisoners only under guard required more armed guards; when they were not available, working time was lost. Political prisoners with skills were employed less productively because they were now barred from responsible positions.

In the autumn one of the most effective incentives used to motivate the forced labourers was removed. This was the promise of early release in return for satisfactory work. On October 21, 1937, the GULAG prohibited camp commandants from offering early release to prisoners sentenced under Order no. 00447. Effectively, this was extended to all political prisoners, who made up a growing proportion of the camp population (Table B.3).

That anything was achieved in this setting is remarkable. While construction costs rose, achievements lagged behind plans. The overall fulfilment of the GULAG construction plan in 1937 was 71.6%, made up of 80.5% for hydro plants, 63.2% for industrial facilities, and 62.7% for railways. The Noril'sk combine reported 50%, and the Volochaevka-Komsomol'sk railway only 44.5%.[25]

The NKVD economy saw a few successes in 1937, but every success had its downside. For the value of industrial production the NKVD exceeded its quota: 945.4 million rubles compared with 931.7 million

[25]GARF, 9414/4/3: 19.

in the plan.[26] (But the context of this achievement was the unplanned growth in the labour resources of the GULAG.) The Ukhta-Pechora trust increased oil deliveries dramatically: 50.8 million tons, up from 31.1 million tons in 1936. (But the trust made a 22.7-million-ruble loss on all products, and its total capital spending of 66.5 million rubles included 17.6 million overspent.)[27] In the Far East, Dal'stroi's mining operation exceeded the target with 51.5 tons of pure gold. In addition to the gold deposits of the Kolyma region, geologists found rich tin deposits there.[28] (But diminishing returns were setting in. Dal'stroi proposed to maintain gold production up to 1939 at the cost of sharp increases in exploration and investments in infrastructure—1.6 billion rubles in three years, compared with 460 million over the five years from 1932 to 1936—as well as an enlarged workforce.)[29]

The difficulties of the NKVD sector in 1937, like those of the economy as a whole, reflected two basic factors. One was the very sharp increase of investments and the unsustainable mobilisation of labour that began in 1936. The other was the onset of the terror.

3 Industrial Production

In 1937 the rate of growth of industrial production declined sharply. According to the official index for large-scale industry, it amounted to a little over 11% as compared with 20% in 1934, 23% in 1935, and 30% in 1936 (see Table B.11 and Vol. 6: 399). The increase fell far short of the planned 23%. The most dramatic decline in the growth rate was in heavy industry. While the gross value of production of the Commissariat of Heavy Industry had increased by over 30% in 1936, in 1937 the output of the two commissariats into which it was now divided increased by only 10.2% (Machine Building) and 7.4% (Heavy Industry) respectively.[30] At the heart of this deceleration was the extremely slow growth of the key

[26] GARF, 5446/22a/142: 5.

[27] RGAE, 7733/36/77: 182; GARF, 9414/1/2947: 51, 53.

[28] Gold, from GARF, 5446/20a/249b: 2; 5446/17/313: 140 (Sovnarkom resolution of April 3, 1936); Shirokov (2014): 141. Tin: a mine would later be opened at Butugychag, made infamous by Zhigulin (1989).

[29] GARF, 5446/20a/949a: 66, 82; Khlusov (1998): 74–77. This document, written in 1936, was dated 1937 by mistake.

[30] *Industrializatsiya 1933–1937* (1971): 145–146.

industrial materials, iron and steel, coal and oil, and the decline in the production of building materials (Table 5). According to Gosplan, 'the lag in the production of fuel, metal and timber has affected the whole course of production and construction.'[31] The immediate reason for this slowdown was the low level of investment in these industries in previous years, which meant that in 1937 relatively little new plant was being completed.

In the case of iron and steel, for example, far less new capacity was brought into use during the second five-year plan than had been scheduled in the plan. This shortfall was partly compensated in 1934–1936 by the more efficient use of equipment. But by 1937 the possibilities of increasing the return from existing plant were being exhausted. At the same time the new equipment received was very limited. The plan for the supply of equipment in 1937 was modest to begin with, and in the outcome the Chief Administration of Metallurgy received equipment valued at less than half the plan: 92.9 million rubles out of 210.6 million. The major sites, with the exception of Kuznetsk, were particularly badly hit: Magnitogorsk, for example, received only 27.9% of its planned allocation. This was because the machine-building plants supplying iron and steel equipment, such as Uralmash, the giant engineering works in Sverdlovsk, were increasingly converted to production for defence; and because priority in the import of equipment was also given to defence needs.[32] In 1937, investment in metallurgy and the amount of new capacity brought into operation were both smaller than in any other year of the second five-year plan.[33] A Gosplan survey at the beginning of 1938 (Table 4) showed that the plan to introduce new iron and steel capacity in 1937 had utterly failed.

Another factor in the poor performance of the iron and steel industry was a decline in efficiency, no doubt a result of the upheaval in the industry associated with the repressions. The yield from blast and open-hearth furnaces had been steadily improving from 1933 onwards, but in 1937 the blast-furnace coefficient (which declines with increased efficiency)

[31] RGAE, 4372/92/63: 422 (G. I. Smirnov, September 17, 1937).

[32] For a detailed account of investment in the Chief Administration of Metallurgy in 1937, see RGAE, 4086/2/4009: 2–38 (especially 4–7).

[33] RGAE, 4086/2/4009: 76–77.

Table 4 New iron and steel production facilities in 1937 (units)

	Target	*Outcome*
Blast furnaces	5	1
Open-hearth furnaces	10	0
Rolling mills	13	6

Source GARF, 5446/22a/1091: 14–17.

rose from 1.09 to 1.11, and the output of open-hearth furnaces fell from 4.60 to 4.55 tons per square metre.[34]

The decline of efficiency was a general feature of 1937. In a striking draft memorandum Gosplan complained that control over the technical norms which set out standards for the use of equipment had been greatly weakened:

> technical norms are not managed either by the commissariats or the chief administrations, and the factories have demoralised a huge number of the staff responsible for the norms.

The quality of coal had deteriorated, and more coal was being used per unit of metal output than in 1936. Moreover, according to the administrations responsible for machine building, the norms for the consumption of metal had been exceeded by 6–7%.[35]

The shortage of iron and steel had repercussions throughout heavy industry. The director of the Chelyabinsk tractor factory complained that 'they [metal suppliers] accept orders but do not supply the metal; you can't close your eyes to the fact that if there is no metal we can't meet [our own] order.' The factory could not establish proper standards with cast iron (*lit'e*) because 'we have to adjust ourselves to the material we get,' which came bit by bit from different factories, although it should have come from Magnitogorsk, next to the tractor factory.[36] On September 20, 1937, Mezhlauk, now people's commissar of Machine-Building Industry, wrote to Stalin and Molotov complaining that his commissariat had received only 800,000 of the 1,495,000 tons of

[34] See Clark (1956): 254. *Promyshlennost'* (1957): 122, claims, however, that the productivity of open-hearth furnaces increased in 1937.

[35] RGAE, 4372/92/88: 10–11 (July 31, 1937). On the norms, see Vol. 6: 162–164.

[36] RGAE, 7295/2/25: 200–201.

structural steel and 120,000 of the 269,000 tons of wire rod to which it was entitled, and that this was a major reason for its failure to fulfil its plan.[37]

The high priority afforded to the production of armaments also affected the whole of heavy industry. At a meeting discussing the 1937 annual report of the Stalingrad tractor factory the rapporteur stated that 'many of our resources are used for special [i.e. defence] production'; tractors constituted only 20% of the programme.[38] Throughout 1937 the Commissariat of Heavy Industry issued decrees imposing priority for defence needs on its civilian factories. On February 7, for example, it ordered Glavspetsstal' (the Chief Administration of Special-Purpose Steels) and several big factories (Uralmash, Krasnoe Sormovo, the Ordzhonikidze machine-tool factory, Elektrostal', the Stalingrad and Chelyabinsk tractor factories, and the main ball-bearing factory) all to give priority to supplying components for improved aircraft propellers.[39] On February 28, reinforcing a government decision, it instructed the Commissariat of Water Transport to give first priority to those of its shipments relating to defence. On June 2 it declared that orders from the aircraft industry were not being met, and instructed its head of material budgets to ensure that Glavspetsstal' received nickel, molybdenum and other metals in sufficient quantities to fulfil these orders. On July 14 it put into practice a decision of the Defence Commission that Uralmash should carry out orders to produce howitzers, and that to this end the Chelyabinsk tractor factory, Uralvagonzavod, and the Zlatoust and other factories should supply Uralmash with the necessary components.[40]

For its part the Commissariat of Defence Industry reduced the plan for bicycle and automobile lamps, and other industrial goods, and even tried, unsuccessfully, to give up the production of consumer goods altogether.[41]

[37] GARF, 5446/20a/377: 77–86.

[38] RGAE, 7295/2/25: 104 (February 22, 1938).

[39] Uralmash was the giant engineering factory in Sverdlovsk (Ekaterinburg); Krasnoe Sormovo was a shipyard on the Volga in Gor'kii (Nizhnii Novgorod); Elektrostal' was a steelworks in the Moscow province.

[40] RGAE, 7297/38/305: 22–30, 93, 154–160, 225–230. Uralvagonzavod was an engineering factory in Nizhnii Tagil.

[41] RGAE, 4372/92/63: 428 (September 17, 1937); Gosplan objected on the basis that the Commissariat of Defence Industry was the sole supplier of these items.

The consumer industries also expanded far more slowly than in the previous three years. The production of all consumer goods increased by 15% in 1937, as compared with 26% in 1936 (Table B.11). This slower rate of increase was primarily a result of the relatively poor performance of the textile industries, the production of which increased by 9.0%. The production of raw cotton and the supply of wool increased slowly in 1937, and as a result the output of cotton and woollen textiles increased by only 6%. On August 7, 1937, an unsigned memorandum in Mikoyan's files savagely criticised the performance of light industry and accused the leadership of the Commissariat of Light Industry, including Lyubimov, of 'surrounding itself with conservative elements and wreckers, and blindly trusting them'. With a wealth of detail, the memorandum claimed that there had been a steady increase in the production of spoiled and low-quality cotton textiles, reaching 21.4% of production by May. Nothing had been done to bring equipment into order. The productivity of labour was lower than in the previous year. In short:

> In the cotton-textile, linen, knitwear, glass and other branches of the industry the practice is widespread of fulfilling plans with poor-quality goods, requiring only a small amount of labour, and simple to produce.[42]

Later in the month the party's Central Committee convened a conference, attended by Stalin and Molotov, to discuss light industry. At the conference, Yeremin, a deputy head of the industry, reported that after the NKVD had exposed the presence of 'wreckers' in the industry, some officials had tried to protect themselves by turning in on themselves and surrounding themselves with documents and memoranda, and Lyubimov acknowledged that 'in the past six months discipline has been disrupted more than ever before.'[43] Both Lyubimov and Yeremin were dismissed from their posts on September 7.

With the boost to agricultural production from the good harvest in the second half of 1937, the food industry performed much better than light industry: its output increased by 18.1%. The production of the meat and dairy industry increased somewhat less rapidly than the

[42] GARF, *fond* Mikoyana, *delo* 960: 21–15.

[43] RGASPI, 17/120/273: 23–25, 203–205.

average, at 15%, but the increase in flour and bread production reached 22% and of fruit and vegetables as much as 54%.[44]

The most successful industrial performers in 1937 were the cooperatives. In the first eleven months of 1937 their production was 24% higher than in the same period of 1936, and their most rapid increase was in the production of consumer goods. Output of the tailoring industry increased by as much as 90%, and of 'cultural goods' by 46.6%. About one-sixth of the production of cooperative industry consisted of food products, which increased by 22.2%.[45]

4 The Defence Industries

The plan for armaments, as for industry as a whole, was carried out less successfully than in the previous year: only 68.4% of the military contracts issued by the Defence Commissariat to industry were fulfilled as compared with 77.5% in 1936. And the actual production of armaments increased much less rapidly than in 1936. The various measures of growth show startling differences. The value of military orders calculated in current prices increased by 23.3%; and production in plan prices of 1926/27 by 17.2%.[46] But the Harrison index, which is based on the number of weapons of various types, and does not reflect improvements in quality and sophistication within types, increased by only 6.2%. Although armaments production did not attain the plan target, it was responsible for approximately one-fifth of the increase in the production of large-scale industry in 1937.

The aircraft industry was the major exception to this general pattern. On December 19, 1936, Voroshilov convened a commission of the Defence Commissariat to approve the 1937 plan for the industry. Reflecting the great importance attached to the industry, the commission included Stalin, Molotov, Mezhlauk, Ordzhonikidze, Rukhimovich and a number of leading designers, including the chief designer Tupolev.[47]

[44] RGAE, 1562/329/2383, 7.

[45] *Osnovnye pokazateli* (November 1937): 16.

[46] Defence production increased in 1937 by 20.3%, according to M. M. Kaganovich (*Pravda*, April 3, 1938); it is not stated whether this figure refers to the total production of the Commissariat of Defence Industry, or only to its military production.

[47] Cited by Rodionov, 'Chronology' (2016), at http://warwick.ac.uk/aviaprom (for 1937).

Table 5 Aircraft produced by type and model, 1936–1937 (units)

	1936	*1937*
Fighters	957	2,072
Of which		
DI-6	10	112
I-16	906	1,887
Other models	41	73
Bombers	414	996
Of which		
TB-3	115	23
SB	268	926
DB-3 and 3F		45
Other models	31	2
Reconnaissance	1,139	818
Trainers	968	1,937
Passenger and other	796	210
All aircraft	4,274	6,033

Source As Table B.19.

The plan it approved corresponded remarkably closely to the actual results. It called for the production of 5196 aircraft, including 1800 I-16 fighters, 900 SBs (fast bombers) and 900 DB-3s (long-distance bombers). In numbers of aircraft the plan was exceeded: 6033 aircraft were produced altogether, more than the targets for the SBs and I-16s (Table 5). The long-distance DB-3 bombers fared much worse. The plan was apparently reduced to 300, but only nine were produced in the first six months of 1937, and a mere 45 in the year as a whole (including the DB-3F). This was a familiar pattern. The DB-3 had been approved for batch production only in August 1936, and, as usual, the teething difficulties took much longer to overcome than was hoped.[48]

The 1937 aero-engine plan, on the other hand, was virtually fulfilled in quantitative terms: production reached 15,410, as compared with the plan of 15,950.[49] But, as we shall see, this figure concealed a serious problem of quality. And in terms of the value of orders placed by the military, only 66% of the engine plan was fulfilled.

While the aircraft industry expanded somewhat less rapidly than in 1936, the increase was still very large. The number of aircraft produced

[48] Byushgens, ed., *Samoletostroenie* 1 (1992): 344–345 (Yu. E. Egorov).

[49] Byushgens, ed., *Samoletostroenie* 1 (1992): 429 (G. F. Kostyrchenko).

increased by 41%, the value of orders by 64.5%, and the Harrison index by as much as 97%. The share of all military orders placed with the aircraft industry increased from one-quarter to as much as one-third of the total (from 24 to 32%). The production of the new I-16 fighters more than doubled. Bomber production increased even more rapidly, by 141%, a consequence of the dramatic expansion in the number of SB fast bombers, produced for the first time in the previous year. The production of training aircraft also nearly doubled. However, although passenger and other civilian aircraft received great publicity in 1937, the number produced declined rapidly, and remained at a low level until after the Second World War.

At the end of 1936 and during 1937 the military effectiveness of Soviet aircraft against their opponents was tested for the first time, when both the Axis powers and the Soviet Union sent substantial numbers of aircraft to Spain. Soviet aircraft performed generally well in the first months of the conflict. The main fighter sent to Spain was the I-15, which ceased production in 1936 but was still in full active service. This was a biplane, light and manoeuvrable, and the military considered it was the appropriate fighter for direct conflict with the enemy. The main German fighter, the Heinkel He-51, also a biplane, was slower than the I-15, and the ceiling it could reach was lower. The Germans soon decided that it must be replaced. Another biplane was the Italian Fiat CR-22; like the He-51, it proved somewhat slower than the I-15, and much less manoeuvrable.[50]

The days of the wood-and-fabric biplanes that dominated the skies in the First World War were about to end, however. The Soviet Union also sent the new I-16 monoplane fighter to Spain. It was much faster than the I-15, and the military considered that it was primarily useful against enemy bombers and reconnaissance aircraft. When engaged with the He-51 and the CR-22, it proved markedly superior. The Axis plane equivalent to the I-16, the Messerschmitt Me-109 monoplane, began to appear in Spain in April 1937. The Messerschmitt fighter was more stable and easier to fly than the I-16, but its early version was markedly slower, and was soon replaced by a new model.[51]

[50]Byushgens, ed., *Samoletostroenie* 1 (1992): 132–139 (K. Yu. Kosminkov); this source provides considerable technical detail about the rival aircraft.

[51]Byushgens, ed., *Samoletostroenie* 1 (1992): 163–166 (K. Yu. Kosminkov).

Tupolev's SB bomber also got its first battle test in Spain. In the autumn of 1936 the first SBs were despatched to Spain, and were manned by both Soviet and Spanish Soviet-trained aircrew. They proved faster and reached a higher ceiling than the equivalent German (Junkers) and Italian (Caproni and Savoy) bombers, and were able to fly without fighter cover for a time. The SBs were the first Soviet aircraft to be licensed for manufacture abroad, and over 100 were produced by the Czechoslovak industry. From the autumn of 1937 the SB was also used successfully in China against Japanese aircraft. But, as with fighter aircraft, the German industry was soon re-equipped to supply the means to defeat them: new anti-aircraft guns and a new model of the Messerschmitt fighter, the Me-109B.[52]

The SBs were equipped with M-100 and later, M-100A aero-engines, based on the French Hispano-Suiza engine, and these on the whole coped well with their tasks. But this proved to be an exception. It was already clear that Soviet aero-engines, unlike airframes, were lagging behind their foreign equivalents. On May 17, 1937, Alksnis, the head of the air force, sent an extensive report to Voroshilov, which was forwarded to Molotov, comparing the most advanced Soviet experimental engines with the current French and United States models. He concluded that large engines were at least three or four years behind their Western equivalents, and that the Soviet engines had advanced less rapidly than their Western equivalents since 1933–34. Alksnis emphasised that 'such a lag undoubtedly influences the flying characteristics of our military aircraft in respect of speed, height, distance travelled and load carried.' According to Alksnis, a major cause of the lag was the 'almost monopoly centralisation of the strongest design organisation in TsIAM [the institute for aero-engines] and the concentration there of the overwhelming majority of research and experimental work, and the extremely slow modification of batch-production aircraft'. He added that 'some other designers lack a production base and their design bureaux are weak, making it difficult to present their alternative concepts and innovations.' He recommended a radical solution, which found official favour later in the 1930s:

[52] Byushgens, ed., *Samoletostroenie* 1 (1992): 237 (Yu. A. Egorov).

Table 6 Tanks produced by type and model, 1936–1937 (units)

	1936	*1937*
T-38 (small tank)	1,046	216
T-26 (light tank)	1,313	550
BT-7/7M (light tank)	1,063	788
T-28 (medium tank)	101	46
T-35 (heavy tank)	15	10
Total	3,948	1,610

Source As Table B.20.

> It is necessary to organise state competitions for design tasks among factory design bureaux, backing up the work with appropriate material incentives.[53]

Following this démarche, on June 7 Rukhimovich sent a long, detailed letter to Molotov on behalf of the aircraft industry. He argued, in implicit refutation of Alksnis, that the main engines had been progressing rapidly, and that the principal bottleneck was the poor quality of fuel, oil, sparking plugs and magnetos. He failed to address the organisation of the industry and the behaviour of its design departments. But he called for the funding of research and development in the industry to be increased from 196 to 290 million rubles. Four days later, on June 11, coincidentally the day on which Tukhachevskii and his colleagues were executed, the Commission of Defence approved both the plan for aero-engine R&D and the grant of 290 million rubles.[54]

In stark contrast to aircraft, the number of tanks produced fell in 1937 by over 60%, a steeper decline than in any other year (Table 6). All types were affected. This semi-collapse requires further investigation. Three factors seem to have been most important. First, at this time the effort to strengthen tanks and improve their performance came up against serious technical obstacles. In the case of the T-26, forcing the engine to work faster and bear heavier loads led to a series of faults, including the frequent failure of valves. The overloading of the BT-7 led its rubber tracks to break, and the pressure on the engine to work

[53] Cited by Rodionov, 'Chronology' (2016), at http://warwick.ac.uk/aviaprom (for 1937).

[54] Cited by Rodionov, 'Chronology' (2016), at http://warwick.ac.uk/aviaprom (for 1937).

faster and cover greater distances caused the gear boxes to malfunction. The amphibious T-38 small tank, which replaced the T-37, proved very difficult to manoeuvre in water if it carried more than two soldiers. Three T-35 heavy tanks broke down in military manoeuvres, and had to undergo major repairs. The experimental T-46, intended to combine the virtues of the T-26 and the BT-7, proved too complicated and expensive, and was abandoned. The attempt to develop a diesel engine, strenuously pursued throughout the second five-year plan, did not come to fruition, partly because the shortage of aluminium meant that the experimental diesels were extremely heavy.[55] And as early as January 17, 1937, the Tank Administration of the Red Army recognised that the thin armour of Soviet tanks gave them no protection against anti-tank guns, which were increasingly coming into use.

A second reason for the collapse of tank production is that these serious technical obstacles and defects emerged in the context of growing repression, which affected the tank industry earlier than the aircraft industry. In the Red Army, Khalepskii, who had been in charge of the Vehicle, Armour, and Tank Administration (ABTU) since 1934, was nominally promoted to be in charge of all armaments in April 1936, and was replaced by his deputy Bokis. In April 1937, before his arrest in August, Khalepskii was transferred out of the Red Army altogether to the lethal post of People's Commissar of Communications, previously held by Rykov and Yagoda.[56]

These uncertainties at the top were accompanied by drastic changes of personnel in the design bureaux and the factories. Even before the repressions got under way, in September 1936, Tukhachevskii, dissatisfied with the work of S. A. Ginzburg, dismissed him from his post as chief designer of the T-26. At about the same time, in the summer of 1936 A. O. Firsov, chief designer of the BT series, was also dismissed when the gear boxes of a large number of BT-7s failed. At the Military Council in June 1937, Bokis vividly described the situation in the industry. His own deputy had been arrested. In many factories there was no firm leadership. The director of the Voroshilov works 'in the new situation is so demoralised that he is not in a fit state to manage the factory'. The designer of the T-46 was working badly after his brother in law had

[55] See Svirin (2006): Chapter I.1.

[56] In June Stalin said of Khalepskii's appointment to ABTU 'I don't know how he got there, he is a drunkard, not a good man' (*Voennyi sovet iyun' 1937* (2008): 140).

been arrested.[57] A recent Russian specialist on the industry summarises the general situation:

> At the beginning of 1937 a large number of trials took place exposing real and alleged wreckers and spies. In consequence decisions that previously took a month were now dragged out over two or three months, and there was no confidence in the future. New developments were at a standstill ...

A large group of 'wreckers' was dismissed and arrested—from factories no. 17, 174, and 185 (the 'Kirov' works), and the Khar'kov locomotive works—as well as a number of military officials responsible for the procurement of tanks and the management of ABTU.[58]

A third factor in the difficulties faced by the tank industry is that tanks received far less attention from Stalin and the Politburo than aircraft. For tank production there was no equivalent of the detailed discussion of the 1937 plan for aircraft, which was attended by Stalin and other members of the Politburo. Stalin met Bokis, the head of ABTU, only once in 1937, on November 19, four days before his arrest.[59] In contrast, Alksnis, the head of the air force, met Stalin as many as nine times in 1937 before his arrest on the same day as Bokis.

Turning from tanks and aircraft, the production of armament and ammunition also expanded less rapidly in 1937 than in 1936. The orders placed by the Defence Commissariat for these items increased by 28% in value terms, and numbers produced by 25% (the changes in values and in weighted numbers are much closer for guns and ammunition than for aircraft and tanks, perhaps because product changes were was slower, so that unit prices increased less rapidly). Naval orders placed with the shipbuilding industry increased more slowly, by only 11% in value terms. The tonnage of ships entering service in 1937 declined from a record

[57] *Voennyi sovet iyun' 1937* (2008): 292–294.

[58] Svirin (2005): 327; Svirin (2006): Chapter I.1.

[59] This meeting, which lasted two hours, was also attended by Molotov, Voroshilov, Yezhov and, Zhdanov, M. M. Kaganovich, recently appointed Commissar of the Defence Industry, and Kulik, head of the Red Army Artillery Administration. N. V. Barykov, a young designer who had worked in the industry since the beginning of the 1930s and now held the post of director of the Kirov experimental works, was also present. For unknown reasons Stalin held Barykov in high regard at this time, calling him a 'good lad' at the Military Council of June 1937, even though, at the same time, Bokis described him as a former Trotskyite who did not deserve confidence (*Voennyi sovet iyun' 1937* (2008): 293).

32,000 tons in 1936 to a mere 7000; because warships were built over several years, this slowdown cannot be interpreted straightforwardly as a measure of value added by the industry in one year. The construction lag for submarines was shorter, and the decline in the number of submarines produced in 1937, from 46 to 9, when numbers had been increasing steadily in previous years, suggests that shipbuilding too underwent a crisis. Repressions certainly played a major part. The plan to produce ten experimental mini-submarines in 1937 came to nothing after the arrest of the chief designer and the closing of the relevant design bureau. In the case of destroyers, the principal designer of the main surface vessel under construction, V. L. Bzhezinskii, who had worked closely with the Italian firm Ansaldo since 1933, was arrested together with three other leading designers, and two of them were executed.[60]

5 Labour and Labour Productivity

As in 1936, production norms were increased generally in the spring of 1937 as part of the drive to increase labour productivity (output per worker). The norms were raised by a modest amount, somewhat less than 20%, and by June the overwhelming majority of workers were already reaching or surpassing the new norms.[61] The norms were sometimes fixed somewhat arbitrarily, and then had to be revised.[62] A Commissariat of Heavy Industry report on the results of 1937 stated that 'the multiplicity of norms and wage rates has not been eliminated, confusing correct norm fixing and making it more difficult.'[63] Gosplan criticised 'a number of serious faults' in norm fixing, including inappropriate wage rates, which in several industries had unjustifiably compressed the range from lower to higher earnings.[64]

[60] Slavin (2005): 362–363, 371–373.

[61] See Siegelbaum (1988): 261–262.

[62] Thus, two inspectors in Glavredmet, the Chief Administration of Rare Metals, found that in the mining department of Turgaistroi (in Kazakhstan) 'the overwhelming majority of workers did not reach their norms because tools were not available or were of poor quality, and compressed air, timber props and other materials were not available' so that the previous norms and rates for the job were restored until the faults were corrected. See RGAE, 7297/28/136: 6 (no date but summer 1937).

[63] *Pravda*, January 29, 1938.

[64] RGAE, 4372/92/88, 138 (1937).

In 1937 the measured increase in labour productivity in industry was far less than in previous years. While reported output grew more slowly, the total of employees and, within the total, the number of manual workers continued to increase almost at the pace of 1935 and 1936 (see Table B.12). Only about 40% of the increase in production in that year was due to increased output per person employed, as compared with between two-thirds and three-quarters in the previous three years.[65] Gosplan attributed this poor performance to 'weak leadership of the Stakhanov movement' and 'numerous cases of weakening of labour discipline in production and weakening of the struggle with those who violated discipline'.[66] At the same time industrial costs (so-called commercial costs, including price rises) increased for comparable goods by 10.7%, compared with the planned reduction of 2%.[67]

6 Agriculture: Plans and Policies

Through the 1930s, grain remained the most important commodity in agricultural production. It was by far the largest food item for the population, urban and rural. Within agriculture the best 15% or so of grain was cleaned and sorted for seed in the following year. Grain was also a critical component of livestock feed, especially in winter conditions. In industry, grain was also significant for brewing, distillation, and starch. It was also, potentially, a major export item. In transport, grain was by far the most widely marketed agricultural product. The major decline in livestock numbers in the early 1930s had made grain even more predominant despite moves to increase the sowing of other crops (Table B.29). But by the late 1930s the grain harvest was becoming less dependent on livestock. The application of tractors and harvesters to field cultivation weakened the historical complementarity of arable crops and livestock

[65] The role of productivity growth varied across industries. In the Commissariat of Heavy Industry, which now excluded machine building and most of the defence industries, output increased by 6.8%, almost all of this being due to the 6.7% increase in output per worker (*Pravda*, January 29, 1938).

[66] RGAE, 4372/92/88, 10 (July 31, 1937). On the Stakhanov movement, see Vol. 6: 160–172.

[67] *Industrializatsiya 1933–1937* (1971): 145 (from the report on the fulfilment of the state budget for 1937).

husbandry, by which farmers fed grain to the animals that ploughed the fields and reaped the grain.

In 1937, the main issue in agriculture arose from the abundant grain harvest. The government was unprepared for this, and had reduced its targets for the harvest following the poor outcome of 1936. The harvest coincided with a purge of the leaders in the agencies responsible for agriculture, procurement, and planning. (The relationship between the purge and the reduction of targets remains unclear.) At all events, the government then suffered a partial loss of control over the disposition of the unexpected surplus of grain. Much more grain remained in the hands of the farmers than would have been considered normal. The private holdings of collective farmers showed unusual growth of non-grain sowings and of livestock. As a result, one source of official anxiety, the fear of harvest failure and food shortages, was replaced by another: the fear of a renascent private sector. We will discuss each of these matters in turn.

The 1937 harvest was planned at a time when cross-cutting pressures were in play. According to the second five-year plan, the Soviet Union was to harvest 110.6 million tons of grain in the terminal year, 1937. But in December 1935 Stalin had issued a public call for a higher target, 115–131 million tons (7–8 billion *puds*) within three to four years (Vol. 6: 263). In public, Stalin never retreated from this enthusiasm. In private, he appeared complacent. As news of the poor harvest of 1936 came in, he advised his close colleagues against over-reaction (Vol. 6: 319). In April 1937, we will see below (Sect. 7), as food shortages materialised, he rejected a proposal to raise the price of grain sold by the state.

Preparations for the 1937 control figures began in July 1936 when the Politburo had discussed Mezhlauk's proposals. At this time it was becoming clear that the ambitious target for the 1936 harvest would not be met. The Politburo projected that the grain yield would rebound in 1937 to the level originally planned for 1936, and called for a small increase in the area sown to grains.[68] The implied harvest was not stated, but can be calculated as 106.5 million tons.[69] This target was slightly above the annual plan target for the year before, but it was well below the five-year plan target for 1937, and fell even further below

[68] RGASPI, 17/3/979, point VI.

[69] RGAE, 4372/35/467: 85–86. The calculation is based on 104.4 million hectares sown to grain and a yield of 10.2 centners per hectare.

115 million tons, the lower limit of Stalin's range. (In 1935 Stalin had expressed his target not in tons but as '7–8 billion puds'; this may have helped to avoid direct comparison with figures expressed in tons.)

On December 23, 1936, however, Gosplan proposed to raise the target to 108.5 million tons.[70] By this time it was obvious that the 1936 harvest was a disaster, but that circumstance was ignored. A table in the Gosplan document showed a column for expected results in 1936; the column was left empty. The target that was eventually adopted by the government and appeared in the final version of the plan in March 1937 was 108.3 million tons.[71]

The most unusual feature of the 1937 plan was the absence of targets for grain collections and livestock.[72] The archives show that the grain collection target in use at the time was 28.3 million tons, 14% below the 33 million tons written in the Second Five Year Plan for 1937.[73] A revised livestock plan of June 1937 (produced in Gosplan by Kviring) cut the targets for horses, sheep and goats by a similar amount, and for large horned cattle, cows, and pigs by much more (Table B.38).

The officials responsible for agricultural production and procurement had reason to fear the consequences of repeated failure of the harvest. The Soviet economy could normally withstand one year of failure. The failures of 1890, 1920 and 1931 did not lead to devastating shortages. Famine followed the second consecutive year of failure in 1891, 1921 and 1932. Chernov, chief of Komzag (the Committee for Agricultural Procurements) in 1932/33, was now the people's commissar of Agriculture. Kleiner, deputy chief of Komzag in 1933, was now its chief. Kviring, chair of the committee of commodity funds under the Council of Labour and Defence in 1932–1934, was now first deputy

[70] RGAE, 4372/35/452: 20.

[71] This figure was given as 6.613 billion puds in *Narodno-khozyaistvennyi plan na 1937 god* (1937): 25. Targets of 103.96 million hectares for the area to be sown to grain and of 10.4 centners per hectare for the grain yield were given separately (ibid.: 106, 109); in combination, these implied a harvest of 108.3 million tons. The decree was dated March 20, 1937 (ibid.: 40).

[72] Until this time, grain collections were included within the section of the plan dealing with commodity turnover (*tovarooborot*). In the 1936 plan commodity turnover was covered in 14 pages (*Narodno-khozyaistvennyi plan na 1936 god* (1936): 332–336), four of them were devoted to grain collections. In the 1937 plan, grain collections were omitted and a short commodity turnover section covered only retail trade and communal dining.

[73] RGAE, 8040/8/360: 65–69. See also Table B.35.

chair of Gosplan. These had all lived through the famine of 1921/22 and were centrally involved in managing the famine of 1932/33. It is not surprising that such specialists advised caution as the 1937 harvest approached.

Stalin appears to have been in two minds. Previously, he was enthusiastic for higher targets and disdained the advocates of caution. Now, in the early summer of 1937, he allowed caution to prevail. This was reflected not only in a somewhat restrained target for grain production, but also in the relatively modest targets that were in use at the time for the things that relied most directly on the grain available after the harvest: the grain to be collected by the state, and also the increase in livestock herds, which depended on the fodder crops available after the harvest and the collections.

In the record of Stalin's Politburo, this was a rare example of willingness to compromise over planning targets. When aspirational targets were set, and inevitably missed, the leaders' normal response was to push back so that they would set still more ambitious plans and expect the lagging economy to catch up. At a moment like this, the strategy of pushing back would have meant ignoring the difficulties with the harvest, while continuing to inflate the plan for the following year, lifting it towards Stalin's aspirational goal of at least 115 million tons. Pushing back also implied greatly increased procurement targets. In 1936/37, in contrast, the planners took the logical, yet unprecedented, step of responding to the disappointment of 1936 by reducing the plans of the following year for both production and procurement of grain.

While Stalin evidently acquiesced in this accommodating approach, he did not endorse a more cautious stance in public. When the harvest turned out to be much larger than had been expected, those responsible for the more cautious approach were accused of 'wrecking' and of causing losses to the state (see Sect. 2 in Chapter 3).

We now turn from the plans to changes in the factors of production that might have affected the 1937 harvest. Some of these were directed by policy interventions; they included capital investments in agriculture and especially the availability of draft power, the supply of fertilisers, the availability of improved seeds, and the improvement of crop rotations. After them, we consider a variable factor that no one directed but that turned out to be decisive: the weather.

In the mid-1930s the government's greatest concern over agricultural technology had been the shortage of draft power caused by the widespread loss of horses that accompanied collectivisation and the famine of 1932/33. The shortage of horses greatly affected the timeliness and speed of field operations throughout the agricultural year. Great emphasis was placed on farm mechanisation under the control of the state-owned MTS (machine-tractor stations) (Vol. 5: 437–439). In the mid-1930s the horse population stabilised at a low level. Meanwhile industry delivered a greatly augmented flow of tractors and other equipment to agriculture. By 1937, as a result (Table B.27), although the number of horses remained less than half the level of the late 1920s, animal losses were at last fully replaced by machines. At this point the authorities began to downgrade the priority of agricultural equipment, and targets for tractors and combine harvesters were scaled down.[74] At all events, sowing in the autumn of 1936 and the spring of 1937 was done efficiently and on time, as was the harvesting from August to October 1937.

If any capital item was neglected at that time, it was the construction element of agricultural investment. As a symbol of agricultural progress, the importance of tractors was easy to grasp. Repair facilities and storage were relatively mundane items, but of no less importance for securing the harvest. For 1937 Chernov, as Commissar of Agriculture, proposed a massive leap in the funding of agricultural investment (4.7 billion rubles, compared to the 2.4 billion outcome then expected for 1936); expenditures on construction and on power machinery would have doubled.[75] Instead, the allocation to agriculture in the 1937 investment plan was a small increase on the previous year's allocation and less than was actually spent by the end of the year (Tables B.5 and B.7).

Some months of infighting ensued. Chernov emerged not with the 85% budget increase he sought, but a 10% cutback.[76] The burden of the cut was shifted onto construction; the supply of power machinery to agriculture was apparently defended by the powerful industrial ministries that supplied it. This meant that the MTS and state farms had to stop building garaging, repair, and storage facilities, and irrigation works were also cut back. This meant a large increase in incomplete work on projects that had just been initiated and now could not be finished.

[74] RGAE, 7486/4/571: 266. See also Table B.19.

[75] RGAE, 7486/4/465: 70 (not dated but probably October 1936).

[76] RGAE, 7486/4/571: 219–234 (October 1937); also RGAE, 7486/4/571: 174–183 (Frolov).

The first and second five-year plans assumed that grain yields were on an upward trend; the expected gain was 30–35% by 1932, and a further 25–40% by 1937.[77] The prospective increase would come from improved seeds, better techniques for working the land and rotation of crops, more winter ploughing, and more intensive use of fertilisers and manure.

Fertiliser production was growing in these years (Table B.22), although little was used for grain. The targets to apply manure and other natural produce to the land were generally underfulfilled, not least because livestock herds fell short. The quantity of land in use for arable cultivation was rising slowly; the proportion that was winter sown increased only marginally (Table B.30). Because of the pressure to maintain the area under harvested crops, there was no improvement in crop rotations. And seed quality also did not improve.

The story of Soviet policies for agricultural improvement in our period is tortuous. In the 1930s, Soviet science was blessed by an abundance of world-class agricultural specialists: the biologist Vavilov, with the world's largest collection of seed types; the chemist Pryanishnikov, who studied plant feeding and fertilisation; pupils of the soil analyst Dokuchaev, the plant breeders Meister and Davydov in Saratov; and the livestock breeder Ivanov, who pioneered artificial insemination. The politics of the time were against them, however, expressed by the various campaigns that pitted Bolshevik militancy against expert knowledge, and the weakness of the Bolshevik leaders for false experts who would tell them what they wanted to hear.

Nowhere was this more evident than in seed selection. If one considers only the science, then the scientists were far ahead of their time, for they envisaged the high-yielding varieties of cereals that would form the basis of the Green Revolution 30 years later. During the 1930s, however, the seed selection system suffered two blows. First was the disruption of specialist seed farms by collectivisation. On the heels of this setback came political demands, led by Yakovlev, to accelerate progress in seed

[77]The rate of increase was based on arguments that Yakovlev had made in the 1920s. At the time he was the main critic of the agricultural statistics of TsSU and of moderate agricultural plans. In TsIK in 1927, he introduced a law prohibiting plans that were *not* based on the target of raising the grain yield by 35% in five years. See *Slavic Review*, 34(4) (1974): 790–802 (S. G. Wheatcroft and R. W. Davies).

selection and plant breeding; the failure of real scientists to deliver quick results created an opening for the exaggerated claims, based on false science, of T. D. Lysenko.[78] A war of attrition ensued.

Meanwhile, the diffusion of improved seeds fell back. The second five-year plan projected that by 1937 sorted seed would be applied to three-quarters of the land sown to grain.[79] But achievement of the target relied on the protection of seed stocks and their gradual multiplication on approved farms. In practice seed stocks were frequently broken into by official bodies for seed loans, because the collection agencies had taken ordinary seed stocks for human consumption, and also by thieves.[80] The figure achieved in 1936 was only 42%.[81] Meanwhile (as discussed in Sect. 2 in Chapter 3), Yakovlev, now chief of the Central Committee's Agricultural Department and first deputy chair of the Party Control Committee, blamed the specialists, accusing them of sabotage as well as incompetence.

During 1937 measures were taken to remove seed reproduction from the hands of the scientists. A Politburo decree of April 7 authorised the removal of high-quality grain seed testing from Vavilov's All-Union Institute for Plant Breeding. Instead, every second or third administrative district should maintain a plot of land for the purpose under an agronomic specialist. A special commission of the Commissariat of Agriculture would exercise central oversight. The change was to be

[78] On the influence of Michurinism and Lysenko, which persisted officially until the 1960s and unofficially even beyond that, see Joravsky (1986) and Graham (1993). Lysenko's pretension to quick results was based not only on the assertion of scientific breakthroughs but also on his claim to have developed new procedures for verification that bypassed the need for lengthy trials in the field.

[79] Of 104.8 million hectares to be sown to grain in 1937, 80 million were to be sown with high-quality seeds. See *Vtoroi pyatiletnii plan* 1 (1934): 209–210.

[80] Seed loans issued after the 1936 harvest, from Vol. 6: 374–383. Seed shortages in early 1937, from *Tragediya*, 5(1) (2004): 187–191 (cases from various agricultural provinces in the spring of 1937). Thefts from seed stores, from ibid.: 192–193 (cases in Stalingrad province at the same time).

[81] With 102.2 million hectares sown to grain in 1936, the target for high-quality sowing was 46 million hectares (i.e. 45%) and the outcome was 43.4 million hectares (42%), based on the then-current Gosplan draft of the 1937 plan (RGAE, 4372/35/452: 5). For 1937 the target was at first 66.1 million hectares, given in the same Gosplan draft, and later 57.7 million hectares (RGAE, 4372/35/452: 20, 22), a figure that eventually appeared in the published version of the plan (*Narodno-khozyaistvennyi plan na 1937 g.* (1937): 110–111).

implemented by a group headed by Yakovlev, including Mikoyan, Osinskii, Vavilov, Lysenko, Chernov, and Kleiner among its members.[82]

At the June 1937 Central Committee plenum, while Yakovlev ranted about sabotage in seed selection, Chernov highlighted the failure to improve crop rotations; he suggested that a third of collective farms did not have correct systems.[83] Perhaps Chernov was defending himself against Yakovlev who, as his predecessor, had failed to register the advance expected. There was a tradition of blaming one's predecessor for such shortfalls; In due course, Chernov's successor would blame him, alleging that the true proportion of farms with 'correct' rotations was only one-fifth (see Sect. 1 in Chapter 7).

To summarise, nothing in the plans and policies of 1936/37 explains the unexpected success of the 1937 harvest. The decisive factor was the weather.

There is no doubt that the growing conditions of 1936/37 marked a dramatic improvement. The poor harvest of the previous year was preceded by drought. Unfavourable weather continued through the late summer and autumn of 1936. August temperatures were relatively high and October temperatures very low. But in the following spring, April was abnormally warm and May and June were cool, a pattern that was ideal for the flowering and maturing of grain. In fact, every producer region but Ukraine registered a large improvement in meteorological conditions. The improvement was greatest in the regions affected by drought in 1936: the Central Black Earth, the Volga, the Urals, and Kazakhstan. Finally, good growing conditions were complemented by a dry harvesting period. This was particularly fortunate because a more abundant harvest necessarily took longer to reap and thresh. Damp conditions in the late summer could still have ruined it—but they did not.

Our estimates of the predicted impact of weather on grains yields (Table 7), suggest that the drought of 1936 was most intense in the Urals and Volga regions, where it was comparable with the droughts of 1891, 1921 and 1931. Across the country the growing conditions of 1936 were in the bottom 20% of the century (Table B.28). In 1937,

[82] RGASPI, 17/3/985: 2–3 (agenda item III). The evolution of responsibility for seed testing is outlined in *Tragediya*, 5(2) (2006): 593n.

[83] RGASPI, 17/2/618: 112–130.

Table 7 Predicted weather effects on grain yields across regions in 1936–1937 (per cent)

	1936	*1937*	*Change*
Ukraine	−2	−8	−6
North Caucasus	+31	+54	+23
Central Blacksoil	−9	+7	+16
Volga	−47	+24	+71
Urals	−48	−2	+46
Siberia	−18	0	+18
Average, all regions	−14	+10	+23

Note The figures show the net impact on grain yields in the given year from weather conditions through the growing season. The unit of measurement is per cent of the yield under average weather conditions. In Ukraine in 1936, for example, the impact of weather conditions during the growing season was to reduce grain yields by 2%, and across the country by 14%.
Source Table B.28.

conversely, the growing conditions were in the top 20%. The predicted harvest was greater in every region but Ukraine. The yield should have been higher in the Volga region by more than 70%, and in the Urals by more than 40%. Across the country as a whole, the projected improvement was nearly one-quarter.

7 Agriculture: Operations and Outcomes

The field operations that led to the harvest of 1937 were closely monitored. The progress of ploughing, sowing, reaping, and threshing, measured by the area subject to each operation, was among the very few aspects of the agricultural calendar that government officials could control day by day through the year. By the time of the 1937 harvest, each of these operations had been reported meticulously through the year, the results being published every five days in the government press.

The figures on autumn sowing had been broadly favourable; month by month, figures were slightly in advance of 1936, and the final figure claimed was around 250,000 hectares (a fraction of 1%) up on the previous year (Table B.30). This varied somewhat from the story emerging from reports on winter sowing, which frequently mentioned problems with the supply of seed (discussed above). The pace of autumn ploughing in preparation for spring

Table 8 The progress of spring sowing: all crops, 1936 and 1937 (thousand hectares)

	1936	*1937*	
		Initial	*Revised in 1938*
March 15	4,008	734	–
April 1	9,639	5,766	–
April 15	13,927	19,711	–
May 1	34,711	49,670	47,848
May 15	73,002	72,797	68,719
June 1	88,216	87,645	81,612
June 15	91,075	90,361	83,888

Note and Source 1936 and 1937 (initial): compiled from *Izvestiya*, which published reports at five-day intervals during the growing season, comparing results with the same period in the previous year. For 1937 (revised): on May 5, 1938, *Izvestiya* announced that all the figures for the previous year from May 1 onward should have been revised downwards, as shown, to exclude sowing by kolkhoz peasants on their personal allotments, by state farms other than those subordinated to the People's Commissariats of Agriculture, State Farms, and the Food Industry, and by the few remaining individual peasant farmers. For discussion, see Sect. 2 in Chapter 7.

sowing, although well below the planned figure, was nonetheless reported as following an upward trend and well in advance of previous years.[84]

Conditions in the spring of 1937 were adversely affected for a time, perhaps by the legacy of the poor 1936 harvest, perhaps by the intensified search for saboteurs. In March and early April the reported progress of spring sowings lagged behind the poor results in 1936, a source of anxiety in the tense conditions of the great purge year. Then, the pace was restored and in the remaining weeks of the campaign the sowers ran neck and neck with the benchmarks of the previous year, ending up less than one percentage point down on June 15 (Table 8).

[84]Reports of progress with ploughing were published in *Izvestiya* each year at frequent intervals through the season. These showed a monotonic increase of land under the plough by November 15 each year from 23.9 million hectares in 1932 to 44.5 million in 1935 and 54.8 in 1936.

In the spring of 1937 the task of evaluating the scale of the coming harvest was in progress. In March the special state commission (TsGK) for harvest evaluations was abolished, and the task of harvest evaluation was returned to the regular statisticians of TsUNKhU (Vol. 6: 361). As head of TsUNKhU, Kraval' warned of the need to rebuild the lower levels of the statistical apparatus to carry out this function.[85] But he made no progress before his arrest on May 31. His replacement, Vermenichev, was from Gosplan, where he had been the major commentator on the agricultural plan in 1936. Vermenichev now blamed his predecessor for the lack of readiness in TsUNKhU for harvest evaluations and warned of delays.[86]

Reports of the harvesting campaign of 1937 suggest that reaping began slowly. Coinciding as they did with the height of the nomenklatura purge, these reports quickly engendered an atmosphere more of imminent disaster than of a bumper harvest. At first the figures seemed to point to disastrous inactivity in Saratov province.[87] The Saratov party secretary, a senior figure with close links to Yakovlev, was detained.[88] Andreev was despatched to Saratov to investigate. Following a brief telegraphic exchange with Stalin, Andreev set about arresting large numbers of local officials and specialists, some of whom went on to incriminate the Soviet Union's leading specialists in seed selection and planting.[89]

Meanwhile, however, the reaping campaign moved ahead, caught up with the rates of the previous year in mid-September, and ended a month later more than 4.1 million hectares ahead of the 1936 rate. This was said to be very close to the plan—99.9% (Table B.32).

[85] RGAE, 1562/84/1: 227–228ob (April 20, 1937).

[86] RGAE, 1562/1/982: 138 (June 5, 1937).

[87] *Izvestiya*, July 20, 1937. These figures showed that in Saratov only 0.3% of the reaping plan had been fulfilled by July 15, compared with 10% on the same day of the previous year. Accompanying figures for other provinces were curiously selective, perhaps with the intention of placing the Saratov officials in a bad light.

[88] In the early 1930s, through the famine period, A. I. Krinitskii (1894–1937) was head of the Agriculture Commissariat's Political Administration and Yakovlev's deputy as commissar for Agriculture, as well as deputy chief of the Central Committee's Agricultural Department.

[89] *Tragediya*, 5(1) (2004): 279, 606. In turn, the specialists Meister and Tulaikov were arrested; the way was being cleared for the anti-scientific views of Lysenko to prevail over Soviet genetics.

The final stage of field operations before the completion of the harvest was threshing. In 1937 threshing began more slowly than in the previous year and, in contrast to other operations, it fell behind more and more as the season progressed. On October 15, the last date for which results were published, the lag of threshing behind reaping stood at 7 million hectares (Table B.32). Most likely the harvest, being unexpectedly large, overwhelmed the threshing capacity.

In 1937, the middle of October was a dangerous moment. Damp weather at that time could have still ruined the harvest, as it did in Ukraine in 1932. As it turned out, the harvesting weather was excellent and harvest losses were much less than otherwise, but the leaders were lucky that there was no disaster. Others were not so lucky, for the moment was dangerous in other ways as well. It was also dangerous for many officials responsible for agriculture and agricultural statistics, who were not so lucky. Yakovlev, previously a leading advocate of over-ambitious agricultural targets, was arrested on October 12; Osinskii, who had resisted him more than anyone, was arrested the following day.[90] Demchenko, formerly the People's Commissar of Agriculture for Ukraine, and now of State Farms for the USSR, was also arrested on October 12. October 17 saw the arrest of Smirnov, head of Gosplan. Chernov, who succeeded Yakovlev as Commissar of agriculture, was dismissed on October 29 before being arrested on November 7 (see Sect. 2 in Chapter 3). By this time the proportion of the harvested area that had been threshed already showed a large improvement.

How large was the bumper grain harvest of 1937? The question looks simple; the complicated answer is summarised in Table 9. Associated with each estimate of the harvest (in million tons) was an estimate of the yield (in centners per hectare). With just over 100 million hectares sown to grain, each one-centner change in the estimated yield was associated with a change in the estimated harvest of just over 10 million tons. As early as August 5, as harvesting began, Stalin was informed that the first indications were excellent. Vermenichev reported to Stalin that that visual inspections taken on July 15 by local statisticians were projecting a yield of 10.8 centners per hectare (110 million tons), but that central field inspectors (many of them former staff of the TsGK) were

[90]Yakovlev was appointed to be the first People's Commissar of Agriculture on December 8, 1929 (Vol. 1: 169); Osinskii became the first head of TsUNKhU on January 11, 1932 (Vol. 4: 201).

Table 9 The grain harvest, 1936 and 1937: from plans and reports based on biological yield to grain available for use (million tons)

	1936	*1937*
Target in annual plan	104.8	108.3
Harvest outcomes		
Preliminary evaluation of TsGK/TsUNKhU during harvesting	84.8	120.0
Final evaluation of TsGK/TsUNKhU after harvest	77.4	114.0
—Revised by Voznesenskii (February 1939)	82.7	120.3
Grain available for use		
In annual TsUNKhU grain-forage balances	62.9	105.0
—Revised by Pavlov (July 1941)	–	98.4
Barn yield estimated by Wheatcroft and Davies (1994)	56	97

Source Tables B.33 and B.34. TsGK was responsible for evaluating the grain harvest until its final evaluation of 1936; it was then dissolved and its work was handed over to TsUNKhU.

proposing to raise the estimate to 11.7 centners (120 million tons).[91] This was a remarkable figure, 42 million more than the 77.6 million tons then accepted for the 1936 harvest. Perhaps most significantly, it reached above the lower limit of 115 million tons that Stalin had previously proposed. Thus, the different estimates of the grain yield made the difference between satisfying Stalin's aspiration and falling below it. In his letter, Vermenichev warned that, on the experience of the previous two years, the final evaluation could fall below the preliminary figure by 1–1.3 centners per hectare, that is, by 10–13 million tons. But this did not put off the optimists. The claim of 120 million tons was strongly defended in the following months; attempts to submit figures below Vermenichev's preliminary figures were often treated as prima facie evidence of sabotage.[92]

After the harvest was in, however, so that the target had lost its operational significance, TsUNKhU succeeded in reducing the estimated yield to 10.7 centners per hectare and the aggregate harvest estimate to 114

[91] RGAE, 1562/1/982: 156–168 (August 5, 1937); also *Tragediya*, 5(1) (2004): 288, 292. The figure of 120 million tons was given as 7.3 billion puds, for comparison with the 7–8 billion range that Stalin had demanded.

[92] RGAE, 1562/84/1: 18, 194–195, and 202–203 (August 25, 1937).

million tons, a figure that fell just short of Stalin's aspirational goal.[93] This conformed to a longstanding pattern of making triumphal claims while the harvest was in progress, followed by the acceptance of more 'realistic' claims when looking forward to the next year's prospective achievements (e.g. Vol. 5: 443–444).

The story does not stop there. The following year, in June 1938, the party leaders ordered Voznesenskii to review the harvest statistics. In his report (not dated, but early in 1939) Voznesenskii criticised Osinskii severely for the methodology applied. The harvest estimates used in 1937, and as far back as 1933, purported to represent the 'biological yield': the size of the crop standing in the field or 'on the root', with a modest allowance (in reality, a large underestimate) for harvesting losses (Vol. 5: 442–447). Voznesenskii not only condemned the allowance for harvesting losses, but also recommended adding a further sum to the harvest estimate to account for grain lost when standing in the field as a result of livestock grazing on it.[94] He concluded that the officially accepted harvest figures should be raised, in 1936, from 77.6 million to 82.7 million tons, and, in 1937, from 114 million to 120.3 million tons (Table 9).

In reality, the Soviet economy did not dispose of anything like 120 million tons of grain in 1937. The biological yield estimates were exaggerated, and the losses of all kinds were greatly understated. When the year's grain-forage balances were drawn up in secret within TsUNKhU, the total of grain available for use was found by making a series of deductions from the declared harvest figure: losses from the crop standing in the field, losses during harvesting, and losses in storage. The second of these was, basically, a made-up figure (previously known as the *nevyazka*, or discrepancy), designed to bring the number down to something more realistic. On that basis, the quantity of grain available for use in 1937 was estimated as 98.5 million tons.

All the estimates agree, however, that the harvest of 1937 was better than the previous year's by an extraordinary margin: at least 30 million tons. This very large windfall was of great importance from several points

[93]RGAE, 4372/36/1407: 10. This figure was based, also, on an increase in the estimate of the area harvested; otherwise, the harvest figure would have been reduced by even more.

[94]Voznesenskii's file on this matter (RGAE, 4372/36/1407) was opened on June 20, 1938, and closed on February 19, 1939. The file includes a copy of his report to Stalin and Molotov in response to their request, but none of the documents is dated.

of view. First, it illustrates how the weather continued to dominate agricultural production (and this implies that agricultural production was less damaged by the mass repressions of the time than industrial production or transport). Secondly, it endowed the economy with much more food than the state had anticipated, and so it raised the question of who would benefit.

The unexpected character of the abundance of 1937 was reflected in the state plan for grain collections for 1937/38 (i.e. from the 1937 harvest), set at 24.3 million tons. This was below the 1936 plan by three million tons, and less than one million tons above the level achieved in the previous year. An increase in state purchases of two million tons was also written in the plan (Table 10). In the end a record was achieved: 28.3 million tons collected, or 31.9 million including state purchases. However, the increase in collections over the previous year was only a small fraction of the increase in the harvest. The fact that grain collections were not easily increased in proportion to the harvest in a good year followed the general pattern, for grain collections were also not reduced in proportion in a bad year, such as 1932/33 (see Vol. 5). If the collections were a tax, then the tax was consistently regressive; it left the farmers fully exposed to particular risks while the public sector protected itself. The peculiarity of 1937/38 is that the upside risk was realised, and the farmers appropriated the benefit.

Table 10 Grain collections, 1936/37 and 1937/38 (million tons)

	1936/37	*1937/38*	
	Outcome	*Plan*	*Outcome*
All compulsory deliveries (*postavki*)	11.0	9.7	10.3
Payments in kind to MTS (*naturoplata*)	6.5	9.1	11.3
Milling levy (*garntsevyi sbor*)	1.1	0.5	1.7
Returned seed loans	1.8	1.2	1.2
Deliveries by state farms	3.1	3.2	3.9
Rescheduled debt repayments	–	0.6	–
Subtotal of collections, exc. purchases	23.5	24.3	28.3
State purchases (*zakupki*)	2.0	4.0	3.6
Total of collections	25.5	28.3	31.9

Source Tables B.35 and B.36.

The procurement campaign began in a spectacular manner: on July 28, a column in the government newspaper asked why Kleiner, chief of the Committee for Procurement, had failed to improve the quality of bread provided to consumers, when the government had ordered him to do so.[95] The column was signed by nine bakery industry officials from big industrial towns. Kleiner was arrested on August 4, charged with wrecking, and executed.[96]

For the general population, in contrast, the grain collections of 1937/38 passed without great drama, the first time this had happened since 1925/26. While millions of people were exposed to traumatic experiences for other reasons at this time, the collection targets were easily achieved, and afterwards there appeared to be ample grain left over in the collective farms, and particularly in the hands of the peasant households. The government did not try to collect or export all the extra grain available, and this was mainly to the benefit of the consumption of grain by farm animals, many of them in private hands.

This conclusion can be supported in various ways. The increase in grain supposedly available for use (around 15 million tons) after the 1937 harvest far exceeded the increase in government collections and purchases (6.4 million tons). When TsUNKhU statisticians came to estimate the grain stocks in the hands of collective farm households, they found more than 12 million tons (Table B.37), compared with two to four million tons normally. Collective farm household stocks remained high through 1939, returning to normal only in 1940. No doubt a more ambitious state collections target could have reduced the grain surplus left in private hands. It is possible, though unproven, that for this reason Stalin came to regret the relative caution of the 1937 harvest and collection plans in hindsight, and this fuelled his mistrust of the officials, such as Chernov and Kleiner, whose moderation had held back his instinctive optimism.

Soviet citizens did not live by bread alone. Potatoes and vegetables, which probably accounted for around one-tenth of agricultural production (valued at plan prices of 1926/27), were grown mainly on kolkhoz peasant households' allotments. State collections and purchases of these

[95] *Izvestiya*, July 28, 1937.

[96] *Tragediya*, 5(1) (2004): 556.

commodities increased markedly in 1937.[97] The yield of other arable products also increased in 1937, but more slowly, and the livestock sector marked time.[98]

This was not what the government had in mind. For 1937 the plan was to increase the aggregate number of livestock by around one-quarter. Targets included 13% growth for horses and cows, and 25% for sheep and goats, and nearly 40% for pigs. In the outcome, the numbers of all types of livestock increased only modestly. All targets were missed but for sheep and goats. Within the broad aggregates, the only striking increases were for the kolkhoz peasants' personal holdings of horses and oxen (Table B.39), a factor that may have contributed to the subsequent tightening of kolkhoz regulations to be discussed below. Not only did livestock numbers fail to expand at the expected rate; the health of animals deteriorated somewhat, with increased incidence of infections, especially brusellosis.[99] (In due course the security organs searched for the wreckers and foreign agents responsible.) The state collected or purchased no more milk in 1937 for resale to consumers, and less meat.[100]

The most important factor in the stagnation of livestock was the legacy of the drought of 1936 in fodder shortages and poor pasture. In the twelve months that began with the harvest of 1936, just 15.2 million tons of grain were used for the maintenance of livestock and this was nearly two million less than in the previous year. But in 1937/38, the allocation of grains to the livestock sector nearly doubled, shooting up to 27.8 million tons. On the private holdings of collective farmers, the increase of fodder consumption was threefold.[101]

The larger stocks of grain held by peasants after the 1937 harvest, the increased use of grain to feed peasant livestock, and also the increased

[97] RGAE, 8040/8/308: 3, 22, 25, 62.

[98] According to a re-evaluation of Soviet agricultural production in terms of barn yield, carried out in TsSU in 1953 (RGAE, 1562/83/38: 1), grain production increased by 47% in 1937 over 1936; total arable production increased by 41%, and livestock production by 4%. The year-on-year expansion of agricultural production as a whole was put at 30%. These figures seem likely to have overstated the growth of the non-grain arable sector, however, and therefore also of agriculture as a whole.

[99] *Tragediya*, 5(2) (2006): 97 (April 8, 1938).

[100] On government procurements in 1937 compared with the previous year, see RGAE, 8040/8/308: 3, 22, 25, 62.

[101] Grain for fodder in 1935–1936, from RGAE, 1562/3/383: 1; in 1936–1937, from RGAE, 1562/3/434: 2, 5, 8, 11, 14; in 1937–1938, RGAE, 1562/329/3110: 30.

sales of potatoes and vegetables by peasant households were all signs of a growing role for peasant household activities within the kolkhoz system.

8 Internal Trade and Consumption

The level and trend of the Soviet standard of living in our period have been much debated. The pioneering work on the subject by Janet Chapman suggested that, across the entire population, consumption per head of goods and services (including communal services) in 1937 was 10% greater in real terms than in 1928, before collectivisation and the first five-year plan (Table B.48).[102] This result, implausible at first sight, was to be explained entirely by the great increase in the working population and its movement from farms to factories between the two years.

The starting point was that living standards declined unambiguously over the period for the average farmer and also for the average worker. In the countryside, peasant households were dramatically impoverished by collectivisation and its consequences. In the towns, workers' wages were savagely cut by inflation—by more than 40% on Chapman's estimate.[103] But for the population in the aggregate, these adverse trends were fully offset by two factors. One was the gain to many urban households from the disappearance of unemployment and the movement of family members, previously unemployed or employed in the home, into factories where their additional wage earnings compensated the family for the loss from inflation. The other was the gain to many peasants who, by leaving the countryside and becoming workers, were able to escape from rural poverty and attain the much higher living standards in towns. These movements were so large that, comparing 1937 with 1928, living standards averaged across the whole population were at least maintained.

In the years between 1928 and 1937, much happened that scholars of the time of Bergson and Chapman were unable to address (for lack of

[102] Chapman's results coincide with those reported by Bergson (1961): 255. According to Chapman (1963): 166, household purchases of goods per head of the population rose by 10% (at 1937 prices) and purchases of services by two-thirds.

[103] Chapman (1963): 166 (at 1937 prices); Bergson and Kuznets, eds. (1963): 237 (Chapman) (at 1937 prices). New research by Allen and Khaustova (2017), working paper, suggests declines of 50% or more: 'The effect was to push Russian real wages back to where they had been around 1880.'

data available at the time). Living standards at first fell with the onset of forced industrialisation, and collapsed in 1933, a time that was terrible everywhere, but particularly in the countryside, in the south of Russia, in Ukraine, and in Kazakhstan, where millions died of hunger (see Vol. 5). After that, living standards gradually improved (see Vol. 6).

As for 1937 itself, more recent research has added to our picture, although not without controversy. Robert Allen's reassessment of Soviet industrialisation provided a more optimistic picture of consumption per head in the late 1930s as more than 20% higher than in 1928 (Table B.48). This uplift was a product of several revisions, combining an improved methodology for calculating index numbers with new data on the consumption of goods. While Allen's index number methodology has been rightly seen as an improvement, however, some of his findings regarding the increased availability of consumer goods, and especially of food, have been contested.

Much of the literature on Soviet food availability in the 1930s has started from the supply side, aiming to estimate the residual of agricultural produce available for human consumption in each year after losses and requirements for seed and livestock have been deducted. Using this method, Allen found a large increase in food availability per head of the Soviet population, rising from around 2500 calories in the mid-1920s to around 2900 in the late 1930s.[104] With food outlays counting for 60% of working class household budgets, this would have been a major boost to living standards. The method of identifying calorie consumption from the supply side is inherently risky, however. One risk arises from the official manipulation of harvest reports to create the appearance of growth in the 1920s relative to pre-revolutionary times, and in the 1930s relative to the 1920s.[105] Another is the risk of understating losses and other uses

[104] Allen (2003): 135.

[105] Reviewing Allen (2003) in *Slavic Review*, 63(4) (2004): 844–845, Michael Ellman raised the issue of inflated Soviet-era harvest figures and their lack of comparability with pre-revolutionary data. In *Explorations in Economic History*, 46(1) (2009): 26, Wheatcroft, one of the present authors, noted that, comparing food availability in the 1930s with pre-revolutiomary data, Allen appeared to neglect the 'Ivantsov correction,' which was used in the 1920s and 1930s to inflate Soviet-era grain harvests by nearly one-fifth relative to uncorrected pre-Revolutionary figures. Later, Soviet statisticians removed the unjustified 'correction' from the Tsarist-era data, but not from the Soviet data, creating the impression of an upward leap in yields even greater than that claimed at the time.

Table 11 Energy consumption from food: survey-based estimates for the mid-1920s and 1937 (calories per person per day)

	1925/26–1926/27 average	*1937*
Wheatcroft (2009)		
Peasant households	3,039	2,175
Manual worker households	3,792	2,637
Nefedov (2012)		
Peasant households (February)	2,981	2,373

Source Table B.49. 'Peasant households' refers to individual family farm households in the 1920s, and to collective farm households in the late 1930s.

of food.[106] The historian Sergei Nefedov has criticised Allen's estimates for greatly understating the quantities of food consumed by livestock in the late 1930s; he finds that, when the understatement is removed, the excess of Allen's figures over previous estimates disappears.[107]

Under these circumstances, a better way would be to measure food consumed in households directly and convert it into calories for an estimate of energy consumption. Household food consumption was surveyed regularly in the 1920s and 1930s although the record found in the archives shows many gaps. Two estimates have been made, one by Wheatcroft, an author of the present volume, and the other by Nefedov. In addition to other differences, the estimates use different calorie conversion schemes. The estimates agree on two things. Considering the starting point, they show that in the mid-1920s the average household was generally well clear of the subsistence minimum for Russia, which can be set at around 2000 calories.[108] When comparing 1937 with the mid-1920s, the estimates agree in finding large declines in energy consumption from food (Table 11) of the order of 30% (Wheatcroft) or 20%

[106] In another review on EH.net in June 2004, Davies, an author of the present volume, noted that, comparing the late 1930s with the 1920s, Allen's hypothesis of greater food availability in the later period was not confirmed by the evidence of peasant household budgets.

[107] *Vestnik Tambovskogo universiteta* (2011), no. 6: 208–213 (S. A. Nefedov).

[108] For the FAO, Sedik, Sotnikov, and Weisman (2003): 33, give 1970 calories, which they compare with the higher figure of 2275 set by the Russian government.

(Nefedov, considering the farm population only).[109] While urban households were better fed than rural households at both ends of the period, the declines are so large that they could not have been compensated by rural–urban migration.

Within Bergson's team it was generally thought that 1937 was the best year of the decade for the Soviet consumer (a view shared by Allen, as can be seen in Table B.48). But this judgement seems to have been based largely on the abundant harvest of that year combined with an easy assumption that grain would be eaten as soon as it was produced. In fact, the harvest arrived only in the late summer of 1937, was first added to stocks, and was then released for human consumption gradually over the next two years, for only in the summer of 1939 did grain stocks fall back to the level that was normal in the mid-1930s (Table B.37). The part of the increment to the harvest of 1937 that was fed to animals also contributed to human consumption, but with a still longer lag. Thus, the consumer benefits of the 1937 harvest would be felt as much or more in the following years, and this is what we will find when we come to 1938 and 1939.

Within the calendar year 1937, until the harvest was gathered and became available for distribution, the growth of retail trade and consumption was constrained by the disappointing harvest of the previous year. With slower expansion of the production of food and industrial goods, state retail supplies of goods increased in 1937 by 16.2 billion rubles (Table 12) at current prices, or 17%; this compared with 36% in the previous year.

Although the priority of the defence sector was high and rising, the Politburo still sought to improve retail trade facilities; on March 13 it approved the construction of 26 new specialised food stores.[110] As in previous years, retail trade in the countryside increased more rapidly than retail trade in the towns, by 22.3% as compared with 16.1% (though of course the level of turnover per head of the population was far below

[109] As Table B.49 shows, the estimates disagree on the trend for worker households. Wheatcroft considers that all the years of the late 1930s were unambiguously worse than the 1920s for all social groups; Nefedov finds that manual worker households in 1938 and 1939 registered a small improvement. The reasons for this gap have not been identified.

[110] RGASPI, 17/3/984: 22.

Table 12 Money incomes and outlays of the Soviet population, 1936–1937 (million rubles)

	1936	*1937*	*Change*
Household incomes			
Incomes from the public (state and cooperative) sector			
—Wages	86.1	93.0	6.9
—Other incomes	30.0	42.3	12.3
Incomes from the public sector, subtotal	116.1	135.3	19.2
Incomes from private (household) activity			
—Kolkhoz market incomes	7.2	12.2	5.0
—Other incomes	2.7	2.5	−0.2
Incomes from the private sector, subtotal	9.9	14.7	4.8
All incomes	126.0	150.0	24.0
Household outlays on goods and services			
Outlays on public sector products			
—Goods	95.7	111.9	16.2
—Services	8.5	10.0	1.5
Public sector goods and services, total	104.2	121.9	17.7
Outlays on private sector products			
—Kolkhoz market goods	7.2	12.2	5.0
—Private services	2.7	2.5	−0.2
Private sector goods and services, total	9.9	14.7	4.8
Outlays on goods and services, total	114.1	136.6	22.5
Other uses of household incomes			
Subscriptions to public organisations	0.9	0.7	−0.2
Share contributions to cooperatives	–	0.1	–
Taxes and other payments	5.1	5.1	0.0
Acquisition of state loans	3.6	4.4	0.8
Savings bank deposits, increase	1.1	1.0	−0.1
All outlays	124.8	147.9	23.1
Public sector incomes, less outlays on public-sector goods and services	11.9	13.4	1.5
All incomes, less all uses of incomes (net cash accumulation)	1.2	2.1	0.9

Source Tables B.43 and B.44, abbreviated and rearranged.

that in the towns).[111] The rural trade network also increased more rapidly: 13,000 trading units were opened as compared with 6000 in the towns. But the number of rural shops did not return to the level reached in 1936, before the closing down of state shops in the countryside (described in Vol. 6: 420).

It was a long-standing dogma of the Soviet government that the economy in general, and retail trade in particular, should be based on a ruble that was stable or increasing in purchasing power; and that this improvement should be achieved by price reduction. Rising output per worker should be compensated by lower prices as well as by higher money wages. A major attempt to this end, first made in 1927, was belatedly abandoned in 1930 under the inflationary pressures of rapid industrialisation (Vol. 3: 62–63, 300–303, and 355–358). In 1935 the abolition of consumer rationing was followed immediately by attempts to set aside funds which would allow retail price reduction to be resumed (Vol. 6: 142–150). The prices of food products in state and cooperative trade were fixed so that supply was roughly sufficient to meet demand. The prices of industrial consumer goods, however, remained generally too low to balance supply and demand. Nevertheless, in 1937 the authorities decided to resume the policy of price reduction for these goods. On April 28 Sovnarkom issued a far-reaching decree on 'the reduction of retail prices of mass consumption industrial goods'. This provided for prices to be reduced in two stages. On June 1 prices in state and cooperative trade should be reduced by 5–15% for a variety of textiles and footwear, and for furs, perfumes, sewing machines, gramophones, sports equipment, window glass, light bulbs, and high-grade cigarettes. Then on July 1 the prices of knitwear, higher-grade clothing, drapery, some musical instruments, school stationery and toys should be reduced by similar amounts.

The decree announcing these measures explained that 'the successes of industrial production and the achievement of the second five-year plan ahead of schedule have enabled the accumulation of new resources by

[111] According to *Po stranitsam* 1 (2006): 22, outlays in state and cooperative trade by rural households in 1936 were 27.2 billion rubles, compared with 65.6 billion rubles by urban households. But the rural population reported by the census of January 6, 1937 (*Vsesoyuznaya perepis' naseleniya 1937 g.*, 2/e (2007): 58), was 110.1 million, compared with 51.9 million in towns. Thus, for every ruble that an urban resident spent in state and cooperative stores in 1936, a rural resident spent only 20 kopecks.

the state, and have created the possibility of a further reduction in the prices of industrial mass-consumption goods.'[112] It did not specifically state that the goods for which prices were being reduced were in relatively abundant supply, though the reduction of the price of matches, which were in surplus, by as much as one-third indicated this intention. In an article of August 7 about the reforms, Veitser stated somewhat cautiously that the size of trade mark-ups depended on a number of factors including the demand for a particular good, and that 'we increase or reduce the trade mark-up or mark-down so as to increase the demand for it.'[113]

On June 2, in the days after the first batch of measures had been put into effect, an enthusiastic editorial in *Pravda* on 'the undeviating policy of price reduction' greeted these developments with enthusiasm, and publicity for them continued during the summer. The sum of reductions was substantial. The price index for industrial consumer goods declined by 3.8% in 1937.[114] Veitser claimed that in 1937 price reductions 'mainly for industrial consumer goods' had amounted to 1450 million rubles. But within a few months any advantage obtained by these measures was swept aside by the growing inflation. And the reforms were limited in scope. In April Veitser wrote to Stalin and Molotov suggesting that the price of grain sold by the state should be temporarily increased:

> The pressure for grain consumption at present is considerable. There are queues in a number of places. The demand for grain is growing locally. Part of the grain is being used to feed animals. Although the amount of grain issued is increasing all the time, the pressure is not reduced. Shouldn't we now increase grain prices until the new harvest?

Stalin refused.[115]

Simultaneously with the price reductions for industrial consumer goods, the authorities embarked on the rationalisation of their prices with measures which brought about greater centralisation and inflexibility. Veitser acknowledged in his article of August 7 that it was anomalous for prices charged for the same good by Union and local industry

[112] SZ (1937), no. 28: art. 116 (April 28, 1937).

[113] *Pravda*, August 7, 1937.

[114] Cited by Malafeev (1964): 205.

[115] APRF, 3/43/60: 121.

to differ from each other. The reorganisation of the prices of industrial goods not only eliminated the many complexities and anomalies which had grown up since the beginning of the 1930s, but also established the central fixing of retail prices for a much wider range of goods.[116]

Trade in agricultural goods in the second half of the year was particularly satisfactory. The good harvest of 1937 swept aside the food crisis resulting from the poor harvest of 1936. Following a sharp rise in prices on the kolkhoz market at the beginning of the year, in August the economic newspaper triumphantly published an article headed 'Fall in prices on the markets', containing reports from its correspondents in Leningrad, Khar'kov, Gor'kii, Kiev, Minsk and Rostov-on-Don, reporting increased sales of food by kolkhozy and by collective farmers, and substantial reduction in prices.[117] In the third quarter, kolkhoz market prices were lower than state and cooperative prices in 75% of the places where prices were registered in the case of rye flour and in 47% for wheat flour.[118] But for 1937 as a whole, the increase in average kolkhoz market prices still amounted to 12.6% as a result of the substantial increases at the beginning of the year.[119] Prices of grain, potatoes and meat and dairy products increased, and prices of fruit and vegetables declined.[120]

The overall result of all these price changes was that in 1937 the incomes that the population earned from the state and cooperative sector increased by 16.5%, somewhat more rapidly than the increase in their expenditure on retail trade. In consequence, the population's holdings of unspent cash were estimated to have increased by 2.1 billion rubles, as compared with 1.1 billion in 1936 (Table 12). The total of currency in circulation grew by 21%, or 2.3 billion rubles (Table B.47). In 1936, a year in which there had been a much greater increase in production, the monetary expansion had been only 15.9%.

[116] This reorganisation, which began at the end of 1937 and continued until 1939, is described by Malafeev (1964): 209–215.

[117] *Ekonomicheskaya zhizn'*, August 12, 1937.

[118] RGAE, 4372/92/63: 421–436 (September 16, 1937).

[119] Malafeev (1964): 207.

[120] For details, see RGAE, 1562/12/2122: 29; 1562/12/2322: 77.

9 Foreign Trade

Bolshevik leaders had traditionally regarded foreign trade as an important instrument. By exporting food and raw materials, the Soviet economy could gain access to the means of industrialisation: capital goods and foreign technology. By 1937, however, the Soviet Union's foreign economic relations had suffered years of atrophy. Behind this lay several factors, all of them negative. One obstacle was the wrenching and profoundly adverse shift in the terms of trade facing primary exporters to the world market in the Great Depression. Another obstacle was the disintegration of global markets and the rise of protectionism. An atmosphere hostile to the Soviet Union specifically prevailed in the Soviet Union's most important export markets. In any case it was difficult, under Soviet arrangements, to incentivise the provision of exportables, such as food and timber, which were in short supply at home, so that only Moscow's coercion could ensure their availability. By the late 1930s, as a result, the Soviet Union came as close to a closed economy as can be found in modern economic history. The share of imports in GDP in 1937 cannot have much exceeded 2%.[121]

The fact that foreign trade was now such a small part of the Soviet economy did not make it unimportant to the leaders. On the contrary, imported goods were now so scarce that they had become extremely valuable. As a result, matters such as plans for earning foreign currency and the allocation of goods obtained in the world market were highly sensitive. As the 'supreme arbitrator' in conflicts among government departments, including competing claims for foreign currency, Stalin was closely involved in all such matters.[122]

The foreign trade and foreign currency plan was, with some difficulty, drawn up in February 1937 with a slight surplus (see Sect. 1 in Chapter 3).

[121] A back-of-the-envelope estimate goes as follows. In 1913, Russia's GDP was 20.3 billion rubles, while merchandise imports were 1.4 billion (Gregory 1982: 57, 314), so 7% of GDP. Between 1913 and 1937, the GDP of the Soviet Union (within constant post-war frontiers) increased by 70% (Maddison 2010), while real imports (within constant 1925 borders) fell by 50–60%, depending on the standard of valuation of machinery (*Studies in East European and Soviet Planning* (1973, no. 21): 27 (Dohan)). Therefore, the share of imports in Soviet GDP in 1937 cannot have been much more than 2%. This ignores trade in services (tourism, for example), but in 1937 the Soviet Union imported no services to speak of. The same calculation based on exports gives similar results.

[122] *Stalin i Kaganovich* (2001): 16–17.

Table 13 Export prices from Soviet customs data, 1929 and 1935–1937 (rubles)

	1929	*1935*	*1936*	*1937*
Wheat, per ton	225	126	163	220
Rye, per ton	142	97	96	173
Sawn timber, per cubic metre	426	188	217	330
Petrol, per ton	273	83	97	113
Manganese ore, per ton	86	34	35	51

Source RGAE, 4372/92/159: 6 (April 29, 1938).

As usual, considerable changes took place in the course of the year. On the import side, the Politburo or Sovnarkom authorised a number of additional purchases, mainly associated with defence needs. These included road-making equipment, aircraft hangars, and non-ferrous metals.[123] Some additional imports were authorised for civilian industry, including coal-mining equipment and 'the latest' Caterpillar tractor.[124] On the export side, the good harvest led to the decision to export 1475 thousand tons of grain by the end of 1937.[125] In fact 1277 thousands were exported (Table B.51). But, counteracting this, goods valued at 270 million rubles were excluded from the original plan because of pressing internal needs; among those excluded in whole or in part were butter, flax, coal and oil.[126]

These changes made it look as if the plan was in jeopardy. On October 21 the export–import plan for the October–December quarter of 1937 estimated that imports scheduled for the quarter would result in the annual import plan being exceeded by 59 million rubles, and that exports in the quarter would need to be pushed at the expense of available stocks.[127] In fact, export revenues exceeded expectations because of a sudden improvement in world prices for Soviet export commodities (Table 13). The relative deterioration in the world price of agricultural

[123] GARF, 5446/1/490: 46, 8 (decree of February 22, art. 308/67); 5446/1/494: 115–116 (July 29, art. 435); 5446/1/494: 119–120 (August 1, art. 1255/287).

[124] GARF, 5446/1/495: 146–147 (decree of October 5, art. 1749/385); 5446/1/495: 176 (decree of October 10, art. 1784/392).

[125] GARF, 5446/1/494: 137, 178 (decree of August 3, art. 496).

[126] GARF, 5446/22a/410: 175 (January 8, 1938).

[127] GARF, 5446/1/496: 47 (art. 1866/415).

Table 14 Expenditures on imports: plan versus outcome, 1937 (million rubles)

	Target	*Outcome*	*Saving*
Orders delayed—payment in 1938	1,010	960	50
Overheads	–	–	26
Remainder from supplementary imports not yet paid	–	–	20
Advance payments for 1938	45	15	30
Foreign technical assistance	31	16	15
Interest on foreign credits	25	18	7
Purchases in East	26	4	22

Source Targets, from GARF, 5446/1/490: 277–278 (art. 272/59, February 17, 1937). Outcomes and savings, from GARF, 5446/22a/410: 176–175 (January 8, 1938). The items listed in the final column cover 170 of the 199 million rubles by which imports fell short of the plan.

commodities had been the bane of Soviet foreign trade since the 1920s, and their restoration substantially improved the Soviet balance of payments.

More surprisingly, in view of the great pressure from Soviet industry for imports, payments for imports were lower than planned by 199 million rubles. A statement sent from the Commissariat of Foreign Trade to Stalin, Molotov, Mikoyan and Chubar' attributed half of the under-spending (100 million rubles) to deferred payments for 1937 or smaller advance payments for 1938 than expected (Table 14).

Thus, at the end of 1937, the Soviet foreign-trade balance appeared to be in a more healthy state than it had been throughout the 1930s. But not many weeks would elapse before the authorities were again troubled about the weakness of the foreign currency reserves.

CHAPTER 5

The Soviet Population and the Censuses of 1937 and 1939

1 The Much-Delayed Census of 1937

The outcome of the population census of January 6, 1937, was a predictable disaster. The census takers made a reasonable attempt at their task, which was to enumerate the population present on the census date. But the results were denounced and suppressed, and those directly responsible were mostly killed or imprisoned. The roots of this disaster were deep, extending many years back into the past.

In 1918, on the foundation of the Soviet Central Statistical Administration (TsSU), its first director P. I. Popov proposed that a population census should be carried out every ten years starting in 1920.[1] The first census was held in 1920, but did not cover the entire country because the Civil War was still in progress. The first complete census was held in December 1926; it was a delayed mid-term census that Popov had proposed as necessary to support the demographic basis of

[1] Popov (1918). P. I. Popov was born in 1872 and died in 1950. Born into the family of a clerk, he worked as a local government (*zemstvo*) statistician until March 1917, when he joined the Ministry of Food of the Provisional Government. Lenin appointed him the foundation director of the USSR Central Statistical Administration (TsSU) in July 1918; Stalin dismissed him in December 1925. Popov worked in the Central Statistical Administration of the Russian Republic in the late 1920s and then headed the Agricultural Department of the Russian Republic's Gosplan from 1931 until his retirement in 1948 when, against all odds, he became one of the few people in our story to collect his pension.

R. W. Davies et al., *The Industrialisation of Soviet Russia Volume 7: The Soviet Economy and the Approach of War, 1937–1939*,
https://doi.org/10.1057/978-1-137-36238-4_5

planning. A decennial census should have been held in 1930, but was cancelled when TsSU was merged into Gosplan in late 1929. At the time it was asserted that statistics, censuses, and surveys, all bourgeois concepts, were to be replaced by socialist accounting. As a result, the statistical economic sector of Gosplan was subsequently renamed its Administration for National Economic Accounts (UNKhU Gosplana).

In 1930 there was no prospect that the census for that year, now cancelled, would ever be reinstated. The first retreat from this extreme position came with the reintroduction of livestock censuses in 1931.[2] Later that year UNKhU became TsUNKhU (the Central Administration for National Economic Accounts) and was granted somewhat greater autonomy within Gosplan. Early in 1932 Osinskii, TsUNKhU's first director, promised to end the political manipulation of statistics and listed an early population census as one of his first aims. At this time he proposed the census for December 1932 or not later than March 1933.[3] A few months later he extended his deadline to the winter of 1933/34.[4] Thus, a full census was now in prospect once more, but was subject to continual postponement.

While the census was postponed, the population figures in use for planning were inflated. They were being overstated already before the harvest failed in the autumn of 1932. The *UNKhU Gosplana* figure for the population on January 1, 1932, was 165.7 million, slightly ahead of the original population plan of 165.6 million. But the latter was in all probability ahead of reality by several millions. Several years later, applying the numbers of births and deaths registered annually to the December 1926 census population, Popov argued for a figure of 160.4 million on the first of 1932.[5] This was 5.2 million less than was accepted at the time.

[2]This might have reflected the Red Army's concerns about the quality and quantity of cavalry mounts, the same logic that led the Tsarist government to carry out regular military horse censuses. Marshal Budennyi was temporarily appointed to the collegium of the Agriculture Commissariat at this time: SZ (1931), no. 12: art. 171 (August 1, 1931).

[3]Osinskii (1932b): 15 (based on his speech in TsUNKhU on February 17, 1932). For Osinskii's dismissal from TsSU in 1928, and his return to carry out a short statistical renaissance in TsUNKhU in 1932, see Vol. 4: 201–202.

[4]Osinskii (1932a): 22 (authorised for printing on July 7, 1932).

[5]RGAE, 1562/329/279: 114 (February 21, 1939).

At the time, a compromise figure of 162.1 million was adopted for July 1, 1931.[6] This figure, which would have been roughly midway between plan and reality, then served as a benchmark from which to extrapolate the forecasts officially incorporated into the second five year plan: 165.7 million for the first of 1933 (or the end of 1932) and 168 million for the end of 1933.[7] Stalin used the latter figure for his political report to the seventeenth party congress in January 1934.[8] But this compromise did not clear the way for a more complete correction. Instead, the very high mortality following the 1932 harvest failure, and a sharp decline in fertility, drove a wedge further into the gap between population projections and realities. The problem changed from concealing unexpectedly low growth of the population to concealing an absolute decline.

In 1933, Stalin and the Politburo understood that a famine was taking place. Behind closed doors, prompted by reports of the security police and inspections by senior party leaders, they eventually approved measures for famine relief (Vol. 5: 211–230). But these secret measures were not integrated into the planning process nor were they reflected in the planning documentation. In public, the government did not acknowledge the famine or the unexpected mortality. Preliminary TsUNKhU reports of elevated numbers of deaths in 1933, well above the level of births, were dismissed on the grounds that they were based on preliminary and incomplete data (This was in spite of the fact that the preliminary reporting system was designed to be informative precisely when data were incomplete). The population forecasts were not changed.

The final report on births and deaths in 1933 became available in early 1934. It showed a deeper catastrophe than could have been inferred from preliminary indications. The provinces with worst results, perhaps reluctant to be first with bad news, had held back to the end. Instead of the planned natural increase of two to three millions per year, in 1933, deaths had exceeded births by 1.5 million. The final report

[6] *Narodnoe khozyaistvo SSSR* (1932): 401.

[7] One of the advantages of 165.7 million as a figure for the end of 1932 was that it was so close to the 165.6 million figure previously planned for the first of the same year. Thus, *Vtoroi pyatiletnii plan* 1 (1934): 501 gives 165.7 million for 1932 and at the same time switches from a January 1 basis to a December 31 basis.

[8] Stalin, *Sochineniya*, 13 (1951): 335 (report to the XVII Party Congress, January 26, 1934).

went first to Kuibyshev, head of Gosplan, who did not accept it but instead referred it to the State Control Committee. There the young Voznesenskii began his rise to power; he claimed that wreckers within TsUNKhU were double-counting deaths and under-recording births to falsify the growth of the population. On that basis the report of a 1.5 million excess of deaths over births in 1933 was suppressed and consigned to the archives. Gosplan and the government continued to work on the assumption that the population had grown as planned.[9]

Behind the scenes, the confrontation unfolded. The party leaders and security police picked up Voznesenskii's charge that TsUNKhU was staffed by wreckers. In 1934 the newly established All-Union NKVD became responsible for coordinating the registration of births and deaths in the provinces, and warned the registrars and statisticians against under-reporting the growth of the population. In September 1935 a joint decree of Sovnarkom and the Central Committee, prepared by Yezhov, repeated Voznesenskii's allegations and ordered that from now on the registration of each birth or death should be marked by issuing a certificate to the household.[10]

Stalin made his own views clear at the end of 1935, putting the natural increase of the Soviet population at 'about three million'. He added: 'This means that each year we receive an increment the size of Finland.'[11]

[9] See *Golod v SSSR*, 3 (2012): 719–772 (S. G. Wheatcroft); the Voznesenskii report of August 10, 1934 is reproduced in the same volume as document 503. The charges of sabotage were repeated in a decree of Sovnarkom and the Central Committee 'On the situation of accounts of the natural movement of population', dated September 21, 1935 (SZ (1935), no. 53: art. 432, also reproduced as document 512 in *Golod v SSSR*, 3 (2012): 640–641).

[10] SZ (1935), no. 53: art. 432 (August 21, 1935). The decree gave Yagoda and Vyshinskii one month to prepare the appropriate registration certificates, but nearly a year passed before TsIK affirmed them on July 26, 1936 (SZ (1936), no. 44: art. 369). For Yezhov's involvement, see RGASPI, 671/1/71: 121–133. In response to Yezhov's query, Kraval' wrote to him that there were no official figures other than those published; all data after 1933 were secret. Kraval' added that the data were bound to be approximate, given the passage of nearly ten years from the last census. He stated, perhaps warily, that after the poor harvests of 1931 and 1932 the number of births in 1933 had been low, but the situation was now better. He noted that the next census, due on July 1, 1936, would give full results. He concluded that, in Osinskii's absence, 'we are not able to give a full response.' But the file contains nothing from Osinskii.

[11] *Soveshchanie peredovykh kombainerov* (1935): 118.

Despite such pressures, the registration data reported by TsUNKhU at this time continued to show much smaller increases, closer to two million per year than to three (see Table B.54). While Kraval' did little to support his demographers, he allowed them to continue to work and he himself continued to forward their reports of relatively slow population growth to the authorities.

Meanwhile, the census was further delayed. It had been planned again for late 1935. The date was put off to 1936, and was finally set for January 6, 1937.[12] If the Soviet population was indeed 168 million at the end of 1933, as Stalin had claimed in 1934, and if it was growing at three million a year, as Stalin had claimed in 1935, then the figure to be expected for the beginning of 1937 was 177 million, or thereabouts.

2 Carrying Out the 1937 Census

Three officials were designated to lead the preparations for 1937, including TsUNKhU chief Kraval' and two distinguished demographers, O. A. Kvitkin and his deputy, L. S. Brandgendler. Kvitkin, a former zemstvo statistician, had retained his position although he had previously been seriously targeted by Voznesenskii and others as politically unreliable.[13]

As far as the public was concerned, the campaign for the census began in April 1936, with nine months still to go. It was repeatedly stated that the census was being carried out on Stalin's personal initiative and with his direct participation. In fact, the census questions were considered in three separate drafts in 1935 and 1936 by a special commission led by Mezhlauk, with Bulganin, Kaganovich, Mikoyan, and Molotov. Stalin was involved to the extent that he personally reviewed the third and final draft.[14]

By design, the 1937 census was unlike those held earlier and later in two respects. It was intended to record only the people on hand in each locality, whether urban or rural, at a fixed moment, and not to measure the permanent resident population—a huge issue for a country where millions migrated annually between country and town. (In

[12] *Vsesoyuznaya perepis' naseleniya 1937 g.*, 1/e (1991): 4 (V. B. Zhiromskaya and I. N. Kiselev). The authors assert that Stalin chose the final date, but do not provide a source.

[13] As reported by Yakovlev in his report following the census: RGASPI, 82/2/531: 47–55.

[14] *Vsesoyuznaya perepis' naseleniya 1937 g.*, 2/e (2007): 21 (Zhiromskaya).

addition to the population on hand in both towns and the countryside, the 1926 census aimed to record the people permanently resident in towns. The censuses of 1939 and later years aimed to measure both the permanent population and the population on hand in all localities.) The new census also introduced a question about respondents' religious belief, 'in all probability' on Stalin's initiative, according to the historian Valentina Zhiromskaya.[15] Faced with such a question, respondents who thought of themselves as believers would have been reminded of the harsh repression of the Christian and other faiths in the course of mass collectivisation (Vol. 1: 118, 255–256), and of the continuing official disdain for believers as backward and prejudiced. The question was made more pointed by the fact that the census date was Christmas Eve in the Orthodox calendar, a time at which the state often engaged in atheistic propaganda.

As preparations for the census were finalised, and the census was actually carried out, there were no signs of serious misgivings. The population figure to be expected, based on preliminary calculations in Gosplan, was no less than 180.7 million.[16]

It is true that, in a speech of late 1936, Kraval' noted difficulties arising from 'the need to gather full and exact data about 170-plus millions (*o 170 s lishkom millionakh*) of the population spread over one sixth of the globe'.[17] Kraval's figure was echoed three days *after* the census by M. Mudrin, head of UNKhU of the Russian Republic. Writing in *Izvestiya* on the need for census controllers to go back over the work on to make sure no one was left out, Mudrin once again emphasised the magnitude of the task of covering in one day 'such a huge country as the USSR with a 170-million population', repeating Kraval's figure while dropping the 'plus'.[18]

Were these, as Valentina Zhiromskaya has suggested, early attempts to lower expectations from the expected 180-plus million figure?[19]

[15] *Vsesoyuznaya perepis' naseleniya 1937 g.*, 2/e (2007): 17 (Zhiromskaya).

[16] RGAE, 4372/92/161: 40.

[17] *Plan* (1936), no. 21: 8 (Kraval'). The author noted the importance of the census and cited Stalin's speech to the Seventeenth Party Congress on the advances experienced by the Soviet population and its growth in recent years.

[18] *Izvestiya*, January 9, 1937 ('Vsesoyuznaya perepis' naseleniya: Stalinskoe zadanie vypolnit' v tochnosti').

[19] *Vsesoyuznaya perepis' naseleniya 1939 g.* (1992): 4 (V. B. Zhiromskaya).

Perhaps so, although another explanation is available. In his article Kraval' noted that the personnel of the Red Army, those employed (and held) by the NKVD, and those in transit on trains and ships would be counted separately from the rest of the population, which would be enumerated by the census officials. These numbers could account for a large part of the 10-million discrepancy between the aggregate figure that was officially anticipated and Kraval's evaluation of the census takers' task. And we could extend the same explanation to Mudrin's figure.

There were few other signs of misgiving. On January 4, 1937, with two days to go, *Izvestiya* and other national newspapers announced that 'the country is ready for the census.' Kraval' wrote the lead article, entitled 'A matter of huge political and economic significance'.[20] He ended by confirming that census data would be used only for statistical purposes. Apparently not everyone believed this, however. In Arkhangel'sk, it was reported the next day, a census recorder had been beaten by thugs.[21] On the day of the census itself, it was reported that the question on religion was being misunderstood: some recorders were ascribing religious affiliation on the basis of ethnicity.[22] Two days after that, on January 8, the deputy head of TsUNKhU (confusingly named A. Popov) reported how well the census had been carried out.[23] And on January 10, *Izvestiya* gave new details of how the census data would now be processed. The data were to reach the provincial governments by January 16 or 17 and, on being added up there, were to arrive in Moscow by January 20. The paperwork would weigh 400 tons and the results would take up 60 volumes.[24] At this point, everything seemed utterly routine.

[20] *Izvestiya*, January 4, 1937.

[21] *Izvestiya*, January 5, 1937 ('Khuliganskoe napadanie na schetchika').

[22] *Izvestiya*, January 6, 1937. Under the heading 'It is necessary to correct mistakes', a special correspondent from Bryansk notified readers that some non-religious respondents were being wrongly classified as believers. Despite official claims that census returns would be used only for statistical purposes, the correspondent had been given names of persons who had been recorded as believers. On investigation, he found that the records were erroneous. As an example, the census taker asked a young man whether he was an Orthodox Christian. The youth retorted that he was obviously not a Tatar (and so perhaps Muslim). The census taker, who ought to have explained that ethnicity does not decide religion, recorded this as a 'Yes'. Another article on the same day explained how well the census was going in the Arctic region.

[23] *Izvestiya*, January 8, 1937 ('Kak proshla perepis,' by A. Popov).

[24] *Izvestiya*, January 10, 1937 ('60 tomov materialov perepisi').

3 The 1937 Census Outcomes Suppressed

It is unclear when the party leaders were first made aware that the results of the census would fall far below forecasts. The first formal report was not made until January 25, which was eighteen days after the census. Evidently, however, Stalin and Molotov were notified informally considerably beforehand. This is shown by the fact that on January 16, only 10 days after the census, the Politburo requested Yakovlev to undertake an investigation. The investigation was to include both professional apparatchiks (Vermenichev and Tsaguriya, who would soon be promoted to the leadership of TsUNKhU, and also Gegechkor), and expert statisticians (P. I. Popov, Smulevich, and Nemchinov).[25] The investigation quickly assembled reports from a number of localities that were critical of the census, but it would not conclude for several months.

The first report, by TsUNKhU chief Kraval', indicated a figure of 155.6 million, but this figure was a partial count, excluding several categories: the 'special contingents' under the control of NKVD and the Defence Commissariat, passengers on trains and ships, and also the populations of regions so distant that they were not counted on time.[26] In order to make up the total population, Kraval' suggested adding around six million (comprised of 5.5 million under the control of NKVD and the Defence Commissariat, 350,000 persons in transit, and 300,000–400,000 others).

The preliminary report therefore implied an overall total of 155.6 + 6 = 161.6 million. This was a shocking figure. It was more than eight million below the minimal 170-million figure floated ambiguously by Kraval' and Mudrin, and 19 million below the officially projected 180.7 million. Perhaps worst of all, any Soviet citizen who recalled and believed the 168 million figure that Stalin had declared for the end of 1933 would understand that over three years of outstanding economic achievements the Soviet population had inexplicably declined.

In his report, Kraval' tried to put a good face on the disaster. He placed emphasis on the population's expansion since the 1926 census:

> This is about 162 million, compared with 147 million in the census of December 17, 1926, an increase of 15 million, or 10.2 per cent over ten

[25] Blum and Mespoulet (2003): 135.

[26] *Vsesoyuznaya perepis' naseleniya 1939 g.* (1992): 4 (V. B. Zhiromskaya).

> years. This is about 1 per cent per year, which is significantly more than for most capitalist countries (0.7 per cent for Germany, 0.3 per cent for England, 0.95 per cent for France), and is exceeded only by the USA and Japan (1.3 per cent for 1933).

Although he omitted to mention the large shortfall below the expected 180 million, Kraval' did suggest that deaths over the preceding decade had been substantially under-recorded in ZAGS, the state system for changes of 'civil status' (i.e. births, marriages, and deaths). By implication, the growth of the population would have been overstated in the current demographic accounts. Earlier, when his own statisticians had warned about this, and had asked him for support against Voznesenskii's allegations of sabotage, Kraval' had been unsympathetic. Now his fate was linked to theirs, and he had little choice but to take their side.[27]

At about the same time, however, Yezhov was reporting a different story to Molotov. An NKVD investigation, led by Yezhov's deputy L. N. Bel'skii, purported to show that that the TsUNKhU demographic model was understating, not overstating the underlying growth of the population. According to Bel'skii, the numbers of both births and deaths in 1935 and 1936 had been greater than Kraval' had allowed, but Kraval' had understated births by more. The margins were small, and Bel'skii's estimate of the natural increase still did not reach Stalin's 'three million', but his report fell nonetheless into line with the leaders' narrative of professional statisticians bent on selling short the country's demographic achievements.[28]

Meanwhile, a fuller set of preliminary census results was prepared for Stalin and Molotov, who received them not later than March 3. The results, which were in line with the disastrous first indications, were now supported by a regional breakdown of the census returns.[29] But Stalin's

[27] Harris, ed. (2013): 725–728 (S. G. Wheatcroft).

[28] RGASPI, 82/2/538: 5 (Yezhov to Molotov, February 2, 1937); 6–17 (Bel'skii to Yezhov, January 27, 1937). The TsUNKhU and NKVD estimates of births and deaths in 1935 and 1936 are compared directly in Table A-26: Kraval' (January 5, 1937), and Bel'skii (January 27, 1937). The next row of this table (Sautin, February 1937) shows that, in the following month, with Kraval' arrested, his successor Sautin signed off on new TsUNKhU estimates of the natural increase that raised the estimated numbers of both births and deaths in 1935 and 1936, but raised births by more, more or less in line with the NKVD prescription.

[29] For the documents, see *Vsesoyuznaya perepis' naseleniya 1937 g.* (1991).

immediate response remains unknown. Around this time, Stalin and the Politburo were organising the Pyatakov trial (January 23–30, 1937) and were about to order the arrest of Bukharin and Rykov (February 27, 1937). There could have been no more unwelcome distraction than the release of news that the population had grown much less than the leaders had claimed. No further public announcement was made until the end of September.

In secret, frantic activity proceeded along three lines. Efforts to explain the census results continued within TsUNKhU for a short while. At the same time TsUNKhU was subjected to two overlapping inquisitions, with the Yakovlev investigation of the census (created on January 16) joined by a separate commission to verify the staffing of TsUNKhU; the latter was in the hands of a security policeman, S. F. Redens, chief of the NKVD for Moscow province, who was to report through Yakovlev.

Within TsUNKhU Kraval' obtained a report on the causes of the census shortfall.[30] Its author, M. V. Kurman, a seasoned demographer, was head of the TsUNKhU department of current population statistics and deputy head of the sector of population and health. As shown in Table 1, Kurman put the apparent size of the shortfall at 6.3 million, based on a forecast figure of 168.3 million (already far below the previous planning estimate of 180 million) and a census outcome of 162 million. He went on to explain that the true gap was more likely to be 8 million, because some births would inevitably have escaped registration. Taking the gap as 8 million, Kurman then broke down its likely elements as follows. Because three weeks had been allowed for the 1926 census in rural areas, migrants on the move within that period could have been double-counted, he suggested, by 1.5 million. Perhaps 2 million had fled abroad in 1930–1933 (i.e. because of collectivisation and the famine that followed, but Kurman did not state this) from Kazakhstan and other Central Asian republics. In 1933 (which was at the height of the famine, but again Kurman did not state this) one million deaths might have gone unrecorded. In other years between the censuses, there might have been three million unrecorded deaths, around half of them among detainees of the NKVD and the rest in civil society. Finally, a million people might

[30] 'On the natural movement of the population in the period between the censuses of 1926 and 1937', reproduced in *Vsesoyuznaya perepis' naseleniya 1937 goda*, 2/e (2007): 285–288. See also Davies et al., eds. (1994): 75 (Wheatcroft and Davies).

Table 1 The Soviet population in the censuses of 1926 and 1937: the Kurman gap (millions)

		Million
	The shortfall	
1.	Census population, December 1926	147.0
2.	Registered births, less deaths, 1927–1936	21.3
3.	Expected population, January 1937	168.3
4.	Census population, January 1937	162.0
5.	Net shortfall to be explained (the Kurman gap)	6.3
	Explaining the net shortfall	
6.	Unregistered births, 1927–1936	1.7
7.	Gross shortfall, corrected for unregistered births	8.0
8.	Temporary absentees double-counted in 1926	1.5
9.	Unregistered emigrants from Kazakhstan and elsewhere, 1930–1933	2.0
10.	Unregistered deaths in 1933	1.0
11.	Unregistered deaths in other years	1–1.5
12.	Unregistered deaths in GULAG and NKVD, 1930	1–1.5
13.	Under-counted population in 1937	1.0
14.	Explained components of gross shortfall, total	8.0

Note The figures in this table are provided not as the best estimates available but to represent the thinking of an expert insider of the time. For post-Soviet estimates see Andreev et al. (1993).

Source All figures are taken from the report of M. V. Kurman 'On the natural increase of the population in the period between the two censuses of 17/XII-1926 and 6/I-1937,' reproduced in *Vsesoyuznaya perepis' 1937 g.*, 2/e (2007): 285–288, except as follows. Row 3 sums rows 1 and 2. Row 5 takes the difference of rows 3 and 4. Row 6 is implied in the source, but not stated, and is calculated here as the difference of rows 5 and 7. Row 14 sums rows 8 to 13, evidently taking the combined subtotal of rows 11 and 12 as 2.5 million.

have avoided registration by the census takers in 1937. Taken together, these would sufficiently explain the shortfall.

Kurman's report, dated March 14, 1937, was circulated to the Yakovlev Committee and the political leadership. Their response came on March 21: Kurman was arrested, charged with defaming the NKVD. Brandgendler's turn came on March 28.[31] The latter's position as deputy head of the census office was filled by Starovskii, now on his way to becoming the grand old man of Soviet statistics.[32]

[31] Blum and Mespoulet (2003): 159, 161.

[32] Volkov (2014): 152.

During this time, the Yakovlev investigation continued. It is not clear how the investigation proceeded, but its character is suggested by an allegation that Kraval' appears to have made afterwards: that Yakovlev had put pressure on the TsUNKhU staff to agree that the census had missed 4% of the population (i.e. a number close to the 6.3 million), the Kurman gap.[33] It is not clear, also, what influence was allowed to the statisticians among the members of the Yakovlev committee. Popov, the most experienced of them, appears to have played an ambiguous role at this time. On one hand, he reported to Yakovlev that the underlying problem was not inaccurate census data but overly optimistic population forecasts.[34] On the other hand, sent to audit the census data in Odessa province, Popov reported that faulty census work had led the returns to understate the true population by around 4%.[35] Whatever the process, in the outcome, Yakovlev ignored Popov's warnings about over-optimistic forecasts and reported to the leadership that the census had been wrecked by class enemies in TsUNKhU.[36]

Yakovlev's report to the party leaders on the census coincided with that of the Redens commission, which reported back (also through Yakovlev) on April 3, 1937.[37] Redens's task had been to verify the staffing of TsSUNKhU. He found that TsUNKhU had been penetrated by a group of spies over many years, and that consciously or unconsciously Kraval' had enabled their activities. As a result, it was alleged, the census had been placed in the hands of figures hostile to the party, such as the

[33]We know this not directly, from Kraval', but indirectly, from Yakovlev, who wrote to Stalin and Molotov on May 18, 1937, to refute Kraval's charges (RGASPI, 82/2/537: 124). For the Kurman gap, see Table 1.

[34]These notes in Popov's personal file (RGAE, 1562/105/1/10: 1–9; 105/1/441a: 1–12) are consistent with the position he took in January 1939, discussed below.

[35]RGAE, 1562/105/1/82: 1–16 (February 1937).

[36]RGASPI, 82/2/537: 124 (May 18, 1937).

[37]RGASPI, 82/2/531: 47 (letter of transmission from Yakovlev to Molotov); 48–55 (the report of the Redens commission). The first page of the report lists the commission members as Redens, Grossman, and Gegechkor. Strangely, the letter of transmission names Peters in place of Redens. At this time S. F. Redens was chief of the Moscow province NKVD, whereas A. A. Peters (Zdebskii) was an NKVD officer in charge of police matters in the Ukrainian province of Chernigov, an unlikely position from which to be assigned this task.

lapsed Old Bolshevik Kvitkin.[38] According to the Redens report, Kvitkin had declined to join the trade union and refused to have Bolsheviks working in his office. When asked why the census results fell short of the projected population, Kvitkin was alleged to have replied (with appalling frankness) that it was a result of collectivisation.

Kvitkin was not the only target to be singled out in TsUNKhU. The census group, according to the Redens report, had worked alongside the department of population and health accounts and therefore with its deputy chief Kurman, who had attempted to 'explain' the population shortfall to Kraval' before his arrest. Kurman was described as a 'fascist' and his explanations as a 'fascist myth that two million had emigrated from the USSR, and that 1.5 million unregistered [deaths] were held by the NKVD, etc.' Kurman's direct chief was allegedly a Hungarian (most likely, a Soviet citizen of Hungarian origin) and his recently appointed successor was said to be a former Socialist Revolutionary (i.e. a non-Bolshevik socialist). Using the sinister language of the time, the report noted that 'the most important departments of TsUNKhU are to a high degree in the hands of suspicious foreigners.' Thus Kurman and Kvitkin were both guilty, but at the same time neither was ultimately in charge. That person was TsUNKhU chief Kraval', who, in the eyes of the Redens committee, had colluded with the saboteurs and failed to restrain them.

Kvitkin was arrested at some point, and this was followed by the arrest of Kraval' on May 31, 1937.[39] Kraval' was replaced as head of TsUNKhU by Vermenichev, a member of the Yakovlev commission.[40]

[38] O. A. Kvitkin (1874–1937) joined the Bolshevik Party in 1904, and was a delegate to the third, fourth, and fifth party congresses, but had allowed his membership to lapse in 1908. He had worked in zemstvo statistical offices from 1901, but then went abroad and graduated in mathematics from the Sorbonne in Paris in 1913. He returned to Moscow in 1915 and revived links with his former statistical colleagues (but not his former party comrades). In 1919 he joined the Soviet statistical administration and took a lead in the urban censuses of 1920 and 1923 and the national 1926 censuses. A most valuable skill was his understanding of mechanical data processing. In the early 1930s Trilisser had tried to have him dismissed but Osinskii and Kraval' kept him in charge of the census office.

[39] For Kraval's arrest, see *Golod v SSSR*, 3 (2012): 857. Volkov (2014): 151, reports that he was suspended from his position on May 23 and dismissed on June 2.

[40] I. D. Vermenichev (1899–1938), born in Turkestan of peasant origin, served in the Cheka and as a political commissar in Central Asia during the Civil War. Afterwards he entered the Timiryazev Agricultural Academy, graduating in 1926, before joining both Rabkrin (the government inspectorate) and TsSU and also the editorial boards of the agricultural newspaper and the party newspaper *Pravda*. From February 1933 he was deputy chief of Rabkrin and a member of the Presidium of the Party Control Commission. From

Vermenichev asked to bring two other members of the Yakovlev commission into TsUNKhU: Tsaguriya of the Commissariat of Heavy Industry, as his first deputy, and P. I. Popov of Gosplan RSFSR, to head the census office and act as another deputy. The higher party officials approved Tsaguriya's transfer and rejected that of Popov.[41] So Popov was allowed to remain in Gosplan RSFSR.

With the TsUNKhU purge under way, no progress was made on the substantive outcomes of the census. As the summer wore on, one new proposal was put forward: in August 1937, Kurman's successor Khotimskii proposed to fill the Kurman gap by adjusting the 162 million figure upward by 4% (making 168.5 million) and by scaling up all the subtotals at different levels. But with September, the party leaders decided instead on a more radical measure: to write off the 1937 census completely. This was implemented by a Sovnarkom decree, 'On the defective character of the All-Union census of population of 1937', published on September 26—after more than eight months of silence, the first public announcement that anything had gone wrong. TsUNKhU, it was said, had carried out the census 'in gross violation of the basic foundations of statistical science, and also in violation of the instructions of the Council of People's Commissars of the USSR'. The census would be re-run in January 1939.[42]

The calculations behind the decision to discard the 1937 census remain uncertain. The decision meant that Stalin did not have to accept in public that the population of the USSR was around 162 million. Still, there were other options short of cancellation. The party leaders could, for example, have chosen to publish the results after scaling them upwards by some small factor, such as 4%, the adjustment proposed within TsUNKhU in August. This would have brought the population total to 168.5 million, which was neither so high as to lose all touch with reality, nor so low as to fall beneath the 168 million figure that Stalin had previously claimed for the end of 1933. Of course, even a compromise

1934 he worked in Gosplan as head of the Departments of Agriculture and State Farms. In 1937, as head of TsUNKhU and deputy head of Gosplan from May 31 until his arrest on December 4, he was active in purging TsUNKhU in Moscow and the localities. Volkov (2014): 152–153, provides a list of regional statisticians purged at this time.

[41] RGASPI, 82/2/531: 56–60 (June 11, 1937).

[42] *Pravda*, September 26, 1937, reproduced in Polyakov et al. (2007): 288.

figure could still have prompted difficult questions about the underlying trend in Soviet mortality.

In choosing to discard the census results entirely, the party leaders could have calculated that a repeat census two years later could then yield a figure closer to the expected 170 million. But in the summer of 1937 a further consideration might also have come into play: the belief that the state was in the process of permanently cleansing Soviet society of the last traces of opposition and the last of the critics who might have expected to gain from exposing the errors of the party. Once they had been eliminated, it would be safe to answer the question: what was the population of the USSR?

In the meantime, a price was paid for postponing the answer. This price was paid in two instalments. The first part was paid by those punished for answering the question incorrectly on the first occasion. The rest was paid by the state as a whole. The suppression of the 1937 census results forced the entire Soviet bureaucracy to continue its operations for the time being on the unquestioned assumption that the number of people under its control was at least 170 million and up to 180 million, a range that exceeded the truth by 8–18 million, or 5–11%.

4 1938 and Preparations for the 1939 Census

Vermenichev did not remain in charge of TsUNKhU for long. He too was arrested on December 5, 1937. Formally speaking, TsUNKhU remained without a chief until January 7, 1938, when the position was filled by I. V. Sautin, an outsider with no previous experience of statistical work.[43] Looking at the work done in TsUNKhU at this time, one

[43] Ivan Vasil'evich Sautin (1903–1975), of peasant origin, served in the Red Army Air Force in the 1920s and then trained as a teacher, joining the party in the process. In the early 1930s he taught in a teacher training college, and a technical college, and then became a deputy director of a Leningrad party distance learning college, responsible for the teaching of political economy. In 1935 he became an affiliate of the Institute of Red Professors and in 1937 became its deputy director for teaching. Nothing in this early career seems to have prepared him professionally for sudden elevation to the chief statistician of the Soviet Union. He was chief of TsUNKhU for the best part of three years, from January 7, 1938, to October 10, 1940. Unlike his predecessors he was not arrested, but spent the rest of a long career in less prestigious roles. At TsUNKhU he was replaced by his deputy, V. N. Starovskii, who was chief of the census office during the 1939 census. Starovskii remained in charge of TsUNKhU (renamed TsSU in 1948) until 1975.

supposes that the main burdens were carried by Sautin's more experienced deputies, such as Starovskii in the census office.

In February 1938 Sautin, the new head of TsUNKhU, reported to Molotov on preliminary estimates of the natural increase of the population (see Table B.54). These figures showed that the number of births registered in 1937 had risen to 6.3 million (from 5.4 million in 1936 and 4.7 million in 1935). One factor in the increase would have been the severe restrictions on abortion, put in place in June 1936 (Vol. 6: 289). The number of deaths registered in 1937 was 2.9 million (stable by comparison with 3.0 million in 1936, but above the 2.5 million of 1935). Taking the difference, Sautin's report showed that the natural increase in 1937 was 3.4 million.

At last, evidence had been found to support Stalin's claim, made in 1935, that the population's natural increase was three million a year (see Sect. 1), although the natural increase had been well below that level at the time he made it (2.4 million in 1936 and 2.2 million in 1935).

Meanwhile, the government press continued to project high rates of population growth and to highlight the risk of sabotage of the new census. On December 3, 1938, a leading article in *Izvestiya* repeated Stalin's three-million-a-year claim.[44] On that basis, the expected population increment from December 1926 to January 1939 would be 36 million. With 147 million as the starting point, the projected 1939 census population would be 183 million. The same forecast arose from adding a 15-million increment to Stalin's announced figure of 168 million as the population at the end of 1933. The editorial warned:

> It is well-known that the results of the 1937 census were declared defective. Wreckers from the Trotskyist-Bukharinist gang present at the time in TsUNKhU ignored government instructions and the elementary foundations of statistical science.

The editors clearly signaled a census population of more than 180 million.

The scheme of the 1939 census restored the conventions breached by its predecessor. The census was designed to record not only the population on hand in each locality on the census date, but also the permanent resident population in both towns and countryside. This implied

[44] *Izvestiya*, December 3, 1938.

the need for a system to cross-check the returns made for people temporarily absent from their places of residence on the census date against the returns for those on hand in each locality but not resident there. For enumeration of the total population, the two should cancel out, unless mistakes were made, and this possibility would play a small but significant role in the census outcome.[45] And, in another return to convention, the sensitive question on religion was dropped.

Concerns about the planning of the census were aired in public. A month before the census, a senior economist of the census office was allowed to publish a defence of the plans in *Izvestiya*. Previously, an article in the trade union journal had criticised the plan of the 1937 census as a 'wrecking plan'. The article explained that this was incorrect: the census had failed, not because of sabotage at the planning stage, for there was nothing wrong with the plan. The problem (it was said) was caused by wrecking at the stage of implementation.[46]

A few days after that, on December 23, *Izvestiya* carried another editorial calling for intensified census preparations; an announcement of the census date, January 17; and an article posing the question 'Why we need the census'.[47] It was explained that the census data would be collected over seven days in the towns and ten days in the countryside; legal sanctions would be applied to anyone refusing to cooperate.

5 Popov's Warning

In the moment before the census, a surprisingly important role was played by the veteran statistician P. I. Popov, who had been rejected for the position of head of the Census Office in July 1937. A biographical dictionary of leading Russian and Soviet statisticians states that in 1938 and 1939 Popov 'participated in the preparation and carrying out of the All-Union Census in 1939'.[48] It is not clear whether Popov's 'participation' was formalised. Popov's biographies list him only as head of the

[45] The 'control measures' adopted in 1939 to avoid double-counting are discussed in *Vsesoyuznaya perepi' naseleniya 1939 goda*, (1992): 12 (T. Labutova).

[46] *Izvestiya*, December 15, 1938 (A. Vaganov).

[47] *Izvestiya*, December 23, 1938. The article was signed by 'Professor Starovskii', most likely V. N. Starovskii, deputy head of the census office at the time, who had been made a professor in 1934.

[48] Kornev (1993): 121.

agricultural sector of RSFSR Gosplan from August 1931 to November 1948, when he retired at the age of 76.

That Popov survived at all is a surprise in itself. In 1937 economic and statistical officials were felled left and right. The purge of those directly connected with the 1937 census did not stop at Kurman, Kvitkin, and Kraval'. Yakovlev was arrested on October 12, 1937. This might have encouraged Popov, who later claimed to have opposed Yakovlev's negative verdict on the 1937 census. On December 5, 1937, moreover, Vermenichev too was arrested. Vermenichev, who had replaced Kraval' as head of TsUNKhU, had unsuccessfully nominated Popov to be head of the census office. Popov's chequered past made him a natural choice to join his former colleagues behind bars.

The ascent of Voznesenskii at this time was another danger sign for Popov and other professional statisticians. Voznesenskii had been particularly hostile to TsUNKhU's estimates of famine deaths in 1933, promoting the bizarre allegation that the registration system had double-counted deaths and under-reported births. When Voznesenskii became deputy chief and then chief of Gosplan in the winter of 1937/38, the prospects for restoring statistical integrity appeared more remote than ever.

Although Popov did not succeed to the census office, and had powerful enemies, those charged with carrying out the 1939 census may well have consulted him for advice. Given the inexperience of Sautin, the new head of TsUNKhU, the burden of preparation must have fallen on Sautin's junior colleagues, Starovskii and Borzin. If they needed advice, Popov was one of the few survivors with the experience to give it.

In the weeks before the census took place, as we have seen, the government-controlled press was indicating that the country's leaders expected a population of over 180 million from the forthcoming census of 1939. It was in these circumstances that Popov took a great personal risk by writing directly to Stalin and Molotov. His purpose was to warn them that the new census would again show a population of around 170 million (despite its growth of five to six million since the 1937 census); and that this low outcome would be a sign not of wrecking in the census, but that Gosplan's previous forecasts had been greatly overstated.

In his letter, dated January 15, 1939, Popov introduced himself as a party member and a specialist statistician 'who had been requested by Lenin' to set up a national statistical service (then TsSU) in 1918. Understandably, he did not mention the clash with Stalin that led to his dismissal in December 1925 (see Sect. 1, footnote 1). He also did not mention the 1937 census or his role in the investigation of it. Instead he went straight to the point:

> The census for 1939 will record the size of the population on January 17. Gosplan and TsUNKhU have calculated the growth of population from the census of 1926. These calculations are not comparable with the level of population that will be recorded in the census, and the difference is very large, more than 10 million … Gosplan's calculation of the population for the beginning of 1939, based on the TsUNKhU figure [for 1933] is 180.7 million. Gosplan's estimate based on their own figures is 183.7 million. The census of 1939 is unlikely to give a figure of more than 170 to 175 million. The gap is 14 to 18 million and may be a little more. The annual population growth for this period does not exceed 1.5 per cent whereas it was planned to grow at 2.2 to 2.3 per cent in the first five-year plan and 1.82 per cent in the second five year-plan.[49]

Popov suggested that 'enemies' would try to take advantage of the situation by pointing to a large population loss, and that it was important to establish the real reason for the discrepancy, which arose from the inflated population forecasts made by Gosplan and TsUNKhU.

The context explains Popov's language. One of those most responsible for the inflated population forecasts was Voznesenskii, recently promoted to the head of Gosplan. Voznesenskii was following a script provided by Yakovlev and Kuibyshev, based on the story that these two expected to win Stalin's approval. Popov could not expect Stalin to listen to allegations against his most trusted subordinates. Instead, Popov began to 'speak Bolshevik'.[50] Using the only terms that would win him a hearing, he explained the background:

> Gosplan and TsUNKhU, when they were led by enemies of the people, carried out their calculations without any scientific basis or without using the empirical data collected on population movement. Their calculations were consciously wrecking and statistically incorrect.

[49] RGAE, 1562/329/279: 58–61 (Popov to Stalin and Molotov, January 15, 1939), reproduced in *Golod v SSSR* 3 (2013): 647–650.

[50] As described by Kotkin (1995): 198–237.

Popov argued that the forecasts should now be corrected. He proposed a population forecasting commission of officials and scholars appointed by the Central Committee and Sovnarkom from the Academy of Sciences, Gosplan, and TsUNKhU. He added, ingratiatingly, that the chair of the commission should be advised by the party and by Stalin personally because, otherwise, specialists were liable to lapse into 'scholasticism'.[51]

Popov wrote, apparently, on his own initiative. Those formally responsible for the census were Voznesenskii (for Gosplan) and Sautin (for TsUNKhU). If they had known, Sautin would surely have discouraged Popov from an intervention calculated to alienate Voznesenskii, his immediate superior; and Voznesenskii would surely have intervened to stop Popov in his tracks. But Popov's letter was copied to these two only on January 26.[52] Possibly, Voznesenskii found out on January 22, when he met with Stalin and Molotov.[53] This was after the census but still before the first preliminary notification of the census outcomes, which Sautin sent to Stalin and Molotov on February 1.

It is not known how Stalin and Molotov reacted to Popov's bombshell. It is known only that their response to the census outcomes shifted, unexpectedly, from denial to grudging acceptance.

6 Outcomes of the 1939 Census

From the first reports, it was made clear to the country's leaders that the final population total would be even lower than Popov had advised.

Stalin and Molotov received their first warning, as far as we can tell, in a report by Sautin dated February 1.[54] This report, classified top secret, was extremely brief and gave preliminary, incomplete results, with

[51] Scholasticism: here Popov echoed a charge that Lenin had levelled at him in 1921: 'Statisticians must be our practical assistants and not scholastic'. For his self-criticism, see *Vestnik statistiki* (1924), no. 1–3: i–viii (Popov). Popov had recalled the episode in *Izvestiya* as recently as January 8, 1937, in an article 'Kak proshla perepis'.

[52] RGAE, 4372/92/161: 36 (January 26, 1939).

[53] Stalin's meetings day by day, at the Melbourne Gateway to Research on Soviet History, http://www.melgrosh.unimelb.edu.au/.

[54] RGAE, 1562/329/279: 10–11 (Sautin to Stalin and Molotov). This is more than a week before the report of February 9 which Zhiromskaya gives as the date of the first communication to the leadership.

no attempt to suggest their implications. But the well-informed reader would easily have drawn the necessary inferences, which were shocking.

Sautin's preliminary notice (Table 2) gave 161.1 million as a subtotal of the population without the 'special contingents' registered separately by the Defence Commissariat as soldiers, and by the NKVD as security officers, troops and their families, and detainees. The reconciliation of returns for temporary absentees from places of permanent residence was also awaited.[55] On February 9, the addition of 3.7 million for the NKVD contingent allowed a new (but still incomplete) estimated subtotal of 165.2 million. Seemingly, a figure for the military contingent arrived that day, for a day later, on February 10, Sautin circulated a revised total of 167.3 million. This was perhaps as close as we will get to the true census total.

In the early hours of February 12, 1939, Voznesenskii and Sautin were summoned to a meeting with Stalin and other top leaders: Kaganovich, Mikoyan, Molotov, and Zhdanov. The meeting lasted nearly two hours.[56] It seems likely that the outcome of the meeting was to instruct Voznesenskii and Sautin to look into the census together and report back, as they did six weeks later.

Over the weeks following this meeting, two things happened. The final total of the Soviet population arising from the census drifted upwards, but the drift was much less than was required to meet the leaders' previous projections. At the same time, the leaders became reconciled to a population figure well short of the 180-plus million that they had previously anticipated.

Within the apparatus, the statisticians quickly converged on a figure of 170 million, or slightly more, but not by much. Thus, on March 5, responding to a request from Molotov (seeking information on the social composition of the population), Sautin mentioned that his answers were based on a possible census total of around 170 million. He did not

[55] The 'special contingents' and their role in the 1939 census are discussed by Bogoyavlenskii (2013) at http://demoscope.ru/.

[56] Stalin's meetings day by day, at the Melbourne Gateway to Research on Soviet History, http://www.melgrosh.unimelb.edu.au/. The meeting was held in Stalin's office. Stalin, Molotov, Mikoyan, and Zhdanov were already present when Voznesenskii and Sautin arrived at 00:15; Kaganovich joined them at 00:30. Voznesenskii and Sautin left at 02:00, and the others remained to discuss matters with Stalin for a further 25 minutes.

Table 2 The Soviet population in the census of 1939, preliminary and final reports (thousand)

Date	*Authority*	*Thousand*	*Notes*
1939			
Feb. 1	Sautin	161,100	Preliminary census returns, exc. NKVD and NKO contingents, not adjusted for temporary absentees
Feb. 9	Sautin	165,174	Adjusted census returns, still exc. NKO contingent and not adjusted for temporary absentees
Feb. 10	Sautin	167,305	Final census returns, still not adjusted for temporary absentees
Mar. 5	Sautin	170,000	Approximate final total
Mar. 10	Stalin	170,000	Speech to party congress
Mar. 21	Voznenseskii	167,300	Final census returns from Feb. 10
	and Sautin	+ 1142	Temporary absentees 4,459,000, under-counted by 25%
		= 168,442	Subtotal
		+ 1684	Subtotal 168,442,000, under-counted by 1%
		= 170,126	Final total
Apr.	Voznenseskii and Sautin	170,467	Final total, adjusted for the population of the Far North
June 2	*Pravda*	170,467	Final total
1940			
Apr. 5	Starovskii	170,560	Final total, further adjusted

Source February 1, 1939 (Sautin), from RGAE, 1562/3 29/279: 10–11. This figure comprised a preliminary count of 106,700,000 rural inhabitants and 52,107,000 urban dwellers, and an estimated 1,500,000 in less accessible regions and 800,000 in the Far North. In addition, 2,729,844 control forms (946,445 urban and 1,783,399 rural) were issued for temporary absentees, as discussed in the text. February 9 and 10 (Sautin), from *Vsesoyuznaya perepis' 1937 g.*, 1/e (1991): 7 (Zhiromskaya). March 5 (Sautin), from RGAE, 1562/329/279: 15–16. March 10 (Stalin), from *XVIII s"ezd* (1939): 18. March 21 (Voznesenskii and Sautin), from RGAE, 1562/329/256: 38–43. April (Voznesenskiii and Sautin), from RGAE, 1562/329/279: 20–28 (the total population of the Far North was adjusted to 965,867). June 2 (*Pravda* and *Izvestiya*), as published on that date. April 5, 1940 (Starovskii), from RGAE, 1562/329/536: 44–77 (see the text for the basis of this revision, which was revealed later, and appeared to repeat the adjustment to the total population of the Far North already made in April 1939).

explain whether this was to the nearest ten million, or whether it signalled an upward revision from the previous figure of 167.3 million.

On March 10, however, reporting to the eighteenth party congress, Stalin made a definitive claim: he declared the Soviet population to be 170 million. This arose, almost incidentally, in a section of his speech that contrasted the situation of the Soviet Union to that of the capitalist countries; Stalin did not mention the subject when turning to internal affairs, a point at which he had previously emphasised the rapid growth in population. Evidently, Stalin now accepted the lack of foundation of 180-plus million. The figure he now endorsed was in line with the possible total that Sautin passed to Molotov on March 5, but was still 2.7 million more than the one that Sautin had previously reported on behalf of TsUNKhU on February 10.

Two weeks after this, Voznesenskii and Sautin gave their evaluation of the census to Stalin and Molotov. Their report, dated March 21, told the leaders that the census had been carried out correctly, but further analysis showed the need to correct the previous total of 167.3 million by adding 2.8 million. The new figure was 170.1 million, as Sautin had guessed and as Stalin had then claimed.[57]

The way in which the extra 2.8 million were found is consistent with a process of fabrication. Voznesenskii and Sautin began from the 167.3 million reported by Sautin on February 10. Still awaited on that day were the results of cross-checking the returns made for people temporarily absent from their places of residence on the census date. The forms issued for those temporarily absent totalled 4.6 million (Table 2 shows more exact figures). Although missed at their places of residence, they should have been recorded as on hand somewhere else. Only if missed in the places where they were actually present on the census date, would they have been under-counted. A more likely scenario was double-counting, in which households in one location recorded resident members who were actually temporarily absent, while the same people were counted as residents in their true (but temporary) locations. In that case, it would have been necessary to scale the final total down, not up. Despite this, Voznesenskii and Sautin claimed that the population previously reported as 167.3 million should be adjusted upwards in two stages, first on the basis that one-quarter of the temporary absentees had

[57]See Table 2. By convention the draft document as typed was not dated; the date would be entered by hand when the draft was accepted—in this case, on March 21. But the draft found in the TsUNKhU files shows a handwritten instruction dated March 13 (RGAE, 1562/329/256: 43) to circulate five copies (to Stalin, Molotov, Voznesenskii, and Sautin, and to the file). Most likely the issue was so sensitive that Voznesenskii and Sautin wanted to ensure that their recommendations would be acceptable to Stalin and Molotov, who saw and approved them before the document was signed on March 21. See also RGAE, 4372/92/161: 43–49 (this version, from the Gosplan files, includes a draft Sovnarkom decree announcing that the census had been correctly carried out).

not been recorded elsewhere by the census takers, and then by 1% of the new total to allow for general undercounting. This gave 170.1 million, slightly above the figure Stalin had announced in his speech to the party congress.

In April the total went up again to 170.5 million. This figure came from an update provided to the leadership by Voznesenskii and Sautin. The further revision was occasioned by a new subtotal for the population of the Far North, given as just under one million.

A brief summary of the census outcomes was finally made public on June 2, 1939, filling two broadsheet pages of the national press (This marked the growing secretiveness of the Soviet state, for the two pages were all of the 1939 census that was ever published during Stalin's lifetime. By comparison the final results of the 1926 census were published in 24 volumes). The total, supported by a regional breakdown, was 170.5 million, as previously reported by Voznensenskii and Sautin. By this time the original census total of 167.3 million had been inflated by 3.2 million, or 2%. In addition, the regional subtotals had also been manipulated to avoid exposing particularly severe losses of the population in Ukraine, Kazakhstan, and some of the Russian provinces. This was done by redistributing parts of the 'special contingents' of NKVD and the Defence Commissariat away from the regions where they were actually located on the census date to other locations where they would fill embarrassing holes. The largest adjustments were made to the rural male populations of Ukraine and Kazakhstan: +11.5 and +21.9% respectively.[58]

The story of the census population of January 1939 took one more turn. On April 5, 1940, when Starovskii took over TsUNKhU from Sautin, he reported to the Sovnarkom that the census population had been through further correction and now stood at 170.6 million. An extra 93,000 had been found, but Starovskii did not explain where. An 'explanation' was offered the following year in a secret handbook of local population numbers.[59] The editors claimed that the increment was required to accommodate the population of the Far North, giving

[58] Bogoyavlenskii (2013) at http://demoscope.ru/.

[59] RGAE, 7971/16/54: 1–263 ('Chislennost' naseleniya SSSR na 17 yanvarya 1939 g. po raionam, raionnym tsentram, gorodam, rabochim poselkam i kruppnym sel'skim naselennym punktam: po dannym Vsesoyuznoi perepisi naseleniya 1939 g.' (1941)); the 1940 revision is explained on p. 3.

their number as just under one million. But the latter figure was already included in the Voznesenskii-Sautin update of April 1939, so this was really no explanation at all.

7 The Two Censuses in Retrospect

Four conclusions may be drawn from the experience of the two censuses of 1937 and 1939. First, our story testifies to the persistent struggle of the Soviet rulers to obscure the demographic consequences of their policies of forced industrialisation, the confiscation of food produce from the countryside, the imprisonment and resettlement of millions of farming families, and other widespread repressions. The heightened mortality arising from the famine of 1933 was most acute in Ukraine, Kazakhstan, and some of Russia's provinces, but the effects were more than merely local. Their impact was perfectly visible in the course of the population as a whole.

Second, the different outcomes of the two censuses show the Soviet rulers moving from outright denial to grudging acceptance. In 1937 a compromise outcome of 168.5 million—well above the actual census figure of 162 million—was completely intolerable. In 1939, 170 million—only a little above the actual census figure of 167.3 million—was just acceptable. By confirming a figure of 170 million in 1939, the authorities showed a substantial (although still incomplete) accommodation to reality.

Third, the attempts to fudge the outcomes of the 1937 census, and the successful fudging of the 1939 census, should not prevent us from acknowledging the basic soundness of the work of enumeration in both censuses. In an atmosphere of relentless intimidation, the Soviet statisticians designed and executed nationwide population censuses twice in two years that were reasonably accurate and free of major distortion. This was a remarkable achievement.

Fourth, when biases were introduced, this was done in response to political intervention at the final stage, after the data collection had been done. By removing these interventions, therefore, it is possible to see what the unadorned census outcomes would have been. In 1937 the outcome would have been 162 million. Two years later, in 1939, it would have been 167.3 million.

A postscript is also necessary. The rough treatment meted out to the censuses and those responsible for them at the time was entirely focused on concealing bad news: the high levels of policy-induced mortality in Soviet society during the 1930s.

Somewhat better news was buried deep in the two censuses. This was evidence that Soviet society was continuing its demographic transition from the high rates of fertility and mortality that characterised medieval Europe to the much lower rates of more recent times. On the side of mortality, in spite of mass killing and dying in famine and terror, life expectancy at birth quietly improved in the middle and late 1930s, exceeding 40 years for the first time in 1938 (Table B.55). Women's survival chances improved more rapidly than those of men. The gender gap, already two to three years in women's favour in the mid-1930s, rose to four years by the end of the decade. The existence of the gap reflected both the greater physical robustness of women at every age and the greater exposure of men to violence and to self-destructive patterns of drinking and smoking. The widening of the gap was not predetermined but would continue through the lifetime of the Soviet state. Underlying improved life expectancy was a gradual reduction in infant mortality, which fell below 180 per thousand in 1938, and so to the lowest level yet seen under Soviet rule.[60]

Longer life expectancy was won in the face of considerable obstacles. The greatest of these was the rapid movement of millions of workers and their families from the countryside to towns and cities that grew and multiplied with extraordinary speed. The new urban environment was marked by cramped, low-quality housing and poor sanitation. For the people who crowded into the towns, morbidity and mortality were consistently higher than in the countryside, a feature of all industrial revolutions, accentuated in the Soviet context by the rapidity of change. From June 1936, the struggle to control infant mortality was also hindered by the sudden imposition of severe restrictions on access to abortion.[61]

In the circumstances of the time, therefore, the fall in the number of infant deaths is to some extent surprising. Behind it lay a tremendous

[60] Andreev et al. (1993): 57.

[61] On the effects of the ban, see Vinogradov, *Rukovodstvo*, 1 (1974): 85 (E. Sadvokasava). Based on a study of 400,000 spontaneous and induced abortion in 30 Russian provinces, Sadvokasava concluded that the law resulted in widespread illegal abortions. There was also a temporary increase in the number of births, but this reflected an increase in the number of unwanted or untimely pregnancies, risking the health and sometimes the life of mother and child.

public health effort, the aims of which were to clean up the city environment, educate Soviet citizens in personal and food hygiene, control infectious and contagious diseases, and provide antisepsis in child birth.[62] This effort began to give returns in the 1930s, was maintained as far as possible in the wartime 1940s, and would go on to transform the lives of Soviet children and their mothers in the 1950s.

Associated with the reduction of adult and infant mortality was a continued decline in fertility (Table B.56). For women of all child-bearing ages, fertility took a hard knock in the famine of 1933, and was then slow to recover. When it did recover, prompted in part by the restriction of abortions, it returned to a level distinctly lower than in the 1920s. The decline was most marked for women aged 30–34 years. In the early and middle 1920s their fertility ran consistently above 250 per thousand, but this was a level that they would never approach again, struggling to reach 190 per thousand in the later 1930s. Even this was a disappointment for those party leaders who saw a burgeoning population as a success indicator.

[62] Filtzer (2010).

CHAPTER 6

The Partial Recovery of the Economy in 1938

1 The Temporary Collapse and Revival of Planning

At first the preparation of economic plans for 1938—the annual plan and the plan for the first quarter—seemed to proceed normally. In the spring of 1937, Gosplan was engaged in preparing the third five-year plan, due to begin on January 1, 1938 (see Chapter 8). On June 26, 1937, G. I. Smirnov, head of Gosplan, issued a three-page order in 50 copies, 'On work on the ceilings (*limity*) for the 1938 plan'.[1] This required Gosplan departments and sectors to prepare the ceilings by July 10–15, 'guided by the directions (*ustanovki*) adopted by Gosplan in preparing the third five-year plan and the conclusions emerging from the fulfilment of the 1937 plan'. The memoranda submitted to Gosplan were to propose numerical indicators including production targets, numbers to be employed, labour productivity, wages, costs, investment and the main relationships with other branches of the economy. Smirnov's order set out in some detail the issues to which particular attention should be paid, including bottlenecks, spare capacity and 'measures to eliminate the consequences of wrecking'. The submission of the ceilings would be preceded by a meeting of the department heads with Smirnov on July 3. This procedure would normally have been followed by a submission

[1] RGAE, 4372/36/203: 43–45.

R. W. Davies et al., *The Industrialisation of Soviet Russia Volume 7: The Soviet Economy and the Approach of War, 1937–1939*,
https://doi.org/10.1057/978-1-137-36238-4_6

from Gosplan of draft directives to Sovnarkom and the Politburo, including, particularly, the capital investment plan.

The directives for the 1936 plan were submitted by Gosplan on July 19, 1935, and the directives for the 1937 plan at the beginning of July 1936, and in each case revised directives were approved by the Politburo before the end of July (Vol. 6: 264, and Sect. 1 in Chapter 3). In 1937, when Stalin met senior economic officials for about forty minutes on July 27, those present in addition to Molotov (prime minister), Smirnov (Gosplan), and Grin'ko (finance) were the senior agricultural officials: Yakovlev (head of the party's Agricultural Department), Chernov (Agriculture), Yurkin (State Farms), Kleiner (Agricultural Collections), and Yakimovich (Forest Management).[2] There was no representation of industry, transport, or trade. The meeting was held three days before the launch of the mass operations by NKVD Order no. 00447. After that, and over the next few months, Smirnov met Stalin on several occasions, but no Sovnarkom or Politburo directives for the 1938 plan were approved.

In September, on behalf of Gosplan, Smirnov sent Stalin and Molotov a memorandum on the 1938 plan and 'Directives on the preparation of the national-economic plan for 1938'.[3] The directives were prepared as a seven-page draft decree ready for signature by Stalin and Molotov, and were issued in 75 copies, the number needed for distribution to the government departments and other agencies which would receive a figure of their own in the national economic plan. The directives proposed that the production of Union and local industry should amount to 87.7 billion rubles in 1938, 16.3% more than the 75.4 billion expected in 1937, and that as part of this total the three Commissariats for Heavy Industry, Defence Industry, and Machine Building should together produce 45.3 billion rubles. As in previous years, most of this increase was planned to be obtained by higher labour productivity. The average daily load on the railways would amount to 102,000 wagons, an increase of 13%. Capital investment would amount to 30,385 million rubles. Stalin and Molotov

[2]For Yakimovich, this was his only private meeting with Stalin. Mikoyan also attended, but did not arrive until the main economic officials had left, and was present for only ten minutes. See Stalin's meetings day by day, at the Melbourne Gateway to Research on Soviet History, http://www.melgrosh.unimelb.edu.au/.

[3]Smirnov's memorandum, from RGAE, 4372/92/88: 136ff. The Directives, from GARF, 5446/22a/1092: 142–136 (September 1937).

did not sign the document, and we do not know if the 75 copies were actually distributed.

In the previous three years, the Politburo approved the directives for capital investment in the summer before, and this was followed by much bargaining, so that the revised investment plan was approved before the beginning of the year to which it applied (Vol. 6: 39 and 268, and Sect. 1 in Chapter 3). But in the second half of 1937 the repressions struck at the heart of the planning apparatus. Of those who met Stalin on July 27, 1937, Grin'ko, Chernov and Kleiner were arrested in August, and Yakovlev in September. Then on October 17 Smirnov was dismissed from his post and arrested.[4] (All were subsequently executed.)

This was a fateful day in the history of Soviet planning. Smirnov's departure, together with the arrest of a number of other senior Gosplan officials, resulted in months of chaos in the planning system. Mezhlauk was immediately transferred back into Gosplan, but he was already under a cloud, and was himself arrested on December 1, 1937. Voznesenskii was appointed deputy head of Gosplan on November 23, but Gosplan remained without a chief for seven more weeks, until Voznesenskii was promoted to the post on January 19, 1938. In the same month, Sautin was appointed head of TsUNKhU and Zverev became the commissar of Finance, so the key figures in planning were now again in place.[5]

[4]A professional economist, Smirnov had worked in Gosplan since 1930, as head first of its Capital Construction Department and then of its Department of Comprehensive Planning. He was placed in charge of Gosplan in February 1937, when Mezhlauk was appointed commissar of Heavy Industry, following the death of Ordzhonikidze. In a statement to the NKVD on July 1, while under arrest, A. I. Gaister, who worked in Gosplan in 1931 to 1935, claimed that he had attended informal evening meetings of Gosplan staff, including Smirnov. He alleged that these discussed and criticised the party line on industrialisation and rural policy (Shikheeva-Gaister (2012): 234–235). This evidence would have been sufficient to condemn Smirnov.

[5]N. A. Voznesenskii (1903–1950) was from a white-collar family; his father had a post in a timber office. As a young man, Voznesenskii worked as a carpenter and printer. Joining the party in 1919, he became an organiser of the Komsomol. He graduated from the Sverdlov Communist University in 1924 and worked as a party organiser in the Donbass from 1924 to 1928. He entered the Economic Institute of Red Professors as a student in 1928, graduated in 1931, and continued to teach there until 1936. He worked in the Leningrad planning department from 1935, moving to Gosplan in 1937. For much of the 1930s he also worked in Rabkrin (the government inspectorate) and KSK (the Commission of Soviet Control), two of the organisations responsible for curbing corruption, abuses, and (of course) 'wrecking'. He was arrested in October 1949, and executed in September 1950; A. G. Zverev (1900–1969), was the sixth of thirteen children; his father was a

In 1937 the only public appearance of the 1938 plan was on November 29, when a published decree of Sovnarkom set out the plans for 1938 and the first quarter of that year for the main supply ministries, covering industrial production, output per worker, and wages. At this point Mezhlauk was temporarily in charge of Gosplan. The decree took account of the poor performance of industry since September, when Smirnov's draft directives had been issued. According to the decree, production in 1938 would increase not by 16.3 but by 15.3% and would reach only 84.3 billion rubles as compared with 87.7 billion in the draft directives. As in the draft, the increase was to be obtained very largely by the rise in output per worker, but the decree was somewhat more modest. In heavy industry as a whole (combining the Commissariats of Heavy Industry, Machine Building, and Defence Industry), output per worker was to increase by 14.4% and the average wage by 10.1%, with similar figures for the other commissariats, Production costs would decline between 1.9 and 3.4%, depending on the commissariat. The decree proposed that the average daily load on the railways would amount to 95,000 wagons, a sharp reduction of the 102,000 in the draft directives.[6]

But no directives for investment were included in the decree of November 22 or approved by the end of 1937. In consequence, on December 20, 1937, Sovnarkom approved emergency measures for capital spending: until February 15, each commissariat could fund capital works up to 40% of the level planned for the fourth quarter of 1937.[7] It soon transpired that that no investment plan would exist by February 15. On January 28 Sovnarkom extended the emergency horizon to the

peasant and worker in a small village in the Ivanovo textile region. Zverev worked in the textile industry before the revolution, joined the party in 1919, and after service in the Red Army as a cavalryman, he held local financial posts in the 1920s. He studied at the Moscow Financial Economic Institute from 1930 to 1933 and headed the financial department of Moscow's Bauman district from 1932 to 1936. He was the people's commissar of Finance from 1937 to 1960 continuously, but for a short break in 1948.

[6]SZ (1937), no. 75: art. 364 (November 29, 1937). A secret decree on the same date specified that the production of the Commissariat of Defence Industry would amount to 10.5 billion rubles out of the total for the heavy industry group of 43.9 billion rubles (GARF, 5446/1/496: 151–152, art. 2090).

[7]SZ (1938), no. 1: art. 6 (December 20, 1937).

end of the first quarter, and lifted the ceiling to half the level of the fourth-quarter plan of the year just ended.[8] Still, the situation was not as serious as might appear, and the limits were not as draconian, for little building work was normally done in the first quarter because of the cold weather.

Meanwhile, a curious thing happened: Smirnov's draft directives again appeared on Molotov's desk. The copy in Molotov's files bears both the original date of September 1937 and two new dates inserted by the Sovnarkom secretariat: December 4, 1937, and May 9, 1938. These estimates were still in use though their author languished in prison as an enemy of the people.

Following his January 19 appointment, Voznesenskii hastened with Molotov to present the long-overdue outline capital investment plan for 1938 to the next full session of the Politburo, which assembled on February 9 (the first full session since September 21). The Politburo resolution reveals that much negotiation had gone on behind the scenes, because it now stated that total investment was to rise to 37 billion rubles compared with the 30.4 billion in the September draft directives. The cost of investment would decline by 7% below the estimate prices prevailing on December 1, 1936. Sovnarkom was instructed to determine the final plan and submit it to the Politburo.[9]

The 1938 plan figure of 37 billion rubles was greatly above the volume of investment realised in the previous year. As a baseline, a comparable figure for the latter may have been 25.1 billion rubles, implying a planned year-on-year increase of almost one-half.[10]

The 1938 investment plan was eventually approved by a full session of the Politburo, which met on February 23, and subsequently by Sovnarkom on February 28 (see Table 1). A five-page document, it listed the allocations to over fifty government departments, amounting to 36.4 billion rubles in all; cost reductions in building were to amount to 6.7%.

[8] GARF, 5446/1/142: 205 (art. 86).

[9] RGASPI, 17/3/995: 1–2; this was item V on the agenda.

[10] In 1937, investment had amounted to 27,519 million rubles (excluding extra-plan and above-limit outlays), but this figure was calculated on a somewhat different basis from the 1938 plan. Voznesenskii later reported that that capital investment in 1938 would amount to 28.4 billion rubles, and this was 13% greater than investment realised in 1937, implying that in 1937 investment in comparable terms was 25.1 billion rubles. RGAE, 4372/57/243: 1–2 (not dated but October 1938).

Table 1 Capital investment; the 1938 plan compared with 1937 outcomes (million rubles)

	Outcomes, 1937	*Plan, 1938*	*Planned change, per cent*
Capital outlays, total	32,029	36,378	13.6
Of which, by commissariat			
—Heavy Industry	9,266	6,032	–
—Machine Building	–	2,000	–
—Defence Industry	–	5,000	–
Defence and heavy industry, subtotal	9,266	13,032	40.6
—NKVD	2,031	2,970	46.2
—Transport	4,217	5,030	19.3
—Timber Industry	786	850	8.1
—Education	746	807	8.2
—Light Industry	1,233	1,265	2.6
—Local Industry	552	500	−9.4
—Agriculture	2,209	2,100	−4.9
—Health	805	790	−1.9
—Food Industry	1,368	990	−27.6
Other investment	10,847	8,044	−25.8

Source Tables B.6 and B.7.

A similar breakdown was given for the first quarter of 1938. Despite the delay of several months in the annual cycle, the degree of detail was similar to that found in the investment directives of previous years, but the plan was still incomplete, and several major items were given in figures that were obviously very rough.[11] The most significant increase over 1937 was for investment in the Commissariat of Defence Industry, planned to grow from 2.2 to 5 billion rubles.

In the first few months of 1938 the system of annual and quarterly plans remained in considerable disarray. The approval of the investment plan, although very belated, marked a step forward. But the officials in Gosplan and the economic commissariats were obviously under

[11]RGASPI, 17/3/996: 1, 42–46; GARF, 5446/1/143: 266–273 and 5446/1/498: 101–102 (art. 239). The plan did not include investment in the electricity industry, or defence industry investment in the Commissariat of Heavy Industry, so the total investment planned would be higher than these figures.

considerable strain at this time. Professionally, they struggled to decide the allocation of resources in the absence of the usual planning landmarks. Personally, they were haunted by the continuing purge. They might have comforted themselves with the knowledge that they had not committed any crime. But they knew from what happened to their colleagues that this was no protection; each of them might be arrested at any moment. Even the officials newly appointed at the end of 1937 and early in 1938 were not free from danger. This is demonstrated by the case of K. P. Kasatkin, who was appointed to the collegium of Gosplan on April 21, 1938, promoted to a deputy vice-chairmanship on July 1, and then dismissed from his post on December 27; according to his granddaughter, after his dismissal, he was detained for 15 years.[12]

The draft state budget and the foreign trade plan were not approved until the Politburo session of April 25. The Politburo did not at this stage approve the normal quarterly state budget for April to June; it decided merely that it would be approved later. The decision on foreign trade included both the annual plan for 1938 and the quarterly plan for January to March (retrospectively) and for April to June. A few days after this session the plans were approved in more detail by Sovnarkom.[13] Thus it was not until May that normal planning processes resumed.

The proliferation of commissariats, which was well under way by the beginning of 1938, meant that the establishment of an administrative machinery to coordinate their economic activity was urgently necessary, and in 1938 Voznesenskii embarked on an ambitious effort to improve the status and functions of Gosplan in the machinery of state. A new statute of Gosplan was adopted on February 2, 1938, some days before Voznesenskii was appointed to the senior post, and one of its clauses provided for the establishment of Gosplan commissioners (*upolnomochennye*) to the republics and provinces.[14] The commissioners answered directly to Gosplan in Moscow, by-passing the local authorities.

The scheme to establish regional commissioners was slow to develop. Even by the summer of 1939, only three had been established, for the Urals, the Volga region and Zaporozh'e, and eight more were about to

[12]For Kasatkin's dismissal, see RGASPI, 17/3/1004: art. 177.

[13]For the Politburo session and the Sovnarkom decisions, see RGASPI, 17/3/998: 2, 60–69; 17/162/23: 1–2, and GARF, 5446/1/499: 12–56 (art. 582/120ss).

[14]GARF, 5446/1/142: 286–295. The statute was published at the time.

be established.[15] But there is much evidence that Gosplan officials now became much more closely involved than their predecessors in checking and attempting to improve what was happening in industry and other sections of the economy.

Gosplan also sought to bring the statistical agency TsUNKhU (the Central Administration for National Economic Accounting) firmly under its control. TsUNKhU was formally a part of Gosplan already (it was TsUNKhU Gosplana, an administrative section within Gosplan, rather than the administratively more independent TsUNKhU pri Gosplane, a section 'attached to' Gosplan). But in practice it had a considerable amount of autonomy. A Gosplan report declared of the proposed change:

> The reorganisation of TsUNKhU from an independent government department into a section (*upravlenie*) of Gosplan, directly subordinated to it, is a most important organisational measure, being carried out by Gosplan on the instructions of the party and government.[16]

However, the administrative position of TsUNKhU remained unchanged until after the war. And then, in 1948, developments went in the opposite direction to that proposed by Gosplan 10 years earlier. TsUNKhU was separated from Gosplan and attached to the Council of Ministers as an autonomous organisation, resuming its pre-1930 title of Central Statistical Administration (TsSU).

While 'normal' planning processes were revived, the plans themselves were continually supplemented by decisions that by-passed the planning cycle, an aspect of the administrative system that was also 'normal'. The growing likelihood of war in 1938 led to the adoption of a series of measures designed to strengthen the defence sector; these were tinged with the irony that the savage repressions had greatly weakened the army and the defence industries.

The measures adopted were of four kinds: First, as in previous years, the size of the military was maintained at its already enhanced level, and in some respects further increased. A decision of April 20, 1938,

[15] GARF, 5446/1/142: 6. A year later, 14 had been established, each with a staff of 10–14 (Harrison, 1985: 20).

[16] RGAE, 4372/37/95 (memorandum of Gosplan's department of the comprehensive national-economic plan, dated August 16, 1939).

increased the size of the NKVD armies to 280,800, of which 117,500 served in the frontier troops, 148,200 in the internal security troops, 13,200 in military training establishments and 1900 in the stores. The cost of this deployment would amount to 1044 million rubles, the bulk of which (85.8%) was to be borne by government departments, and the rest by the state budget, Simultaneously, the number of NKVD soldiers working in industry was to be cut by 20,000, and they were to be replaced by wage workers.[17] On August 12, a Politburo decision fixed the annual call-up for the armed forces at 936,000 (the 1917 and part of the 1918 cohorts).[18] This would maintain the armed forces at the higher level of 1,500,000 men, as approved in 1935 (Vol. 6: 95–96). Then, on September 29, 1938, reflecting the growing threat of war in Europe (the Munich agreement was signed on September 30), the Politburo authorised a temporary partial mobilisation: in the Leningrad province, Belorussia and Karelia. Including 38,000 officers, 180,000 soldiers were called up from the reserve, as well as 22,000 horses and 3400 goods vehicles from the civilian economy.[19] On October 16 the exercise was concluded, and the demobilisation of the officers, soldiers, horses and goods vehicles was approved.[20]

Secondly, even firmer control was imposed over military establishments. On March 7, a decree signed by Stalin and Molotov, while acknowledging the historical value of the existence of national military formations, declared that in future all national units were to be absorbed into the All-Union Army.[21] On the following day, the frontier zone of Ukraine was enlarged by the inclusion of a number of districts

[17] RGASPI, 17/162/23: 15–16 (art. 184III).

[18] RGASPI, 17/162/23: 142 (art. 96).

[19] RGASPI, 17/162/24: 14 (art. 108).

[20] RGASPI, 17/162/24: 17 (art. 182). In his diary A. G. Man'kov, a Leningrad postgraduate and teacher, described how he learned about a 'concealed mobilisation' on September 29. He was called up on October 2, and demobilised on October 24. Students from his faculty were called up, and a large number of workers from Leningrad factories. According to his account, their uniforms and footwear were poor and they slept in tents; during the night the rain soaked their blankets, but they merely reported this to the authorities, 'half-joking, half serious': 'The submissiveness, tolerance and patience of the Russian soldier is a pledge that he is unconquerable.' The young lieutenants were limited in their knowledge and competence, leading to confusion and disorder (Man'kov 2001: 191–196).

[21] GARF, 5446/1/498: 111–112 (art. 278/52s).

of Zhitomir and other provinces, and control in the frontier zone was greatly strengthened by ordering that photographs were to be attached to the internal passports of inhabitants of the zone, and by expelling to Kazakhstan the families of persons found guilty of espionage and of persons who had at any time fled abroad, and by expelling from the zone all criminals and politically unreliable persons. The number of NKVD troops in the Ukrainian and Moldavian frontier zones was increased by 3578.[22] On March 23, a particularly severe and undoubtedly counter-productive decision noted the 'large number of Germans, Poles, Latvians and Estonians' who worked in the Commissariat of Defence Industry. Describing this as 'abnormal', it instructed Yezhov, Malenkov and M. M. Kaganovich to 'cleanse the defence industries from persons of these nationalities'.[23] Meanwhile on March 21 the list of defence and heavy industry factories which were to be controlled by a 'special regime' was expanded to include power stations and factories in the northern region.[24] On July 28 and 31, funds were provided for the establishment of new fortified districts in Belorussia, Murmansk and elsewhere.[25] On September 20, the category of 'responsible officials' whose appointment was to be confirmed by the party's Central Committee was greatly widened in the army and navy, in the Commission of Defence, and in the Commissariat of Defence Industry. It was henceforth to include all personal assistants and secretaries to people's commissars and deputy people's commissars, local agencies down to the regional level, and in the defence industry, 'heads of trusts, directors of factories, assistants concerned with hiring and firing, factory party organisers, heads of building sites, and directors of higher educational establishments and research institutes'. The procedures for checking staff were described at length, and 52 senior staff were to be appointed to deal with this issue in the department of leading party organisations of the Central Committee.[26]

Thirdly, measures were adopted to strengthen defence capacities. As in previous years, the resources allocated to the defence industries were increased piecemeal in the course of the year. These measures frequently failed to be carried out on time, but their general effect was to increase

[22] GARF, 5446/1/498: 116–119 (art. 287/54s).

[23] RGASPI, 17/162/22: 157 (art. 256).

[24] RGASPI, 17/162/22: 154, 165 (art. 231).

[25] RGASPI, 17/162/23: 127–128, 131 (arts. 19 and 39).

[26] RGASPI, 17/3/1002: 18–20 (art. 20).

the proportion of national resources allocated to defence purposes as compared with the plans drawn up earlier in the year. During 1938 the Politburo or Sovnarkom agreed to proposals by the Commission for Defence (1) to enlarge the capacity to manufacture aircraft bombs, including the construction by the end of 1939 of a model bomb factory in the Urals;[27] (2) to construct military petrol stores and defence research facilities, the most important of which was the construction of a new TsAGI (research institute for aerodynamics) at a cost of 408 million rubles;[28] and (3) to restore the Vladivostok dry dock and the Novomoskovskii welding factory.[29] Substantial additional funds were allocated for aero-engine R&D in 1938.[30] And on October 31 the substantial sum of 290 million rubles, nearly all from the Sovnarkom reserve, was allocated to the state reserves for the acquisition of mobilisation stocks.[31]

Fourthly, additional money was allocated to encourage better performance in the defence sector. The tighter controls over the army were partly compensated by the allocation of an additional 30 million rubles for the construction of clubs and other communal facilities,[32] Wage rates were increased on building sites and in armaments factories where labour turnover was interfering with efficient performance. A Politburo decision of August 5 permitted the Commissariat of Defence Industry to increase wage rates for building workers and engineering and technical staff by 15% 'to avoid labour turnover on the sites of armour-plating factories' at Chelyabinsk, Mariupol' and Izhorsk, and that a new scale was to be adopted increasing wages by 10% 'to attract and consolidate engineering and technical staff at torpedo factories, especially in design bureaux, and assembly and experimental shops'.[33] From November 19 onwards, a series of decrees increased pay in the armed services.[34]

[27] RGASPI, 17/162/22: 14 (art. 184II, dated April 20).

[28] RGASPI, 17/162/23: 86–90, 115–118 (art. 77, dated June 17), which lists 13 items of new military-related investment.

[29] RGASPI, 17/162/23: 101, 102 (dated July 5).

[30] RGASPI, 17/162/23: 148–150 (art. 191, dated September 3).

[31] GARF, 5446/1/501 (art. 1179/290ss).

[32] RGASPI, 17/162/22: 15 (art. 195, dated April 21).

[33] RGASPI, 17/162/23: 135–136 (art. 67).

[34] GARF, 5446/1/501.

2 The GULAG Economy

During 1938 the NKVD plan of capital works continued to grow. Its initial scale exceeded the previous peak in 1936, unsurprisingly, perhaps, given the sharp increase in the NKVD workforce. On February 23 its volume was fixed at 2.97 billion rubles (Table 1), and this sum was confirmed on April 27.[35] In addition the NKVD was assigned 566 million rubles of capital works to funded from the budgets of other ministries, mainly the Transport Commissariat (doubling lines in the Far East, and from Birobidzhan to Blyukherovo, and the new line from Volochaevka to Komsomol'sk).[36]

The largest projects in the 1938 plan were those begun in previous years, such as the Uglich and Rybinsk hydro power projects, and two hydro power projects at Kuibyshev (Samara). The Kuibyshev projects, with a provisional budget of eight billion rubles, designed for a combined capacity of 3.4 million kilowatt-hours, were the world's biggest undertaking of their kind, as noted in the Soviet documentation, with a volume of earthworks more than twice that of the Panama canal.[37]

Once the NKVD plan of capital works had been confirmed, it was rapidly overtaken by new decisions. These decisions loaded additional assignments onto the GULAG over and above the plan. In March 1938 the NKVD was allocated a huge project for the Archangel shipyard, until then managed by the Commissariats of Heavy and Defence Industry. The budget for this project and the town around it was 1.65 billion rubles.[38] The reason for the transfer was that the work had fallen six months behind schedule. The old civilian and new NKVD managers operated side by side for several months, until the NKVD became the sole proprietor in July 1938. In the transition, repressions were directed against the former bosses, now accused of sabotage. The waged workers and salaried engineers and technicians were replaced by detainees of the Yagrinsk camp (in the region of Molotovsk). The camp acquired a 'special-purpose bureau' (*spetsbyuro*) for imprisoned shipbuilding

[35] GARF, 6757/1/7: 13–56.

[36] *Glavnoe upravlenie lagerei* (2000): 709–712; GARF, 9414/1/2947: 71–79. Railway construction was assigned to no less than six camps in the Far East (GARF, R-5446/22a/89, 255).

[37] *Glavnoe upravlenie lagerei* (2000): 770–771.

[38] *Glavnoe upravlenie lagerei* (2000): 772.

specialists. These harsh measures failed to resolve the difficulties, which had external causes such as the lack of infrastructure, power shortages, poor mechanisation, and low productivity. Construction continued to lag behind the plan through 1938 and 1939.[39]

On May 16, a joint resolution of Sovnarkom and the Central Committee directed the NKVD to build ten sulphite pulp mills, each with a budget of 3.5 to 4 million rubles, to open no later than February to April 1939.[40] The following day, a decision of Sovnarkom transferred the Archangel and Solikamsk pulp and paper mills to NKVD based on 'the impossible situation regarding the completion of construction'. The mills were to be operational by the following year.[41]

On August 29 a joint decree of Sovnarkom and the Central Committee added the Voroshilov-Ussuriisk-Pos'et railway (construction project no. 206) to the NKVD capital works agenda for 1938. The transfer of prisoners to this project was to begin on September 25, and the work was to be finished in less than a year: by August 1, 1939.[42]

The addition of the Archangel shipyard and the new timber camps (see Sect. 2 in Chapter 4) required amendment of the NKVD plan for capital construction. Actual outlays on the Archangel shipyard during 1938 were 190.2 million rubles, or more than 10% of the GULAG's capital works by value. Capital outlays on the timber camps came in at 183 million rubles, compared with only 50 million in the initial plan. To compensate, there were savings elsewhere. Work was cut by 92 million rubles on the Kuibyshev hydro power projects (178 instead of 270 million in the plan), by 100 million on the Baikal-Amur Mainline (250 instead of 350 million), and by 89 million on the dredging of the Amur (11.1 instead of 100 million).

The final value of NKVD capital works in 1938 was 3.073 billion rubles. In addition, the Transport Commissariat subcontracted a further 320 million rubles to NKVD for building railways in the Far East.[43]

[39] Upadyshev (2007): 167, 168, 172.

[40] GARF, 5446/1/498: 76–78.

[41] GARF, 5446/1/498: 80.

[42] GARF, 5446/1v/500, 159.

[43] This is the difference between 730 million rubles, the value of all railway construction carried out by the NKVD in the Far East in 1938 (reported in February 1939 by Beria, GARF, 5446/24a/2332, 59), and 410 million rubles, the value of Far Eastern railway construction carried out in 1938 within the budget of the NKVD itself (GARF, R-5446/24a/18, 111).

If we take into account that the NKVD also built a number of other smaller facilities that were financed by other agencies, it follows that NKVD capital works reached approximately the same value as in 1936, although somewhat less in volume because of increased costs.[44]

During 1938, despite the huge pressure for capital construction, the expanding NKVD economy became more diversified, moving into new activities and new regions. At the end of December 1937, in view of the growing flood of detainees, despite the dismal experience of the first timber camps, the government ordered the establishment of six more timber camps, to hold around 150 thousand people.[45] By March, 54,000 had already been assembled and 22,000 were in transit.[46] From 1938 the timber industry was one of the NKVD's most important branches, exporting 22.9 million cubic metres of timber in that year, three times more than the 7.4 million of 1937.[47] During 1938 and 1939 the NKVD supplied 13% of all Soviet timber deliveries.[48]

The forced growth of timber cutting substantially altered the structure of the NKVD economy. Before the Great Terror, the greater part of NKVD activity consisted of construction projects for industry and transport. As of the first of 1939, such projects employed 630,000 prisoners, but this was now less than half (47.7%) of the camp population; the timber camps alone held 273,000, or one in five camp detainees.[49] Diversification can also be seen in a decree of March 5. 'On the production of furniture' directed the NKVD to supply 150 million rubles of furniture to the domestic market within 1938, including 1.12 million chairs, 280,000 tables, 190,000 metal bedsteads, and 100,000

[44]As of November 1936, the plan for the value of capital works by the NKVD in that year, including work funded from the budgets of other commissariats, amounted to 3.57 billion rubles (GARF, 5446/20a/461: 40; also R-5446/20/62: 170), and the comparable outcome anticipated at that time (in estimate prices of 1935) was 3.38 billion (GARF, R-5446/20a/461: 1).

[45]GARF, 5446/22a/134: 17.

[46]GARF, 5446/22a/134: 41.

[47]GARF, 5446/24a/18: 69; 5446/22a/142: 5.

[48]GARF, 9414/1/368: 124.

[49]Based on GARF, 9414/1/1155: 20–22. In May 1938 the Ukhta-Pechora camp was subdivided into four separate camps for oil (Ukhta-Izhma), coal (Vorkuta), timber (Ust'-Vym), and railways (the Pechora railway). These were all included within the Ukhta-Pechora complex, although the Ust'-Vym camp should be counted as a timber camp.

wardrobes.[50] The linkage from diversification to spatial dispersal of the NKVD economy is illustrated by a decree of February 11, which transferred the Raichinsk and Bukachacha coal mines in the Far East and Siberia from the Commissariat of Heavy Industry to the NKVD.[51] These mineral deposits were seen as a long-term resource for the energy and transport of the Far East.

During this process, the GULAG workforce expanded by less than might have been expected. The underlying driver of expansion was the mass repressions, which continued through the year at high intensity, being curtailed only in November on instructions from Moscow. Across the country from October 1936 to November 1938, 1.7 million people were arrested, of whom 1.5 million were convicted and sentenced, 740 thousand to death and a similar number to detention in camps.[52]

On the first of 1939 the NKVD held more than two million persons including 1317,195 in labour camps, 355,243 in labour colonies, and 352,508 in prisons.[53] But this was a year-on-year increase of only 150,000. The modest growth of the population behind bars or barbed wire is explained by elevated death rates, attributable partly to executions, and partly to other causes. Mass killings took place in the camps, as elsewhere. On February 1, 1938, for example, the Politburo authorised 12,000 additional executions in the Far Eastern camps.[54] It is not clear whether such mass killings were a response to the crisis of overcrowding, or were based on some other calculation. There was also rising mortality among detainees from other causes. In 1938 the NKVD recorded 90,546 deaths in camps (up from 25,376 in 1937) and 36,039 in prisons and colonies (up from 8123).[55] These figures exceeded all previous years except the famine year of 1933.

The dreadful mortality among detainees took place at a time when consumers in the rest of the country were enjoying relatively favourable

[50] GARF, 5446/22/36: 1–2.

[51] GARF, 5446/1/497: 56 (decree of Sovnarkom and the Central Committee, February 11, 1938).

[52] *Tragediya*, 5(2) (2006): 567–568 (A. Roginskii and N. Okhotina).

[53] *Otechestvennaya istoriya* (1997), no. 4: 77 (V. N. Zemskov).

[54] *Lubyanka* (2004): 469–470.

[55] Camps, from GARF, 9414/1/1155: 2. Colonies and prisons, from GARF, 9414/1/2740: 41, 50. On the deficient coverage of these figures, see the note under Table B.4.

conditions, after the unexpectedly bountiful 1937 harvest. There was barely enough clothing for prisoners: in the first months of 1938, at a time when the aggregate population of camps, prisons, and colonies was close to two million, the detainees were allocated 422 thousand pairs of shoes and 213 pairs of felt boots.[56] On average 9.1% of camp prisoners, more than 100,000 persons, were unfit for work because of illness, feebleness, or disability.[57]

The repressive atmosphere directly affected the management capacity of the GULAG. In the camps, repression was directed against managers and employees as well as prisoners. During 1938 the troika of Dal'stroi alone sentenced 12,566 persons, among them 5866 to death. Those sentenced included both detainees and salaried staff.[58] The spring of 1938 saw the arrest of Ya. M. Moroz, chief of the Ukhta-Pechora trust, and his subordinates. In April V. Z. Matveev, the first chief of construction of the Noril'sk combine was also dismissed and arrested.

During 1938 the general tightening of rules and repressions in labour camps was accompanied by a campaign to end the system whereby many detainees were allowed out to live in labour colonies. Those who had had settler status for some time, and had been joined by their families, were taken back into the camps.[59] The restriction of early release in return for productive achievement was maintained, damaging the incentives that camp labourers faced. Tighter security impeded work. In the coal-mining camp of Raichinsk, in the Far East, it was estimated that five to six hours per day were lost in roll-calls and the control of prisoners' movements.[60] Stricter regulation led to the appearance of a remarkable phenomenon, prisoners unable to attend work for lack of authorisation. In 1938 this category exceeded one per hundred in the total GULAG population.[61]

[56] GARF, 9414/1/19: 412–414; also 9414/1/17: 20–21.

[57] GARF, 9414/1/1140: 83. The figures for 1938 here and below exclude the North-Eastern camp, which supplied labour to Dal'stroi. They are most likely understated. In April 1939, Beria reported to the government that the camps held a further 150,000 prisoners classed as 'weakened and less than fully fit' (GARF, R-5446/23a/76: 6–7).

[58] GARF, 8131/37/145: 24, 26–28.

[59] On the settlers in the Ukhta-Pechora trust, see Okhotin and Roginskii, eds., *Zven'ya*, 1 (1991): 349 (Kaneva).

[60] GARF, 5446/30/1742: 28.

[61] GARF, 9414/1/1140: 83.

How well did GULAG managers match their growing resources to the priorities imposed upon them? The evidence suggests: not well. In the first seven months of 1938, GULAG completed only 42% of its annual plan of capital works. For some projects the figure achieved was even worse: 33% for the Kuibyshev hydro plants, and 33.1% for the GUSHOSDOR (Highway Administration) projects.[62] Meanwhile, in 1938 as in 1937, the NKVD capital projects exceeded budgeted costs and incurred large losses.[63]

A major source of poor work was the NKVD economy's low level of mechanisation and poor use of equipment. A Gosplan audit of the Kuibyshev projects found overwhelming reliance on hand labour. The diggers, vehicles, and other equipment that were available stood idle.[64] In the Raichinsk coal mine, diggers were used up to half their capacity.[65] Typical of GULAG construction work was that work was poorly organised and skills were in short supply, while machinery that would have compensated for the scarcity of labour was underutilised.

When the value of capital works completed is compared with the number of prisoners, it emerges that the construction targets for 1938 were met by applying more labour, while productivity fell and the number of non-working prisoners grew. In the Far East, for example, the value of railway investments in 1938 was 37% greater than in 1936, while the number of prisoners held in BAMLag, the camp supplying labour to these projects, increased by 60% over the same period, implying a 17% fall in the value of capital works per prisoner.[66] A similar trend was at work in Dal'stroi.[67] Gold extraction in 1938 was 20% greater in 1938 than in 1937, but in the same period the prisoner population of the North Eastern camp serving Dal'stroi rose by around 40%.[68] Gold was

[62] GARF, 5446/22a/41: 5–6.

[63] Poor quality of GULAG construction: GARF, 9414/4/3: 25–26. Financial losses of GUSHOSDOR projects: GARF, 5446/23a/134: 4–7.

[64] *Zaklyuchennye* (2008): 190–192.

[65] GARF, 5446/30/1742: 28.

[66] Calculated from GARF, 9414/1/1155: 20. Railway investments: 533.7 million rubles in 1936, 730 million in 1938. Prisoners held in BAMlag: 157,500 and 252,800.

[67] Gregory and Lazarev, eds. (2003), 115–116 (Nordlander).

[68] Chemically pure gold: 51.5 tons in 1937, 62 tons in 1938 (Shirokov, 2014, 141). Prisoners held in the Far Eastern camp: 138,200 on January 1, 1939; 90,700 one year before; and around 70,000 one year before that (GARF, 9414/1/1155: 20); the implied change in annual averages for 1938 over 1937 is 40%.

not the only Dal'stroi product, but again the figures are suggestive of a decline in productivity. On Dal'stroi's own account, overspending on labour stood at 44.7% of the plan.[69]

For Dal'stroi, an immediate cause of declining productivity was the deteriorating gold content of the gravel, leading to a 40% increase in the volume of material extracted. But Dal'stroi itself considered that other factors also lay behind the adverse productivity trend. There was a lack of equipment. Managers and technicians were in short supply, so that the work was badly organised. And there was another matter, on which Dal'stroi reports were silent: the skill shortage of 1938 was made worse by the mass repressions. The composition of the North-Eastern camp population changed radically. At the beginning of 1937 those sentenced under the 'non-political' clauses of the Criminal Code were 48% of the camp population. A year later they were down to 12%. In 1938, the Dal'stroi report comments, those arriving in the camp were mainly 'counter-revolutionary elements of middle and older age, little suited to physical work'.

In that situation the Dal'stroi leaders set out to exploit their workforce to the full. From December 1937 all camp privileges were eliminated; a 12-hour working day was instituted; a night shift was introduced; and there were no more suspensions of work because of the cold, the prisoners being sent out to work in temperatures as low as minus 57 degrees.[70] Among the consequences were rapid exhaustion and high death rates among the prisoners. In 1938 there were 17,800 deaths in the North-Eastern camp, placing it far above all others in mortality.[71] Meanwhile, seven out of ten Dal'stroi labourers did not achieve the work norm set for them, and half of them did not reach even 30%.[72]

The record of Dal'stroi typifies the pattern of the NKVD economy during the Great Terror. As the workforce grew, its productivity fell. The camp authorities responded by escalating the pressure on the labourers, so that mortality rose, while the exhaustion of the survivors further reduced their productivity. The share of the Soviet camp population available for work, which stood at 74.7% in 1934, fell back to 71.9%

[69] The information here and below is taken from the report of work by Dal'stroi for 1938 (RGAE, 7733/36/99: 1–12).

[70] Shirokov (2000): 116–117.

[71] Polyakov, ed., *Naselenie*, 1 (2000): 321 (V. N. Zemskov).

[72] RGAE, 7733/36/99: 12.

in 1938—and even this figure was boosted by mobilising the sick, the disabled, and the half-clothed for the sake of the plan. In some camps the results were catastrophic. An inspection of Ushosdorlag, engaged in highway construction in the Far East, found that in May 1938 more than a quarter of all prisoners were sick. In June, a time of the most favourable weather, only 50.5% of prisoners were working. Of these, half were unable to reach their work norms. This added a further twist to the downward spiral. An NKVD decree on the situation remarked: 'Because of the underfulfilment of norms, a significant share of the workforce receives only the minimal ration, which, in the context of malnutrition, is leading to rapid deterioration of the stock of labour.'[73]

During 1938, therefore, while the number of prisoners rose, the NKVD leaders complained continually about shortages of labour and made attempts to remove prisoners from the projects of other agencies (212,000 in July 1938, for example) to work on the NKVD's own assignments.[74]

To summarise, the experience of the NKVD economy during the Great Terror shows clearly that Stalin's repressions had political objectives. Their scale was not in any sense caused by NKVD demands for additional labourers. For one thing, in the course of the mass operations around 700,000 people, most of them able-bodied and fit for work, were executed or confined in prisons. For another, the massive inflow of detainees to the camps and GULAG enterprises did not stimulate the NKVD economy. If anything, the NKVD economy was thrown into crisis. The indicators of this crisis were high mortality among the detainees, the exhaustion of the survivors, the disruption of management, and the worsening of performance indicators such as labour productivity.

3 Industrial Growth

Data for industrial production in plan prices are available in some detail for the first five months of 1938 (see Table 2). These data bear the marks of the plan delays of these months; a footnote states that in the first quarter the monthly plan was obtained by dividing the quarterly plan by three, as no monthly plans existed; monthly plans were not prepared

[73] GARF, 9401/1a/20: 284–285 (NKVD Order no. 00518, August 11, 1938).

[74] GARF, 9414/1/17: 162–164; also 9414/1/18: 343–346.

Table 2 Plans and results for Union and Union-republican industrial commissariats, January to May 1938 (production measured in plan prices of 1926/27 and per cent)

	Jan.	*Feb.*	*Mar.*	*Jan. to Mar.*	*Apr.*	*May*
Per cent of plan						
Gross production	90.6	88.2	100.7	92.9	96.3	97.7
Number of workers	97.9	97.6	97.8	97.8	95.4	95.5
Output per worker	92.6	90.3	103.0	91.3	100.6	98.8
Total wage bill	99.6	93.2	101.9	97.3	98.5	–
Change over same period of 1937, per cent						
Gross production	5.6	9.0	12.0	9.7	15.3	16.5
Number of workers	1.5	1.3	2.6	2.1	3.0	2.6
Output per worker	4.0	7.7	9.3	7.4	12.2	13.7
Average monthly wage	2.3	−4.5	4.1	−0.8	3.6	–

Source: *Pokazateli vypolneniya* (1938); some figures are handwritten. This document was issued in 100 printed copies marked 'not for publication'. A longer document appears to exist with the same name, published in 1939, but we have not seen it.

until April. The figures show that production as a whole was less than planned. By May it had reached 16.5% above the level of May 1937. By far the larger part of the increase in production in these four months was due to an increase in the value of output per worker; the number of workers increased only slightly. On average, wage increases lagged behind output per worker.

In the first quarter of 1938 capital construction also proceeded reasonably satisfactorily. According to a Gosplan report to Sovnarkom, the amount spent was 9% greater than in the first quarter of 1937. This fell short of the planned value by 40%, but a slow start in these winter months, though always strongly criticised, was normal. Adequate building materials and equipment were made available from stocks, and sufficient labour was also apparently available.[75]

An optimistic editorial in *Pravda* on May 22, obviously using the official returns shown in Table 2, stated that industrial production in January had been 5.5% greater than in January 1937, and that the equivalent figures had been 9% in February, 12% in March, and 16% in April. The acceleration had been particularly rapid in the producer goods industries: in the three heavy industry commissariats (including

[75] RGAE, 4372/36/256: 1–2, 14.

the defence industry and machine building), year-on-year growth had increased from 6.5% in January to 18% in April. 'Our industry', the editorial claimed, 'has almost reached the rate of growth called for in the annual plan.'

A further editorial on June 2, 'The socialist economy is advancing to new victories', heralded a major return to normality. The editorial announced that Sovnarkom had approved the quarterly plan for July–September 1938, and this plan proposed that production in the third quarter should be as much as 28% higher than in the same period of 1937, and that capital investment should amount to 12,659 million rubles (one-third of the annual plan). Oddly enough, this was a matter of days before the quarterly plan was actually approved by Sovnarkom and endorsed by the Politburo.[76] The plan was an immense document of a couple of hundred pages, including 45 appendices. A short memorandum appended to it, dated June 13, drew attention to differences between the quarterly plan and previous decisions; in every case the plan was less optimistic. A handwritten note by Voznesenskii suggested how these differences should be reconciled, with Molotov's further comment, 'I do not object.'[77] After the months of chaos, this was a return to bureaucratic order.

Business as usual included a return to the normal optimism, which continued during the summer. On July 4 and 5, a month after the quarterly plan was adopted, Sovnarkom and Politburo decisions replaced the previous plan for industrial production in 1938, adopted on November 29, 1937, by a substantially increased plan. Industrial production in 1938 as a whole was now to increase not by 15.3 but by 21%. This was a result of the increase in the plan for the heavy industries by 3.1 billion rubles; the latter was mainly due, in turn, to an increase in the plan for defence industry production by 2.5 billion rubles.[78] The decree quietly

[76]The Sovnarkom decree was approved on June 4 and endorsed by the Politburo the following day (GARF, 5446/1/146: 72–138 (art. 720); RGASPI, 17/3/998: 5). The brief announcement of the quarterly plan to the public, before it had been approved by Sovnarkom and the Politburo, seems to have been without precedent. This practice was repeated with the plan for the fourth quarter.

[77]GARF, 5446/1/146: 78.

[78]RGASPI, 17/3/1000: 31 and 17/162/23: 96 (decision of July 4); GARF, 5446/1/500: 48–49 (decree of July 5, art. 813).

reduced the plan for the timber industry, the performance of which was already clearly abysmal.

Three months later, on September 4, an editorial in *Izvestiya*, entitled 'The plan for the IV quarter', cited figures for January to July as compared with the same seven months of 1937: heavy industry had increased by 16.6%, food industry by 17.6%, light industry by 7.5%, and local industry by 10%.[79] Later in the month, an article by Kasatkin stated that in July year-on-year growth had fallen to 14.2%, though it dismissed this as a seasonal decline.[80] These figures clearly implied that both the plan for the third quarter and the revised annual plan of July 4–5 had been too optimistic. The plan for the fourth (October–December) quarter proposed more modestly that industrial production should be 21% above the October–December 1937 level, as compared with the 28% growth scheduled for the third quarter. The plan for the fourth quarter was adopted by a Sovnarkom decree dated September 10. This cited the figures for January to July given in the *Izvestiya* article and also reported that several industries were 'continuing to work unsatisfactorily and lagged considerably behind the plan'. It specifically reproved the commissariats concerned for the 'major lag' in eleven chief administrations, which were responsible for industries including copper, aluminium, rubber and cotton textiles. it reserved its strongest admonition for the timber industry, where the fulfilment of the plan had been 'completely unsatisfactory'. The decree stated that industrial production as a whole would be 20.1% greater than in October–December 1937.[81] But for heavy industry, according to Kasatkin, this meant that the year-on-year growth of production in the fourth quarter would be as much as 30%. The decree of September 10 also called for the accumulation of higher stocks of coal, cotton yarn, wool and leather, which had fallen to low levels at the beginning of the year. It concluded by reproving the industrial commissariats for overspending on wages even though their production plans were not being achieved.

The quarterly figures for industrial production in 1938 were not published at the time, but eventually appeared in the press in the course of 1939 (see Table 3). They show the extent of the stagnation in the

[79] *Izvestiya*, September 4, 1938.

[80] *Pravda*, September 24, 1938.

[81] GARF, 5446/1/500: 163–178 (art. 989).

Table 3 Gross value of industrial production, 1938, by quarters (million rubles and plan prices of 1926/27)

	Quarter 1 (Jan.–Mar.)	*Quarter 2 (Apr.–June)*	*Quarter 3 (July–Sept.)*	*Quarter 4 (Oct.–Dec.)*	*Year in total*
Defence industry and machine building	4,848	5,752	5,315	6,214	22,129
Other heavy industry	4,803	5,600	5,110	5,157	20,670
Defence industry and machine building, subtotal	9,651	11,352	10,425	11,371	42,799
Timber industry	805	655	701	687	2,848
Light industry, subtotal	3,962	3,962	3,780	4,443	16,146
Food industry, subtotal	3,186	3,530	3,558	4,714	14,987
Local industry, subtotal	706	560	514	632	2,413
Agricultural procurements	473	440	509	651	2,073
Total	18,783	20,498	19,487	22,498	81,266

Note Q2 is found by subtracting Q1 from Q1–2, Q3 by subtracting Q1–2 from Q1–3, and so forth. All growth rates are recalculated.

The aggregate is the gross value of industrial production of the All-Union and Union-Republic industrial commissariats. It excludes 2.6 billion rubles of industrial production of the non-industrial commissariats (most importantly the railways, but also the commissariats for various other modes of transportation, communication, health, finance, and cinematography), 270 million rubles of the Union-Republican commissariats of the local fuel industry, and 15 billion rubles of gross output (at 1932 prices) of industrial cooperatives.

The data in the original sources are divided among the people's commissariats, many of them established in 1939, but the four defence industries are consolidated in the annual data, and in the quarterly data they are further aggregated with the three engineering industries. We ourselves group the seven remaining commissariats for heavy industry as one line. The two commissariats for light industry, the three commissariats for the food industry and the eleven republican commissariats for local industry are also consolidated into three groups.

Source Q1 (January–March): ***Pravda***, April 18, 1939; Q1–2 (January–June): ***Pravda***, July 12, 1939; Q1–3 (January–September): ***Pravda***, October 12, 1939; year in total (January–December): ***Pravda***, January 15, 1940.

basic heavy industries, particularly in the second half of the year. While the production of armaments and machinery increased substantially, the production of the other heavy industries, after an increase in the second quarter, declined in the second half of the year. This reflected the general crisis in these industries, which had already emerged in 1937. The commissariats concerned were responsible not only for coal, iron, and steel, but also for non-ferrous metals, essential for the production of armaments, which had been given top priority. They were also responsible for electric power, chemicals, and building materials. In the second half of 1938, the production of non-ferrous metals increased by only 6.7% and of chemicals by less than 2%.

In the light and food industries, on the other hand, production rose substantially. After a decline in the third (summer) quarter, in October–December the production of the light industries increased by 17.6% and of the food industries by as much as 32.5%.

On January 17, 1939, *Pravda* published a short table prepared by TsUNKhU, which showed 'preliminary data' for 1938 compared with 1937 for the Union and Union-republican industrial commissariats (see Table 4). Production had increased by only 12.0% in 1938, at rates varying from 15% for the heavy industry group of commissariats and for the Commissariat of Food Industry to a decline of 3.9% in the timber industry. Output in 1938 was thus lower than both the revised plan for 1938, which proposed an increase of 21%, and the original plan of November 1937, which proposed an increase of 15.3%.

The increase in production in 1938 overwhelmingly depended on the increase in output per person employed. The labour force in industry increased by a mere 2.4%, less than a quarter of a million people, only 107 thousand of which were workers. Output per worker increased by 10.1%. However, the average wage increased by as much as 20%, with damaging financial consequences to be considered below (see Sect. 6).[82]

The table in *Pravda* did not give figures for the production of the separate heavy industry commissariats, because the data for the Commissariat of Defence Industry were classified top secret. The defence industry figure was, however, unexpectedly published in the planning journal in 1940, and showed an increase in 1938 of as much as 37.6%.[83] This meant, as is shown in Table 4, that the year-on-year increase in

[82] *Industrializatsiya 1938–1941* (1973): 145 (report by Voznesenskii, dated October 4, 1940).

[83] The publication of these previously top-secret figures was an anomaly in a time when the appearance of any statistics in the press was increasingly restricted. Only two years before this, Kraval', then head of TsUNKhU, had protested vigorously because the Commissariat of Heavy Industry had issued figures from which it was possible (using methods familiar to Western Sovietologists) to deduce the amount of armaments production. The incident is described in Barber and Harrison, eds. (2000): 23 (Barber, Harrison, Simonov, and Starkov). That the Soviet authorities had decided to reveal the rapid expansion of the industry as a warning to the aggressive powers is possible, although unsupported by evidence.

Table 4 Gross industrial production, 1938: plans and performance (million rubles)

	1937 outcomes	*1938*			
		Plan		*Outcomes*	
		Initial, Nov. 29, 1937	*Revised, July 4, 1938*	*Prelim., Jan. 17, 1939*	*Final, Jan. 15, 1940*
By commissariat					
Heavy Industry	(29,165)	16,861	17,280	–	20,670
Machine Building		16,200	16,800	–	10,573
Defence Industry	7,759	10,500	12,986	–	11,556
Defence and heavy industry, subtotal	36,924	43,900	47,065	42,517	42,799
Light Industry	14,508	16,520	16,520	15,301	16,147
Food Industry	12,803	14,000	14,100	14,747	14,988
Timber Industry	3,006	3,840	3,316	2,891	2,848
Agricultural Procurement	1,948	2,200	2,200	2,065	2,073
Union and Union-republican commissariats, subtotal	69,189	(80,460)	(83,201)	77,521	78,855
Local Industry	3,864	3,840	3,840	–	2,683
Industrial commissariats, total	(73,053)	84,300	87,520	–	81,538

Source Outcomes of 1937 and preliminary outcomes of 1938: ***Pravda***, January 17, 1939, except as follows: in 1937, for Defence Industry see Table B.13, and for Local Industry see ***Tretii pyatiletnii plan*** (1939), 201 (includes industry of district executive committees). Figures in brackets are calculated from data in the source. Note also that this source reflects the division of commissariats as they existed in the spring of 1939. We combine them by incorporating separate items for the Commissariat of Textile Industry into that of Light Industry, and for the new Commissariats of Meat and Dairy Industry and Fishing Industry into that of Food Industry. Initial 1938 plan: SZ (1937), no. 75: art. 364, except figures for Heavy Industry, Machine Building, and Defence Industry separately, from GARF, 5446/1/496: 151–152 (art. 2090). Revised 1938 plan: GARF, 5446/1/500: 48–49 (art. 813, July 5), except figures for Heavy Industry, Machine Building, and Defence Industry separately, from RGASPI, 17/162/23: 96, but note that the sum of these is 46,966, not the 47,065 reported in the source as the subtotal for defence and heavy industry and shown in the table. Likewise, the sum of all subtotals in the table is 87,041, not the 87,520 reported in the source as the total for all industrial commissariats and shown in the table. Final outcomes of 1938: ***Pravda***, January 15, 1940, but note that other figures for production of the Commissariat of Defence Industry in 1938 have been cited from the archives: 10,673 (Samuelson, 2000: 194), and 11,530 (Stepanov, 2009: 492).

production in the two mainly civilian Commissariats of Heavy Industry and of Machine Building was only about 7%. In particular, in 1938 as in 1937, production of the main industrial materials expanded very slowly.

Perhaps the most startling figure is for iron and steel. Following the underinvestment in the industry in previous years, production expanded extremely slowly in the whole period 1937–40. A Gosplan report stated that this 'is one of the most backward industries, restricting the growth of the economy and particularly of machine building and capital construction'.[84] An editorial article in the planning journal frankly admitted that the better performance of the industry required not only improved efficiency but also 'a considerable extension of its productive base, founded on the expansion of capital construction'.[85] Pig iron, crude steel and rolled steel expanded by a trivial amount from 1937 to 1939, the poorest result since the crisis of 1931. The only product of the industry which expanded more rapidly was high-quality steel, which increased by 32% in these three years (Table B.14).

The rapid expansion of armaments production, which will be considered in the next section, meant that an increasing proportion of all industrial materials was used by the Commissariat of Defence Industry, and a much lower proportion was available for civilian engineering. In 1938 as much as 42.8% of high-quality steel was consumed by the defence industry, and the proportion certainly increased in 1939 and 1940. And although the production of coal, oil and electricity increased, the increase was insufficient to meet the pressure of demand from machine building and especially armaments. Moreover, construction absorbed two-thirds of capital investment costs, and building materials were also in crisis. The output of mineral building materials fell well below the peak year of 1936, and did not recover before the outbreak of the Second World War. Thus, brick production declined, and although cement production was greater than in the previous year, it did not reach the 1936 level, and the production of window glass declined to a mere two-thirds of the 1936 peak. The production of timber, much of which was used for building, also declined substantially (Table 5).

In contrast to the civilian branches of heavy industry, the consumer industries performed well. The final figures showed that the production

[84] *Industrializatsiya 1938–1941* (1973): 135.

[85] *Planovoe khozyaistvo* (1940), no. 1: 12.

Table 5 Industrial production of intermediate goods, 1938 (in plan prices of 1926/27 and per cent of 1937)

Rubber and asbestos	15.5
Oil refining	10.3
Electricity	9.2
Glass	9.2
Chemicals	8.5
Chemicals extracted	8.1
Oil extracted	6.1
Non-ferrous metals (inc. ores extracted)	5.6
Coal	5.1
Peat	1.7
Iron and steel	0.1
Mineral building materials	–3.0
Non-metallic minerals	–6.2
Iron ore	–7.7
Manganese ore	–19.5

Source Calculated from data in RGAE, 4372/36/871: 1–45 ('Itogi vsesoyuznoi perepisi sotsialisticheskoi promyshlennosti 1938 god').

of the Commissariat of Light Industry increased by 11.3% and that of the Commissariat of Food Industry by as much as 17%. Light industry almost reached the planned figure for 1938, and the food industry exceeded it by 6.2%, a rare event in the history of Soviet planning. The increased production of light industry was not due primarily to the rise in the supply of materials: Measured in physical terms, the production of woollen fabrics increased by 4.6%, of cotton fabrics by only 0.3%, silk fabrics remained unchanged, and linen fabrics declined by 5% (Table B.14). But there was a substantial increase by over 18% in the production of socks, stockings, and outerwear.[86]

For the food industry, following the fine harvest of 1937, this was a year of considerable success. The production of meat rose by 44%. Sugar production reached its pre-war peak: the output of raw sugar increased by 4%, and granulated sugar by 10.1%. The production of butter, vegetable oil and tinned food also increased substantially. Fish was the only major food the production of which declined (Table B.14).

[86]For these figures, measured in value terms, see RGAE, 1562/329/2383: 7, 9.

Table 6 Gross value of output of the armament industries, 1937–1939 (million rubles at current prices and per cent)

	Gross value of output					*Harrison index*	
	Million rubles			*Change over previous year, per cent*		*Change over previous year, per cent*	
	1937	*1938*	*1939*	*1938*	*1939*	*1938*	*1939*
Aviation	2,345	3,238	4,883	38.1	50.8	38	57.5
Shipbuilding	1,726	2,011	2,866	16.5	42.5	–	–
Armaments	2,127	3,001	4,432	41.1	47.7	133.6	34.3
Ammunition	1,561	2,424	3,719	55.3	53.4	122.4	42.7
Total	7,759	10,673	15,900	37.6	49	71.4	43.5

Note The statistics for the later 1930s are usually subdivided by the four commissariats for the defence industries into which the industry was divided in January 1939 (see Appendix A) and are therefore not exactly comparable with the division of previous years. Alternative totals for 1938 (11,556 million) and 1939 (16,935 million) are given in *Planovoe khozyaistvo* (1940), no. 1: 10.

Source Gross value of output from RGAE, 4372/92/265: 1 (July 13, 1940), cited by Samuelson (2000), 194; also by Mukhin (2006), 68. Harrison index from *Europe-Asia Studies*, 49(3) (1997): 374 (Davies and Harrison).

4 The Defence Industries

While the economy as a whole did not return to the rapid expansion of 1934–1936, the production of armaments increased far more rapidly in 1938 than in the previous year. The increase measured in current prices amounted to 37.6%, against an increase in Group A production as a whole by only 12.3%. In the number of weapons the increase was more than 70%. Moreover, capital investment in the defence industries, measured in current prices, rose by 68.5%, against a decline of investment in the economy by 10%. Thus the defence industry continued its rapid expansion, and accounted for an increasing proportion of industrial activity. The increase in 1939 was even more rapid than in the previous year.

All branches of armaments increased substantially (Table 6). While the gross production of the shipbuilding industry grew more slowly than the other defence industries, the number of ships completed and handed over to the navy increased very rapidly. In 1937 only seven thousand tons of ships entered service with the navy, but in 1938 this increased sevenfold to 49,000 tons, the highest figure so far in the 1930s.[87]

[87] *Europe-Asia Studies*, 49(3) (1997): 375 (Davies and Harrison).

Table 7 Aircraft produced by type and model, 1937–1938 (units)

	1937	*1938*
Fighters		
I-15bis	–	1,104
DI-6	112	100
I-16	1,887	1,175
Other models	73	–
Fighters, total	2,072	2,379
Bombers		
TB-3	23	1
SB	926	1,427
DB-3	12	204
DB-3F	33	195
Other models	2	–
Bombers, total	996	1,827
Reconnaissance, total	818	479
Trainers, total	1,937	2,695
Passenger and other, total	210	310
All aircraft, total	6,033	7,690

Source Table B.19.

As in previous years, investment in aircraft production increased more rapidly than in other defence industries, rising to 40% of all armaments investment as compared with 33% in 1937 (Table B.9). Aircraft production also rose rapidly, the increase being greater than for other armaments except artillery (on which see below). As in the previous two years, the achievement of world records by Soviet aircraft was widely publicised. On January 20, 1938, addressing the deputies of the Supreme Soviet, Stalin declared amidst extravagant applause:

> After the heroes of the civil war, I love our aviators most of all. Forgive me, comrades, but that's my weakness. I can make all kinds of compromises, but I cannot allow our aviators to be belittled.[88]

During 1938 the number of fighters and bombers produced substantially increased (Table 7), and, in spite of the bloodshed in the major

[88] Reprinted in Nevezhin (2003): 174.

design organisations, the quality of the aircraft continued to improve. A modified I-16 fighter monoplane was produced in somewhat smaller numbers than in 1937, but this decline was compensated by the surprising re-emergence of the I-15 biplane, which had ceased production at the end of 1935. The I-15b, designed by Polikarpov, included a more powerful engine, the M-25, which it enabled it to manoeuvre better and climb faster than the I-15; its performance was superior to the contemporary Japanese I-95. But Polikarpov realised that Japanese fighters would soon prove superior to the I-15b, and designed a new biplane fighter, the much faster I-153. The I-153 was successfully tested in October 1938, and over a thousand of the new fighters were produced in 1939.[89] On October 26, a Politburo decision resolved in measured terms that a major advance in the sophistication of fighters was required:

> Contemporary single-seater fighters, including those constructed according to the 1938 plan of experimental work, have secured success against fighters and other forms of aircraft. But they are not completely fulfilling the task of successful struggle with modern high-speed bombers, because they do not have an overwhelming advantage in maximum velocity, speed of ascent, ceiling reached, manoeuvrability at great heights and fire power.

The Politburo therefore authorised priority for construction of the twin-engined, single-seater fighter designed by V. K. Tairov, a pupil of Polikarpov, the first example being completed as early as May 1, 1939.[90] This proved to be the first of many efforts to produce an up-to-date fighter, accomplished only after the outbreak of war.

In 1938 other designers moved towards preparing a new generation of fighters. Thus Mikoyan's brother A. I. Mikoyan, who had written a thesis on single-seater fighters in 1936, after working in Factory no. 1, took a major part in the design of the I-15b and I-153 fighters, for which Polikarpov was the principal designer. But no fundamentally new fighter designs emerged until the end of 1939 or 1940.

The greatest success of the aircraft industry in 1938 was the production of large numbers of bombers. Although Tupolev was already in

[89] Byushgens, ed., *Samoletostroenie*, 1 (1992): 142–143.

[90] RGASPI, 17/162/24, 20–21 (art. 250). The first flight of this fighter did not take place until January 21, 1940; it crashed in January 1941, and Tairov himself was killed in an air disaster in October 1941.

prison, 1427 of his SB (fast bombers), with more powerful engines and a heavier bomb load, were produced in 1938, as compared with 926 in 1937 (Table 7). The SBs could fly a distance of some 1500 km, and the SB-bis, produced from the second half of 1938, could carry a bomb load of 1500 kg, compared with 600 kg in previous models of the SB.[91]

Since 1932, under the general supervision of Tupolev, Soviet design bureaux had also been seeking to produce a long-distance bomber, the DB. Produced in small numbers, the DB achieved records for non-stop distance and altitude by 1936. The DB-3, nearly 400 of which were produced in 1938, was faster and achieved a considerably greater range than the equivalent German Heinkel 111 and Junkers 86D. In June 1938 the plane *Moskva* travelled 7580 km non-stop from Moscow to a town near Vladivostok, at an average speed of 307 kilometres per hour. (This was the prerequisite for non-stop flights between Moscow and New York, the first of which took place in April 1939.) Then, in September 1938, three Soviet women aviators flew the DB-2 *Rodina* (*Motherland*) a distance of 5947 km and thus achieved the women's world record for a non-stop flight (see Sect. 3 in Chapter 2).

Despite these successes, on October 13–15 the GVS summoned meetings to discuss 'measures to eliminate the defects of the DB-3', attended by more than 30 representatives of the air force and the defence industry.[92] Voroshilov stated that the crucial problem was that the plane was often flown at 6000–7000 metres and 'this height is fatal' because 'Japanese, and of course not just Japanese but no doubt German as well, can reach over 8000 metres.' Voroshilov acknowledged that the problem for the DB-3 designers was to achieve an altitude of 9000 to 11,000 metres without reducing the range: 'It is necessary to maintain this height not for an hour or two but for the time needed to fly to the territory of the enemy and then keep this height for a further period of time.' This proved difficult to achieve.

In spite of the temporary removal of Tupolev from the scene, the design bureaux continued to produce innovative types of aircraft. In 1937 Il'yushin had produced a preliminary version of a single-engined attack aircraft designed to avoid the faults of its predecessors by being reinforced against anti-aircraft fire. On January 27, 1938, he wrote a

[91] Byushgens, ed., *Samoletostroenie*, 1 (1992): 238–241.

[92] *Glavnyi voennyi sovet 1938–1941* (2004): 151–152.

Table 8 Tanks produced by type and model, 1937–1938 (units)

	1937	*1938*
T38 (small tank)	216	–
T26 (light tank)	550	1,054
BT7/7M (light tank)	788	1,221
T28 (medium tank)	46	100
T35 (heavy tank)	10	11
Total	1,610	2,386

Source Table B.20.

letter to Stalin describing the aircraft as a 'flying tank' and successfully secured his own release from administrative duties in order to work full-time on the project.[93] The attempt to provide the necessary armour plating, without overloading the aircraft, proved very complicated, and the prototype, the TsKB-55, was not flown until October 1939. More or less simultaneously, Petlyakov and his colleagues, working with Tupolev, had begun to design a three-seater dive-bomber, the 100, eventually transformed into the Pe-2 dive bomber. Petlyakov was arrested with Tupolev and other designers in October 1937.

The tank industry, in the doldrums in 1937, recovered remarkably in 1938 (Table 8). The number of tanks produced increased by 48%; this would certainly underestimate the real value of output, because the production of the much cheaper small tanks temporarily ceased in 1938 (but we have not found data for the value of output of tanks and armoured vehicles and for the value of investment in this industry in 1938). Even more important, by the end of the year the authorities had embarked on a co-ordinated programme for the design of new tanks. These developments followed the appointment (after the arrest of Bokis) of General D. G. Pavlov as head of ABTU in November 1937. Pavlov, a vigorous administrator, had experience both as commander of a mechanised brigade and as an organiser of Soviet military aid to Spain.[94] On February 21, 1938, Pavlov sent a report to Voroshilov calling for a fundamental

[93] Chuev (1998): 87.

[94] On the eve of the war Pavlov was placed in charge of the Western front. Made a scapegoat for the catastrophic failures of the first weeks of the Nazi invasion, he was executed on July 22, 1941. His conduct at that time is discussed in *Voprosy istorii* (2010), no. 5: 41–51 (I. A. Basyuk).

reorganisation of tank production, arguing that the large variety of tanks with incompatible characteristics made the joint military use of them very difficult. He proposed that the production of the T-26 and the BT should be continued with substantial modifications, though the BT should eventually be replaced by a more advanced tank with a (long-awaited) diesel engine. The present medium T-28 and heavy T-35 should gradually give way to a single caterpillar tank with armour resistant to shells. Production and work should cease altogether on the tank being designed by the Stalingrad tractor factory to replace the T-26, and also on the T-29, intended to replace the T-28. A new small amphibious tank should replace the T-38, which had ceased production in view of its many faults.[95] Two months later, on April 20, the GVS approved a somewhat modified version of the conclusions of this report.[96] Pavlov introduced the report to the GVS in a positive spirit:

> We now have tanks and armoured cars whose fighting characteristics are better than most of the models in capitalist countries ...
>
> The BT-7 is faster than all the tanks of the old world and equals the American M-1. The tank gun has better characteristics than the guns on this type of tank throughout the world and equals the 47 mm gun on the British heavy tank. The armour plating is inferior only to the Czechoslovak VZOR-35 and somewhat inferior to the American M-1. The operating range of the BT is superior to that of any other tank.
>
> The T-26 is better armed than similar tanks. Its operating range is superior to Czechoslovak and Swedish tanks and only a little inferior to the British Vickers
>
> Apart from us only the British have amphibious tanks. The characteristics of our tanks are almost the same as the British, although ours are slightly slower.

Pavlov continued, however, by stressing that technology was continually advancing, so Soviet tanks must be redesigned and modernised. The decision adopted by GVS on the basis of his report stressed the importance of strengthening the armour for the T-26 and the BT-7, and the urgency of introducing a diesel engine for the BT.[97]

[95] *Glavnyi voennyi sovet* (2004): 336–341.

[96] *Glavnyi voennyi sovet* (2004): 37–40.

[97] *Glavnyi voennyi sovet* (2004): 47–49.

Further meetings, sometimes involving the tank factories and designers as well as the military, sought to reach an agreed programme for the future development of the industry. Eventually, a meeting of GVS on December 9–10 approved the four main types of tanks to be developed. These included: the T-40, a new version of the small amphibious tanks which the Soviet Union had been producing for many years; a heavy 55–57 ton tank, the SMK, with stout armour and a diesel engine, for which the Leningrad Kirov factory would be responsible; and a tank designated the A-20, to be manufactured in Khar'kov at Factory no. 183. The A-20, weighing 16.5 tons, and thus half-way between the light BT-7 and the T-28, was to be armoured against large shells, and heavily armed, and was to be able to reach a maximum speed of 65 kilometres per hour. Two versions were to be produced, one which could run on wheels or caterpillar tracks, and the other to run on tracks alone.[98]

Another important development in 1938 was an attempt to deal with the vast variety of tanks which had accumulated since the early 1930s. In his February 1938 report Pavlov pointed out that there were now nine types of tanks and 11 types of armoured cars, apart from hundreds of early tanks which were no longer manufactured and for which spare parts were not available. Moreover, seven new types of tanks were scheduled to be produced:

> Such a variety of types of tanks causes great difficulties in the work of the motorised and mechanised armies, complicating their operation and repair, the supply of spare parts, and the training of cadres. The variety of technical and tactical performance indicators (for speed, distance covered, armour plating and weapons carried) of these combat vehicles when acting in a single unit results in their incorrect use in battle.

The report therefore proposed that some older tanks (notably 822 T-18s) should be taken out of use, that the 2960 T-27 'tankettes' should be used in separate army units and for communications, and that the 3851 T-37s and T-38s, which were no longer produced, should placed in a reserve. Spare parts should continue to be produced for the T-37s and T-38s.[99] These changes were a useful step forward. But the main problem was not solved. This was the large number of obsolescent tanks

[98] *Glavnyi voennyi sovet* (2004): 160–163.

[99] *Glavnyi voennyi sovet* (2004): 335–344.

in use, including thousands of T-26s and BTs, which lacked adequate protection against shellfire, and had many other defects. The resources required to modernise them would be enormous.

In 1938 considerable emphasis was also placed on the armaments and ammunition industries, which of course provided not only infantry and artillery armament but also the weapons and ammunition used by aircraft, tanks, and ships. In 1938 arms and ammunition production grew even more rapidly than the rapidly growing production of aircraft. Stalin, in his speech in praise of aviation and aviators on January 20, 1938, emphasised the importance of artillery in a passage not published at the time, citing the experience of the Napoleonic wars and the First World War:

> In the last resort the side which has good artillery defeats its opponent … I drink a toast to our artillery being first-class, to its being better than the German artillery, better than the Japanese, better than the British artillery … I drink to our artillery being successful, and showing that it is the foremost artillery in the world—both inside the country, and outside it, on territories far from our state.[100]

The authorities had evidently decided that it was important to build up stocks of weapons in preparation for war, and on April 10 GVS submitted an appropriate claim.[101] GVS also decided that 'untouchable' stocks (the Nepfond) and mobilisation stocks (the Mobfond) should be centralised in order to prevent their misuse. It claimed that 'commanders of divisions and regiments often borrow weapons, equipment and other items from the untouchable and mobilisation stocks for current use, and often exchange current property in poor condition for items in good condition'; these illegal actions meant that the Nepfonds and Mobfonds were inferior in quantity and quality to what was shown in the official records. From this time the stocks were to be transferred to the military districts and kept in special stores; they were to be used only by permission of the People's Commissar of Defence in the case of the Nepfonds, and of the government in the case of the Mobfonds.[102]

[100] Recorded by his stenographer A. A. Khatuntsev, and reprinted in Nevezhin (2003): 176–177. Other records of this passage are reprinted in Nevezhin (2003): 179, 183.

[101] *Glavnyi voennyi sovet* (2004): 35.

[102] *Glavnyi voennyi sovet* (2004): 22–23 (March 29–April 1).

In 1938 the army and industry also embarked on an intense effort to modernise army equipment. The first item on the agenda of the first session of the new GVS, on March 19, 1938, was the profile of small arms.[103] Much of this weaponry was rooted deep in pre-revolutionary history. The main rifle was a 1930 modification of the standard 1891 Russian rifle. The decision of March 19 proposed the introduction of a self-loading rifle; the Tokarev SVT-38 was approved in 1938, and began production in the summer of 1939. It proved cumbersome and difficult to maintain, and an improved version was introduced in 1940. The decision also proposed to replace the Nagan revolver, famous in the history of Bolshevism because it was carried and often displayed by army officers and others, by an automatic pistol, and to stop production of the Nagan. However, the GVS did not resolve until December 29 that the new pistol design, based on the German Mauser, should be ready by April 1, 1939, and the decision to abandon production of the Nagan was accordingly rescinded.[104]

In 1938 further steps were taken to modernise artillery. The F-22 76 mm divisional gun designed by Grabin at Factory no. 92 in Gor'kii began batch production in 1936, and 807 units had been produced by June 1938. Meanwhile the military ordered an alternative gun to be designed by the Kirov factory in Leningrad. This gun, known as the L-12, and its rival, the F-22, were both considered at the GVS on June 19 and on the following day by a conference of the army and the defence industry chaired by Voroshilov. The F-22 had shown a number of defects, and a Major Zhevanin reported at the GVS, alarmingly, that the F-22 'is not ready for battle and [therefore] the Red Army does not have a divisional gun'. But the conference resolved that the faults of the guns could be corrected without returning them to the factory.[105] The conference also received a report dated June 17 from Kulik, head of the Red Army Artillery Administration, about the L-12, which criticised defects, but described it as 'a contemporary model of a divisional gun' praising the advantage of its lighter weight than the alternatives.[106] Accordingly, the conference, as well as endorsing the F-22, approved arrangements to

[103] *Glavnyi voennyi sovet* (2004): 21.

[104] *Glavnyi voennyi sovet* (2004): 199.

[105] *Glavnyi voennyi sovet* (2004): 400–402.

[106] *Glavnyi voennyi sovet* (2004): 394–398.

prepare the L-12 for production.[107] In the next few months Grabin and his team designed a new version of their gun, known as the USV.

5 The Railway Crisis

On August 22, 1937, A. V. Bakulin took over the post of people's commissar of Transport from Kaganovich, who became the people's commissar of Heavy Industry.[108] Developments on the railways proceeded more or less normally in the first three months of Bakulin's appointment, but in December the daily freight carried fell sharply, and for the first time for some years was lower than in the same month of the previous year (see Table B.26). On January 7, 1938, a decree signed by both Bakulin and Kaganovich announced that 'in view of difficulties of a seasonal character and the need to improve goods turnover as much as possible', Kaganovich was assigned to support the Transport Commissariat for the period January 1 to May 1.[109] However, the poor performance continued in the first quarter of 1938: freight carried was appreciably lower than in the same quarter of 1937. In consequence, on April 5, 1938, Commissar Bakulin was removed from his post for 'not coping with his work', and Kaganovich again took over transport, holding that position jointly with his post in heavy industry.

The performance of the railways under Bakulin was very strongly criticised in the deed (*akt priemki*) that transferred responsibility for the Transport Commissariat to Kaganovich, signed by both parties.[110] According to the text, in the first quarter of 1938 the stock of railway wagons had been 47,000 greater than in the same period of 1937, but in the months since October 1937 the wagons had been badly distributed between different regions so that some railroads were short of wagons while others were congested by wagons that could not be used. As a result, all technical performance indicators on the railways had worsened. There was also an increase in accidents and crashes after a sharp decline

[107] *Glavnyi voennyi sovet* (2004): 398–399.

[108] Bakulin had joined the party in February 1918, and he followed this with a varied career in the army, graduating from the Far East Military Academy in 1929. In September 1933 he became a political commissar on the railways, and served on the railways in various political capacities until his appointment as a people's commissar.

[109] GARF, 5446/1/142: 57 (art. 26).

[110] GARF, 5446/22a/402: 42–1 (sent to Molotov on May 23).

in 1937. The deed admitted that many difficulties had occurred in 1937 before Bakulin had taken over; and that in the process of purging the railway staff 'excesses and crude distortions' had occurred. It blamed these not on the NKVD but on the railways' personnel departments and on key railway officials, even claiming that some of the dismissals had been brought about by 'enemies of the people' in order to disrupt the railways.

During his period of office Bakulin had confronted the problem of increased accidents on the railways, and had placed part of the blame on embittered former employees. In a memorandum of October 4, 1937, he stated that 46,278 persons working on the railways had been dismissed and that a survey of 34,000 of those dismissed had shown that over 11,000 continued to live in railway accommodation or near the railways. He produced a number of examples purporting to show that some of these people had deliberately caused accidents, and he asked that they should all be resettled by the NKVD, with their families, in remote areas. Krylenko on behalf of the Justice Commissariat accepted this proposal with various amendments, but Yezhov (a busy man in those days) failed to respond, in spite of requests by Molotov.[111]

Although Bakulin's dismissal was said to be a result of his inefficiency, he was arrested on July 23, 1938, and condemned to death on March 7, 1939. However, the problems on the railways proved not to be due to Bakulin's deficiencies. Throughout the rest of 1938, except for the single month of November, the daily freight carried was less than in the equivalent period of the previous year (see Table B.26), so that the total freight carried during the year was 516.3 million tons as compared with 517.3 million in 1937.[112] This was the first year-on-year decline since the early 1920s. A number of other indicators showed a decline in performance in 1938. The average commercial speed declined from 19.5 to 19.1 kilometres per hour; and only 60 kilometres of new line were completed, after 1937, when no new lines at all were completed, this was less than in any previous year since 1929.[113]

[111] GARF, 5446/22a/408, 17–1. We have not found out what happened to these railway workers and their families.

[112] *Zheleznodorozhnyi transport* (1970): 413. Measured in ton-kilometres, the volume of freight increased by 4.4%. This was because of the continued increase in haulage over longer distances. The volume of passenger traffic increased slightly.

[113] *Zheleznodorozhnyi transport* (1970): 351, 412–413.

A Transport Commissariat report explained that the continued decline in freight carried in the fourth quarter was due to 'sudden frosts and snowstorms'.[114] But this does not explain the decline in the rest of the year. The explanation lies almost certainly in the effect of the wholesale repressions on the railways. A table prepared by the commissariat's personnel group shows that, of the 2968 top railway officials in place on November 13, 1938, as many as 42.7% had been appointed since April 1 and a further 33.0% between November 1, 1937, and April 1, 1938. A mere 24.3%—723 of the total 2968—had been in post before November 1, 1937.[115] The technology and management of the railways is of course a complicated business. Because of inexperienced managers, it is not surprising that the railways took a year to recover. From the beginning of 1939 the volume of freight improved steadily.

6 Internal Trade

While the supply of food and industrial consumer goods increased in 1938, the purchasing power of the population increased far more rapidly. Household incomes from the public (state and cooperative) sector increased by 20.5 billion rubles, and the public sector supply of retail goods and services by only 14.7 billion (Table 9). In a single year, therefore, the excess of household purchasing power from public sector incomes over the value of retail products made available by the public sector, which was already 13.4 billion rubles in 1937, rose to 19.2 billion rubles in 1938—namely, by 5.8 billion rubles.[116]

The growing excess of demand over supply was covered partly by increased taxes (2.3 billion) and semi-compulsory state loan subscription

[115] *Zheleznodorozhnyi transport* (1970): 309.

[114] *Zheleznodorozhnyi transport* (1970): 311.

[116] There is some uncertainty about the value of private-sector transactions in 1938 shown in Table 9 (for explanation, see the note to Table B.43). This depended largely on the value of trade in the kolkhoz market, where collective farm households sold private produce to urban households at unregulated prices. Other sources suggest that the value of kolkhoz market trade in 1938 could not have been less than in 1937. Correcting this figure would not change the point made in the text, however: the source of inflationary pressure in 1938 was the excess of purchasing power created in the public sector. Recording a higher value for kolkhoz trade in 1938 would increase the sums of private sector incomes and outlays by the same amount; it would reduce the share of the public sector in retail transactions, but not its role as the origin of retail shortages.

Table 9 Money incomes and outlays of the Soviet population, 1937–1938 (million rubles)

	1937	*1938*	*Change*
Household incomes			
Incomes from the public (state and cooperative) sector			
—Wages	93.0	112.5	19.5
—Other incomes	42.3	43.3	1.0
Incomes from the public sector, subtotal	135.3	155.8	20.5
Incomes from the private (household) sector			
—Kolkhoz market incomes	12.2	11.8	–0.4
—Other incomes	2.5	4.5	2.0
Incomes from the private sector, subtotal	14.7	16.3	1.6
All incomes	150.0	172.1	22.1
Household outlays on goods and services			
Outlays on public-sector products			
—Goods	111.9	124.1	12.2
—Services	10	12.5	2.5
Public-sector goods and services, total	121.9	136.6	14.7
Outlays on private-sector products			
—Kolkhoz market goods	12.2	11.8	–0.4
—Private services	2.5	4.5	2.0
Private-sector goods and services, total	14.7	16.3	1.6
Outlays on goods and services, total	136.6	152.9	16.3
Other uses of household incomes			
Subscriptions to public organisations	0.7	1.3	0.6
Share contributions to cooperatives	0.1	0.1	0.0
Taxes and other payments	5.1	7.4	2.3
Acquisition of state loans	4.4	5.4	1.0
Savings bank deposits, increase	1.0	1.5	0.5
All outlays	147.9	168.6	20.7
Public-sector incomes, less outlays on public-sector products	13.4	19.2	5.8
All incomes, less all uses of incomes (net cash accumulation)	2.1	3.5	1.4

Source Tables B.43 and B.44, abbreviated and rearranged. On kolkhoz market incomes in 1938, see the note to Table B.43.

(1 billion); households also deposited an additional half billion in savings banks. A gap remained. In the course of the year, the population retained an additional 3.5 billion rubles in currency that could not be spent, an unusually large sum.

These years saw an endemic shortage of industrial consumer goods in retail trade, because their prices remained relatively low when food prices were substantially increased at the time of the abolition of rationing. But with the inflationary pressures of 1938, a much greater shortage of consumer goods developed. A Moscow diary of March 28, 1938, reported that 'there's a shortage of manufactured goods right now and it's difficult to get your hands on anything of any kind ... The line starts forming outside the [army goods] store at about 2 in the morning...after 4 days I finally managed to get two saucepans.'[117] A Leningrad diary of August 11, 1938, similarly complained, 'There are no consumer goods, finished clothing or knitwear.' On December 29 not even socks could be found: people bought up everything they could get hold of, stood outside the shops at night and hurled themselves into them when they opened, breaking the glass.[118]

Growing inflationary pressure was associated with the increase in the stock of currency in circulation (Table B.47). During 1936, a year of relatively calm market conditions, the increase had amounted to 16%. In 1937, the very poor harvest of 1936 resulted in food shortages and a sharp increase in the price of grain and potatoes, and of meat and dairy products on the kolkhoz market. The currency stock increased by one-fifth. But in 1938, as shortages became more general, currency increased by more than one-quarter.

7 Foreign Trade

Although the foreign trade plan was not approved until April 25, the Commissariat of Foreign Trade and Gosbank were already working with an informal plan for the first quarter of 1938. On March 3, Grichmanov, the head of Gosbank, and his deputy sent a memorandum to Mikoyan, who was the Politburo member responsible for trade, in which they expressed alarm about 'the acute underfulfilment of the trade section of the foreign-currency plan of the present quarter'. They explained that 'the intensive expenditure of foreign currency on payments for imports for the present year and for past years has created considerable tension in the foreign currency reserves of Gosbank.' The memorandum anticipated that by the end of the quarter the deficit would amount to 90

[117] Garros et al. (1995): 214–215 (diary of Galina Shtange, wife of a professor of railway engineering).

[118] Man'kov (2001): 186, 207.

million rubles, which Gosbank could not fully cover, so it would be necessary to export gold to the value of £2 million to 2.5 million.[119]

The foreign-trade and foreign-currency plan approved by the Politburo and Sovnarkom was more optimistic. It assumed that income would exceed expenditure, resulting in a small surplus of 25 million rubles. New import orders would amount to 864 million rubles, including a sum labelled 'unplanned payments for imports on the basis of government decrees', which was presumably an estimate of orders mainly for the defence industries. In addition, a substantial sum—537 million rubles—would be needed for payments for imports ordered in previous years. Interest and repayments of foreign loans would amount to the small sum of 29 million rubles, a contrast with earlier years, when these repayments took a large part of foreign currency expenditure.[120]

The import plan anticipated that the cost of raw materials, semi-manufactured goods and equipment would amount to 608 million rubles as compared with the 1937 plan of 683 million, but this reduction was largely due to the reduced international prices for these goods. Imports of most non-ferrous metals, and of wool and other materials for light industry, were planned to increase in physical terms. Thus the imports of nickel, tin, lead and aluminium would all increase: the main reductions were for zinc—the import of which would cease altogether—rubber and jute. While reducing substantially the import of rolled steel and high-grade steel and ceasing to import cables, the plan also proposed to increase greatly the import of ferro-alloys including molybdenum and wolfram concentrate, needed for the defence industries. In many cases the plan stated the proportions designated for the Commissariat of Defence Industry, which were often large: 94% of cadmium, 80% of ball bearings, 36% of industrial diamonds and 27% of all chemical imports.[121]

During 1938, as the plan forecast, a large number of import items were additionally authorised by the Politburo and Sovnarkom, mostly for the defence industries (but not exclusively; see below the decision of September 21). The United States was one of the countries that were more frequently mentioned as sources of supply. Others were

[119] GARF, 5446c/22a/424: 1–3.

[120] RGASPI, 17/162/23: 1–2 (Politburo session of April 25, item V); GARF, 5446/1/499, 12–56 (Sovnarkom decree of April 28, art. 582/120ss). There were small changes betweeen April 25 and 28.

[121] For the import figures see GARF, 5446/1/499: 17–20.

Czechoslovakia and China, victims of Axis aggression; and Spain, an Axis power. Britain and France, with which the USSR had trade problems, appeared rarely, and Germany only once[122]:

- February 3: purchase of additional machine tools.[123]
- February 13: purchase of seven to nine Douglas passenger aircraft in the United States.[124]
- February 21: purchase of equipment for the Commissariat of Defence Industry.[125]
- March 17: contract with the Škoda works, Czechoslovakia, in US dollars, for howitzers and 76 mm guns, to be managed by a commission of six persons including Vannikov (the chief of the armament industry) and led by Kulik (the Red Army chief of artillery). The contract, made in US dollars, could allow for payment of 50% in raw materials.
- March 17: arrangement for Czechoslovak assistance in manufacturing nitroglycerine powder.[126]
- March 28: purchase of equipment for manufacture of mirror reflectors for the Commissariat of Defence Industry, which, with the Commissariat of Machine Building, was to send 5 to 10 people to the factories concerned to purchase equipment and to study (i.e. copy) it with a view to removing these products from imports.[127]
- April 20: Contracts with Caudron-Renault for technical assistance to build aircraft were deemed 'completely unsatisfactory'. It was decided to refuse to assist them in building aircraft, to complete work at own factories and, if necessary, completely break off relations with the firm.[128]

[122]The Soviet Union sought negotiation of a new 200-million-mark credit from Germany, but this came to nothing (*Moskva-Berlin*, 3 (2011): 254–259. 261–262, 265–266).

[123]RGASPI, 17/162/22: 116 (art. 60).

[124]RGASPI, 17/162/22: 124 (art. 30).

[125]RGASPI, 17/162/22: 132 (art. 133).

[126]RGASPI, 17/162/22: 151 (art. 167).

[127]RGASPI, 17/162/23: 4 (art. 1).

[128]RGASPI, 17/162/23: 13 (art. 184).

- June 2: import of equipment for the Elektrosila aircraft forgings factory.[129]
- June 2: import of an additional quantity of lemons.[130]
- June 1: imports from China, an authorised list, including cotton, wool, and skins.[131]
- June 16: a barter deal with Spain, supplying artillery in return for textiles.[132]
- June 17: import of equipment for armour-plating factories of the Commissariats of Defence Industry, Heavy Industry, and Machine Building.[133]
- July 5: import of turbine parts, etc., from Brown-Bovery in Switzerland.[134]
- July 9: provide US dollars to NKVD to buy technical documentation for six-cylinder Dodge automobile, and for equipment for naval vessels.[135]
- July 22: imports to the Commissariat of Defence Industry for cellulose-fibre factory.[136]
- July 27: commission of seven people under D. F. Ustinov (director of the Bolshevik factory, Leningrad) to visit Czechoslovakia for 10 days to discuss ordering naval artillery system.[137]
- July 28: discuss extending trade agreement with the USA to 1938–1939. If the USA reduces customs duties on Soviet fur, promise to place orders in USA valued at $50 million to $60 million a year. If not, continue with the present level of $40 million.[138]

[129] GARF, 5446/1/499: 106–107 (art. 694/152ss).

[130] GARF, 5446/1/499: 108 (art. 695/153ss).

[131] GARF, 5446/1/499: 110 (art. 697/155ss).

[132] RGASPI, 17/162/23: 84 (art. 69).

[133] RGASPI, 17/162/23: 90 (art. 77).

[134] RGASPI, 17/162/23: 101–102.

[135] RGASPI, 17/162/23: 104.

[136] RGASPI, 17/162/23: 120 (art. 223).

[137] RGASPI, 17/162/23: 125 (art. 10). Ustinov (1908–1984) later became the People's Commissar of Armaments; in 1965 he became a candidate member and in 1976 a full member of the Politburo, and Minister of Defence of the USSR.

[138] RGASPI, 17/162/23: 127 (art. 17).

- September 20: decree of Sovnarkom and Central Committee listing orders from USA to be obtained by May 1, 1939, for the Norilsk nickel combine.[139]
- September 21: list of equipment to be imported for the Commissariats of Heavy Industry, Machine Building, Light Industry, Food Industry, and Health. For the food industry, for example, the list includes 'samples of latest equipment' for refrigeration and the sugar industry.[140]
- September 21: non-ferrous imports in the fourth quarter: reduce planned import of lead and nickel, increase copper, aluminium, antinomy, molybdenum concentrate, wolfram, resulting in a net increase of the import bill for the year.[141]
- October 13: advance of US dollars to the Škoda works: a commission to be sent to purchase machine tools, guns, and explosives for immediate delivery.[142]
- October 22: import of equipment for the cellulose-paper industry, partly to the NKVD, partly to the Commissariat of the Timber Industry.[143]
- October 22: import of equipment for Factory no. 82 (an aero-engine plant) of the NKVD in 1939, to be paid out of the 1938 foreign-exchange plan.[144]
- November 14: provide US dollars for purchases for Factory no. 19 (an aircraft plant), largely from the United States, with small amounts from UK, Germany and Czechoslovakia.[145]
- December 16: contract with Firestone for a new tyre factory with capacity to produce 600 units per hour.[146]

In the outcome the import volume (measured by weight) of non-ferrous metals, ships and metalworking equipment substantially increased, and the import of ferrous metals and building materials declined; the

[139] GARF, 5446/1/500: 182–185 (art. 1008/242ss).

[140] GARF, 5446/1/500: 189 (art. 1010/244ss).

[141] GARF, 5446/1/500: 182–185 (art. 1018/246ss).

[142] RGASPI, 17/162/24: 17 (art. 176).

[143] GARF, 5446/1/501: 58–64 (art. 1038/277ss).

[144] GARF, 5446/1/501: 65 (art. 1139/278ss).

[145] RGASPI, 17/162/24: 32 (art. 93).

[146] GARF, 5446/1/501: 184 (art. 1325/313ss).

import of equipment for the light and food industries virtually ceased. Total imports increased, and as in previous years exports declined. As a result, the foreign trade balance, measured in constant world prices, was in deficit for the first year since 1932. But data have not been available on the value of imports for the defence industries in 1938, or on the balance of foreign exchange.

CHAPTER 7

Agriculture in 1938 and 1939

Faced with smaller harvests in 1938 and 1939, the government worked to regain control over the distribution of the harvest. The harvest of 1938 fell short of the previous year's by 20 million tons or more, but the state's grain collections fell by only three million tons. This was achieved at the expense of the private stocks held on farms, which had been boosted by the ample harvest of 1937, and were now were squeezed by more than 5 million tons. After the squeeze, peasant stocks were still larger than normal, especially in the Urals. Collective farm peasants continued to feed more grain to animals so that the livestock sector was able to expand. These positive developments were not prevented by a continuing purge of the agricultural officials at the centre, where the senior figure, Eikhe, was suddenly removed on April 29, 1938. The unintended growth of the private sector within the collective farms may have contributed to the purge; it would continue to be a major concern into 1939, as we will document.

In 1939 the government fully reasserted its grip on the grain collections. The harvest remained poor, despite more optimistic official evaluations. Despite the poor harvest, grain marketings were maintained and collective farm peasants' grain stocks now fell back to the level of the mid-1930s. Additional pressures on the private sector adversely affected other branches of farming, where production and sales marked time or fell back.

R. W. Davies et al., *The Industrialisation of Soviet Russia Volume 7: The Soviet Economy and the Approach of War, 1937–1939*,
https://doi.org/10.1057/978-1-137-36238-4_7

Throughout this period the authorities remained keenly interested in the availability of food for the urban centres of industrial production, but food production itself was never a priority. Rearmament, in particular, claimed a growing share of resources that might otherwise have contributed to agricultural growth. The economy's resources in the aggregate were fully employed, if not efficiently so, and every new allocation to defence meant less for other sectors. More specifically, rearmament competed with agriculture for a wide range of intermediate goods that were potentially usable for both peaceful and warlike purposes: metal goods of all kinds, especially motor vehicles and equipment, the associated maintenance and repair services, and fuels and chemicals, especially unstable compounds such as nitrates which were equally demanded as fertilisers and explosives.

1 The Agricultural Officials

The agricultural leaders were targeted repeatedly over this time. Former Commissar of Agriculture Yakovlev, who continued to be intimately involved in agricultural policies in the Central Committee apparatus, was arrested on October 12, 1937. Chernov, who had replaced Yakovlev as commissar of Agriculture in 1934, was sacked (Sect. 2 in Chapter 3) on October 29 and arrested on November 7. Chernov was replaced in turn by Robert Eikhe, a leading official of the party in Western Siberia and a candidate member of the Politburo.[1]

While no firm conclusions can be drawn, it is useful to consider whether Eikhe's replacement of Chernov had some wider significance for the status of agriculture and the way agriculture would be managed. First, in Soviet bureaucratic infighting, the status of the ministry mattered, and so did that of the minister. In the 1920s, agriculture was weak in part because its ministry was of low status. At that time, the People's

[1] Robert Indrikovich Eikhe, born in 1890, was an Old Bolshevik of Latvian ethnicity. He was a full member of the Central Committee from 1930 and a candidate member of the Politburo from 1935. As a leading official in Western Siberia, he was involved in preparations for the collectivsation of peasant agriculture (Vol. 1: 234, 249), and in management of the ensuing famine (Vol. 5: 85, 97). Before the Great Terror, he worked actively with state security officials in his region, calling for extra-judicial killings, organsing show trials and exposing plotters in the local Agriculture Commissariat office (*Tragediya*, 5(1) (2004): 256–259, 489; see also Wheatcroft, ed. (2002), 134–135 (S. G. Wheatcroft)). Appointed the people's commissar of Agriculture on October 29, 1937, Eikhe was arrested and dismissed on April 29, 1938, and sentenced to death on February 4, 1940.

Commissariat of Agriculture was an agency not of the Union but of the Russian Republic; the commissar was able to attend meetings of the All-Union Sovnarkom, if at all, only by means of some bureaucratic device.[2] This problem was fixed in December 1929, when agriculture became an All-Union ministry. Meanwhile, however, the ministers—Yakovlev from 1929 and Chernov from 1934—were secondary figures, clearly outside Stalin's inner circle of power. Here Eikhe presented a contrast: as a candidate Politburo member, his rank made him the most senior party figure to have held the post up to that time.

Now, however, a second factor came into play. Not only did status matter, but also the relationship of the minister to power. The promotion of agriculture to an All-Union commissariat in December 1929 did not bring new resources into the farming sector, because, loyal to the encompassing interests of the party, Yakovlev's ministerial goal was to extract resources from agriculture to support industrialisation. Here Chernov appeared to present a contrast. When in charge of food procurements, Chernov also worked to squeeze agriculture. But on becoming commissar of Agriculture, he appeared to switch to the defence of agricultural interests. In 1934 he was in a weak position to do much, because Yakovlev was now head of the Central Committee's Agricultural Department, a position from which he could breathe down Chernov's neck. But in 1936 Yakovlev became more engaged with Yezhov in directing purges from the party's Control Commission, and this likely released Chernov from close supervision for a time.

At the June 1937 Central Committee's plenum, Chernov found himself facing a new enemy: Eikhe. Eikhe repeatedly interrupted Chernov's speeches on agriculture. Eventually Chernov counter-attacked, telling the Central Committee that in 1935 and 1936 Eikhe had forced the Commissariat of Agriculture to fund assistance to Western Siberia by making claims of a shortage of equipment that turned out to be false. Chernov used this story to make the case for the Commissariat to retain oversight of local agencies.[3] Eikhe fought back. Unfortunately, no record was made of Stalin's summary of the exchange.[4] Possibly, the idea of replacing Chernov with Eikhe came to Stalin at this time.

[2] *Slavic Review*, 34(4) (1974): 790–802 (Davies and Wheatcroft).

[3] RGASPI, 17/2/623: 29.

[4] RGASPI, 17/2/620: 1.

What, then, did it mean for agriculture in 1938 that Chernov, one of more than 70 members of the Central Committee, had gone from the position of commissar for Agriculture, with his place taken by one of the handful of candidates and full members of the Politburo? Did it mean new status or new resources for agriculture? At first this was unclear. More than likely, Eikhe himself did not know.

In hindsight, the status and aspirations of Eikhe look to have been irrelevant to the fortunes of agriculture in 1938. By then, nothing mattered more than loyalty to Stalin, who had not finished with purging the agricultural officials. Eikhe made his first major speech on agriculture to the Central Committee's plenum on January 18. On that occasion Stalin prodded him to call for more purges, and Eikhe willingly complied.

The arguments for more purges that Eikhe offered to the Central Committee show how he distanced himself from his predecessor, whose fate he no doubt hoped to avoid. His objective, he said, was to 'quickly and finally liquidate the consequences of wrecking in the land organisations'.[5] He compared wrecking in the Agriculture Commissariat with that in the cooperative system, notorious at the time for the prevalence of sabotage. He suggested that wrecking in Agriculture was worse. According to the secret transcript, Stalin interrupted to egg him on: 'They [i.e. the wreckers in Agriculture] are ahead.' Details followed. Eikhe alleged that the previous leaders of the Agriculture Commissariat, now under arrest, had awarded themselves millions of rubles in bonuses (this was omitted from the *Izvestiya* report). He attacked the Agricultural Research Institutes for working on topics that were trivial or irrelevant. He blamed saboteurs for the slow spread of improved crop rotations, a problem that (he said) was worse than previously acknowledged by Chernov. Progress in issuing title deeds granting land use rights in perpetuity had been overstated, and some had been issued corruptly, granting land use rights to saboteurs. Wreckers had worked in breeding stations to spread animal diseases, and in MTS to damage repair facilities. With Eikhe's charges and Stalin's support, the purges continued.

[5] The words quoted were used as a headline in the version of Eikhe's speech published in *Izvestiya* on January 22, 1938 (reproduced in part in *Tragediya*, 5(2) (2006): 28–33). The full transcript, with interjections by Stalin and others, is available in RGASPI, 17/2/635: 4–25. The published text omitted the interjections.

Not long after, it was Eikhe's turn; he was arrested on April 29. Where previous commissars for agriculture and for state farms had been dismissed and replaced before arrest, Eikhe had the distinction of being arrested while in office. Unexpectedly, he was not formally condemned for his role in agriculture. The charge was that he was leading a 'Latvian fascist organisation'.[6] Apparently, therefore, it was Eikhe's Latvian ethnicity that caught up with him. His was not an isolated case; the NKVD's 'Latvian operation' had been running for five months.[7] The fact that Eikhe lasted so long into the purge of Latvians implies that Stalin protected him at first, and then lost trust in him for some reason. That reason might have been some personal incident, but it might also have been related to developments in agriculture. As we will document below, there was a sudden rise of official anxiety concerning the private sector in agriculture, and Agriculture Commissariat officials had to admit to providing erroneous data which could be interpreted as an attempt to conceal the growth of the private sector.

Arrested on April 29, 1938, Eikhe was not replaced for more than six months. On November 15, Ivan Benediktov was appointed to the vacant post. Benediktov had served previously as the commissar of State Farms, but he was still a junior figure, not even a member of the Central Committee.[8] Appointed, in March 1938, as Eikhe's first deputy when Eikhe was the commissar of Agriculture, Benediktov had worked in that role for just a month when Eikhe was suddenly arrested. This was likely too brief a probation for the rank of a people's commissar, so he was made to wait until November for his promotion to be confirmed. The

[6]'Eikhe, Robert Indrikovich,' at https://ru.wikipedia.org/.

[7]The Latvian campaign was launched by NKVD Order no. 49990 on November 30, 1937 (*Istoriya Stalinskogo Gulaga*, 1 (2004): 285). In 1938, 11,490 Latvians were arrested and charged with espionage under various sections of Article 58 of the criminal code (Mozokhin (2011): 464).

[8]Ivan Alexandrovich Benediktov (1902–1983) was born into a family of post office employees in Kostroma province. In the 1920s, after a period of employment, he studied agricultural economics at the Timiryazev Academy. He was involved in the collectivisation of peasant farms in Uzbekistan; after a period of military service, he returned to Moscow to work as the director of a local state farm trust (it was here that he came into contact with Khrushchev, as explained in the text). In August 1937 Benediktov was appointed the people's commissar of Grain and Livestock State Farms in the RSFSR, where he worked until April 1938. In March 1938 he also became first deputy to Eikhe, when he became the people's commissar of Agriculture of the USSR.

status of the Agriculture Commissariat was now clear: It was an underdog once more. Agriculture would be pressed to do more (for example, to supply the state with more grain) for less (for example, with reduced capital investment).

Benediktov's associations are not without interest. Working in the mid-1930s in the Moscow province as director of a local state farm trust, he encountered Khrushchev, then Moscow city party secretary, in connection with the supply of vegetables to the city. Khrushchev evidently came to see Benediktov as his client, but it is not clear that Benediktov recognised his patron. In his memoirs Khrushchev recalled being consulted by Stalin on whether Benediktov could do the job at Agriculture, to which Khrushchev said yes.[9] Benediktov recalled a different story: his appointment was a complete surprise, coming at a time when he had been shown an accusation against him by the NKVD and was expecting to be arrested.[10] Meeting to talk about the appointment, he told Stalin of his situation. According to Benediktov, Stalin expressed surprise and said he would stop the investigation. A possible interpretation is that Stalin used the opportunity, or created it, to place Benediktov under an obligation to him. If so, it was remarkably effective because, to the end of his long life, Benediktov considered that Stalin was innocent of most of the crimes of the period, for which he blamed Yagoda and Yezhov. He rated Khrushchev as much more dictatorial than Stalin in his relations with other senior officials. He continued to think that, overall, Lysenko had done more good than harm. These professions served to identify Benediktov as a sincere Stalinist.

Benediktov's ascent marked a return to stability in the agricultural leadership. Only 35 at the time of his appointment, he was a typical member of the generation of the future prime minister, Kosygin, and defence minister, Ustinov. Born between 1902 and 1906, he was promoted early to high offices because of the nomenklatura purges, and continued in these offices for the next forty years. This generation was less experienced but more professionally educated than the old revolutionaries it displaced. It was still vulnerable to the influence of cranky

[9] Khrushchev, ed. *Memoirs*, 1 (2004): 195.

[10] Before his death (the date is not given), Benediktov gave a long autobiographical interview in *Molodaya Gvardiya* (1989), no. 4: 12–65.

ideas. Lysenko was also promoted, joining the board of the Agriculture Commissariat on June 23, 1939.[11]

While the purge of agricultural officials slowed, agriculture continued to suffer from mass repressions. In the first half of 1938, more than 28,000 collective farm peasants and more than 13,000 individual peasants were arrested. The monthly rate of these arrests was slightly above that of 1937 and several times the rate for 1936 (Table B.2). At the end of the year the NKVD mass operations were stopped. In 1939 the level of political repression amongst the peasantry fell back: only 3100 collective farm peasants and 4600 individual peasants were arrested. This was the lowest level since the 'extraordinary measures' of 1927.

2 The Private Sector After 1937

Agricultural policies in 1938 and 1939 were dominated by a legacy of the unexpectedly abundant harvest of 1937. There was anxiety that, having failed to anticipate the size of the harvest, the state had lost control over its disposition. Too much grain had been left in peasant hands, and the private sector in agriculture had reaped the benefit. In the spring of 1938, steps were taken that were apparently intended to conceal the size of the private sector, but these efforts were poorly calculated and can now be disentangled. During the 1938/39 agricultural year, the state set further limits on the sphere of private agriculture, imposing heavier taxes on the few remaining independent farmers and tightening limits on the livestock that collective farmers were permitted to maintain in their private activities. While projections of future harvests remained cautious, the fear of underestimating current harvests led again, in the summer of 1939, to measures designed to further puff up the biological yield methodology of harvest evaluation. In association with these measures, the authorities restored their former control over the disposition of the grain harvest.

The core of the 'State plan for agricultural work for 1938', issued that year on January 27, was the plan for spring sowing. It marked an imperfect attempt to conceal the persistence of private activities in agriculture. According to the plan (Table 1), the area to be covered in the spring sowing of 1938 was to be 90.8 million hectares, 3.7 million less than in

[11] SP (1939), no. 40: art. 308 (June 23, 1939).

Table 1 The spring sowing plan, 1937 and 1938 (thousand hectares, excluding previously sown perennial grass)

	1937	*1938*	*Change*
Targets given in sources			
Area sown, total	94,495	90,805	−3,690
Of which			
State farms	9,855	7,509	−2,346
Collective farm sector (farms and households)	83,857	–	–
Collective farms	78,715	77,309	−1,406
Independent households	783	704	−79
Given in sources but not included in above			
'Manual and office workers'	–	1026	–
'Organisations and institutions'	–	1,223	–
Calculated subtotals			
Socialised sector			
(A) State and collective farms	88,570	84,817	−3,753
(B) State, collective farms, other organisations	88,570	86,040	−2,530
Private sector			
(C) Collective farm households	5,142	5,284	+142
(D) Collective farm and independent households	5,925	5,988	+63
(E) Collective farm, independent, and employee households	5,925	7,014	+1,089

Source SZ (1937), no. 10: art. 34 (Sovnarkom decree 'On the state plan of spring sowing for 1937', February 3, 1937) and SZ (1938), no. 2: art. 5 (Sovnarkom decree 'On the state plan of agricultural work for 1938', January 27, 1938). Year-on-year changes are calculated from the figures for each year, and subtotals (A)–(E) are calculated from the data given by the sources in preceding rows. Socialised sector: (A) the sum of state farms and collective farms. (B) for 1937, as (A); for 1938, as 1937 plus 'organisations and institutions'. Private sector: (C) for 1937, the collective-farm sector as a whole, less sowing by collective farms; for 1938, as (D), less collective farms. (D) for 1937, as (C) plus independent households; for 1938, the plan total, less (A). (E) for 1937, as (D); for 1938, as (D) plus 'manual and office workers'.

the previous year. But the total for 1938 was also 5.3 million more than the sectors into which it was broken down: 7.5 million hectares for state farms, 77.3 million for collective farms, and 700,000 for the individual sector. In previous years, such as 1937, the separate parts had added up to the given total. Within the collective-farm sector broadly defined, the previous practice had also been to distinguish the collective farms more narrowly, leaving a residual of four to five million hectares in 1936 and 1937. This residual would have been the individual sowings of kolkhoz peasants on their household allotments.

Separately, the plan document also listed 2.2 million hectares to be sown by 'manual and office workers', and by 'organisations and institutions', a distinction that was not previously reported.

The changed format of these figures from one year to the next appears designed to obfuscate something—most likely, the unwanted persistence of the private sector. The figures may be interpreted in two ways, as shown in the calculated subtotals. The socialised sector was projected to decline—by as much as 3.8 million hectares, if we count only the sowing attributed to state and collective farms (subtotal A), or by a smaller amount, 2.3 million, if we allow that the 1.2 million hectares projected separately under 'organisations and institutions' were more than likely incorporated under state farms in 1937, probably those belonging to non-agricultural ministries (subtotal B).

While the socialised sector was expected to shrink, the private sector was expected to persist or expand. Subtotal (C) shows that collective-farm households were slated to increase their sowing, something that the plan concealed. Subtotal (D) shows that, while independent peasants' sowing was to continue to decline, the shrinkage would be more than offset by the collective-farm households' additional sowing. On a minimal interpretation, therefore, there was no trend to increased socialisation, for the private sector was holding its ground while the socialised sector gave way. Subtotal (E) shows that, if the sowing anticipated by 'manual and office workers' had been previously incorporated into the statistics of the independent sector, then the private sector would have been forecast to expand by a million hectares, reaching a size comparable with that of the entire state farm sector.

In short, the reporting format of the 1938 sowing plan concealed an embarrassing development from which officials would certainly have wished to distract public attention. If this was the intention, however, the enterprise was flawed. Later in the spring, they would have to engage with the regular practice of reporting the progress of spring sowing every five days in the columns of *Izvestiya*. The 1938 figures would be compared automatically with those for the same period in the previous year. As the spring developed, the consequences of shrinking the boundaries of the state plan for spring sowing became embarrassingly obvious in a large shortfall of sowing behind the previous year's achievements. On May 6, in the middle of the sowing campaign, the editors of *Izvestiya* announced that the figures previously reported for 1937 had been inflated by wrongly including various categories of sowing that did not belong in the state plan.[12] The revision (Table 7 in Chapter 4) was large: for the end of the 1937 sowing campaign, the revised total was cut by 6.7 million hectares, or more than 7%. The correction took the entire private sector out of the state plan (4.5 million hectares sown by kolkhoz peasants on their personal allotments, and 0.8 million sown by the individual peasant farmers) and also the state farms owned by non-agricultural ministries (1.4 million hectares).

This admission of error came shortly before Eikhe's downfall. Did the first cause the second? Trying and then failing to hide something embarrassing from the public was sufficient cause to dispose of a people's commissar. Trying and then failing to hide something embarrassing from Stalin, if that was the crime, was surely sufficient for a death sentence. But the documents do not reveal the arrow of causation. On the face of it, Eikhe was condemned as a Latvian. He was already known to be Latvian when appointed, so something more than his ethnicity was required as the trigger for his demise. The important thing for an official's survival was to retain Stalin's trust. Evidently, Eikhe lost Stalin's trust at this time, and his being exposed in trying to conceal the spread of private agriculture is one possible cause.

More generally, April 1938 saw a clear uptick in official anxieties about the private sector in agriculture. The evidence stemmed from the successful harvest of 1937 and the inflationary pressures of 1938. The larger stocks of grain held by peasants after the 1937 harvest, the increased use of grain to feed peasant livestock, and the increased sales of potatoes and vegetables by peasant households, were all signs of the growth of household activities within the kolkhoz system. Not only were peasant household activities growing, but they were becoming more profitable, as suggested by the trend of prices for potatoes and vegetables on the kolkhoz market, which rose markedly in the second half of 1938 compared with the same months of 1937 (see the note to Table B.43).

In the mid-1930s, the compromises reached with the peasantry had left more than half the farm animals (excluding horses) in the hands of the collective farm households, and collective farmers received twice as much income through the private sale of produce from their household plots as from their work on the kolkhoz.[13] The Bolsheviks' clear and

[12] *Izvestiya*, May 6, 1938.

[13] Davies et al. eds. (1994): 127, 289.

Table 2 Cattle and pigs, December 31, 1935–1937 (per cent of previous year)

	Cattle			*Pigs*		
	1935	*1936*	*1937*	*1935*	*1936*	*1937*
Animals, total	118.2	103.3	107.2	151.3	77.4	128.3
Of which						
Socialised animals	130.1	107.8	102.1	145.3	104.4	117.3
Collective farm households' animals	133	104.8	112.8	180.8	70.6	145.3

Source *Tragediya*, 5(2) (2006): 90–97. The source misprints the total of pigs in all categories in 1936 as 177.4, an error that we correct above.

consistent preference was that the compromise, although necessary for a time, should not persist, and that the socialised sector of agriculture should grow steadily at the expense of the private sector. But the anxiety that the persistence of the private sector caused was practical as well as ideological. It was feared that increased private activity, by attracting the efforts of collective-farm households, was undermining the collective farms' ability to monopolise and mobilise their members' labour.

The issue emerged strongly with the results of the livestock census of January 1, 1938. They indicated that the growth in livestock numbers had been lower than expected in the socialised sector and much higher in the private sector. In a memorandum to Stalin, Molotov, and others, dated April 8, 1938, TsUNKhU reported that in 1936 the numbers of socialised livestock had increased more rapidly than private livestock, but in 1937 the ratios had been reversed (Table 2).[14] The numbers of socialised animals had declined absolutely, moreover, in 21 provinces in the case of cattle and 10 provinces in the case of pigs, while in all these provinces the numbers held by the collective farm households had increased.

These startling results focused the minds of the party leaders. At first, they aimed to restrict the activities of state farm workers and the remaining individual peasant households outside the kolkhozy. On April 14, 1938, Stalin signed a Central Committee decree placing limits on the size of livestock holdings for state farm workers and employees.[15] Five days later a decree of Sovnarkom and the party's Central Committee strongly criticised local party and government agencies for failing to

[14] RGAE, 1562/1/1051:135–121 (April 8, 1938); *Tragediya*, 5(2) (2006): 90–97.

[15] Reproduced in *Tragediya*, 5(2) (2006): 98.

enforce existing laws on the taxation of individual peasants. According to the decree, these peasants were 'in an advantageous position in relation to the kolkhozy, which is fundamentally in contradiction with existing laws'. The decree also claimed that the horses held by individual peasants were used not only to cultivate their own land, but also 'for speculation and profit'. It proposed to introduce a tax on these horses.[16] The tax was enacted, with considerable publicity, at a new session of the Supreme Soviet on August 21. The debate was marked by enthusiastic unanimity. The first horse owned by a household was taxed from 275 to 400 rubles, and second and subsequent horses between 450 and 800 rubles.[17]

The campaign against private farming continued through 1938 and into 1939. On November 28, 1938, the NKVD reported more signs of the spread of private agriculture to the Central Committee's Agricultural Department: collective farm peasants were showing increased acquisition of private property and were increasingly trying to opt out of the collective farms.[18] On December 1, TsUNKhU reported to Voznesenskii that in 'almost all' republics and provinces some collective farmers held more animals than was permitted; in a number of districts more than 10% of households held animals in excess of the norm.[19] This was the prelude to a secret decree of Sovnarkom and TsIK, dated January 21, 1939, which affirmed that 'violation of the statute on the agricultural artel by exceeding norms for livestock and for sideline activities in the personal use of collective farmers is occurring to some degree in all republics and provinces.' The decree demanded that the norms should be enforced. Collective farmers were to be informed that failure to comply would result in their expulsion from the kolkhoz without compensation.[20] The following spring, in connection with discussions on the third five-year plan, Agriculture Commissariat officials proposed that the norms in the kolkhoz statute should be not merely enforced, but also revised.[21]

Regulation of the amount of land collective farmers could hold in private allotments was also tightened. On January 15, 1939, the Central Committee told Benediktov to withdraw an instruction issued by the

[16] SP (1938), no. 18: art. 117 (April 19, 1938).

[17] *Finansovo-khozyaistvennoe zakonodatel'stvo* (1938), no. 24: 9–10.

[18] *Tragediya*, 5(2) (2006): 311–317.

[19] *Tragediya*, 5(2) (2006): 319–321.

[20] *Tragediya*, 5(2) (2006): 338–339.

[21] *Tragediya*, 5(2) (2006): 361 (March 4).

Commissariat of Agriculture in the previous April, which allowed market-garden plots up to one hectare in addition to allotted land: the limit was too high, and should be offset against allotment land.[22] A week later, on January 21, another decree demanded that excess allotments should be eliminated by April 15, 1939.[23] But on May 15, the NKVD reported that excessive allotments remained, and amounted to 5.3 million hectares. This was more than half of the total allotment area of 8.3 million hectares. The most important private crops were potatoes (2.9 million hectares), grain (1.2 million), vegetables (700,000) and fodder (300,000). In 1938, 10.4% of collective farmers were avoiding work on the collective. While this was down from 12.8% in 1936, rates were particularly high and rising in particular provinces: Voronezh, Kuibyshev, the Krasnodar district.[24]

The eighteenth party congress, held in March 1939, provided the occasion for public announcement of new policies towards collective farmers. At the session of March 12 Andreev, the Politburo member responsible for agriculture, declared that in the early stages of collectivisation the kolkhozy were too weak to satisfy the needs of the collective farmers but that 'now the emphasis must be placed on strengthening and extending the socialised kolkhoz economy,' and 'the personal economy of the collective farmers must increasingly acquire a narrow auxiliary character.' As well as restrictions on personal livestock and the household plot, he also insisted that collective farmers must work a minimum number of labour days for the kolkhoz.[25] Economically, the introduction of a minimum number of labour-days was equivalent to a further compulsory tax on the kolkhoz household sector.

Following the congress, the party leaders called a Central Committee plenum for May 21–22, 1939. The plenum was prepared by three small conferences at which Andreev, Kalinin, Khrushchev and Benediktov met with local kolkhoz officials.[26] In the conferences, limits on allotment size were much discussed; the highest figure proposed was 0.4 hectares, and the lowest was 0.05 hectares (500 square metres), but there was general agreement that the typical peasant plot should be reduced.

[22] *Tragediya*, 5(2) (2006): 337.

[23] *Tragediya*, 5(2) (2006): 338–339.

[24] *Tragediya*, 5(2) (2006): 413–416.

[25] *XVIII s"ezd* (1939): 118–119.

[26] Zelenin (2006): 244.

Low participation in collective farm work by the kolkhoz members was directly linked to excessive allotment size. From Ukraine, Khrushchev was particularly critical of the Moldovan kolkhozy where, he claimed, only the head of the family worked on the collective while the others worked in the family vineyards.

At the Central Committee plenum, Stalin appeared to be shocked to hear the facts. When Andreev reported on collective farmers' unwillingness to work in the collective, Stalin interrupted him no less than seven times, asking 'How can this be?' The transcript records that eventually many voices chimed into the effect that Andreev was right.[27]

In his reply, Stalin demanded action to stop the erosion of the socialised sector, but he also insisted that the existing structure of the agricultural artel should be preserved, and there should be no transition to a 'commune' structure—namely, to complete socialisation. He called for the convening of a peasant congress to give the peasants a say in the amount by which their allotments should be reduced. Finally, he advocated more regulation of kolkhoz labour to ensure that no one could get away without contributing—in other words, to set a minimum number of labour-days, as Andreev had proposed at the party congress.

The Central Committee plenum was followed on May 27, 1939, by a decree of the party's Central Committee and Sovnarkom 'On measures to protect the socialised lands of the kolkhozy from dispersal (*razbazarivanie*)'. The Agriculture Commissariat and TsUNKhU estimated that the total area of the household plots of collective farmers amounted to 8,251,000 hectares in 1937, and that 1,189,000 hectares were removed as exceeding the norm.[28]

3 Plans and Policies, 1938

In 1938 there was a return to ambitious targets for production and procurement. The grain harvest fell short, while the state's grain levies were intensified. The difference was covered by a decline in household grain stocks. These had risen suddenly, following the unexpectedly abundant harvest of 1937, to a level that the party leaders undoubtedly considered to be excessive; after the 1938 harvest, they declined. This turnaround

[27] RGASPI, 17/2/643: 1–46.

[28] *Tragediya*, 5(2) (2006): 413, 482. Land was also removed from individual peasant households and from other peasants who were not members of kolkhozy.

is confirmed by the secret grain forage balances prepared by the sector of the balance of the national economy in TsUNKhU, and also by the unpublished results of peasant household budget studies.

In the Gosplan draft directives for the 1938 plan, sent to Stalin and Molotov in September 1937, Smirnov proposed that in 1938 the overall sown area should rise by three million hectares (from 135.2 to 138.2 million), but that the land sown to grain should decline by 2.1 million hectares (from 104.1 to 102 million). The grain yield now planned for 1938 was 10.8 centners per hectare.[29] This was slightly above the 10.7 centners that TsUNKhU was seeking to defend at the time (see Sect. 7 in Chapter 4). The target implied for the grain harvest (but not stated) was therefore 110.2 million tons. The directives also indicated that 300 new MTS (machine-tractor stations) were to be built in 1938. In the chaos of the time, described above (Sect. 1 in Chapter 6), this draft was not accepted, but lay on the table.

At the time of his arrest on October 29, 1937, Commissar for Agriculture Chernov was assailed by criticisms for his conduct of agricultural policy. Among the issues was the alleged failure of autumn ploughing. His successor, Eikhe, made his first major statement at the Central Committee meeting held on January 18, 1938. His enthusiasm was not damped by circumstances. As already discussed, much of his speech was devoted to the exposure of widespread sabotage (see Sect. 1). Despite this, he assured his audience, the 'grain problem' was now solved.[30] Outcomes for agriculture, he said, depended entirely on good leadership at the centre and high morale in the localities. (Apparently, the weather would have nothing to do with it.) He reported that the spring sowing had been badly prepared, but the situation would be turned around: agriculture in 1938 would yield more produce than in 1937.

Eikhe cited Stalin's 1935 call to raise the harvest to at least 115 million tons within three to four years, and claimed that in 1937 this goal had been reached. (The text published in *Izvestiya* claims that 'in 1937 agricultural production was nearly one and a half times the good harvest of 1935.') Once the sabotage had been overcome, it would be possible 'to produce in 1938 even larger growth of agricultural production than in 1937'. Thus, Eikhe's words appeared to argue for a target

[29] RGAE, 5446/22a/1092: 138 (September 1937). No figure for the 1937 harvest was given in the directives.

[30] *Izvestiya*, January 22, 1938.

of more than 115 million tons. Despite this, no more authoritative figure emerged for the harvest plan than the 110.2 million implied by Smirnov's draft of the previous autumn.

Eikhe's optimism was evidently based on the expectation of higher yields. Set against Smirnov's recommendations of the previous September, Eikhe proposed to increase overall sowing by 1.7 million hectares (instead of three million) and to cut the area sown to grain by three million (instead of 2.1 million). He did not state a figure for the expected yield, but reduced sowing was a necessary condition for improvement of the crop rotation which, if done, could increase the yield substantially.

After the Central Committee's January plenum, Molotov, as head of the government, issued instructions on the 'State plan for agricultural work for 1938', the document discussed above for its subterfuge regarding private sowing.[31] Despite its grand title, the spring sowing plan was its core, supplemented by a plan for the autumn sowing for the 1939 harvest. There was no livestock plan, no harvest plan, and no detail of the grain collections plan, beyond the observation that collective farms' grain obligations to the state would be fixed in relation to the state sowing plans, not by the harvest achieved. In other words, as usual, the farmers would bear the risk arising from harvest fluctuations, not the state. For the harvest itself, the messages were that 'the most important task is to increase yield in 1938, especially from sorted seed' and that 'this year it is necessary to ensure an even higher growth of agricultural production than in 1937.'

Agricultural investment also featured strongly in Eikhe's January speech to the Central Committee. For context we return to the autumn of 1937 when, before his arrest on October 29, Chernov and his deputy Paskutskii assembled the final draft of the Agriculture Commissariat proposal for capital investment in 1938.[32]

The investment plan drafted by the Agriculture Commissariat asked for a large sum: 3.5 billion rubles. This sum was a billion less than the previous year's request, but a billion more than was allocated in the

[31] SZ (1938), no. 2: art. 5 (Sovnarkom decree 'On the state plan of agricultural work for 1938', January 27, 1938).

[32] Two copies of substantially the same draft plan are in RGAE, 7486/4/571: 251–260 (undated, in the name of Chernov) and 219–250 (dated October 1937, in the name of Paskutskii, including additional and other material).

Table 3 Capital construction for the Commissariat of Agriculture, January to September 1937 (million rubles)

	Total	*From central accounts: tractors, vehicles, and equipment*	*From decentralised accounts: construction, capital repairs, agricultural machinery*
Investment planned	1676.3	1116.8	559.5
Investment funded	1607.8	1115.7	492.1
Funds utilised	1415.3	1065.6	349.7
Funds utilised, per cent of plan	84.4	95.4	62.5
Funds not utilised	192.5	50.1	142.4

Source RGAE, 7486/4/571: 1. The final row is calculated from the source.

previous round. Once again the draft stressed the importance of construction: one billion rubles' worth of garages, repairs shops, and stores that were needed by the MTS and state farms. Much new machinery was rusting in the open or was lying unused for lack of repair facilities. Much fertiliser, stored without protection, was going to waste.

The need for investment funding was not the only problem of the day, however. At the end of 1937, the Commissariat of Agriculture was terrorised, humbled, and generally deficient in capacity. Regardless of the sums allocated, the Commissariat could not ensure that its investment plan would be fulfilled. This problem is diagnosed from a report by Frolov, chief of the Commissariat's sector of capital investment. He showed (Table 3) that by the last quarter of 1937 the Commissariat was struggling to complete construction work. Compared with spending on machinery of various kinds, the much larger sums unspent from the relatively small construction budget suggests that it was easier to acquire machinery from centralised suppliers than to coordinate construction work that required the cooperation of a variety of local subcontractors.

The difficulty of coordinating planned construction was not Frolov's only concern. He also worried about what was not foreseen in the plan: the flow of new, unexpected requirements that the government loaded onto the existing obligations of the Commissariat of Agriculture through 1937, particularly towards the end of the year, as the government tried to meet its objective of covering the whole country with machine-tractor stations. He listed:

- Orders of August 14 and September 20 to establish new MTS in Voronezh and Kursk provinces by breaking up the assets of existing ones.
- An order to establish new MTS from the assets of state farms that were being dissolved in the Belorussian Republic.
- An order to organise five new MTS in Kalinin province and to release money for new barns and garaging facilities elsewhere (not yet carried out).
- An order to organise 10 new MTS in the Kirgiz Republic (partly carried out).
- An order to rebuild the Moscow Hippodrome (not carried out for lack of funds).
- An order of January 29, 1938, to build elevators and stores for centralised seed agencies (delayed for lack of funds).
- An order to release money to the Kazakh Republic's Commissariat of Agriculture to build equipment facilities there.

Meanwhile, the leaders considered the overall situation of government funding, which involved balancing external priorities (such as the needs of rearmament) against internal constraints (such as the need to feed the country). While Chernov was being softened up for his part in the public show trial of Bukharin and others that began on March 5, 1938, his draft plan for 3.5 billion rubles to be invested in agriculture was sent to the government, where Chubar' was charged with cutting it down to size. This was evidently no secret within the administration, for the records show that once Eikhe was in the saddle, he was barraged by subordinates expressing panic about the prospect of investment cuts, in particular from officials responsible for irrigation, land amelioration, and electrification.[33]

This was the somewhat chaotic setting for Eikhe's remarks at the January plenum of the Central Committee, which amounted to a renewed bid for investment funding. There, he claimed that that 500 new MTS would receive tractors of more than a million horsepower. That number was 200 more than Smirnov's September draft directives had envisaged.

[33] RGAE, 7486/4/571: 133–136 and 171–173.

The effort was in vain. On February 28 the Sovnarkom adopted an investment plan that awarded the Agriculture Commissariat only 2.1 billion rubles (Table B.6). Two-thirds was for machinery: 1.4 billion or 400 million less than in 1936. Construction was given 200 million rubles, enough to enable a start on covering repair shops and storage facilities. Despite the reduction, the plan was not fulfilled. The outcome was just 1.7 billion (compared with two billion in 1937). Meanwhile, the much smaller sums being invested in state farms remained roughly stable (Table B.7).

In the late 1930s, to summarise, Soviet agriculture had unmet needs for investment in both equipment and structures. Equipment was needed to assist arable cultivation, and structures were needed for the garaging, repair, and storage of equipment and fertiliser. The different kinds of capital works faced specific obstacles. At the centre, agricultural construction was not easily associated with the modernising goals of an aspirant great power, and the authorities were reluctant to budget for it. Because the supply of construction services was relatively decentralised, it was more difficult for a buyer at the centre to contract for them. Mechanisation, in contrast, was more easily associated with modernisation, and the authorities were more ready to budget for its provision. The supply of equipment was also more centralised, easing the buyer's contract problem. But, for that very reason, the centralised supply of equipment was highly exposed to key events of the late 1930s: the nomenklatura purge, and the heightened priority accorded to the mechanisation of the armed forces, which gravely weakened the position of the Agriculture Commissariat. Part of the growth of defence production in the late 1930s was achieved by converting the capacities previously assigned to civilian equipment, which therefore became less available.

The vulnerability of the Commissariat's investment plan was expressed in the shrinking supplies of new agricultural machinery. The number of tractors produced annually (Table B.21) fell by more than half in 1937 and made no recovery before the war. This was offset only to a small extent by the increase in their capacity, measured by horsepower per tractor (as noted below the table); more powerful tractors were part of the Soviet Union's war preparations, anticipating their military uses. The production of combine harvesters declined steeply and steadily.

The supply of new tractors was one problem. Another problem was that old tractors needed to be maintained and serviced, a task on which the MTS were falling behind. There was a plan for repairs, but this was just another missed target: as of January 10, Eikhe told the Central Committee, the 73,000 tractors repaired represented only 30% of the repair plan, with more than 173,000 awaiting repair. Parts were in short supply. Even in full working order, tractors could not be operated without fuel, for which many collective farms lacked funds. (Eikhe added that he had asked Stalin and Molotov for a special loan of 120 million rubles to allow collective farms to buy the necessary fuel; it is not clear whether the money was found.)

Seed and fertiliser continued to present difficulties, as Eikhe reported to the January plenum. Seeds had to be collected, cleaned, sorted, and released for sowing, and there was a target for each of these stages. Predictably, every target was being missed, and the degree of the shortfall increased from stage to stage. On January 1, according to Eikhe, the collection of grain seed was behind by 13%; this was an average, with some seed types and areas ahead and others much further behind. At the other end of the process, the lag was more acute. By January 10, the schedule required Gossortfond and Zagotzerno, the two organisations engaged in this work, to have released just over one million tons of seed, but the total actually released on this date was less than 4000.

At the time, the Soviet chemical industry was expanding rapidly, but the supply of nitrates and phosphates for agricultural fertiliser did not increase (Table B.22). The most important reason was that nitrates and phosphorus had important applications in making explosives and incendiary munitions. Competition from the defence sector caused the supply of fertiliser to agriculture to stagnate in 1938 and 1939 and, by 1940, to decline absolutely.

4 Operations and Outcomes, 1938

The plan for autumn sowing of the grain to be harvested in 1938 was published in a Sovnarkom decree of July 28, 1937 (Table 4). The 37-million-hectare target represented a reduction of 1.4 million versus the previous year. The decline was shared among the three main sectors: the collective farms, the state farms, and the few remaining individual peasants. There was an upward trend in the share of collective farm operations covered by the machinery services of the state-owned MTS, which was planned to reach 93%. The outcome for autumn sowing in 1937 was 36.5 million hectares. Although the target was missed, this was an increase over the previous year's outcome.

Table 4 Autumn sowing, 1936/37 and 1937/38 (million hectares)

	1936/37		*1937/38*	
	Target	*Outcome*	*Target*	*Outcome*
State farms	2.8	–	2.1	–
Collective farms	35.0	–	34.6	–
Of which				
—MTS	30.1	–	32.2	–
—Individual peasants	0.6	–	0.3	–
All autumn sowing	38.4	36.2	37.0	36.5

Note The years shown are agricultural years; in 1936/37, for example, the autumn sowing of 1936 contributed to the harvest of 1937. The plan for state farms in 1936/37 includes 284,000 hectares to be sown by ORSy and other state farms outside the system of the People's Commissariats of State Farms, Agriculture, and Food Industry. These are excluded from the plan for state farms in 1937/38.
Source Plan figures for 1936/37: SZ (1936), no. 44: art. 376 ('State plan for winter sowing for 1937 harvest', July 29, 1936); for 1937/38, SZ (1937), no. 48: art. 197 ('State plan for winter sowing work', July 28, 1937). Outcomes, both years: *Izvestiya*, December 1, 1937 (report for November 2).

While the autumn 1937 sowing was satisfactory, the autumn ploughing (for the spring sowing of 1938) was not. The target was pushed up from the previous year's 68 million hectares (which had been badly missed) to 70.8 million, which would have covered nearly 80% of the land to be sown in the spring of 1938. But *Izvestiya* reported that the outcome fell far below the plan, and even below the poor results of the previous year (Table 5). Instead of the 54.8 million hectares under the plough in the autumn of 1936, by the end of the season, on November 20, 1937, only 48.5 million hectares were ploughed. In his speech to the January 1938 Central Committee plenum, Eikhe warned that the previous year's excellent harvest had engendered complacency; the lag in autumn ploughing meant a greater burden of spring ploughing for the year just beginning.

Tensions ran high as the spring sowing began. First indications, published in *Izvestiya* on March 25, suggested that the campaign had begun on time.[34] But situation reports from the provinces testified to the anxieties that now pervaded the agricultural bureaucracy. A local

[34]By March 20, 1938, according to the reports, 1.7% of the spring sowing target had already been met, and this compared with 1% on the same date in 1937. *Izvestiya*, March 25, 1938.

Table 5 Autumn ploughing, 1936/37 and 1937/38 (million hectares)

	1936/37		*1937/38*	
	Target	*Outcome, Nov. 20*	*Target*	*Outcome, Nov. 20*
State farms	7.5	–	5.8	–
Collective farms	66.1	–	65.0	–
Of which				
—MTS	53.5	–	60.9	–
—Individual peasants	0.4	–	0.0	–
All autumn ploughing	68.0	54.8	70.8	48.5
—Per cent of target	–	81	–	65

Note The years shown are agricultural years; in 1936/37, for example the autumn ploughing of 1936 would be sown in the spring of 1937 and contributed to the harvest of 1937. The plan for state farms in 1936/37 includes 1,424,000 hectares to be ploughed by ORSy and by state farms outside the system of the People's Commissariats of State Farms, Agriculture, and Food Industry. These are excluded from the plan for state farms in 1937–1938.
Source Plan figures for 1936/37, from SZ (1936), no. 46: art. 385 ('State plan for winter ploughing for the 1937 harvest', August 27, 1936); for 1937/38, from SZ (1936), no. 46: art. 385 ('State plan for winter ploughing for the 1938 harvest', August 27, 1936). Outcome: reports every five days in *Izvestiya*.

correspondent asked: 'How can Tashkent "liquidate" the consequences of wrecking?' In the Ordzhonikidze district of Uzbekistan, a report claimed, saboteurs had pushed the sowing targets to impossible levels so that a formerly successful agricultural district was now set up to fail. To meet their sowing obligations, it was alleged, collective farmers were being forced to travel from Uzbekistan to districts in neighbouring Kazakhstan where additional land was available for rent. According to the story, those who raised doubts about the targets had been victimised.[35] For the time, the article was plausible. The fact that it was released to the national press, and ended with a call for investigation, no doubt added to the momentum of the purges already under way.

As the campaign proceeded, the rate of sowing appeared to fall increasingly behind the previous year. The figures published in *Izvestiya* showed a gap of 2.3 million hectares as of April 5, rising to more than six million hectares as of April 20 and 25 (Table B.31). The NKVD looked for causes, finding weakened horses, backlogs of tractor repairs, shortages of fuel and seed, and low-quality sowing work. The report placed

[35] *Izvestiya*, March 25, 1938 (V. Krainev).

Table 6 Predicted weather effects on grain yields across regions, 1937–1938 (per cent)

	1937	*1938*	*Change*
Central Blacksoil	6.9	−3.0	−9.9
Ukraine	−8.0	−1.1	+7.0
Volga	23.6	−11.1	−34.7
Urals	−1.8	13.6	+15.4
North Caucasus	54.1	15.7	−38.4
Siberia	−0.3	32.8	+33.1
Average, all producer regions	9.8	6.5	−3.3

Source Table B.28. The figures show the net impact on grain yields in the given year from weather conditions through the growing season in per cent of the yield under average weather conditions.

these material deficiencies in a frame of sabotage and poor leadership in the localities.[36]

It was at this time that Eikhe was arrested and, as discussed in the previous section, the published reports of spring sowing in 1937 were revised sharply downwards. On the new reporting basis, the progress of spring sowing in 1938 was similar to that made in the previous year.

The last factor in the harvest to be considered was the weather. In its favourability to the harvest across the country, the weather of 1938 was better than average, although not as good as in the previous year (Table 6).

The harvest of 1938 took place during the interregnum at the Commissariat of Agriculture between the arrest of Eikhe in April and the appointment of Benediktov to succeed him in November. At this time, Benediktov, previously Eikhe's first deputy, was no doubt on probation. He was watched over by Andreev who, as a Central Committee secretary, juggled agriculture among many other responsibilities. In 1938 the reaping and threshing campaigns proceeded 'normally', in so far as one can use such a word, and the time lag by which threshing followed reaping was also kept under control (Table B.32). Because the threshing lag was a time in which the harvest continued to be at risk, this must have contributed to lower harvesting losses than in 1937.

For grains, the outcome of the harvest was not as good as in 1937 (Table 7): 95 million tons based on Voznesenskii's biological yield

[36] Reproduced in *Tragediya*, 5(2) (2006): 113–118.

Table 7 The grain harvest, 1938 compared to 1937 (million tons)

	1937	*1938*	*Change*
Biological yield on 1939 basis	120.3	95.0	−25.3
Grain available for use			
—Implied by annual TsUNKhU balances	105.0	80.6	−24.4
—Implied by revised TsUNKhU balances (1941)	98.4	73.9	−24.5
—Barn yield from Wheatcroft and Davies (1994)	97	74	−23

Source Tables B.33 and B.34.

Table 8 Grain collections, 1938/39, compared to the annual plan and the preceding year (million tons)

	1937/38	*1938/39*	
	Outcome	*Target*	*Outcome*
All compulsory deliveries (*postavki*)	10.3	10.3	9.8
Payments in kind to MTS (*naturoplata*)	11.3	12.5	10.1
Milling levy (*garntsevyi sbor*)	1.7	1.7	1.5
Returned seed loans	1.2	1.6	1.2
Deliveries by state farms	3.9	4.4	3.4
Rescheduled debt repayments	–	1.0	–
Collections, exc. purchases, subtotal	28.3	31.4	26.1
State purchases (*zakupki*)	3.6	1.8	3.0
Collections, total	31.9	33.2	29.1

Source Tables B.35 and B.36, using version 1 for 1938/39.

concept that excluded all harvesting and pre-harvest losses, leaving 74 million tons available for use on the estimate of the TsUNKhU sector of balances. This was roughly at the average level of the late 1930s, and so not a failure.

The state took the opportunity to raise its ambition for grain collections (Table 8). If 1937 was a moderate deviation, the procurement plan of 1938 reverted to the earlier pattern, with all targets raised: an additional four million tons from peasant agriculture, and 1.2 million tons more from state farms. With higher targets for the milling levy and seed loans, the total collections plan, excluding voluntary purchases, was 31.4 million tons compared to 24.3 million the previous year. Within the total, the role of kolkhoz payments to the state-owned MTS for

Table 9 Grain stocks held by producers, 1938 and 1939 (million tons on July 1)

	1938	*1939*
State farms	0.2	0.2
Collective farms	15.9	10.5
Of which		
—Farm stocks	3.3	2.3
—Household stocks	12.6	7.2
Individual peasant households	0.1	0.1
Grain stocks, total	16.2	9.8

Source Table B.37.

machinery services was to continue to rise and was expected to become the largest single item.

The plan also reverted to the earlier pattern in its implementation, which fell short of the targets in all categories. Overall collections fell short of the plan by 17%. The shortfall was offset to a minor degree by overachievement of voluntary purchases. Still, to have collected 29 million tons in a year of a rather mediocre harvest was a considerable achievement for the state. This had the desired effect of shifting grain out of peasant stocks into the hands of the state; peasant stocks fell from 16.2 million tons, a very high level, to 9.8 million, which was still high, but was now on the way back to normal (Table 9).

At this time agricultural production, when valued at plan prices, was composed of three roughly equal parts, of which grains were only one. Another part was other arable crops: potatoes, vegetables, and industrial or technical crops. The third part was livestock produce. As Table 10 shows, nearly all grain came from the socialised sector, while the private allotments of collective farmers contributed around one-fifth of other arable crops (including 40–50% of potatoes and vegetables) and around half of livestock produce.

In 1938 the value of output of other arable crops fell back sharply. The fall was roughly in proportion to the decline in the grain sector, and was equally pronounced in socialised agriculture and on peasant allotments.

It was in livestock that trends diverged. Livestock were among the chief beneficiaries of the bumper harvest of 1937, and the value of livestock produce in 1938 was 20% above that of 1937. Both the socialised sector and the collective farm peasants showed large increases in output.

Table 10 Agricultural production, 1938 compared to 1937, total and by collective farm peasants on private allotments (million rubles and plan prices of 1926/27)

	1937	*1938*	*Change*
All agriculture			
Grains	7,779	6,466	−1,313
Other arable produce	7,291	6,076	−1,215
Livestock produce	5,054	6,061	1,007
All produce, total	20,123	18,603	−1,520
Of which, by kolkhoz peasants			
—Grains	80	66	−14
—Other arable produce	1,692	1,086	−606
—Livestock produce	2,524	3,072	548
All produce, total	4,236	4,224	−12

Source RGAE, 1562/83/38: 1.

This was unexpected, because the socialised sector had been expected to outperform the private sector.

As already described, the relationship of the Soviet state to private livestock farming was fraught with tension. An example is found in the state plan for livestock in 1938 which, unlike the 1937 plan, gave a favourable evaluation of progress to date in the numbers and quality of animals.[37] While much of the growth took place in the private sector, the public sector was awarded the credit for assisting the collective farm households, materially and financially, by selling them livestock on advantageous terms. As a result, it was declared, the goal had been nearly achieved of providing every kolkhoz household with at least one cow for milk and manure. But the same plan undermined these claims when it reported targets for young farm animals. These showed that collective farm households would be responsible for rearing between 60 and 80% of calves, lambs, kids, and piglets.

5 Plans and Policies, 1939

The directives of the 1939 annual plan relating to agriculture were issued by Stalin and Molotov in November of the previous year.[38] The target for area sown under all crops by all categories of producers was set at

[37] SP (1938), no. 28: art. 182 (Sovnarkom decree 'On the state plan for the development of livestock for 1938', June 17, 1938).

[38] RGASPI, 17/3/1003: 39 (November 22, 1938).

Table 11 Targets for agricultural production, 1939 compared to the outcomes of 1938

	1938 (preliminary outcome)	*1939 (target)*	*Planned change (per cent)*
Billion rubles and plan prices of 1926/27			
Gross value of agricultural production	18.5	22.1	+19.5
Of which			
—Arable produce	12.7	15.6	+22.8
—Livestock produce	5.8	6.5	+12.1
Production in physical units			
Grain (million tons)	95.0	106.5	+14.0
—Of which, yield (centners per hectare)	9.3	10.6	+14.0
Sugar beet (million tons)	16.7	23.5	+40.9
Cotton fibre (million tons)	2.69	2.62	−2.6
Flax fibre (thousand tons)	54.6	61.0	+10.9

Source Gosudarstvennyi plan (1939): 5. The source gives grain output in puds, and other crops in centners; in the table these are converted to tons.

139.8 million hectares, including 118.9 million for the collective farms. Unlike the 1938 agricultural plan, which was full of omissions, the 1939 plan provided a fuller set of targets for produce (Table 11). At 106.5 million tons the grain target was substantially larger than the 1938 outcome, and it relied on a 14% improvement in the yield. Still, it fell below the 110.2 million set in the previous year and consequently represented a significant moderation.

The plan devoted many fine words to mechanisation, improvement of livestock, crop rotations, and seed. These were traditional concerns that had been raised many times in the past, with only chequered progress to report. Nonetheless, their importance was underscored in Molotov's report on the third five-year plan to the eighteenth party congress in March 1939.[39] There, Molotov left the delegates in no doubt of the priorities of mechanisation, 'scientific farming methods, with special attention to seeds', chemical fertilisers, and rational systems of crop rotation and land improvement.

While field rotations were the last of Molotov's priorities for agriculture, it was the principal topic of the contribution to debate on the

[39] *XVIII s"ezd* (1939): 282–315.

Table 12 Investment in agriculture versus defence and heavy industry, 1936–1939 (million rubles and per cent)

	1936	*1937*	*1938*	*1939*
All capital investment	35,311	27,659	29,314	30,710
Of which				
—Defence and heavy industry	10,099	8,794	10,471	13,240
—Agriculture (collective farms)	3,050	2,007	1,683	1,305
—State farms	579	273	258	260
Agriculture and state farms, subtotal	3,629	2,280	1,941	1,565
Per cent of total				
—Defence and heavy industry	28.6	31.8	35.7	43.1
—Agriculture and state farms, subtotal	10.3	8.2	6.6	5.1

Source Table B.8. Figures are in current prices (1936) or estimate prices (1937–1939); for 1937, the figures of the latest date are preferred.

third five-year plan provided by the new commissar for agriculture, Benediktov.[40] Immediately after the congress, Benediktov followed the matter up with Stalin and Molotov in more detail. In a written report, he warned that the proportion of collective farms operating approved field rotations was as low as 12–15%.[41] This was even less than the 21% claimed by Eikhe when he criticised Chernov for exaggerating progress (see Sect. 1).

The investment plan initially awarded to the Commissariat of Agriculture for 1939 was just 1350 million rubles, the smallest sum since the famine in 1933 (Table B.2). Under the circumstances it is something of a surprise that it was almost fully realised. If we add the shrinking sums also invested in the state farm sector, however, it turns out that agriculture's share in all capital investment in the Soviet economy fell from one-tenth in 1936 to one-twentieth in 1939 (Table 12). Agriculture's decline was absolute as well as relative, for government capital spending in aggregate was under growing pressure from all sides. Ever larger sums were being assigned to the equipment and expansion of the Red Army and Soviet Navy. Meanwhile, the economy's aggregate

[40] *XVIII s"ezd* (1939): 409–416.

[41] *Tragediya*, 5(2) (2006): 384–387 (not dated but before March 26, 1939).

Table 13 Draft power in Soviet agriculture, 1929 and 1938–1939 (million horse equivalents)

	1929	*1938*	*1939*
Horses	34.6	16.2	17.2
Tractors (at 2:1)	0.8	16.8	18.5
Draft power, total	35.4	33.0	35.7

Source Table B.27. In this table, tractors are converted into horse-equivalents at the conservative rate of two horses to one tractor. See the source for alternative estimates.

production capacity was stagnating. While the overall value of capital works fluctuated below its 1936 peak, the share of defence and heavy industry increased over the same period from less than 30 to more than 40%. Inevitably, civilian and consumer-oriented investments suffered, and this applied particularly to agriculture as the one of the larger civilian claimants on investment funds.

Despite the fine words of the plans, the mechanisation of agriculture proceeded more slowly in 1939. This followed from the shrinking investment budget, and from the continuing conversion of the machine-building industries to war production. The supplies of tractors and grain combines continued their downward slide (Table B.21). The slowdown of mechanisation does not mean that no mechanisation took place or that it went into reverse. On the contrary, the overall stock of mechanical draft power continued to increase. Even on a conservative measure of the value of a tractor in terms of the number of horses that it replaced (Table 13), the overall horsepower of Soviet agriculture now exceeded its previous peak in 1929. This was the positive aspect of 1939; on the negative side, the draft stock had marked time for a decade.

Planned deliveries of chemical fertilisers to agriculture also continued to fall (Table 14) Again, the context was one of the conversion of the chemical industry to a war footing. Whereas tractors and combines were durable assets that could be accumulated from year to year, fertiliser was a consumable item, and industrial fertiliser inputs became less available to the farming sector. Supplies of animal fertiliser could not fill the gap without significant increases in livestock numbers, and these were not achieved.

Table 14 Targets for the delivery of chemical fertilisers to agriculture, 1937 and 1939 (thousand tons and per cent)

	1937	*1939*	*Change (%)*
Superphosphate (14%)	2,375	1,668	−29.8
Ground phosphates	835	735	−12.0
Potassium (in 41% eq.)	450	420	−6.7
Nitrogenous ammonium sulphate	998	780	−21.8
Thomas slag (tetracalcium phosphate)	70	50	−28.6

Note The levels and trends in these figures do not bear any clear relationship to the production targets shown in Table B.22. An explanation may be that the present table is concerned not with production in general but with deliveries to agriculture specifically; in the late 1930s increasing quantities of raw chemicals were being taken by the armament and ammunition industries.
Source 1937, from *Narodno-khozyaistvennyi plan* (1937): 114–115; 1939 from *Gosudarstvennyi plan* (1939): 101–102.

Table 15 Autumn sowing, 1937/38 and 1938/39 (million hectares)

	1937–1938		*1938–1939*	
	Target	*Outcome*	*Target*	*Outcome*
All autumn sowing	37.0	36.4	36.5	35.3
By state farms	2.1	–	2.1	–
By collective farms	34.6	–	34.2	–
By individual peasants	0.3	–	0.2	–

Source Plan figures for 1937/38 from SZ (1937), no. 48: art. 197 ('State plan for winter sowing work', July 28, 1937); for 1938/39 from SZ (1938), no. 2: art. 5 ('On the state plan of agricultural work for 1938', January 27, 1938). Outcomes for 1937/38 from *Izvestiya*, November 25, 1937 (report of November 2); for 1938/39 from *Izvestiya*, November 20, 1938 (report of November 15).

6 Operations and Outcomes, 1939

The target for autumn sowing in 1938 (for the 1939 harvest) was set at 36.5 million hectares (Table 15). This figure, being just greater than the previous two years' outcomes and just less than the previous two years' plans, counts as a realistic target by the standards of the time. No target was given for the use of sorted seed.

When accounts were closed on the autumn sowing campaign in mid-November, the outcome was still a shortfall of more than one million hectares below the target, and below the benchmark or the previous

Table 16 Autumn ploughing, 1937/38 and 1938/39 (million hectares)

	1937/38	*1938/39*
Target	70.8	67.9
Outcome, Nov. 20	48.5	43
—Per cent of target	65	63

Source For 1937/38, as Table 5. For 1938/39 target, from SZ (1938), no. 2: art. 5 ('On the state plan of agricultural work for 1938', January 27, 1938). Outcome: from reports every five days in *Izvestiya*.

years. The shortfall was greatest in parts of the Urals, Western Siberia, and Northern Kazakhstan, where it had been hoped to extend the margin of cultivation to virgin soil. In January 1939 the government responded to the repeated failure of the autumn sowing plan in these districts with a special plan for 1940 and 1941.[42]

The ploughing campaign of the autumn of 1938 was still more problematic (Table 16). In previous years the autumn ploughing target had lost all touch with reality, and was consistently missed by a very wide margin. As if in denial, the target was steadily raised. In 1937 the autumn target was missed by more than 22 million hectares. The autumn of 1938 was the first to register a more moderate target; the quota was reduced to 67.9 million hectares from 70.8 million hectares in the previous year. But the lower target was still nearly 20 million hectares above the outcome of 1937. The outcome of 1938 was worse by more than the reduction in the plan, so the lower target was missed by a wider margin than before: nearly 25 million hectares. The poor result did not bode well for the spring sowing campaign.

Eikhe's innovation of a state plan for agricultural work, issued early in the calendar year, which covered the spring sowing (for the current harvest) and the autumn sowing and ploughing (for the next year's harvest), was followed again in 1939.[43] The spring 1939 sowing target was set at 6.6 million hectares less than the quota for 1938 (Table 17); this was almost entirely due to the exclusion of the private sector from the plan (the unattributed residual shown in the table, discussed in Sect. 2). On

[42] *Tragediya*, 5(2) (2006): 330–333 (January 4, 1939). In 1953 these measures would be revived as Khrushchev's 'virgin lands' campaign.

[43] SP (1939), no. 14: art. 88 (February 8, 1939).

Table 17 Spring sowing, 1938–1939 (thousand hectares)

	1938		*1939*	
	Target	*Outcome*	*Target*	*Outcome*
All sowing	90,805	81,900	84,223	81,950
Of which				
—State farms	7,509	–	7,506	–
—Collective farms	77,309	–	76,140	–
—Individual households	704	–	577	–
—Residual not attributed	5,988	–	0	–
Sowing to grain	62,580	65,950	62,660	–
Of which				
—State farms	5,310	6,250	5,440	–
—Collective farms	56,400	58,290	56,900	–
—Individual households	870	1,400	320	–

Source Targets: 1938 plan, as Table 1; 1939 plan, from *Gosudarstevennyi plan v 1939 g.* (1939): 74. Outcomes: all sowing, from *Izvestiya*, June 5, 1939 (report of June 1); sowing to grain, *Posevnye ploshchadi* (1939). For an explanation of the unattributed residual in the 1938 plan, see Sect. 2.

a comparable basis, as the table shows, targets for the spring sowing of grains in 1939 were slightly increased.

As was to be expected, the plan offered lip service to the needs of agricultural expansion and improvement. Two specific measures are worthy of note. One was the support assigned to seeds improved by the methods of Lysenko, now an Academician: 138,000 hectares for his potato seeds, and 14.5 million hectares for his 'yarovised' (vernalised) grains. The other was a target of 570,000 hectares for the virgin lands.

The weather in 1939 was worse than in 1938 in all regions (Table 18), and worse than in 1936 in the Ukraine and the North Caucasus, and also, overall, giving a harvest prediction in the thirteenth percentile over the century of our data (Table B.28). In that context the reported grain harvest of 100.9 million tons (Table 19), five million more than in 1938, was surprisingly large, and this suggests an increased contribution from statistical exaggeration of the yield.

As discussed in the previous section, the harvest plan for 1939 was fixed below the level of 1938. It would normally follow that a smaller target for the harvest would be accompanied by a smaller quota for grain collections. But in 1939 the collections target was raised above the previous level (Table 20). The decisions that led to this are not clear, except

Table 18 Predicted weather effects on grain yields across regions, 1938–1939 (per cent)

	1938	*1939*	*Change*
Central Blacksoil	−3.0	−7.9	−4.8
Ukraine	−1.1	−8.1	−7.0
Volga	−11.1	−34.2	−23.1
Urals	13.6	−42.1	−55.7
North Caucasus	15.7	−16.6	−32.3
Siberia	32.8	3.7	−29.1
All producer regions, average	6.5	−16.4	−22.9

Source Table B.28. The figures show the net impact on grain yields in the given year from weather conditions through the growing season in per cent of the yield under average weather conditions.

Table 19 The grain harvest, 1939 compared to 1938 (million tons)

	1938	*1939*	*Change*
Biological yield on 1939 basis	95.0	100.9	+5.9
Grain available for use			
—Implied by annual TsUNKhU balances	80.6	82.0	+1.4
—Implied by revised TsUNKhU balances (1941)	73.9	73.5	−0.4
—Barn yield from Wheatcroft and Davies (1994)	74	73	−1

Source Tables B.33 and B.34.

for what was now the largest single item: the collective farms' payments in kind for machinery services provided by the state-owned MTS. To determine the rate of payment, collective farms were divided into six bands by grain yield from five or fewer kilograms per centner to 15 or more. In May 1939 Stalin and Molotov signed a decree directing the local procurement commissioners to carry out a re-banding of the collective farms.[44] Five months later, Deputy Commissar of Procurements Subbotin reported the outcomes to Mikoyan. The pattern his commissioners had identified was for farms to underestimate the yield so as to obtain a lower band. On re-evaluation, many farms were moved into higher bands; the data that Subbotin reported show that, whereas in 1937 the median farm was reporting a yield of just over 9 kilograms

[44] *Tragediya*, 5(2) (2006): 424–426 (May 24, 1939).

Table 20 Grain collections, 1939/40, compared to the annual plan and the preceding year (million tons)

	1938/39	*1939/40*	
	Outcome	*Target*	*Outcome*
All compulsory deliveries (*postavki*)	9.8	10.6	9.1
Payments in kind to MTS (*naturoplata*)	10.1	13.4	12.1
Milling levy (*garntsevyi sbor*)	1.5	2.0	1.3
Returned seed loans	1.2	3.0	2.6
Deliveries by state farms	3.4	4.2	3.1
Collections, exc. purchases, subtotal	26.1	34.6	28.3
State purchases (*zakupki*)	3.0	–	2.7
Collections, total	29.1	–	31.0

Source Tables B.35 and B.36, using version 1 for 1938–1939.

Table 21 Grain stocks held by producers, 1939 and 1940 (million tons on July 1)

	1939	*1940*
State farms	0.2	0.2
Collective farm sector	10.5	4.8
Of which		
—Farm stocks	2.3	1.2
—Household stocks	7.2	3.6
Individual peasant households	0.1	0.0
Grain stocks, total	9.8	5.0

Source Table B.37.

per centner, the 1939 reclassification moved this figure up to more than 11 kilograms.[45]

As a result, most farms owed more to the MTS for machinery services. And in 1939, as a result, there was a large increase in collective farm payments in kind to the MTS: 14.2 million tons instead of the 10.4 million tons of the year before. Despite the dismal conditions, state collections

[45] *Tragediya*, 5(2) (2006): 475–479 (October 17, 1939). Between 1937 and 1939 the number of collective farms increased by around 2%, and the change in the land area they occupied was likely similar, with the first efforts to expand agriculture into the virgin lands.

achieved the remarkable overall quantity of 28 million tons of grain, the same amount as in the year following the record harvest of 1937.

Meanwhile, peasant grain stocks fell back to 3.6 million tons, the same level as before the 1937 harvest (Table 21). After two years, the Soviet state had fully restored its control of grain and of the private sector.

Earlier in the year, at the eighteenth party congress, Molotov had outlined his four priorities for agriculture: more mechanisation, improved seed varieties, increased supplies of fertiliser, and better field rotations. As 1939 drew to a close, all of these priorities were compromised. Supplies of machinery and chemicals were being swallowed up by rearmament. The improvement of varieties was taken away from the Grain Administration of the Agriculture Commissariat, and this was a positive step, for the Grain Administration was much more focused on consuming all the possible seeds for this year's harvest than on preserving and multiplying improved seed for the future. Instead, however, the responsibility for seed improvement was given over to Lysenko, a scientific huckster.[46] As for field rotations, no improvements were under way.

At his most optimistic, Molotov told the delegates to the eighteenth party congress that in future the Soviet Union would no longer have to worry about bread. 'In so far as the grain production is already solved,' he said, 'in the third five-year plan the USSR must once and for all solve the livestock problem.'[47] What he did not tell the listeners was that the key to the livestock problem was in the hands of the private sector. But no progress could be expected there, for it was on the private sector in agriculture that the Soviet state was setting new limits and piling new pressures as the 1930s drew to a close.

[46] *Tragediya*, 5(1) (2004): 593 (December 5, 1939).

[47] *XVIII s"ezd* (1939): 298.

CHAPTER 8

The Drive for Growth and the Eighteenth Party Congress, January–March 1939

On November 17, 1938, the Politburo adopted a decree 'On arrests, inspection by the procuracy, and investigation procedures'.[1] This measure brought the mass operations to an end. At the same time, there was a marked reduction in the repression of the nomenklatura. A week later, on November 25, Beria was appointed to replace Yezhov as head of the NKVD.

Some months before this, in January 1938, a new group of key economic officials had been appointed (see Sect. 1 in Chapter 6). Many of these, such as Voznesenskii as head of Gosplan, and Zverev as Commissar of Finance, were able to hold office for much longer than their predecessors. At the same time, as the senior personnel of the economic system were stabilised, the basic processes of economic decision making, which had been partially dissolved by the frenzy of 1937, were consolidated.

The reinforcement of economic planning and policy took place against an international background which became increasingly desperate. The fascist powers were everywhere advancing. While Italy was securing a colonial empire in North Africa, the Japanese had seized large parts of China. The Spanish nationalists were on the point of a victory over the Republic, delayed but not prevented by Soviet military

[1] *Istoricheskii arkhiv* (1992), no. 1: 123–128. For a translation of the decree see Getty and Naumov (1999): 532–537.

R. W. Davies et al., *The Industrialisation of Soviet Russia Volume 7: The Soviet Economy and the Approach of War, 1937–1939*,
https://doi.org/10.1057/978-1-137-36238-4_8

assistance to the Republican side. In a first direct engagement with the enemy, the Soviet Union had temporarily rebuffed the Japanese at Lake Khasan in July 1938, but this success also exposed serious weaknesses in Soviet military preparations.

Meanwhile Soviet efforts to establish collective security with the democratic powers had largely failed. A conference about the Far East in Brussels in November 1937 got nowhere. The Popular Front in France collapsed in June 1938, and in September, Britain and France signed the Munich Agreement with Germany and Italy, which transferred the German-speaking province of Sudetenland from Czechoslovakia to Germany.

In 1938, as we have seen, the Soviet economy, still shaken by savage repressions, was struggling to convert its industrial capacities into military power. For a second year in succession industry grew more slowly than in the mid-1930s, and capital construction in 1938 was probably no greater than in 1936. In the last quarter of 1938, the production of coal, oil, pig iron and crude and rolled steel were all lower than in the same quarter of the previous year, and the Soviet railways carried less freight. Moreover, growing inflationary pressures resulted in an acute shortage of every kind of industrial consumer good, and food prices on the kolkhoz market increased by 14%, after four years of decline.

With the new economic appointments, two aspects of economic policy came into sharper focus. One was preparation of the third five-year plan, which was to cover the years 1938–1942. The other was planning for the current year and its successive quarters. We shall see that these two processes were carried on almost independently of each other. The five-year plan was discussed and compiled primarily in terms of the final years of the second and third five-year plans, 1937 and 1942, with little attention being paid to the years in between. Similarly the annual and quarterly plans were prepared with little regard to the simultaneous work on the five-year plan.

Other measures taken in the months before the eighteenth party congress aimed to regulate more closely the activities of the industrial workers and of the collective farm peasants. These measures were motivated by similar concerns: how to assure the supply of labour to collective agriculture and to state-owned industry, restricting opportunities for absenteeism, shirking, and working on the side in the private sector or in the underground economy. The parallel campaign against employment in sideline farming was described above (Sect. 2 in Chapter 7). Below we describe, in order, the evolution of the third five-year plan, the simultaneous compilation of the current production and capital plans for 1939, and the increasing regimentation of industrial labour, before coming to the eighteenth congress itself.

1 The Third Five-Year Plan

Although the third five-year plan officially began on January 1, 1938, it was not approved until May 1939, seventeen months late. This repeated the experience of the second five-year plan (1933–1937), which was not approved until November 1934. The second plan was delayed by the severe economic crisis and famine, which continued until after the 1933 harvest had been gathered in. The third plan was delayed by the repressions.

At first it seemed as if the third plan would be adopted on time. Early in 1936 preliminary discussions took place.[2] Then on April 28, 1937, a Sovnarkom decree called on Gosplan and government departments to prepare the plan for approval by July 1 of that year.[3] The decree extravagantly claimed that industry 'as a whole' had already fulfilled the second five-year plan by April 1, 1937, and that railway freight had already completed its plan a year in advance. Gosplan and the commissariats set to work feverishly.

Some major targets of the plan appeared in the press in the next few weeks (Table 1), and the archives contain memoranda on different aspects of the plan, with numerous targets for the years 1938–1942.[4] At this point Gosplan was overwhelmed by the purges, and it was not until the appointment of Voznesenskii early in 1938 that activity on the third plan was resumed. On April 25, 1938, the full session of the Politburo which approved the final investment plan and the state budget for 1938 (see Sect. 1 in Chapter 6), resolved in an unpublished decision

[2]Zaleski (1980): 163–165. Zaleski thoroughly examines the various stages of preparing the plan; in the present account we concentrate on the defence aspects of the plan, on which Zaleski, writing before the archives were open, had only limited information.

[3]SZ (1937), no. 28: art. 115 (April 28, 1937).

[4]Memoranda for the defence industries, sent to G. I. Smirnov, then head of Gosplan, are nearly all dated between May 11 and May 20, 1937. The matters they deal with included defence as a whole; aviation; chemical industry; tanks; transport and communications; the work of the GULAG; and agricultural transport (see RGAE, 4372/91/3217 and 4372/91/3222); the memorandum on the GULAG is dated June 13.

Table 1 Drafts of the third five-year plan: industrial targets for 1942

	Proposed, June–July 1937	*Adopted, March 1939*
Gross industrial production in plan prices of 1926/27 and per cent of 1937	200	192
Of which		
—Production of producer goods	185	207
—Production of consumer goods	250	172
Production in physical units		
Coal (million tons)	327	243
Electricity (billion kWh)	85–90	75
Pig iron (million tons)	30	22
Crude steel (million tons)	37–38	28

Source Zaleski (1980): 179.

that Gosplan should present 'draft directives on the compilation' of the third five-year plan to the Central Committee by June 1, together with the results of the second five-year plan.[5] But it was not until January 29, 1939, that a further session of the Politburo resolved to convene the eighteenth congress of the Communist Party, the first since 1934, and that a major item on its agenda would be a report by Molotov on the third five-year plan.[6] On the following day, January 30, *Pravda* published Molotov's 'theses' (draft resolution) on the third five-year plan, and on January 30 it published Zhdanov's theses on the third item on the agenda, 'Changes in the statute of the VKP(b)'. The draft five-year plan was adopted with little change by the congress.

The changes between the 1937 and 1939 versions of the plan (shown in Table 1) were considerable: the new version of the plan was more modest, and placed more emphasis on the producer goods (Group A) industries. The 1939 targets were lower, partly because the 1937 version began from the projections in the annual plan for 1937, and the 1939 version on the outcomes for 1937 and 1938. The results for 1937 fell far short of the plan (except for the grain harvest), and the 1938 results revealed that the rate of growth of industry, particularly the

[5]RGASPI, 17/3/998: 2 (item IV); GARF, 5446/1/145: 83.

[6]RGASPI, 17/3/1005 (item I).

civilian branches of heavy industry, was now relatively slow. The revised draft that was approved by the eighteenth party congress continued to be unrealistic, however. The pace of industrial development since 1936 was entirely incompatible with the expectation that production could be doubled in five years.

A major difference between the two drafts resulted from the rapidly increasing role of the defence industries. This was reflected in a shift of priorities: in 1937 it had been anticipated that the consumer sector would grow more rapidly, but by 1939 attention had swung back to producer goods (which for these purposes included armaments).

The plan for the defence industries secretly compiled in the spring of 1937 proposed that their production in 1942 would be 21,614 million rubles, 239% of the 1937 plan, so that it would increase somewhat more rapidly than industrial production as a whole, which would double in the same period. It also surprisingly incorporated our old friend the 'attenuating curve' (Vol. 3: 334): armaments production was to increase by 29.6% in 1938, and the increase would gradually decline until in 1942 it amounted to only 13.7%. The plan also assumed that the defence industries would continue to produce a considerable amount of civilian goods throughout the five years: civilian goods made up 27.6% of the gross value of output of the defence industries in the 1937 plan, and 30.8% of the total in the plan for 1942.[7] These estimates implicitly assumed that although the threat of war was serious, war would not break out before 1942. The capital plan for the defence industries in the 1937 draft of the five-year plan was even more sanguine. It proposed that investment in the industries, already amounting to 2972 million rubles in the 1937 plan, would increase to 4072 million rubles in 1938, and would then fall absolutely in each year of the plan, until in 1942 it amounted to only 1728 million rubles.[8]

The plan for the defence industries in the 1939 version of the third plan was a world apart. Taking into account the rapid development of armaments in 1938 and in the 1939 plan, the new version proposed that production in 1942 should amount to 25.6 billion rubles, and 330% of 1937, rather than 249%.[9] In fact, by the time the 1939 version of the five-year plan was approved, investment in the defence industries had

[7] RGAE, 4372/91/3217: 118–116 (May 20, 1937).

[8] RGAE, 4372/91/3217: 115 (May 20, 1937).

[9] *Industrializatsiya 1938–1941* (1973): 127–145 (reported by Voznesenskii on October 4, 1940).

Table 2 Drafts of the third five-year plan: agricultural targets for 1942 (in plan prices of 1926/27 and per cent of 1937)

	Proposed, May 1937	*Adopted, March 1939*
Gross value of output	185	152
Arable produce	155	137
Of which		
—Grains	140	111
—Cotton	157	128
—Flax	152	149
—Sugar beet	149	137
—Feed crops		166
—Vegetables and potatoes		149
Livestock produce	262	196
Of which		
—Meat	310	266
—Milk	261	173
—Wool	333	273

Source May 1937, from RGAE, 4372/26/1415: 1–4; March 1939, from *Tretii pyatiletnii plan* (1939): 218.

already outstripped the earlier draft of the plan. We shall see that the capital plan for 1939 was already greater than the largest annual investment proposed in the 1937 version of the five-year plan.

The changing context also altered perspectives on agriculture. In its May 1937 directives for the third five-year plan, Gosplan proposed a massive 150 million tons of grain for 1942, still in line with the growth rates set earlier by Stalin. When work on the plan resumed in March 1939, the agricultural targets were substantially moderated. The harvest expected in 1942 was now only 133 tons (see the note to Table B.33). Instead of doubling, the gross output of agriculture was to expand by one-half (Table 2). While the livestock sector was to nearly double, and feed crops by two-thirds, the arable sector as a whole was to grow by just 37%, and the grain harvest by 13%, still a tough target, because its baseline was the record harvest of 1937, and even 133 million tons would not be achieved until 1958.[10]

The five-year plan submitted to the eighteenth party congress was thus already being overwhelmed by the huge expansion of the defence

[10] *Narodnoe khozyaistvo* (1972): 216.

sector of the economy, which was entirely secret. Nonetheless, the public discussion of the plan remains significant because it outlined and foreshadowed several major changes in economic policy. Most important was the emphasis on the large and persistent lag of Soviet industry behind the advanced capitalist countries in general and the United States in particular. The resolution on the plan pointed out that in output per head of population Soviet electricity amounted to less than half that of France, nearly one-third that of Britain, and less than a third that of the USA, and gave similar figures for iron, steel, and coal. It also stated that the USSR lagged in consumer goods such as textiles, paper, and soap. In his report to the congress, Stalin spelled out what this meant for the future. In the case of pig iron, the USSR produced about 15 million tons in 1938; it would need to produce 25 million tons to overtake the British level, 40–45 million tons to overtake Germany, and 50–60 million tons to overtake the United States. But Soviet production could be expected to grow by only 2–2.5 million tons a year. Based on such estimates, Stalin set the goal for the USSR to overtake the main capitalist countries in 10–15 years.[11]

The resolution on the five-year plan claimed prematurely that 'in the level of its technology of production in industry and agriculture [the USSR] is already ahead of any European capitalist country.' These claims seem to have been based on the idea that Soviet industry, having developed very recently, had a higher proportion of up-to-date equipment than the longer-established industrial economies.

Anticipating a protracted struggle to overtake the West, two further themes played a major part in the third five-year plan and in its proposals for development, and these were evidently based in large part on defence considerations. First, the policy of locating new factories and resources in the Urals and beyond should be pursued with greater determination. The resolution on the plan called for the establishment of duplicate facilities (*predpriyatiya-dublery* or 'shadow factories') for engineering, oil refining, and chemicals in the Urals, the Volga region, and beyond 'in order to avoid unexpected interruptions in supply of some industrial goods from monopoly enterprises'; the following paragraph more explicitly proposed 'a more rapid growth in the volume of investment and the construction of enterprises in *the Eastern and Far-Eastern* regions

[11] *XVIII s"ezd* (1939): 17–18, 27.

of the USSR'—specifically, three-quarters of new blast furnaces should be constructed in the Eastern regions.[12] Secondly, the plan placed great emphasis on moving sharply away from concentrating capital resources on the construction of large enterprises.

Following the precedent of previous congresses, after *Pravda* had published the theses on the five-year plan on January 30, it proceeded immediately to publish a series of 'discussion pages' (*diskussionye listki*) with extensive comments and suggestions on the theses. The first appeared on February 2, and the final, sixteenth issue on March 9, the eve of the congress. The contributions, as with the previous two congresses in 1930 and 1934, were restricted in scope by a censorship which controlled all discussion. But the permitted range of discussion was not clear cut, and within narrow limits, crucial problems of the economy were aired publicly.

The lag of Soviet industry behind the advanced capitalist countries was a central theme of the contributions. The head of the iron and steel sector of Gosplan gave striking examples from each stage in his industry. The dust produced from equivalent US blast furnaces was only one-third of that in the Soviet industry, even though US iron ore was more friable. Although the USSR was relatively short of scrap iron, its open-hearth furnaces used more scrap per unit of crude steel produced. Soviet rolling mills used more crude steel per unit of output of rolled steel than German mills.[13] Another contributor pointed out that in the automobile industry, the Soviet Union had very few repair bases, so that goods vehicles had to be transported long distances for repair, while the USA had 90,000 repair bases; moreover, US spare parts cost only 7–8% per year of the value of a heavy goods vehicle, while the Soviet figure was 25–30%.[14] According to one engineer, the absence of local repair facilities meant that it could take three to six months for a vehicle to be repaired.[15] A leading Stakhanovite explained that in US cotton textile mills the automatic control of moisture and temperature meant that threads broke far less often than in the Soviet industry; automatic signalling that a loom was not working properly, used widely in other countries, meant that the

[12] *XVIII s"ezd* (1939): 660.

[13] *Pravda*, February 13, 1939 (diskussionyi listok no. 5).

[14] *Pravda*, February 4, 1939 (disk. list. no. 2: A. Neverov).

[15] *Pravda*, February 11, 1939 (disk. list. no. 4).

operator responsible for a number of looms did not have to leave her post to fetch a charge hand or engineer.[16] Other proposals sought to fill gaps in Soviet industry. A bus driver claimed that 'the present bus, built on the chassis of a goods vehicle, does not meet the requirements of the population.' What was needed was a high-speed vehicle seating 50–60 people which could be used for both urban and inter-city transport, and this would require a special factory.[17] An engineer proposed that at least two telephone-equipment factories should be built during the third five-year plan.[18] A railway engineer attacked 'enemies of the people' for deliberately discrediting diesel locomotives; after they were built in 1931 they were sent to Central Asia without proper preparation. There were now 40 in Central Asia but only 16 were working; the rest were awaiting repair. The decision of the June 1931 party plenum supporting diesel locomotives should be revived.[19]

A second theme which received much attention was the need to establish small and medium enterprises which would serve their own locality, reducing the need for long-distance shipments, and duplicating capacity in case of need (this was obviously a reference to the war danger). In the Urals, small factories were required to manufacture every kind of fastening and cable which all had to be brought in from other regions, and larger duplicate enterprises were needed for ball bearings (which needed a medium-size factory) and cutting tools, for which a duplicate of the Frezer works in Moscow was needed.[20] The head of the knitwear workers' trade union pointed out that several large knitwear factories had been built during the 1930s, but what were now needed were small factories near the raw material and also close to available female labour—for instance, in the Urals, the Donbass, Uzbekistan and Kazakhstan.[21] Related to these proposals, several contributors called for modification of the centralised control of investment, The resolution on the third five-year plan called for a more rapid increase in local industry and in industrial cooperatives, and in the discussion, the deputy head of the

[16] *Pravda*, February 15, 1939 (disk. list. no. 6: M. Vinogradova and V. Morozov).

[17] *Pravda*, February 11, 1939 (disk. list. no. 4: B. Paskhin).

[18] *Pravda*, March 9, 1939 (disk. list. no. 16: Basaev).

[19] *Pravda*, March 2, 1939 (disk. list. no. 13: D. Shalii).

[20] *Pravda*, February 19, 1939 (disk. list. no. 8: A. Petros'yants).

[21] *Pravda*, February 15, 1939 (disk. list. no. 6: M. M. Kaganovich; despite the name, this was evidently not the recently dismissed commissar of the aircraft industry).

metal cooperatives' union called for the establishment of 'hundreds and thousands of small enterprises', and argued that in order to facilitate this, the maximum amount for 'below-the-limit' investments should be increased from 30,000 to 100,000 or 200,000 rubles, while the construction of larger cooperatives should cease.[22] Malkin, director of the Kerch iron and steel works, complained that after he built a facility for drying clothes and a toilet for 2000 rubles, his decision was condemned by the inspector as 'illegal and anti-state'; he called for the right to invest up to 10,000–15,000 rubles at his own discretion. This indicated that factory directors at that time could not legally undertake the below-limit investments which had been permitted since 1935, but now required the permission of the higher authority.[23]

The familiar theme of the rights of factory directors received much attention. In his article Malkin vigorously demanded greater powers. Directors had no funds from which they could pay bonuses: the chief bookkeeper at Malkin's works had tried to stop him paying bonuses of 100 rubles each to four workers who had remained at their posts during a fire at a blast furnace. He was unable to improve the low wages of engineers in the labour organisation department, and this meant that people would not work there. He also had insufficient powers to appoint staff: the heads of shops were appointed by the people's commissar, and their deputies were appointed by the head of the chief administration responsible for his factory, often without consulting him. Other contributors strongly supported Malkin.[24] At the congress itself, however, Kaganovich did not take up the question of the rights of factory directors, but instead called for increased rights for heads of shops, foremen and brigade leaders.[25]

The shortage of labour, a particularly acute problem in the immediate pre-war years, rather surprisingly received more attention in the discussion pages than at the congress itself. Referring to the 'unceasing complaints about the shortage of labour on building sites', a Kiev engineer called for the adoption of 'accelerated methods of construction': the

[22] *Pravda*, February 19, 1939 (disk. list. no. 8: V. Egorov).

[23] *Pravda*, February 17, 1939 (disk. list. no. 7: I. Malkin).

[24] *Pravda*, March 9, 1939 (disk. list. no. 16).

[25] *XVIII s"ezd* (1939): 246.

more extensive use of pre-fabricated doors and windows, and building machinery, would reduce the building labour needed to one-fifth or one-sixth (he claimed) of the present level.[26] Another contributor suggested that the shortage of labour in the Far East should be dealt with by establishing a central resettlement committee to provide both agricultural and industrial labour, and by passing a law granting advantages to those who resettled.[27] Other contributors argued that greatly improved facilities must be established for training skilled labour. A chief engineer responsible for automobile repairs stated that only 3% of goods vehicle drivers were classified in grade 1, and as many as 86% in grade 3, the bottom grade, and more than 150,000 additional drivers were required, so more training facilities must be established, and a unified training programme must be introduced with training documentation that was not continually amended.[28] Skills and training were also unsatisfactory in farm machinery services. In the Saratov province, there were 166 machine-tractor stations, but only five directors had been through higher education and 12 through secondary education, and 66 directors had to be replaced in 1938, so a special college should be set up for training MTS directors.[29]

Although defence matters remained secret in all specifics, several contributors used the public discussion to call for greater attention to defence. A writer from Leningrad complained that party members did not participate sufficiently in defence measures, and a letter from the Perm province reported that primary party organisations concerned with defence had been closed down because of lack of support. Various suggestions were made to deal with this situation. Provincial party committees should include a department to deal with defence matters. Alternatively, defence departments should be established in the lower district committees. A contributor from the Belorussian railways proposed that every party member should 'properly master one of the

[26] *Pravda*, February 11, 1939 (disk. list. no, 4: Ya. Plaksin).

[27] *Pravda*, March 9, 1939 (disk. list. no. 16: Bogdanevskii, Moscow).

[28] *Pravda*, February 4, 1939 (disk. list. no. 4: A. Neverov of Glavavtoremont, the Chief Administration of Vehicle Repairs).

[29] *Pravda*, February 11, 1939 (disk. list. no. 4: I. Vlasov, secretary of the Saratov provincial party committee).

military specialities'. These varied contributions all gave the impression that defence was receiving rather little attention in the civilian party.[30]

While these discussions were taking place in public, the Gosplan draft, behind the scenes, was strongly disputed. It presented numerous figures for 1937, the year before the plan commenced, and for 1942, but, with rare exceptions, not for the years in between. But by this time the results for 1938 and the plan for 1939 were already known. The five-year plan was effectively making proposals only about the last three years of the plan from 1940 to 1942. Gosbank was one of the principal critics of the Gosplan proposals. Gosbank was headed by the formidable N. A. Bulganin, who was also a deputy chair of Sovnarkom. He assured members of his staff and leading academics specialising in financial questions, who assembled to discuss the five-year plan on January 17:

> The indicators (for the five-year plan) are very controversial. The main thing is that we do not need to make ourselves dependent on the data of Gosplan, Narkomtorg and Narkomfin [the Commissariats of Trade and Finance]. We must propose our own indicators. The indicators of Gosplan are only for orientation.[31]

The published planning indicator in the Gosplan drafts which came in for most criticism was for the wage bill. In January 1939 Gosplan proposed that the number of manual and office workers should increase from 27 to 31 million between 1937 and 1942, and presented two versions of the planned increase of the wage bill: by either 50 or 56.5%. In its draft memorandum to Sovnarkom dated January 15, Gosbank argued that this increase was 'evidently insufficient'. The wage bill had increased by 18.8% in 1938, and was planned to increase by a further 11.6% in 1939. Even if it increased only by a modest 9% a year in the remaining three years of the plan, the cumulative increase in the wage bill over the five years would be 71%. In the discussion on January 17, Yu. E. Shenger, a professor in a Moscow financial institute, argued that

[30] *Pravda*, February 17, 1939 (disk. list. no. 7, a summary of letters entitled 'Strengthen mass defence work').

[31] The Gosbank documents that are quoted here and detailed in the next paragraph are published from the archives in *Po stranitsam*, 4 (2007): 63–68 (draft memorandum to Sovnarkom, January 15, 1939); 69–82 (discussion of January 17, 1939); 84–89 (draft memorandum to Sovnarkom, January 24, 1939); 90–96 (discussion of January 25, 1939); 98–102 (memorandum to Sovnarkom, January 27, 1939).

9% a year was unrealistically small, and L. M. Biderman, a consultant in the Central Planning and Economic Administration of Gosbank, argued that even to limit the annual growth of the wage bill to 12% would be 'a colossal achievement'. Bulganin, in summing up the discussion, agreed that the annual growth in 1940–1942 would be more than 9%. In its second draft memorandum to Sovnarkom dated January 24, Gosbank proposed that the wage bill would increase over the five years by as much as 80.9%, pointing out that the more rapid growth of Group A industries during the plan, where the average wage was higher than in industry as a whole, would also push the wage bill in an upward direction. The final memorandum sent by Gosbank to Sovnarkom on January 27 retained the increase of 80.5%. In the published volume on the five-year plan, Gosplan raised its earlier estimate of the increase in the wage bill from 50 or 56.5%, but only to 62%.[32]

Behind the scenes, a three-cornered dispute about the key question of prices took place between the central government (which meant, in practice, Molotov and Stalin), Gosplan and Gosbank. The second five-year plan had proposed that prices should be reduced by as much as 35%, but in practice, partly because of the decision to abolish all food rationing, prices rose substantially over the five years. There was general agreement that the third five-year plan should be more modest. But the central government took it as an axiom, and Gosplan accepted, that retail prices should fall somewhat over the next five years. It was typical of Gosplan that, in a memorandum dated May 10, 1938, Martynov, deputy head of the financial department of Gosplan, stated that food prices would fall by 25% between 1937 and 1942, and the prices of industrial goods by 10%. Later in the year, an unsigned memorandum to Voznesenskii, dated October 23, probably written by N. Margolin, head of the currency circulation group in Gosplan, proposed more modestly that retail prices would decline by 17%, food prices by 22% and the prices of industrial goods by 10%.[33]

The discussions in Gosbank which preceded the eighteenth party congress reveal that while preparing the plan, Gosplan itself became increasingly sceptical about price reductions. On January 17, V. S. Gerashchenko,

[32] *Tretii pyatiletnii plan* (1939): 28.

[33] *Po stranitsam*, 4 (2007): 106 (Gosplan draft directives on currency circulation, May 10, 1938) and 107–111 (unsigned Gosplan memorandum to Voznesenskii on currency circulation from 1932 to 1942, October 23).

head of the Central Planning and Economic Administration of Gosbank, stated that prices were likely to be reduced by 5% in 1941 and 10% in 1942.[34] On January 25, V. V. Ikonnikov stated that Gosplan now proposed to reduce retail prices by only 10%, but even so its proposals for retail trade allowed for only a quarter of this reduction. According to Bulganin, Voznesenskii had concluded that only a 5% reduction could be achieved, but the government still expected a 10% reduction. Eventually Gosplan's published volume on the plan reported all retail trade figures only in constant 1937 prices, and nothing whatsoever about price reduction appeared in the volume, or in the various reports about the third five-year plan to the eighteenth party congress. The authorities had tacitly agreed that the price question should be shelved.

The plan for currency issue played a major part in the discussions of the third five-year plan, behind the scenes. Neither the first nor the second five-year plan included a plan for currency issue. During the second five-year plan, however, the amount of currency to be issued was planned on an annual basis and was heatedly discussed throughout the year (Vol. 6: 150–153, 188–192). Generally, currency issue greatly exceeded the plan. The quantity of currency in circulation during 1937 was nearly double the average stock in 1932.[35] In preparing the third plan, currency was at the centre of the attention of Gosplan and Gosbank. The draft directives dated May 10, 1938, prepared in Gosplan by Martynov, stated unambiguously that 'currency circulation must be speeded up and no additional currency must be issued during the third five-year plan.' Margolin's memorandum to Voznesenskii on October 23, 1938, insisted more specifically:

> The main task of the third five-year plan in currency circulation must be to eliminate the excess monetary demand which has been carried over from

[34] The senior official who prepared the draft Gosbank memoranda to Sovnarkom was Vladimir Gerashchenko. His son Viktor became the head of the Soviet Central Bank in 1989, and was appointed to lead the Central Bank of post-Soviet Russia from 1992 to 1994, and again from 1998 to 2002. In 1993 the economist Jeffrey Sachs named Viktor Gerashchenko 'the worst central-bank governor of any major country in history' (*The Economist*, October 16, 1993: 90).

[35] The contemporary estimate of the increase was 94% (*Po stranitsam*, 4 (2007): 107). Averaging the monthly figures reported over each of the two years (*Po stranitsam*, 2 (2007): 40–41) gives 87%.

> the second five-year plan, and achieve at least a small surplus of supply over demand. The achievement of this will bring into circulation the currency which is not in use—the equivalent of increasing currency in use by about 50 per cent. Therefore, the third five-year plan must be compiled without any issue of new currency.

When Gosbank discussed currency circulation in January 1939, the draft memorandum prepared by Gerashchenko on January 15 pointed out that currency circulation had increased by 3.5 billion rubles in 1938 and was planned to increase by a further 614 million rubles in 1939. It nevertheless proposed that no net currency issue should take place over the five years as a whole. In the discussion that took place on January 17, Gerashchenko proposed that the 1939 plan should be revised so that no currency issue took place in that year, and that the currency in circulation should be reduced by 4.9 billion rubles in 1940–1942, more than cancelling out the increase in 1938.

During the discussion, N. N. Rovinskii, a prominent academic specialist on financial questions, challenged this position:

> Currency in circulation must increase during the five-year plan. In the second five-year plan it grew by 5 billion rubles and it will be good if in the third plan we keep to an increase of 3–4 billion rubles.

It was essential to avoid a currency famine. Even now, there were cases when 'managers do not have a kopek to pay for minor matters'; a normal rate of issue would enliven the economy.

At the end of a heated discussion Bulganin supported Rovinskii, declaring:

> I cannot imagine that if the amount of commodities in circulation is increasing by 55 per cent, the currency in circulation would remain at the 1937 level ... there is nothing wrong with increasing the currency in circulation if it is on a healthy basis.

The reduction of currency in circulation would put a squeeze on the development of heavy industry, and 'We must also consider the defence capacity of the country.'

In view of Bulganin's attitude, it is not surprising that the second draft of the Gosbank memorandum to Sovnarkom on January 24, prepared by Gerashchenko, now proposed that the currency in circulation should

Table 3 Drafts of the third five-year plan: currency emission, 1938–1942 (million rubles)

	Outcomes		*Targets*				
	1937	*1938*	*1939*	*1940*	*1941*	*1942*	*Total*
Gerashchenko, draft proposal to Sovnarkom, Jan. 25, 1939							
Currency in circulation, Dec. 31	13,582	17,251	17,150	17,450	19,350	21,650	–
Year-on-year increase	–	3,569	–101	300	1,900	2,300	7,968
Gosbank, proposal to Sovnarkom, Jan. 27, 1939							
Currency in circulation, Dec. 31	13,600	17,200	17,800	19,000	21,000	21,600	–
Year-on-year increase	–	3,600	600	1,200	2,000	600	8,000

Source: *Po stranitsam*, 4 (2007): 88 and 101.

increase by 8 billion rubles over the five years. As the increase in 1938 had already been 3.6 billion rubles, however, the remaining 4.4 billion rubles of monetary expansion should be postponed until the last years of the five-year plan, with the money supply remaining roughly level in 1939 and 1940 (Table 3). Thus, Gerashchenko continued to defend austerity in the short term.

In the discussion on the following day, no one defended the previous view that currency in circulation should be reduced over the five years. L. I. Skvortsov, head of the Gosbank department for the credit plan, argued for an even larger increase, 9.3 rather than 8 billion, in view of the estimates made in his department. In fact, the final version of the Gosbank memorandum, submitted to Sovnarkom on January 27, kept the ceiling of eight billion. But it was agreed that the increase of currency in circulation in 1939 and 1940 would amount to two billion rubles; the pain of monetary restraint would be put off to 1942.

Adopted in March 1939, the third five-year plan was soon overtaken by events. In a report of October 4, 1940, Voznesenskii noted that industrial production as a whole 'has not yet reached the annual rate of growth fixed in the third five-year plan'. He went on to point out:

> Nevertheless, the average annual rate of growth of defence industry in 1938–40 amounted to 41.5 per cent instead of the 27.3 per cent envisaged

> by the five-year plan. The total increase of the output of defence industry has already amounted to 180 per cent in three years as compared with the target of the third five-year plan of an increase of 230 per cent in 5 years. This has ensured that the third five-year plan will be achieved ahead of time by the industry of the defence commissariats.[36]

2 Current Economic Planning

Following the arrest of the key economic officials in the autumn of 1937, as we saw in Chapter 4, the preparation of the 1938 plan collapsed. The key targets for 1938 drawn up in July 1937 were never approved, and only a plan for industry was adopted before the end of 1937. Plans for the other sectors of the economy, including capital investment, were not approved until after the appointment of Voznesenskii in January 1938. The capital investment plan was approved in February; plans for some sectors were not approved until April.

The preparation of the 1939 plan was a significant step on the road back to normal economic planning. It was still delayed, however. A firm feature of annual planning in the mid-1930s was the approval of preliminary targets in the previous July, which gave the basis for factories and other enterprises to prepare their own plans well before the end of the year. This stage was entirely neglected in 1937, and was not resumed in 1938. Evidently the plan was first discussed at a meeting between Voznesenskii and Stalin on November 10, 1938. Lasting 3 hours 40 minutes, this was Voznesenskii's only visit to Stalin's office in the year. Voroshilov, Molotov, Yezhov, Mikoyan, Bulganin and Kaganovich were also present. A preliminary version of the plan was then approved at a special meeting of the Politburo on November 22. This plan already included capital investment, unlike the 1938 plan at a similar stage.[37] Despite this, it was still incomplete, lacking plans for the Commissariats of the Army and Navy. These plans were not adopted until March 2, 1939, evidently because agreement had not been reached on the amount they should receive.

The plan adopted in November 1938 assumed that industrial growth would continue at the relatively modest pace of the previous two years.

[36] *Industrializatsiya 1938–1941* (1973): 128.

[37] RGASPI, 17/3/1003: 1, 36–51.

Gross production of the industrial commissariats, including local industry, was planned to increase by 15.5%, and the production of cooperative industry by 14.8%. The combined value of production of the Commissariats of Defence Industry and of Machine Building was planned to increase by 26.3% (the growth of military production alone within this subtotal was not stated but was of course much higher), and the production of the Commissariat of Heavy Industry by 13.5%. The production of the Commissariats of Light Industry and Food Industry, directed to the civilian consumer market, would increase much more slowly, by 9.3 and 7.5% respectively.

For the civilian industries this increase was to be achieved primarily by an increase in labour productivity, which was to be accompanied by an increase in the average wage somewhat below that of productivity. As a result of these developments a modest cost reduction was also targeted (Table 4).

Capital investment was planned to increase at a moderate pace (Table B.2). Within the total, by far the largest increase was investment in the defence industries, which was to rise by 32%, from 3.7 to 4.9 million rubles. The allocation to the Transport Commissariat, substantially reduced in 1938, was planned to increase from 3.7 to 4.2 billion rubles, restoring it to the previous level, while the allocations to education and agriculture were reduced.

When, on March 2, 1939, a decree of Sovnarkom and the party's Central Committee approved the missing estimates for these commissariats, it also approved much larger additions to the sums already allocated

Table 4 Planned industrial production, 1939 (change over previous year, per cent)

	Gross value of output	*Average output per worker*	*Average earnings*	*Unit costs*
By commissariat				
Defence Industry	–	17.0	10.0	−6.0
Heavy Industry	13.5	11.0	8.5	−2.5
Light Industry	9.3	6.0	6.0	0.0
Food Industry	7.5	7.0	5.0	−1.0

Source RGASPI, 17/3/1003: 1, 36–51. The increase in the gross value of output of the Commissariat of Defence Industry was not stated, but its production combined with that of the Commissariat of Machine Building was planned to increase by 26.3%.

Table 5 Plans for defence-related capital construction, 1939 (million rubles)

	Allocations, Nov. 22, 1938	*Additional allocations, Mar. 2, 1939*	*Total*
By commissariat			
Defence (army)	–	976	976
Navy	–	800	800
Defence Industry	4,900	1,050	5,950
NKVD	3,150	803	3,953
Total	8,050	3,629	11,679

Source Table B.8. The March 1939 allocation to NKO included 50 million rubles to Glavvoenstroi, the Chief Administration of Military Construction.

to defence-related investment under other headings.[38] Planned investment in the defence industries was now brought to almost 6 billion rubles, and the total under all defence-related headings to 11.7 billion rubles. This was 35% of the plan for all capital works in 1939, a quite unprecedented amount (Table 5).

3 Managing the Industrial Worker

Against this background, another decision made on the eve of the eighteenth party congress was to increase control over employees at work. In December 1938, the Politburo approved two measures greatly affecting factory life: first, to introduce labour books for all employed persons, and secondly, to tighten labour discipline.

On November 27, 1938, Shvernik, head of the VTsSPS (All-Union Central Council of The Trade Unions), spent half an hour with Stalin in his office, together with Molotov and Mikoyan, and on the following day he visited Stalin for another hour, again in the presence of Molotov and Mikoyan. On this second visit he took with him P. G. Moskatov, secretary of the VTsSPS. These visits evidently prepared for a meeting of the Politburo two weeks later on December 15. The latter meeting approved a draft decree, which was eventually promulgated by Sovnarkom on December 20 as 'The introduction of labour books' and published in the press the following day.[39]

[38] GARF, 5446/1/552: 27 (art. 254/37, March 2, 1939).

[39] RGASPI, 17/3/1004: 24 (art. 113); *Pravda*, December 21, 1938.

Eight years earlier, in the winter of 1930/31, when labour scarcity and a high level of labour turnover seemed to make it urgent to control labour more tightly, the introduction of labour books had been promoted enthusiastically by both the Labour Commissariat and the VTsSPS. The Labour Commissariat submitted a draft decree to TsIK in February 1931 (Vol. 3: 422–423; Vol. 4: 30). For unknown reasons, no decision followed at that time. The labour books approved in December 1938 closely resembled those proposed in 1931 and, in view of the speed with which millions of books were issued, it seems probable that they were the original books which had been kept in store since 1931. They were to be issued from January 15, 1939, by all state and cooperative organisations to all manual and office workers who worked for more than five days, and were to show their 'age, education, trade, and information about their employment records, their transfer from one enterprise or establishment to another, reasons for the transfer, and the rewards and awards received'. Reasons for departure were to be entered in conformity with the Labour Code, and no penalties imposed by the factory should appear in the book. A paragraph in the Code, stating grounds for dismissal, included the significant clause of 'if the person taken on is found to be unsuitable for the work'. No one was to be taken on without the labour book, which was to be presented to the management upon arrival and would be held until the person left the employment.[40]

Most likely, the issue of labour books somewhat restricted the ease with which workers could move from one enterprise to another, but nonetheless it proved to be an interim measure. In 1940 much harsher decrees made unauthorised departure from work a criminal offence, and subjected workers to the compulsory direction of labour.[41]

The introduction of labour books at the end of 1938 was followed closely by a more direct approach to managing labour discipline. On December 27, a month after meeting with Stalin to discuss labour books, Shvernik visited Stalin again, spending 2 hours 20 minutes with him.

[40] *Sbornik zakonodatel'nykh aktov* (1956): 20–21 (text of the decree), 72–74 (grounds for dismissal).

[41] For the decrees of June 26 and October 19, 1940, and other labour legislation issued at this time, see *Bulletins*, series 2, no. 6 (1951): 2–3 (G. R. Barker), and Filtzer (1986): 234 ff.

On this occasion a wider group of political leaders was present, not only Molotov and Mikoyan, but also Voroshilov, Zhdanov, Kaganovich, and Malenkov. Shvernik was accompanied by no fewer than three Komsomol secretaries, one of them a woman (a rare occurrence). The next day, December 28, Shvernik spent a further 35 minutes with Stalin; on this occasion only Molotov was present. That day the Politburo approved a decree which was published on December 29 as a decree of Sovnarkom, the party's Central Committee and VTsSPS: its lengthy title was 'Measures to regulate labour discipline, improve the practice of social insurance and struggle with abuses in this connection'.[42]

The decree proclaimed that 'in the Soviet Union people are not working for capitalists but for themselves, for their own socialist state, for the good of the whole people.' The overwhelming majority worked honestly and conscientiously, the decree continued, but there were also some backward or dishonest people: 'flitters, layabouts, absentees and self-seekers'. These people tried to work less for the state and to grab more for themselves. They worked for only four or five hours a day; if they were dismissed, they tried to be paid for loss of earnings. In most cases, they immediately walked into another job. The decree insisted that absence from work without due cause should result in dismissal, in accordance with existing law. Arriving late for work, lingering over lunch, slacking during working time, and leaving work early were all serious violations of labour discipline. If such violations occurred three times in a month or four times in two months, the employee should be dismissed as an absentee and a violator of labour discipline. In a clause aimed at breaking collusion between managers and employees for the sake of a quiet life, the decree stated that managers should also be penalised by dismissal and prosecution if they failed to carry out the punitive measures against defaulting employees.

The decree also ruled that people leaving a job on their own initiative were henceforth required to give the management notice of four weeks rather than seven days. But perhaps the most significant new measures were those tightening up on social insurance, because they had the effect of reducing expenditures from the state budget as well as discouraging people from changing their place of work. Payments for temporary inability to work were already fixed on a sliding scale related to length of

[42] RGASPI, 17/3/1004: 38 (art. 219).

service at the particular enterprise or establishment. Under the new regulations, the length of service required was increased. For example, under the old regulations, persons unable to work were paid two-thirds of their existing wages if they had been at the enterprise for less than one year; under the new regulations, they were paid only 50% of their wages until they had been working at the enterprise for two years. The period a pregnant woman was required to have worked at a given enterprise in order to be entitled to maternity leave was similarly increased.

The introduction of these measures was evidently influenced by the looming war danger. A clause in the decree of December 28 listed the ways in which labour discipline was being violated and proclaimed that they resulted in 'the disruption of the economic *and defence* power of our country and of the well-being of our people' (emphasis added). But the vociferous campaign against slackers which accompanied and followed the publication of the decree mainly emphasised the general duty of the Soviet citizen. For many weeks it occupied as prominent a position in the press as previous campaigns over Stakhanovism and the major political trials had done. The campaign began at the end of December, before the publication of the decree, with a feature in the industrial newspaper *Industriya* headed 'Manual and office workers propose to introduce changes in labour legislation'.[43] It included suspiciously convenient articles signed by minor figures in industry. Thus 'Reduce pregnancy leave' claimed that all babies of workers in the Krasnyi Treugol'nik factory received places in the crèche, so four months' leave was unnecessary; moreover, the system was abused by women who joined the factory in the sixth or seventh month of their pregnancy and did not return to the factory after they had received their paid leave.

A series of editorials in *Pravda* kept up the pressure in January and February. Their headings convey the flavour of the campaign: 'Work the full eight, seven or six hours'; 'Strictly observe the length of the working day fixed by law'; 'Against the violators of the interests of the state'; 'Observe Soviet labour laws as sacred'; 'Unswervingly strengthen labour discipline'; 'Labour in the USSR is steeped in glory.'[44] But several obstacles hindered the success of the campaign.

[43] *Industriya*, December 28, 1938.

[44] Respectively *Pravda*, January 2, 10, 19, 20, and February 20, 1939.

The easiest task was the registration of absenteeism. But even here problems arose. According to press reports, workers frequently tried to obtain doctors' notes to justify their absence on grounds of ill-health. In the Paris Commune factory, 65 workers reported sick on one day. Only three were certified to be ill, but the others lost much working time waiting to see the doctor, and one of the 65, who had been refused by the factory doctor, managed to get a note from another doctor at her local polyclinic.[45] More difficult than registering absence was to record late arrival or early departure from work. The standard system was to issue each worker with a numbered disc to hang on a board on arrival. The success of this system depended on the clerks responsible for managing it. They were often ill trained, poorly paid and few in number. When they were not at their posts, a worker could hang up discs for his mates who had not yet arrived, or leave early without this being recorded.[46] Moreover, the system was not installed in all factories.[47] Then there were reasons for lateness. A legitimate excuse was delay due to the vagaries of the transport system. According to a *Pravda* editorial, in Khar'kov 'almost all suburban trains are consistently late'; at the Kursk railway station in Moscow, 7000–8000 workers a day reported train delays. *Pravda* demanded that the provincial and urban party committees in Khar'kov put this right.[48] Sometimes the management demanded a note from the transport authorities certifying the transport delay. But to obtain the notes proved to be far too time consuming. Instead, managements attempted to check on the transport delays themselves. Sometimes the delays were misrepresented by the workers. In the Avtosteklo factory in Moscow, 17 workers claimed they were late due to train delays on one day. But when the management asked the workers to state which trains were responsible, it turned out that one of the trains was scheduled to arrive too late for the shift even if it had been on time, and that two

[45] *Pravda*, January 6, 1939 (O. Yakovleva).

[46] See *Pravda*, January 5, 1939 (I. Chernov) for one of many reports on the Gor'kii motor vehicle factory. In one large shop, seven out of nine time clerks had joined the factory only in 1938, and at least two of them had to cope with over 400 workers each, although 150–200 was regarded as a normal work load.

[47] For example, *Pravda*, January 17, 1939 (an order by the Commissariat of Food Industry).

[48] *Pravda*, January 5 and 10, 1939.

others were going in the opposite direction; only 4 of the 17 workers had a legitimate excuse.[49]

More difficult than either absenteeism or lateness was to manage failure to work continuously. In many factories there was no system for recording absence during the lunch hour; and in any factory only a strong and well-informed manager could deal with idling during the day. V. A. Malyshev, director of the Kolomna locomotive factory, who was to be appointed Commissar for Heavy Engineering in February 1939, reported that he had personally gone round the factory talking to people who were chatting instead of working.[50] But this was hardly a general solution for the problem. The role of the foreman, as the person in closest touch with workers on the shop floor from day to day, had been discussed intermittently ever since the 1920s, when foremen had vigorously complained that limitations on their authority hindered them from managing production in the area for which they were responsible.[51] Within a few days of the decree of December 28, a vigorous discussion was launched in the press, dominated by the foremen themselves. Many foremen were long established in their factory, and had been promoted from below. A not untypical example was E. Zhurkov, who had worked in the Dnepropetrovsk iron and steel works since 1908, and was promoted to foreman in 1922.[52]

The foremen had four main complaints. First, their time was preempted by demands unrelated to the organisation of the workforce. These including hunting for materials: four foremen in the Stalin iron and steel works in the Donbass complained that they spent much of their time seeking out metal, or on the telephone trying to secure power or

[49] *Pravda*, January 10, 1939 (V. Saparin).

[50] *Pravda*, January 29, 1939.

[51] Carr and Davies, *Foundations*, 1 (1969): 574n.

[52] *Pravda*, January 8, 1939. On January 1, 1941, 35.7% of foremen had worked in their industry for more than ten years, 28.5% for five to ten years, 15.9% for three to five years, and 19.9% for less than three years (*Industrializatsiya 1938–1941* (1973): 274). Only 3% were graduates with higher education, and 7.5% with secondary special education; 88.9% were 'practicals' with no special training. In 1941 women accounted for 10.3%, compared with only 1.7% in 1933 (Rosenberg and Siegelbaum, eds. (1993): 176 (L. H. Siegelbaum)).

water for their furnaces.[53] 'A foreman or a pusher (*tolkach*)?' asked a headline in *Pravda*.[54] Second, their status was low. They were paid less than the skilled workers, or Stakhanovites, they supervised.[55] They were overlooked in consultations over policy matters such as the 1939 plan.[56] Third, they had little discretion: they could not change a worker's pay grade, or set output norms.[57] Fourth, their notional authority to penalise drunkenness or bad behaviour was often undermined when superiors overruled them.[58]

No doubt there was substance in the general thrust of these complaints. But there was another side that went unsaid. This was the scope for the foreman to exercise favouritism and discrimination on the shop floor. Even if the foreman was often the only person competent to fix a particular norm, the authority to raise or lower a work norm could be abused to favour some workers or harm others.[59] Alternatively, when foremen took the line of least resistance by cutting work norms for everyone, the aggregate effect was to push up wages and add to inflationary pressure.[60]

A few weeks into the discussion of the rights of foremen, an authoritative editorial in *Pravda* on January 25 strongly supported them. It was headed 'Raise the authority of the lower and middle-ranking commanders of production', and stressed the need to increase the authority of the foreman in the eyes of the worker:

> The foremen themselves, and also workers, engineers, heads of shops and directors of enterprises, are raising the question of *the necessity of increasing the rights of foremen,* revising their system of payment, and strengthening the position of foremen as managers in their sections.

[53] *Pravda*, January 7, 1939.

[54] *Pravda*, January 7, 1939.

[55] *Pravda*, January 7 (V. Mikhailov, Kirov works, Leningrad), and January 8 (P. Kozlov, Moscow watch factory).

[56] *Pravda*, January 8, 1939 (A. Piliyenko, Kiev 'Transsignal' factory).

[57] *Pravda*, January 7 (V. Mikhailov), January 11 (P. Romanov, Barnaul weaving factory).

[58] *Pravda*, January 8, 1939 (E. Zhurkov, Stalin iron and steel works; A. Piliyenko).

[59] Rosenberg and Siegelbaum, eds. (1993): 179–180 (Siegelbaum).

[60] Filtzer (1986): 232.

In particular, the editorial pointed out that work norms in the engineering industry had not been re-examined for two years and were too low; foremen must play an active part in revising them. A general increase in work norms soon followed. But no immediate steps were taken to widen the authority of foremen. It was not until May 27, 1940, that Sovnarkom and the party's Central Committee promulgated a decree 'Increasing the role of the foremen in heavy machine-building factories'.[61] This conceded the demands summarised in the *Pravda* editorial 16 months before, including the right of the foremen to impose sanctions, but dismissal or appointment of a worker still had to confirmed by the head of the shop.

The discussions about both the decree of December 28 on labour discipline and the rights of foremen reemphasised the most serious problem which confronted the central authorities in trying to enforce labour discipline. The general shortage of labour, particularly unskilled labour, meant that managers were very unwilling to dismiss workers; a poor worker seemed better than no worker. No matter how hard the authorities sought to penalize unauthorised absence or lateness beforehand, the temptation to excuse it after the event was overwhelming. The senior ministerial officials to whom factory managers were responsible were themselves willing to overlook the delinquency of a factory director if this was the price of getting the plan fulfilled. This was a major reason for the limited effectiveness of the labour legislation of 1932. The problem was still more acute in the late 1930s, when the increase in the size of the armed forces and the enforcement of the internal passport system narrowed the number of potential recruits to industry in many industrial areas.

The central authorities undertook a series of unprecedented measures to cajole and compel factory managers to come to heel soon after the publication of the decree of December 28. On January 5 an editorial in *Pravda* vigorously criticised the railway depot at Barnaul because its first shift started late on January 2 when workers were absent or turned up late. The editorial blamed the head of the depot for the delay, castigating it as '*against the people and the state*' (the emphasis is as in the original;

[61] *Industrializatsiya 1938–1941* (1973): 121–125. We have not been able to establish to what extent this decree was adopted informally by other industries.

the editorial did not mention the obvious reason for the trouble, this being the morning after the New Year holiday).[62]

The next step in dealing with the managers was taken by L. M. Kaganovich, evidently with the approval of Stalin and Molotov. As the commissar of Heavy Industry, on January 13, he issued an order 'On the progress of the fulfilment of the decree ... of December 28, 1938'.[63] The order bluntly declared:

> some of the heads of factory shops, and of enterprises and establishments, have not got down honestly to the fulfilment of the decree ... and have not applied the measures listed in the decree in relation to absentees and violators of labour discipline. Some miserable managers are afraid to dismiss absentees, relying on the mistaken and harmful notion that if they dismiss an absentee they will allegedly have difficulties with [retaining] the labour force. There are still cases of covering up absentees and people who arrive late by seeking out all kinds of 'justifications'.

The order gave a number of examples and took action against the management of three factories. In the Karl Liebknecht iron and steel works the head of the railway depot was dismissed and sent to trial; the head of the open-hearth shop was dismissed from his post and transferred to a more junior post; and the director of the works was given a formal reproof and warning. Penalties were also applied to managers in a mine in the Kuibyshev coal trust and an iron mine in Krivoi Rog.

On January 15, the day after the publication of the order, a *Pravda* editorial cited it at length and called on trade union and party organisations to support the campaign. In the next fortnight the other supply commissariats, including those responsible for the defence industries, issued similar orders. All the orders were considerably longer than Kaganovich's and nearly all sent at least one director or shop head to trial and imposed lesser penalties on others.[64] No comprehensive data have been available on the result of these measures, but the much sterner

[62] On January 2, 1970, one of the authors unwisely turned up at the Saltykov-Shchedrin Library in Leningrad. The librarians were at work, but the workers had not put the central heating on, and he had to retreat from the cold by lunchtime.

[63] *Pravda*, January 14, 1939 (printed in full in with an accompanying order on time recording).

[64] *Pravda*, January 17, 18, 20, 24, and 27, and February 2 and 3, 1939.

measures adopted on June 6, 1940, were evidently based on a judgement that the orders just described were ineffective.

4 The Eighteenth Party Congress

The eighteenth congress, which met from March 10 to 21, was a substantially new body: most of the delegates to the previous (seventeenth) congress held in 1934 had been arrested and very many executed. Molotov reported at length on the five-year plan on March 14.[65] A large part of his report was devoted to the technological lag of the USSR 'behind the level of contemporary technology'; he warned against 'complacency and conceit'.[66] In his own report, as we have seen, Stalin set the goal of overtaking the main capitalist countries in 10–15 years.[67] Later in the congress Voznesenskii proposed that a 'general economic plan' should be prepared, 'covering several five-year plans, and aiming at a transition from socialism to communism, and at completing the task of catching up and overtaking the capitalist countries economically'.[68]

Molotov did not refer in his report to any of the numerous suggestions made in *Pravda*'s 'discussion pages', and on the following day, March 15, the Politburo, on Stalin's initiative, passed an unpublished resolution which most unusually criticised him for this failure—with the purpose, evidently, of keeping Molotov in his place.[69] In his reply to the discussion on March 17, Molotov referred to this failure as an omission which he would correct, and he discussed the proposals made in the discussion pages at some length. He did not, however, attempt to incorporate any of the proposals in the plan.[70] At the congress itself, as

[65] *XVIII s"ezd* (1939): 282–315.

[66] *XVIII s"ezd* (1939): 296.

[67] *XVIII s"ezd* (1939): 17–18, 27.

[68] *XVIII s"ezd* (1939): 340. On February 22, 1941, following the eighteenth party conference, and on the occasion of the twentieth anniversary of the foundation of Gosplan, the party Central Committee and Sovnarkom announced that Gosplan would prepare 'a fifteen-year general economic plan of the USSR, aimed at carrying out the task of overtaking the main capitalist countries in production per head of population of pig iron and crude and rolled steel, fuel, machines and other means of production, and consumer goods' (*Pravda*, February 22, 1941); the plan covered the years 1943–1957. For details see Zaleski (1980): 207–212.

[69] Khlevniuk (2009): 221.

[70] *XVIII s"ezd* (1939): 494–498.

in previous congresses, many speakers were concerned with presenting their own successes and problems, and called for more resources to be devoted to their own regions.[71] On March 20, at the end of the congress, Molotov presented to the delegates the decisions of the congress commission on the five-year plan, which accepted a number of the suggestions on additions to the plan made during the congress proceedings, and incorporated them in the plan by the simple procedure of slightly increasing the already over-ambitious targets.[72]

The congress was addressed by new people's commissars and other leading officials, including Bulganin, Kosygin, Malyshev, Pervukhin and Tevosyan, none of whom had spoken at the previous congress, and who later rose to become leading figures in the post-war Soviet government. Several of these officials raised important issues. Thus Malyshev, recently appointed Commissar of Heavy Engineering, pointed out that collaborative subcontracting (*kooperirovanie*) among specialised industrial enterprises, which had already become a thorny issue when they all fell under a single commissariat, was a much greater problem now that the enterprises were divided up among many specialised commissariats and other government agencies:

> The growth of our economy and particularly its disaggregation into different people's commissariats has undoubtedly complicated collaborative subcontracting ... Our Gosplan does not so far understand the huge importance of establishing correct collaboration among factories, industries and commissariats and is not undertaking specific steps to assist the commissariats in this task. It is evidently necessary to establish a special agency either attached to Gosplan or—even better—to the Economic Council which would sort out the problem of collaboration and supervision of the correct distribution and utilisation of equipment.

He also suggested that prices should be used to encourage collaborative production and that a special bonus system should be introduced for the same purpose.[73] M. M. Kaganovich, who was at this time Commissar for

[71] For examples of these speeches, see Rees, ed. (2002): 201–205 (E. A. Rees).

[72] *XVIII s"ezd* (1939): 633.

[73] *XVIII s"ezd* (1939): 388. In this context the Russian term *kooperirovanie* is imperfectly translated as 'collaboration'; it also has the more specialised meaning of subcontracting among specialised partners in a supply chain.

the Aviation Industry, and had been responsible for the whole defence industry until it was divided up two months before the congress, also emphasised the issue of coordination among the commissariats; he warned of the risk that, rather than rely on the cooperation of others for intermediate goods such as forgings and electrical equipment, each specialised industrial commissariat would prefer to source them internally, leading to the creation of vertically integrated, self-sufficient conglomerates: 'We do not need commissariat-combines, but mutual collaboration between industries.'[74] Replying to the discussion, Molotov emphasised that a major advantage of the increase in the number of commissariats was that they were closer to the factories. But he also agreed that the Economic Council must 'strengthen its staff and manifest considerably more activity in coordinating the work of the commissariats', and that the staff of Gosplan must also be strengthened.[75]

The need for social discipline was a strong theme of the congress. As we have seen, this included the need to shore up the collective farms against the encroachment of private activities. In his report on the five-year plan, Molotov warned that 'in some cases the interests of the side-line business of the collective farmers have begun to be counterposed to the interests of the kolkhoz, not without the influence of alien and directly wrecking people.'[76] This was a somewhat sinister revival of the vocabulary largely abandoned with the end of the mass repressions. Reporting on agriculture, Andreev reinforced the support of the Politburo for limits on personal livestock and the household plot to be buttressed by forcing collective farmers to work a minimum number of labour days for the kolkhoz.[77] This would place the kolkhoz farmer in the same situation as the industrial worker subject to a minimum working week.

Another feature of Molotov's report was support for increased efficiency neatly combined with defence considerations. He insisted:

> The plan requires a decisive rejection of gigantomania [excessive enthusiasm for large-scale projects] in construction, which has become a real disease with some economic managers; the plan requires a steady transition to the

[74] *XVIII s"ezd* (1939): 438–439.

[75] *XVIII s"ezd* (1939): 494.

[76] *XVIII s"ezd* (1939): 299.

[77] *XVIII s"ezd* (1939): 118–119.

> construction of medium and small enterprises in every branch of the economy, starting with power stations. This is necessary to speed up the rate of construction and the completion of new production capacity, and to disperse new enterprises among the main economic regions of the country.[78]

Many speakers responsible for commissariats and other government departments more strongly emphasised the needs of defence. In a long report about the Red Army, Voroshilov stressed that the capitalist countries, particularly the fascist states, were rearming rapidly, with priority to aviation, and that the USSR in turn must have a 'powerful and unconquerable' army and navy. He described in some detail the growth of the military and human strength of the armed forces since the 1934 congress.[79] L. M. Kaganovich claimed that much had been done in the defence preparation of the railways, but many more defence facilities must be constructed.[80] The famous polar explorer I. D. Papanin had taken over the Chief Administration of the Northern Sea Route from Otto Shmidt shortly before the congress on March 4, at a time when, after particularly intensive repressions of its staff, those of its functions not concerned with transport were being transferred to other organisations (Sect. 3 in Chapter 2). Papanin stressed the great importance of the Northern Sea Route in defence:

> By the end of the third five-year plan it (will become) a normal sea route, enabling a planned link with the Far East. The Northern Sea Route is enormously significant for defence. This very short route is within our internal seas, where we ourselves are the masters and do not depend on anyone. In case of necessity, if an enemy dares to attack us from the West or the East, we will be able, without interference, to transfer large vessels very quickly from one sea frontier of our great Soviet Union to another.[81]

Tevosyan, appointed as the first People's Commissar of Shipbuilding Industry, when that commissariat was established on January 11, attacked the principal leaders of the navy before the repressions, Muklevich and

78 *XVIII s"ezd* (1939): 302.

79 *XVIII s"ezd* (1939): 187–204.

80 *XVIII s"ezd* (1939): 260.

81 *XVIII s"ezd* (1939): 330.

Orlov, together with Tukhachevskii, as agents of fascism who had tried to prove that the Soviet Union did not need a powerful surface navy. He called for the development of ports, approach lanes and dock repair bases, and for the transfer of an increasing proportion of the work of the Khar'kov electro-turbine factory and Elektrosila to shipbuilding. He reported proudly that the production of his commissariat in January and February 1939 had been one-third greater than in the same months of the previous year, and two-thirds greater in defence production.[82]

Other speakers paid particular attention to those aspects of the industries for which they were responsible which were of obvious defence application. In his speech Malyshev explained that the output of machine tools was going to increase by 130% and that their output would become more sophisticated and closer to the American pattern. This led Stalin to make his only recorded interruption of another's speech at the congress:

> *Stalin*: And how are you doing with automatic machine tools?
> *Malyshev*: We are making them. But a small number: 2.5 per cent. They are decisive. They are highly productive. In the third five-year plan the proportion will be doubled to 4.5 per cent.
> *Stalin*: That's not much.
> *Malyshev*: It is small in comparison with America.
> *Stalin*: They are the best machine tools?
> *Malyshev*: Certainly, they are the most productive and most precise machine tools. We are backward here. We must catch up.[83]

Opening the congress with political developments since the previous (seventeenth) party congress, Stalin stressed the growing danger of war, the need for the USSR to strengthen its defences, and Soviet support for victims of aggression; and he condemned the aggressive policies of the fascist powers. But he spoke contemptuously of French and British policy in the face of aggression (Sect. 3 in Chapter 2). Turning to internal affairs, Stalin linked the repressions of 1937/38 with the military danger. He insisted that the party purge of 1933–1936, which had greatly reduced the number of party members, although suffering from 'serious

[82] *XVIII s"ezd* (1939): 420–422.

[83] *XVIII s"ezd* (1939): 386–387.

mistakes', had been 'inevitable and in the main gave positive results'. He conceded that 'undoubtedly we shall no longer have to use the method of mass purges.'[84] While admitting some faults in 1933–1936, however, his main political message was that the repressions of 1937/38 had been entirely justified and that those repressed had been a serious danger to the state. According to Stalin:

> The Trotskyite-Bukharinite clique of spies, murderers and wreckers, grovelling to other countries, are imbued with a slavish attitude of kow-towing to every foreign petty official, and are prepared to serve them as spies.[85]

Such imprecations were repeated hundreds of times by delegates to the congress. And in Stalin's report, errors which he and his immediate entourage had encouraged and fostered were presented as treachery carried out by enemies. Thus he condemned the initial extravagant targets for the second five-year plan in the following terms:

> Some officials of the old staff of Gosplan proposed ... to plan the production of pig iron towards the end of the five-year plan at 60 million tons. This of course was a fantasy, if not worse.[86]

(The targets had been prepared by Rabkrin, the government inspectorate, and supported by Kuibyshev as head of Gosplan, though Stalin did not mention this; see Vol. 4: 43–44).

In the final section of his report, modestly entitled 'Some questions of theory', Stalin also discussed the future of the state under socialism in the light of the external situation. In the Soviet Union, exploiting classes had been eliminated, and this had led some comrades to conclude that 'there is no longer a need for the state, it must die.' But they failed to understand the present international situation:

> This overlooks the fact of the capitalist encirclement and underestimates the role and significance of bourgeois states and their agencies, which are sending spies, murderers and wreckers into our country and trying to look for an opportunity to undertake a military attack on us. It equally

[84] *XVIII s"ezd* (1939): 28.
[85] *XVIII s"ezd* (1939): 26.
[86] *XVIII s"ezd* (1939): 18.

> underestimates the role and significance of our socialist state and its military, punitive and intelligence agencies, necessary to defend our socialist country from attack from outside … All of us Bolsheviks were guilty of this oversight to some extent, all of us without exception. It is certainly surprising that we learned about the spying and conspiratorial activity of the top Trotskyites and Bukharinites only recently, in 1937–8.

Stalin concluded that 'the state will continue if the capitalist encirclement is not eliminated,' and proclaimed a stern message about the war danger:

> The function of the military defence of the country from external attack remains in full, as do the Red Army and Navy, and equally the repressive agencies and the intelligence services, necessary to expose and punish spies and wreckers sent into our country by foreign intelligence … The main task of our state within the country is the peaceful economic, organisational, and cultural and educational work. The sharp blade of our army, and our punitive and intelligence agencies, is not pointing within our country, but outside it, against foreign enemies.[87]

The congress was dominated by the threat of war.

[87] *XVIII s"ezd* (1939): 31–36.

CHAPTER 9

The Economy in 1939: Further Moves to a War Economy

In the first half of 1939, Soviet diplomacy continued to seek security from cooperation with the Allied countries—Britain, France, Poland, and Czechoslovakia—but on terms that the Allies did not find acceptable. The situation continued to deteriorate, and in August the Soviet stance shifted abruptly to close association with Germany. This fateful step opened Germany's road into Poland, launching war in Europe with the Allied powers. At this point the Soviet Union sought to obtain advantage by becoming Germany's co-conspirator. The Soviet agreement with Germany was to share domination over all of Poland and the Baltic region, and so it brought the Soviet Union into the war through a series of military occupations. In 1939 and 1940 the Soviet Union annexed bordering territories from Romania and Poland through the Baltic to Finland.

The Soviet Union's position in the international arena was characterised by dramatic displacement, but in economic trends and policies there were no sudden shifts. Rather, the militarisation of the economy continued in the same direction. In 1938, as we have seen, the production of armaments and investment in the defence industries expanded extremely rapidly. In 1939 the gross value of output of armaments increased by 49% (Table B.13), more rapidly than in 1938. The aircraft industry was the largest sector of the defence industries, producing nearly one-third of all armaments by value.

R. W. Davies et al., *The Industrialisation of Soviet Russia Volume 7: The Soviet Economy and the Approach of War, 1937–1939*,
https://doi.org/10.1057/978-1-137-36238-4_9

1 The Growth of Industry

Taking industry as a whole, the year 1939 was by far the most successful since 1936. At the heart of this development was rapid and consistent growth. The defence industries expanded particularly rapidly, but the light and food industries also grew.

As Table 1 shows, industrial production increased steadily throughout 1939, except for the seasonal decline in the July–September quarter. By October–December, it was 25.5% greater than in the previous quarter, and in the year as a whole, it exceeded the 1938 level by 14.7%. The most rapid expansion was in the machinery and defence industry sector, which increased by 30.6%. The textile, light and food industries expanded more slowly, each by between 8 and 9%.

The expansion of the various capital goods industries was uneven. Coal production, which had stagnated in 1937, and increased very slowly in 1938, increased by 9.7%, from 133.3 to 146.2 million tons. But the production of oil, which had increased very slowly in 1936 and 1937, continued to stagnate in 1939, increasing by only 100,000 tons, from 30.2 to 30.3 million tons. The number of new wells brought into exploitation declined in 1939, as it had in the previous year.[1] But the electricity supply continued to grow quite rapidly, as it had throughout the 1930s; in 1939 it increased by 9.6%. However, production did not increase as much as demand. According to the Gosplan report to Sovnarkom, 'in the most important industrial areas (Moscow, Leningrad), the position with industrial supply [of electricity] has continued to remain tense.'

The most ominous development in heavy industry was the failure of the iron and steel industry. The production of pig iron, crude steel and rolled steel, which was stagnant in 1938, declined in 1939 (Table B.14). The Gosplan report to Sovnarkom frankly described the performance of the industry as 'extremely unsatisfactory'. It was 'one of the most backward industries, impeding the growth of the economy, and especially of machine building and capital construction'. The report complained that capital construction in the industry had been extremely slow: in the two and a half years of the five-year plan so far, from 1937 through June 1940, only 2 open-hearth furnaces, 10 crude steel furnaces, and 7 rolling

[1] New oil wells: *Industrializatsiya, 1938–1941* (1973): 127–145 (Gosplan report to Sovnarkom on the results of the third five-year plan, October 4, 1940).

Table 1 Gross value of industrial production, 1939, by quarters (million rubles and plan prices of 1926/27)

	Quarter 1 (Jan.–Mar.)	*Quarter 2 (Apr.–June)*	*Quarter 3 (July–Sept.)*	*Quarter 4 (Oct.–Dec.)*	*Year in total*
Million rubles					
Armament and machine building	6,079	7,413	7,062	8,356	28,910
Other heavy industry	5,199	6,102	5,582	5,394	22,276
Armament and heavy industry, subtotal	11,278	13,515	12,644	13,750	51,186
Timber industry	831	709	727	732	2,999
Light industry, subtotal	4,321	4,318	4,194	4,686	17,519
Food industry, subtotal	3,654	3,980	3,973	4,930	16,536
Local industry, subtotal	812	661	586	644	2,703
Agricultural procurement	604	558	584	700	2,446
Total	21,500	23,740	22,707	25,441	93,389
Change over the same period in 1938, per cent					
Armament and machine building	25.4	28.9	32.9	34.5	30.6
Other heavy industry	8.2	9.0	9.2	4.6	7.8
Armament and heavy industry, subtotal	16.9	19.1	21.3	20.9	19.6
Timber industry	3.2	8.3	3.7	6.6	5.3
Light industry, subtotal	9.1	9.0	11.0	5.5	8.5
Food industry, subtotal	14.7	12.7	11.7	4.6	10.3
Local industry, subtotal	14.9	17.9	14.1	1.9	12.0
Agricultural procurement	27.7	27.0	14.7	7.5	18.0
Total	14.5	15.8	16.5	13.1	14.9

Source: *Pravda*, April 11, July 12, October 12, 1939, and January 15, 1940 (as Table 3 in Chapter 6).

mills had been constructed, out of the 23, 56, and 34 planned for the five years. Meanwhile the capacity utilisation of existing furnaces was declining.[2]

The situation with non-ferrous metals was more favourable. In the first two and a half years of the third five-year plan, the supply of aluminium increased by 33%, and of copper by 60%. The Gosplan report to Sovnarkom pointed out, however, that this was considerably less than planned, and the production of lead, wolfram, molybdenum and zinc had been particularly delayed because of the slow development of capacity. Gosplan anticipated, however, that production of nickel, mercury, tin and antimony would eventually rise to the amounts proposed in the five-year plan.[3]

The production of some important building materials continued to decline in 1939. The supply of cement amounted to only 5.2 million tons as compared with 5.5 in 1937 and 5.7 in 1938. The supply of bricks and alabaster was also lower than in 1937. But within the total figure for cement, the production of high-grade cement increased from 24% of the total in 1937 to 30% in 1938 and 40% in 1939. The production of wooden and reinforced-concrete components also increased substantially. The increased production of wooden components was based on the general improvement of the timber industry in 1938.[4]

The consumer industries expanded much more slowly than the industries for producer goods. The performance of the different light industries was varied. Cotton textiles increased by only 4.4% in 1939. This was a result of the failure to increase the capacity of the spinning industry. The supply of raw cotton increased far more rapidly, and stocks of raw cotton piled up in consequence. In contrast, the woollen industry, where production increased by only 5.4% in 1939, was held back by a shortage of raw material, partly mitigated by increased use of wool substitutes. The increase in the production of leather footwear by a mere 4.7% was also attributed to shortages of raw materials.[5]

The Gosplan report to Sovnarkom stated that 'the production of meat, bread, vegetable oil and soap has developed in 1938–40 at a rate

[2] *Industrializatsiya 1938–41* (1973): 135–136.

[3] Ibid.: 136–137.

[4] Ibid.: 138.

[5] Ibid.: 138–139.

Table 2 Industrial productivity and wages, 1938–1940 (per cent of previous year)

	1938	*1939*	*1940 (expected)*
Average output per worker	110	113	110.0
Average wage	120	117	109.5

Source: *Industrializatsiya 1938–41* (1973): 144–145 (Gosplan report to Sovnarkom on the results of the third five-year plan, October 4, 1940).

which will generally achieve the fulfilment of the third five-year plan.' The supply of meat by the livestock commissariat had increased in 1939 by 28.8%. But 'the plan for sugar, alcohol, preserved foods and particularly for butter and fish has not been achieved. The main reason for the failure to fulfil the plan for the sugar industry has been the failure to fulfil the plan for the yield of sugar beet and large losses of sugar beet when storing it and of sugar in producing it.' The plan for alcohol had not been fulfilled because of the lack of raw material and also of fuel. The plan for preserved foods had failed because of the lack of tins, and the plan for butter because of insufficient milk. The fish catch and the repair of shipping had both been badly organised.[6]

As in 1938, the growth of industry mainly depended on the increase in labour productivity (growth per person employed) rather than the increase in the labour force. In 1939 labour productivity increased by 13%, slightly more rapidly than in 1938; the average wage increase of 17%, although somewhat lower than in 1938, still outpaced productivity (Table 2). The result was to push up unit costs.

During this period the industrial labour force changed in ways that were seen from above as adverse. The number of all employees (including office workers and technical staff) increased, but the number of manual workers employed in industry declined from 7,922,800 in 1938 to 7,791,400 in 1939.[7] The shortage of industrial labour became acute, and the authorities undertook strenuous efforts to recruit more workers. A commission was established under the Economic Council of Sovnarkom for the 'organised recruitment' (*orgnabor*) of labour from the collective farms, covering the RSFSR, the Belorussian Republic and

[6] Ibid.: 139–141.

[7] Ibid.: 248–251 (report of Gosplan department of labour, August 1940).

Table 3 Organised recruitment of labour, 1938 and 1939 (thousands)

	1938	*1939*
Recruitment outside the province	597	850
Recruitment within the province (excluding Belorussia)	1,099	1,330
Total	1,696	2,180

Source: *Industrializatsiya 1938–1941* (1973), 232–233.

Ukraine. It began work in 1938, and by the end of 1939 it had brought nearly four million temporary recruits from the countryside to industry (Table 3).

All was not for the better, however—at least from the perspective of the state's interests in the labour market. On May 4, 1940, the Economic Council received a critical review of these developments from Gosplan.[8] The review strongly condemned the 'unhealthy competition' in which several people's commissariats competed to recruit from each province, rather than each limiting itself to the province allocated to it. This was partly because many new commissariats had been formed since 1938. Moreover, the recruitment agents sent to the districts were inexperienced, and the labourers recruited were not trained for industrial work. Collective farmers did not like these arrangements when the recruitment system operated as intended, because all those recruited from a province were required to work in a designated commissariat, regardless of varying preferences for different kinds of employment. As a result, many farmers, perhaps a majority, chose to seek outside employment independently of the recruitment system. Finally, many local authorities and kolkhoz chairmen imposed limits on the working of the recruitment system by prohibiting the practice of sending their members far away, such as to the Far East, for years at a time. In short, this was an expensive system that worked badly.

2 The Defence Industries

In 1939 defence production grew at an unprecedented rate, absorbing a greatly increased proportion of industrial activity. Measured in plan prices of 1926/27, the value of output of the defence industry

[8] Ibid.: 237–240.

commissariats grew by 49%, as compared with 37% in the previous year (Table B.13). The building of new plane, tank, and gun factories was of obvious importance to this huge increase, and the growth of capacity of the defence industries in 1939 no doubt reflected the great volume of capital works in the industry in the previous year: 3.7 billion rubles in 1938, compared with 'only' 2.2 billion in 1937 (Table B.9). Capital investment in the defence industry continued to grow through 1939, although at a diminishing rate.

Other factors besides the building of new capacities also contributed to the acceleration of defence output. More was made available to the military by squeezing civilian lines out of defence factories. In 1933, as Table 4 shows, civilian products accounted for nearly half the value of output of the defence industry, and as late as 1936 their share was still more than two-fifths. By 1939, the civilian share was planned to shrink to just 13%, so that nearly all defence capacity would be realised for the supply of weapons.

Another factor that boosted defence output was that the civilian supply ministries were increasingly called upon to supply intermediate products and services to the defence industry commissariats. This is illustrated from a report written for Stalin on June 15, 1939, by Aircraft Industry Commissar M. M. Kaganovich. Detailing the plans of the industry to develop capacities rated at 26,540 aircraft per year, he also listed the requirements. The capital works under way would cost two billion rubles over four years. Existing allocations were insufficient. To the 435 million rubles already assigned to building aircraft factories in 1939 must be added a further 88 million rubles for factories and 25.5 million rubles for workers' housing. Given the additional demands, it was also necessary to dictate additional supplies: building materials for new factories

Table 4 The value of civilian products of the defence industries, 1933–1939 (million rubles in plan prices of 1926/27 and selected years)

	1933 outcome	*1936 outcome*	*1939 target*
Civilian products	1,400	2,774	2,403
Share of defence industry production, per cent	48.2	41.3	13.1

Source Outcomes, 1933 and 1936, from *Europe-Asia Studies*, 49(3) (1997): 403–406 (Davies and Harrison). Target for 1939, calculated from data on the four defence industry commissariats in GARF, 8418/28/13: 134–138, 109–113, 140–151, 85–87.

Table 5 Aircraft produced by type and model, 1938–1939 (units)

	1938	*1939*
Fighters		
I-15bis	1,104	1,304
I-153	–	1,011
DI-6	100	–
I-16	1,175	1,835
Fighters, total	2,379	4,150
Bombers		
DB-1	1	–
SB	1,427	1,778
DB-3	204	555
DB-3F	195	404
Bombers, total	1,827	2,737
Reconnaissance, total	479	523
Trainers, total	2,695	2,675
Passenger and other, total	310	251
All aircraft, total	7,690	10,336

Source Table B.19.

and housing for their workers, 4000 building workers from the GULAG, further electric power supplies and a new power station.[9] It went without saying that these resources would be taken from the civilian economy. Chemical factories supplied nitrates to the ammunition industry, not to the fields as fertiliser. Metallurgical factories supplied steel and nonferrous metals to the defence industry, not to make household agricultural implements or household goods. Machine-building factories produced tanks and planes, not tractors or bicycles.

Measured by the value of output at plan prices, the aircraft industry was by now the largest of the defence industry commissariats (Table 5). As in 1938, its output expanded particularly rapidly, by 51.8%. Capital investment in the industry, which had doubled in 1938, was scheduled to grow further, particularly after the boost to rearmament agreed on February 5 (Table B.9), but the outcome probably fell short of the plan, and in practice but much of the expansion proceeded by the conversion of existing factories from civilian to military lines. In production, the main emphasis fell upon combat aircraft. The largest increase was in fighters,

[9] *Istoriya OPK Rossii*, 4 (2015): 338–342 (M. M. Kaganovich to Stalin, July 15, 1939).

the number of which increased by 75%, while the number of bombers increased by 50%. The production of reconnaissance aircraft expanded slowly, and the production of training and passenger aircraft declined.

As important as the numbers produced was their quality, and particularly how this compared with the rapid progress of German and Japanese industry. Soviet fighters varied greatly in quality. The I-15b biplane, which entered production in 1937, was greatly improved by 1939. It could reach 379 kilometres per hour at a height of 3500 metres; its maximum altitude was 9300 metres, and its maximum range was 520 kilometres. A new variant, the I-153, designed by Polikarpov, went into mass production in 1939, and was used successfully against the Japanese in Mongolia in July. But biplanes were now outdated, and the I-15 and its variants were the last of their kind. The future lay with monoplanes. One such was the I-16, first produced as long ago as 1934. Despite many modifications, the I-16 now lagged behind others. By 1939, according to one report, when powered by an M-62 or M-63 engine, its maximum speed reached 462 to 489 kilometres per hour, but this was already slower than the German Messerschmitt fighter.[10] Another report rated the I-16 Type 10 as superior to the Japanese equivalent, but only below 500 metres; above this height it was inferior. Unlike the Japanese plane that it was matched against, it lacked a radio.[11]

As in 1938, the two bombers in mass production were the SB fast bomber and the DB long-distance bomber. The SB began mass production in 1936, and in 1939 as many as 1778 were produced. At 419 to 450 kilometres per hour when flying at 4000 metres, the 1939 version was faster than its predecessor, with a higher ceiling and a longer range. A major defect was its lack of defensive armour. The DB-3, equipped with an M-87 engine from the end of 1938, under the name of *Moskva*, or TsKB-3, became world-famous on April 28, 1939, when V. K. Kokkinaki and M. M. Gordenko flew from Moscow to the United States, landing near New York after a nonstop flight of almost 23 hours. In 1939 the military version was produced in several variants, including the torpedo-carrying DB-3T, which could be launched from water.

Until 1939 a serious gap in the industry's profile was the absence of a dive-bomber for attacking troops on the ground. In January 1939

[10] OPK, 4, 464–485 (Malenkov to Stalin, January 23, 1940).

[11] *Samoletostroenie*, 1: 162–165.

Il'yushin produced an armoured dive-bomber, the TsKB-55. Ground-tested during the summer, it was successfully flight-tested by Kokkinaki on October 2. A second model, the Il-2, was flown in December. In Germany, Focke-Wulf and Heinkel also produced dive-bombers in 1939.

As the year ended, the first Chief Administration of the Commissariat of the Aircraft Industry issued a report on the state of the industry.[12] The report concluded: 'We are considerably behind the German industry.' Soviet fighters and bombers were slower than equivalent German airplanes. The armament of fighters and of the DB-3 bomber was comparable with German equivalents, but the SB bomber had lighter armament. The range of bombers was similar; the range of fighters fell short by up to 200 kilometres. The Soviet Union did not mass-produce dive-bombers, and produced seaplanes only in small numbers and with low speeds. In Germany more than 30 factories were equipped for batch production; in the Soviet Union there were only eight, and repair facilities were much less developed.

The number of tanks produced increased rapidly in 1939, reaching 3107. The T-26 and BT-7 light tanks continued to predominate, increasing by as much as 239%. In 1939 the fire power of the T-26 was substantially increased, and the tanks began to be equipped with radio.[13] In 1939 the velocity and fire power of the BT-7 was also greatly increased, and the tank was produced in a number of variants.[14] As for small tanks, 158 T-28s were produced in 1939, but the T-27, first produced on a large scale in 1936, was about to give way to the more advanced T-40, the first examples of which were produced in the spring of 1939. At the end of the year, the Dodge engine was replaced by the Soviet GAZ-202, and the new tank was ready for mass production by December 19.[15]

The number of T-28 medium tanks produced in 1939 increased from 100 to 140, the largest number in any one year (Table 6). The tank was equipped with the L-10 76.2 mm gun, reported to be a great improvement on the KT-28 which preceded it.[16] But the most important development with medium tanks was the emergence of the T-34, which would prove to be perhaps the most successful Soviet tank design of the

[12] OPK, 4, 447–459 (January 17, 1940).

[13] Baryatinskii (2007): 78.

[14] Ibid.: 119–120.

[15] Ibid.: 52

[16] Ibid.: 160.

Table 6 Tanks produced by type and model, 1938–1939 (units)

	1938	*1,939*
Small tanks		
T-38	–	158
Light tanks		
T-26	1,054	1,399
BT-7/7M	1,221	1,402
Medium tanks		
T-28	100	140
T-34	–	2
Heavy tanks		
T-35	11	6
Total	2,386	3,107

Source Table B.20.

Second World War. On February 27, 1939, Factory no. 183 in Khar'kov submitted two versions of a tank then named the A-20 to the Committee of Defence, one being half tracked and the other fully tracked. In July and August both versions underwent factory tests; they were demonstrated to the military on September 23. It was decided to strengthen the armour of the tracked version, and on December 19 this version was adopted by the army, and renamed the T-34.

The year 1939 saw considerable experimentation with heavy tanks. Only six T-35s were produced; but at the same time three experimental tanks were produced in very small numbers. Each was tried out in the 'winter war' of 1939/40 between the Soviet Union and Finland. The SMK, named after Sergei Mironovich Kirov, and a product of the Kirov factory, was destroyed immediately after going into action on December 19. The T-100, produced at Factory no. 183, made great efforts to rescue the SMK and its crew. It was eventually decided not to proceed with either of these tanks.[17] The KV, named after Defence Commissar Kliment Voroshilov, and also produced at the Kirov works, was completed in August, and underwent factory tests in October, Like the SMK and the T-100, it was sent to the front in December, where it performed much more successfully than the other two.[18] More than 1500 KVs and

[17] Ibid.: 271.

[18] Ibid.: 272.

more than 15,000 T-34s would be produced from 1940 to the turning point of the Soviet-German war at the end of 1942.[19]

In the course of 1939 the capital investment plan, although originally set below the plan for 1938 (Table B.6), was substantially increased as follows:

- March 31: 184 million rubles for various purposes including expansion of the Baikal-Amur mainline railway.[20]
- May 3: 105 million rubles to the industry for construction materials.[21]
- May 19: 17.8 million rubles to the iron and steel industry.[22]
- June 10: 80 million rubles to the aero-engine industry, 22 million rubles of which was set aside for workers' housing.[23]
- June 26: 38.5 million rubles for defence construction by the Communications Commissariat, including investment in the Far East.[24]
- July 4: 119 million rubles for defence construction in the chemical industry.[25]
- September 19: 71.5 million rubles to the Construction Commissariat to cover shortage of working capital up to June 1.[26]

The total increase of over 600 million rubles was not achieved. In 1939, as in previous years, realised investment fell far short of the target, amounting to 30.7 billion rubles, an increase of only 4.7% as compared with 1938. Investment in the defence industries also fell short of the target. However, it still increased by 20% as compared with 1938, from 3.7 to 4.5 billion rubles (see Table B.9). The additional allocations to investment, as we have seen, were mainly defence related, and their net effect

[19] Harrison (1985): 250.
[20] RGASPI, 17/162/25: 12–16.
[21] RGASPI, 17/3/1008.
[22] RGASPI, 17/3/1008.
[23] RGASPI, 17/162/25: 53.
[24] RGASPI, 17/162/25: 78.
[25] RGASPI, 17/162/25: 81.
[26] RGASPI, 17/3/1014: 19–20.

was to increase the investment in the defence industries both relatively and absolutely.

Throughout 1939, as in the previous two years, the Politburo devoted a great deal of attention to defence, adopting over 40 decisions on defence matters. These ranged from major decisions about the size of the armed forces to detailed decisions about the armaments to be produced by particular factories. As before, the aircraft and aero-engine industries received most attention.

One of the most important meetings took place on April 27, when the Politburo approved a range of decisions on the aircraft industry.[27] First, it approved the programme to produce the DB-240. Molotov and M. M. Kaganovich were instructed to secure the supply of personnel and materials to the factory concerned so that the first three planes would be produced by April 1, 1940; the M-105 engines would be replaced by the more advanced M-120.

Secondly, the Yakovlev R-12 would be produced in both a reconnaissance and a bomber version. Three reconnaissance planes would be produced by November 1; the drawings for the bomber version would be completed by June 6 so that the first bomber could also be produced by November 1. Both versions would go into batch production at Factory no. 81.

Thirdly, seven PS-35s were to be supplied to the civilian aviation industry in the second quarter of 1939; this was a twin-engined passenger plane designed by Tupolev, who was now employed in a design bureau of the NKVD as an imprisoned 'enemy of the people'.[28] At least four Douglas aircraft were to be produced at the same time in Factory no. 84.

Finally, the meeting approved the proposal to attempt an international record by means of a 5000-kilometre flight from Moscow to Sevastopol', Sverdlovsk, and back to Moscow.

Six weeks later, on June 10, the Politburo approved a similarly wide-ranging programme for the aero-engine industry.[29] Five factories were to be built or rebuilt in 1939 and 1940. Production of the M-88 engine was to begin in Factory no. 24, leading to its batch production

[27] RGASPI, 17/162/25: 26–27.

[28] The document (previous footnote) refers to '7 shtuk "BS-35"', most likely a typographical error.

[29] RGASPI, 17/162/25: 52–54.

in place of the M-62 and M-63 in the second quarter of 1940. Factory no. 27 in Kazan' was to be completed by 1940, with a capacity of 6000 engines. But the core of the programme was the decision to develop the production of aero-engines in the East, where six new factories were to be established, with a rated capacity of 27,000 engines. As mentioned above, additional capital investment was allocated for this purpose amounting to 80 million rubles. Arrangements were made to import machine tools valued at 31.5 million rubles between October 1939 and March 1940, and to supply 2719 Soviet machine tools, building materials, and petrol. Workers on the programme were to be freed from call-up to military service in 1939 and 1940. The 6000 workers employed from the GULAG at Factories no. 19 and no. 336 were to continue until the factories were completed, and 4500 engineers and technicians were to be supplied by the GULAG for Factories no. 26 and no. 27.

The Soviet defence industry was enormously expanded by all these measures. It was also much more fully focused on military products. Table 4 showed that the share of military products in the output of the defence industry (in plan prices) was pushed up from just over half in 1937 to 87% in the 1939 plan. But in 1939 defence production was now so large that the value of its civilian lines was still much greater than in the early 1930s and fell below the peak of 1936 only by a small fraction.

3 The GULAG Economy

With the ending of the mass operations at the end of 1938, the NKVD economy entered a short period of relative stability. The number of arrests fell sharply, and the number of detainees increased only slowly, by 27,000 from the first of 1939 to the first of 1940.[30] The problem was now to overcome the crisis condition of production. This task fell to L. P. Beria, the new people's commissar of Internal Affairs, who replaced Yezhov (soon to be arrested and shot) in November 1938. Yezhov's legacy was a badly disrupted camp economy. The NKVD was unable to fulfil its production quotas, given the high rates of mortality and disability of the detainees and the mass arrest of camp officials. The new NKVD leadership had no more important task than to show Stalin its organisational competence and capacity to achieve new economic successes.

[30] GARF, 9414/1/1155: 2.

Among Beria's first proposals was the establishment of a Special Technical Bureau (Ostekhbyuro), approved by the Politburo on 8 January 1939, and implemented two days later by an NKVD decree. The bureau's purpose was 'to utilise detainees having specialised knowledge and experience for the design and bringing into production of new types of military and naval armament.' Beria himself would direct the Ostekhbyuro.[31]

The structure of the bureau illustrates its main activities. There were groups for aircraft, aero-engines, naval shipbuilding, explosive powders, guns and shells, armour steel, chemical weapons, and chemical defence.[32] On April 1, the Politburo assigned 36 million rubles to Ostekhbyuro activities. The budget was for design work on airplanes and aviation diesel engines, a torpedo boat, submarines, and the development of explosive powders and chemical weapons. There was also funding for transmitter-receivers for long-distance aviation record attempts, and for heavy bombers.[33] To illustrate, one of the Ostekhbyuro's sub-units was TsKB-29 (Central Design Bureau no. 29). This bureau held the leading Soviet aviation designers, led by A. N. Tupolev, who had been detained in 1937 and 1938.[34]

In contrast to the work of Ostekhbyuro, which depended on small numbers of detained specialists, the achievement of the vast NKVD construction plans required the raw labour of hundreds of thousands of able-bodied prisoners. To find these amongst the camp population was not straightforward. A GULAG report prepared in January 1939 shows only 70% of the 1,130,955 detainees in work. One in ten were sick or disabled; others could not work for lack of clothing.[35] In April 1939 the overall shortage of camp labour was reported as around 10% (143,000 persons).[36]

[31] RGASPI, 17/162/24: 80, 97; GARF, R-9401/1a/32: 12–13; see also *Istoriya Stalinskogo Gulaga*, 3: 443–444. V. A. Kravchenko was appointed chief of the Ostekhbyuro on November 11, 1939 (RGASPI, 17/3/1016: 5).

[32] *Istoriya Stalinskogo Gulaga*, 3 (2004): 445–450 (report of work of the Ostekhbyuro, 1939–1944).

[33] RGASPI, 17/162/25: 4–5. The decision was formalised by the Sovnarkom defence committee (GARF, 8418/28/65: 100).

[34] GARF, 8131/32/4002: 32–34; Ozerov (1971).

[35] GARF, 9414/1/1140: 118.

[36] GARF, 9414/1/1140: 38–41; *Istoriya Stalinskogo Gulaga*, 3 (2004): 158.

Meanwhile, the NKVD was burdened by new assignments. In early March 1939 the year's plan of capital works was increased by 517 million rubles.[37] On March 31 the Sovnarkom and the Central Committee assigned a further 280 million rubles to NKVD for vast railway projects in the Far East.[38] As of April 1939, NKVD was responsible for building defence-related railways and highways, military airfields, the Archangel shipyard, three pulp and paper combines, five pulp mills, the dredging of the Amur, the completion of the Kuibyshev and Rybinsk hydro power projects, design of the Solikamsk hydro power station, and building the Noril'sk combine. The timber procurement quota stood at 51 million cubic metres. Prisoners were mining gold in the Kolyma, working on farms, and manufacturing consumer goods.[39]

Noting the obstacles to the achievement of these immense ambitions, Beria put a number of far-reaching initiatives before the administration. On April 9, 1939, he wrote to Prime Minister Molotov that conditions in the camps would prevent the NKVD from achieving its objectives. A particular problem that he noted was the 'low satisfaction' of prisoners' needs for food and clothing. The basic allowance of 2000 calories per day, he wrote, was based on maintaining a prisoner in the cells, not at work. In fact the prisoners received only 65 to 70% of the allowance. In consequence, a significant proportion of GULAG's workforce 'falls into the category of enfeebled and productively useless people'. On March 1, Beria reported, there were 200,000 detainees in camps and colonies classed as enfeebled; labour utilisation on average across the GULAG population stood at no more than 60 to 65%. He requested the government to approve higher rations.

Beria went on to attack the system of early release which had previously been an important incentive for prisoners to work hard. Under this system prisoners sentenced for non-political crimes, who were judged to work conscientiously, could be considered for early release. This, Beria considered, was a factor in 'the exceptionally high turnover of the camp workforce', adversely affecting the organisation of production cycles and

[37] Decrees of Sovnarkom and the Central Committee in GARF, 5446/1v/503: 27–28 (March 2, 1939), and 5446/1/152: 344–346 (March 4, 1939).

[38] GARF, 5446/1v/503: 73–78. The Politburo approved the decree on March 30 (RGASPI, 17/162/25: 4, 12–16). See also Elantseva (1995).

[39] GARF, 5446/23a/76: 6.

of camp production as a whole.' He proposed an end to early release: 'the convicted person should serve their sentence in full.' Exceptions might be made, but only for 'the highest achieving producers, who deliver high work indicators over long intervals'. Even this exception would be largely nullified by a lengthy bureaucratic process of application for early release: the NKVD board or special assembly would have to approve a joint request of the camp commandant and chief of the camp's political department. The basic incentive to effort, Beria argued, would have to be improved supplies of food and other goods, cash benefits, and a lightening of supervision. Not relying solely on rewards, the new people's commissar also proposed to increase punishments:

> to apply harsh measures of compulsion to absentees, shirkers, and disrupters of production—intensified camp supervision, punishment cells, reduced supplies, and other measures of disciplinary action. To the most malicious disrupters of camp life and production, to apply still harsher judicial measures, in some cases up to and including the supreme penalty [execution]. To publicize all uses of these interventions widely among the camp inmates.[40]

Two weeks later, on April 24, Beria wrote to the government again. This time, he claimed that to fulfil the 1939 programme, the NKVD would require more than 1,550,000 camp workers, compared with 1,264,000 actually on hand; the latter number excluded those classed as disabled, but included 150,000 'enfeebled and partially able workers'. He reported the problem as particularly acute in the Far East, where the workforce numbered half a million compared with the 680,000 to 700,000 required. To manage the growing tensions, Beria proposed not to add to the capital construction plan for 1939, but to cease the subcontracting of GULAG workers to other agencies, and to withdraw some of those already subcontracted to focus their work on NKVD projects.[41]

As was customary, the NKVD proposals were circulated to other interested agencies for their agreement. There was no real opposition to the increases in GULAG rations and funding for GULAG.[42] Controversy

[40] GARF, 5446/23a/121: 6–9; Khlevniuk (2004): 201–203.

[41] GARF, 5446/23a/76: 7–9; also Khlevniuk (2004): 203–204.

[42] GARF, 5446/23a/70: 29–30.

raged, in contrast, over the ending of early release and the introduction of the death penalty for work indiscipline. These ideas were resisted by USSR chief prosecutor Vyshinskii and People's Commissar for Justice Rychkov. They objected that early release was written into the law, that its prospect was a positive influence on discipline and productivity, and that it should be rationalised rather than ended. As for the death penalty, they argued that even 'malicious disrupters' should not be executed unless they had committed crimes for which the criminal code prescribed the death penalty.[43]

The arguments of the judicial authorities found support within the administration. On June 7, Molotov chaired a meeting of his deputies, with Beria present, and it was resolved to curtail discussion of Beria's two proposals (to end early release and bring in the death penalty for indiscipline).[44]

Beria's response to this setback remains unknown. Most likely, he appealed to Stalin personally and enlisted his support. This was all the easier, given that in August 1938 Stalin himself had voiced opinions on early release similar to Beria's. When the presidium of the Supreme Soviet reviewed the early release of detainees who had done outstanding work on a particular project, Stalin commented:

> Is it right that you've proposed a list of these prisoners for release? They'll leave work. Can't you think of some other way to value their work—medals, and so on? We're doing this wrong, we're disrupting the work of the camps. These people have to be released, of course, but it's bad for the business of the state ... Can't you work around this so that these people remain at work, perhaps give them medals or decorations? So we let them go, and they go home and they mix with criminals again and they go back to their old ways. It's a different atmosphere in the camps, it's hard to go wrong there ... Let's not confirm this proposal today, but require the NKVD to work out some other measures that will make these people stay in their place.[45]

Considering Stalin's views, it is no surprise to find that the Politburo eventually supported Beria. A Politburo resolution of June 10, 1939,

[43] GARF, 5446/23a/121: 2–5.

[44] GARF, 5446/23a/121: 1.

[45] GARF, 7523/67/1: 5.

'On the NKVD camps', repeated Beria's proposals of April 9 word for word, including the ending of early release and the institution of harsher punishments including execution for cases of indiscipline. The government was charged with reviewing GULAG allowances for food and clothing.[46] The legal aspects of early release and punishment for indiscipline were then covered by a decree of the Presidium of the Supreme Soviet 'On the NKVD camps', dated June 15. And on July 4, the government's Economic Council confirmed new food and clothing allowances for detainees in camps and colonies. These new allowances also matched the NKVD proposals, with only trivial alterations.[47]

Beria's other proposals of April 1939 were also adopted. On June 17 the Sovnarkom adopted a resolution on the provision of labour to NKVD projects. The NKVD was authorised immediately to cease new allocations of detainees to work on the projects of other agencies and, from the first of 1940, to take back all prisoners previously contracted out in this way. The NKVD was also empowered to transfer 120,000 prisoners to the Far East.[48]

The NKVD failed only in Beria's demand for stability in the plan. After being boosted by more than half a billion rubles in March 1939, the NKVD plan for capital works was then further inflated by a similar additional sum, so more than a billion in total. By the end of the year, the plan was one-third larger than at the beginning.[49] The expansion reflected both the enlargement of established projects and the addition of new ones. Investments in Dal'stroi and in the Noril'sk metallurgical combine were substantially increased. The volume of the NKVD's railway construction activities became so large that on January 2, 1940, the Politburo authorised the NKVD to set up a new Chief Administration for Railway Construction.[50]

The growth of NKVD capital works, at a time of relative stability of the camp population, inevitably complicated the business of NKVD management. Meanwhile, the promises extracted from the government with

[46] RGASPI, 17/162/25: 54–55; Getty and Naumov, eds. (1999): 549–550.

[47] GARF, 5446/23a/70: 31–41, 64–65. For the decree of the NKVD of August 14, 1939, establishing new nutritional and clothing norms, see *Glavnoe upravlenie lagerei* (2000): 476–489.

[48] GARF, 5446/1/503: 4–6.

[49] GARF, 5446/24a/18: 73.

[50] RGASPI, 17/3/1018: 20.

such difficulty, regarding extra funding and the withdrawal of detainees from work for other agencies, were, as usual, only partly kept.

The prisoners' new food rations, approved from the fourth quarter of 1939, were not matched by additional funding. The camps' new food requirements substantially exceeded the supplies allocated. Of the supplies allocated, only a part reached the prisoners, much being lost in transit, spoiled, or stolen. GULAG medical department reports for 1939 show that the camps were poorly supplied with meat, fats, and vegetables.[51] The situation was no better with regard to clothing. Although most camps were located in hostile climatic conditions, a significant proportion of inmates lacked appropriate clothing, especially for deep frosts. The GULAG supply department recorded that in 1939 it received only 73.5% of the leather footwear required, and only 25.8% of felt boots.[52]

The situation of the camp inmates remained grave. On the positive side, mortality in 1939 ran at half the level of the previous year. The NKVD authorities complained continually, however, that a substantial proportion of the prisoners remained unfit for work. Beria's deputy, Chernyshev, reported to the government on September 14 that 50,000 of those detained in camps and colonies were registered as disabled and up to 150,000 as 'partly fit', meaning that they were at the final stages of exhaustion or seriously ill.[53] Despite the prisoners' exhaustion, they were worked ever harder, and this led in turn to their irreversible disability or death. A GULAG order of September 16, 1939, noted attempts of 'some camps' to fulfil quotas 'mechanically' by 'forcing detainees to work for 14 to 16 hours to meet the latest production norms, and also organising work on rest days'. Such a policy, the order declared, 'will lead to the exhaustion of the camp inmates, to rising morbidity, and, in the final outcome, to underfulfilment of plan quotas'.[54]

The hope of making up the numbers of detainees working on NKVD projects by withdrawing from work for other ministries also failed. The Sovnarkom resolution of June 17, mentioned above, infringed on the interests of other powerful economic agencies, which were accustomed to drawing freely on GULAG resources and could not quickly replace

[51] GARF, 9414/1/2989: 84–85.

[52] GARF, 9414/1/2989: 101–104.

[53] GARF, 5446/23a/70: 77.

[54] GARF, 9414/1/24: 195.

them by hired workers. The government was flooded with complaints and lobbies that sought to keep prisoners at work on various projects. Many of these appeals found support. The commitment to withdraw prisoners from outside contracts by the first of 1940 was broken, and the practice continued.

November and December 1939 saw the beginning of the process of reconciling production plans for 1940. It became clear that various targets for 1939 would be substantially underachieved. The value of NKVD capital construction in 1939 would be 3.6 billion rubles, or 83.7% of the planned 4.3 billion rubles. The value of industrial production would be 87.5% of the plan. Timber procurement and coal deliveries were lagging. The extraction of chemically pure gold by Dal'stroi in 1939 reached 66.6 tons, compared with 79.9 tons in the plan (which was much too ambitious, given that in 1938 the achieved level was only 62 tons).[55] A major factor here was the rapacious extraction methods used in previous years, which had quickly exhausted the richest deposits. Remaining deposits were contaminated or otherwise unfavourable for industrial exploitation. Over the years from 1932 to 1937, the extraction of one kilogram of pure gold required shifting 168 cubic metres of soil on average. In 1938–1940 the average rose to 245 cubic metres. Mechanisation, which would have helped, remained at a low level, and the utilisation of the equipment available also remained low: 50–60% on average, and 37% for diggers. The emphasis fell on hand labour.[56]

In order to excuse the plan failures of 1939, the NKVD leadership invoked the substantial inflation of the plan of capital works within the year, and the shortages of labour, equipment, and supplies.[57] Alongside such factors, the documentary record shows that another cause was the ineffective use of GULAG labour and its low productivity. A Gosbank report compared the efficiency of the investment process in the hands of the NKVD, using forced labour, and of the Construction Commissariat with its hired employees. For every ruble invested, GULAG projects accomplished one-quarter of the construction and installation work that was done by the Construction Commissariat. Equipment use indicators in the GULAG were also worse: one-third of the Construction

[55] GARF, 5446/24a/49: 52.

[56] Shirokov (2014): 152, 156.

[57] GARF, 5446/24a/18: 71–73.

Commissariat's level of use of building machinery, and one-half for vehicles.[58] But both the mobilisation character of the Soviet economic system, and the rapid build-up of production as the Second World War broke out, ensured that the forced labour economy would not only be preserved; it would also continue to expand.

4 Internal Trade and Consumption

Official reports suggest that urban living standards continued to improve in the last years of the 1930s. According to the data they relied on, average wage earnings of manual and office workers rose from 3047 rubles in 1937 to 4054 in 1940, that is, by exactly one-third. Between the two years, the official index of prices in state and cooperative trade increased by less than 20%.[59] But this measure cannot be relied on for a full picture. On Janet Chapman's estimate, the state and cooperative trade price index rose by at least 26%. Other prices rose faster. Charges for services in Moscow increased by 42% over the same period. In the collective farm markets, where unsatisfied demand spilled over the state and cooperative stores, unregulated prices doubled. In sum, she found, the cost of living for urban households was 36% higher in 1940 compared to 1937. Inflation thus wiped out the gain of nominal earnings.[60]

After making some allowance for trends in the countryside, Chapman estimated a decline in real household purchases of all goods and services per head of the population from 1937 to 1940 by 4%; this figure did not change when communal services were brought into account. For the years 1937–1939, Robert Allen found a 6% decline (Table B.48). This pattern is generally consistent with other trends described in this volume: in the last pre-war years the harvest was never as good as in 1937, while in 1938 and 1939 rearmament encroached particularly on the metal-using industries that were being converted from civilian machinery and equipment to the supply of weapons.

[58] RGAE, 7733/36c/220: 30.

[59] Malafeev (1964): 407.

[60] Chapman (1963): 81 (prices of services in Moscow); 87 (cost of living, urban USSR and all markets); 97 (collective farm market prices); 157 (state and cooperative trade). The figures that we give are those based on quantity weights of 1940, which are slightly more favourable to the trend of real wages. Chapman's figure for the increase of nominal earnings (1963: 109) was the same as that of Malafeev (1964): 107.

Table 7 Energy consumption from food: survey-based estimates for the mid-1920s and late 1930s (calories per person per day)

	1925/26–1926/27 average	*1937*	*1938*	*1939*
Wheatcroft (2009)				
Peasant households	3,039	2,175	2,311	2,360
Manual worker households	3,792	2,637	2,679	2,696
Nefedov (2012)				
Peasant households (February)	2,981	2,373	2,682	2,614
Manual worker households (October or November)	2,626	–	2,756	2,764

Source Table B.49. 'Peasant households' refers to individual family farm households in the 1920s, and to collective farm households in the late 1930s.

For living standards, it is likely, however, that the comparison is too favourable to 1937, and so overstates the subsequent deterioration. For most of 1937, households suffered from the food shortages that resulted from the failed harvest of the year before. Much of the fine harvest of 1937 was first accumulated in grain stocks and in cattle, with benefits to human consumption that were at first delayed and then flowed through to human consumption in 1938 and 1939 (Sect. 8 in Chapter 4). This is what we find when we consider food consumption measured directly (Table 7). As the table shows, Wheatcroft and Nefedov agree that 1938 was better than 1937 in calories per head for both peasant and manual worker households, and that the trend of the late 1930s was basically flat.

In the 1930s the authorities did not only survey households for food consumption; they also gathered data on money incomes and outlays. These too are revealing (Table 8). The concept of disposable income that we use in the table is total household money income after deducting state loan subscriptions and membership dues, such as trade union levies, which were generally deducted from wages before payment. The underlying magnitudes are nominal, so no account is taken of changing prices or purchasing power. Three categories of household are distinguished, based on the main earner: manual workers, office workers, and engineering and technical workers (ITR). For some reason office worker households were not surveyed from 1935 through 1938. Still, with 1934 as the benchmark year for all three groups, it is possible to reach two conclusions.

Table 8 Relative incomes and non-food consumption of urban households, 1934 and 1937–1939 (per person and per cent)

	1934	*1937*	*1938*	*1939*
Disposable income, per cent of manual workers				
—Manual workers	100	100	100	100
—Office workers	137	–	–	142
—Engineering and technical workers (ITR)	161	138	131	126
Non-food consumption, per cent of disposable income				
—Manual workers	39.6	40.9	40.9	40.8
—Office workers	39.1	–	–	47.2
—Engineering and technical workers (ITR)	45.0	46.1	46.6	44.5

Source Calculated from Table B.50; non-food consumption is disposable income less outlays on food and dining.

First, the table identifies the main losers from the consumption squeeze of the late 1930s as the engineering and technical workers (ITR). In 1934 there was a clear hierarchy: the average office worker household received 37% more disposable income per person than the average manual worker household, and the average ITR household 61% more. By 1939 the office-worker income differential persisted as it was or had widened slightly. In contrast, the position of ITR households had declined substantially; they now received less on average than the office-worker households. On balance, therefore, the technical specialists were the losers.

Second, while the table shows nominal magnitudes, it is possible to use them as a cross-check on real incomes by applying the concept of the Engel curve. The nineteenth-century German statistician Ernst Engel first proposed that spending on items other than food tends to increase more than in proportion as real disposable income rises. Other things being equal, therefore, changes in the share of non-food consumption in household budgets should follow changes in income. Here, 'other things being equal' is an important qualifier: over time, the consumption choices of Soviet households were shaped by the unpredictable appearance and disappearance of goods in government shops, and by rapidly changing prices in the kolkhoz markets.

In the hope that something survived of Engel's law even in the Soviet Union, Table 8 also reports the proportions of income not spent on food across households and over time. The table shows that the share of non-food outlays in manual worker households' disposable income was stable at around 40% from 1934, the year of recovery from the famine of the time of collectivisation, through the late 1930s.[61] In itself, this argues against any upward trend of urban consumption. As for other categories of household, we see that over the same period office worker households substantially increased their shares of non-food spending. ITR households, in contrast, showed no improvement.

In 1939, as in 1938, the purchasing power of households arising from public sector employment increased more rapidly than the supply of goods and services from the public sector. This happened despite measures taken to manage the growth of unsatisfied demand by raising state retail and wholesale prices, a setback for the previous policy of seeking price reductions where possible. On January 5, 1939, a decree of Sovnarkom and the party's Central Committee introduced higher retail prices for cotton, woollen, linen and silk fabrics, and for knitwear and clothing. The bulk of these goods were produced by the Commissariat of Light Industry, and their prices were increased by an average of 38%; the prices of cooperative industry were increased by a smaller percentage. In 10 department stores in Moscow, Leningrad, Khar'kov, Kiev, and Minsk prices were increased by an additional 10%. Simultaneously higher prices were introduced for a variety of previously loss-making industrial consumer goods, and prices were adjusted in order to make scarce and high-quality items more profitable. Lower prices for children's clothes were cancelled. Across 43 provinces and republics, the total value of the higher prices was put at the large sum of five billion rubles.[62]

More increases followed. A Sovnarkom decree substantially increased postal charges with effect from February 6. Letters sent within a town now cost 15 instead of 10 kopeks, and letters to places outside a town

[61]This proportion was close to those observed in British working-class households in 1904, when 1904 skilled, semi-skilled, and unskilled British households spent 40, 38, and 34% of their household incomes on food (*Economic History Review*, 68(1) (2015): 106 (I. Gazeley and A. Newall)). There are many uncontrolled variations in the settings of British and Soviet households, however, not limited to differences in relative prices of commodities. Soviet household preferences differed from those of British households for both cultural and climatic reasons. Soviet households also faced multiple prices of commodities and some commodities were unavailable at official prices, or at any price.

[62]The decree is published in *Istoriya tsenoobrazovaniya* (1973): 84–85. See also Malafeev (1967): 213–216, and Kondrashev (1956): 122, 130.

30 instead of 20 kopeks; the postal charge for newspapers increased from two to three kopeks.[63] A further Sovnarkom decree promulgated before the eighteenth party congress increased rail freight charges with effect from April 1. In 1937 railway income per ton-kilometre averaged 2.0 kopeks, while costs stood at 2.17 kopeks. To cover the losses, charges were increased by 14% for distances up to 50 kilometres, while for longer distances a planned reduction of charges by 70 to 75% was amended to 45% (special rates for the Ural-Kuznetsk combine were, however, retained).[64] From November 16, 1939, the retail prices of vodka, liquors and wine were increased.[65]

The January measures alone were expected to take the large sum of five billion rubles out of household purchasing power.[66] But this was far from sufficient and, despite all the price increases, the gap between household incomes from the public sector and the value of goods and services that the public sector made available to households in 1939 widened further to 23.5 billion rubles, compared with 19.2 billion the year before (Table 9). Corresponding to the real spending gap was a monetary gap: the quantity of money growth accelerated to 29% (from 27% the year before) (Table B.47). There were no further efforts to soak up the excess of purchasing power by levying taxes, by borrowing from households (which was done at the time in a way that amounted to taxation), or by taking in saving bank deposits, which even declined.

As a result, the signs of general scarcity of goods in the market increased. The NKVD reported in the spring of 1939 that in Moscow during the night of April 13–14, queues of 33,000 people formed before the shops opened and that on April 16–17 the number had reached 44,000.[67] In April–May 1939 the Politburo issued decisions on 'the

[63] SP (1939), no. 15: art. 89 (February 1).

[64] SP (1939), no. 25: art. 159 (March 5).

[65] *Istoriya tsenoobrazovaniya*, 1 (1973): 578.

[66] The decree was preceded by a lengthy memorandum from the Economic Council to Sovnarkom and the Central Committee explaining the reasons for the decree and its consequences (*Istoriya tsenoobrazovaniya* (1973), 1: 567–573); we estimate the value of the price increases from this memorandum.

[67] Osokina (1998): 228. The pattern of decline in consumer supplies is supported by much statistical and personal description of growing shortages at the time; see also Osokina (1998): 206–218 and Hessler (2004): 240–243.

Table 9 Money incomes and outlays of the Soviet population, 1938–1939 (million rubles)

	1938	*1939*	*Change*
Household incomes			
Incomes from the public (state and cooperative) sector			
—Wages	112.5	138.3	25.8
—Other incomes	43.3	49.4	6.1
Incomes from the public sector, subtotal	155.8	187.7	31.9
Incomes from private (household) activity			
—Kolkhoz market incomes	11.8	15.7	3.9
—Other incomes	4.5	4.4	−0.1
Incomes from the private sector, subtotal	16.3	20.1	3.8
All incomes	172.1	207.8	35.7
Household outlays on goods and services			
Outlays on public sector products			
—Goods	124.1	148.0	23.9
—Services	12.5	16.2	3.7
Public sector goods and services, total	136.6	164.2	27.6
Outlays on private sector products			
—Kolkhoz market goods	11.8	15.7	3.9
—Private services	4.5	4.4	−0.1
Private sector goods and services, total	16.3	20.1	3.8
Outlays on goods and services, total	152.9	184.3	31.4
Other uses of household incomes			
Subscriptions to public organisations	1.3	1.7	0.4
Share contributions to cooperatives	0.1	0.4	0.3
Taxes and other payments	7.4	9.5	2.1
Acquisition of state loans	5.4	6.1	0.7
Savings bank deposits, increase	1.5	1.0	−0.5
All outlays	168.6	203.0	34.4
Public sector incomes, less outlays on public sector goods and services	19.2	23.5	4.3
All incomes, less all uses of incomes (net cash accumulation)	3.5	4.8	1.3

Source Tables B.43 and B.44, abbreviated and rearranged.

struggle with queues for industrial goods in shops'.[68] In the course of the year the shortages spread to foodstuffs sold by the state and cooperative sector. Visitors to the Belorussian countryside in the summer of

[68] Osokina (1998): 231.

1939 reported that 'there were no sugar, matches, kerosene, industrial consumer goods, or vodka.'[69]

There were several further consequences. The first effect was that unsatisfied demand spilled over from the regulated state sector into the unregulated collective farm markets, where the volume of trade increased only slightly, but prices increased on average by 25% (Table B.46).[70] Potatoes nearly doubled in price. Such price increases protected farmers at the expense of the non-farm population. From the point of view of the macro-economy, higher kolkhoz market prices had a further effect: they raised the demand for money generally, and so helped to reduce the quantity of it that was supplied in excess of demand. Most likely, some excess supply of money remained, and the final outcome was an increase in the rate of accumulation of households' unspent cash: 4.8 billion rubles in 1939 (compared with 3.5 billion in 1938).

5 The Soviet-German Accord

The international effects of the German occupation of Czechoslovakia in March 1939, in violation of the Munich agreement, had profound consequences throughout Europe. For Britain and France, it ended the era of appeasement. These countries now made guarantees to Poland that made war inevitable if Hitler could not be deterred from further territorial encroachments.

In his last days as Soviet foreign minister, on 18 April, Litvinov had proposed a full alliance to the British government. Chamberlain himself put little faith in the military capabilities that the Soviet side would bring to an alliance, and regarded Stalin as no more trustworthy than Hitler. Litvinov's proposal was at first rejected, but a persistent minority within the British cabinet favoured an Anglo-Soviet alliance in principle, and their view gained steadily ground through the summer, eventually becoming a majority.[71] In deference to the majority, the British returned to talks with the Soviet government on 24 May. Chamberlain, however, remained sceptical of the value of a Soviet alliance; in a private letter to

[69] Man'kov (2001): 225.

[70] See also *Istoriya tsenoobrazovaniya*, 1 (1973): 579–580.

[71] Hill (2010): 48–84.

his sister on July 7, he remarked that he did not consider the British position 'greatly worsened' if the attempt failed.[72]

The negotiations that followed were inconclusive. On the British side, one of the sticking points was the Soviet demand for freedom of action against 'indirect aggression' from the Baltic countries. Soviet disquiet at the state of the negotiations was indicated on June 29 by an unprecedented public statement by Zhdanov, which he presented as his personal opinion, concluding that 'the English and French do not want a real agreement acceptable to the USSR.'[73] This had been true: the agreement that the British now wanted would have been unacceptable to Stalin, because it aimed in principle to preserve the independence of the smaller countries of the region. It was also certain to fail in practice, because it aimed to deter Germany from a course of aggression on which Hitler was already determined. But it is also possible that the British negotiations were certain to fail because Stalin prolonged them only to exert leverage on Germany. Consistent with this, as the British side conceded on one point, the Soviet side hardened on another.

The British were content to drag negotiations out, wrongly believing that Stalin would refuse a deal with Hitler for as long as an Anglo-Soviet treaty was in prospect. Chamberlain's last throw was an Anglo-French military mission, which travelled slowly and arrived in Moscow on 11 August with strictly limited authority to negotiate a treaty, but not to conclude it. (On the positive side, the British representative, Admiral Reginald Drax, was one of the Royal Navy's foremost strategists and a determined opponent of appeasement.)[74]

At this moment Hitler, eager to neutralise the Soviet Union before attacking Poland and bearing in mind his expectation of a wider war with Britain and France, made a firm offer of German-Soviet cooperation. On August 14, while the Soviet talks with Britain and France stood still, the German ambassador in Moscow, Schulenberg, was instructed to inform Molotov that in the German opinion there was no question which could not be resolved to the satisfaction of both Germany and the Soviet Union. He should offer to bring German Foreign Minister von Ribbentrop to Moscow to conduct negotiations. On August 20 Hitler

[72] Haslam (1984): 224; for the negotiations in detail, see pages 215–226.

[73] *Pravda*, June 29, 1939.

[74] Maiolo (1998): 126–132.

followed this up with a personal message to Stalin, appealing to him to receive Ribbentrop to agree a non-aggression pact and a secret protocol defining spheres of interest.[75] These were duly signed on August 23. Less than two weeks later, Europe was at war.

The failure of the talks on a Soviet alliance with Britain and France marked a turning point, but the consequences were perhaps not as great as is sometimes thought. Were they a lost chance to avert war? Perhaps not, because, after the occupation of Czechoslovakia, Hitler was already determined to attack Poland, and all that remained was for him to create the most favourable circumstances for the attack.[76] Given a wider war in the West was reasonably sure to follow, however, he would wish to avoid a wider war in the East at the same time, and this opened up the surprising option of a German-Soviet rapprochement.[77]

If the failure did not necessarily bring about the wider war, it did ensure that for two years Hitler was able to wage war with the Soviet Union's active support, rather than without it. Thus, the reasons for their failure are of considerable importance.

Historians have generally concluded that one side or the other negotiated in bad faith. But which side? Did Stalin, through Molotov, continue to work sincerely towards an Anglo-French alliance through the early summer of 1939, abandoning those efforts at the last moment only in the face of British duplicity? This was the interpretation that Stalin offered on September 7, 1939. Summing up his reasons for the turn towards Germany in conversation with Dimitrov, he suggested that collective security had been his fundamental preference and that only the circumstances created by the British and French were to blame for its failure:

> We preferred agreements with the so-called democratic countries and therefore carried out negotiations with them. But the English and the French wanted us for farmhands [Stalin used the Russian term, *batrak*, for a hired farm labourer] and at no cost![78]

[75] Haslam (1984): 226–227.

[76] Weinberg, *Foreign policy*, 2 (1980), 578–583.

[77] Gorodetsky (1999): 4.

[78] Dimitrov (2003): 116.

If this was how it was, then Stalin could hardly be blamed for the eventual breakdown of the international order.

Alternatively, was Litvinov's dismissal back in April the signal that Stalin had already moved his orientation away from the democracies towards cooperation with Germany? In that case, the countdown to war had already begun, because Hitler was determined to attack Poland, and Stalin would not only not stop him, but would help him. This would have meant it was Stalin who negotiated with the British and French in bad faith, using the talks only to increase his advantage in the negotiation with Germany that would follow. Stalin provided some support for this view as well. In July of the following year, he suggested to Stafford Cripps, the British ambassador, that he had come to see German and Soviet interests as fundamentally aligned:

> The USSR had wanted to change the old equilibrium ... but that England and France had wanted to preserve it. Germany had also wanted to make a change in the equilibrium, and this common desire to get rid of the old equilibrium had created the basis for the rapprochement with Germany.[79]

As for the documents more recently available, historians have looked for support on both sides. Some scholars have maintained the traditional Soviet view that Stalin continued to work for collective security and an Anglo-French alliance through the summer of 1939, and abandoned the cause only at the last minute in the face of a lack of seriousness on the British side.[80] Others have concluded that, for a variety of reasons, Stalin formed a definite preference for an agreement with Hitler early in 1939.[81] As the historian Jonathan Haslem came to see it,

> Litvinov's ouster [on May 3] meant the rejection of collaboration with the Western democracies on any terms other than those that explicitly sanctioned the expansion of Soviet influence, and with it military power, into Eastern Europe. Stalin rejected the multilateral and collective security

[79] Cited by Weinberg (1994): 25.

[80] Carley (2000); *Europe-Asia Studies*, 52 (2000): 695–722 (Watson).

[81] Pons (2002); Biskupski, ed. (2003) (A. Cienciala); *Otechestvennaya istoriya* (2005), no. 1 (S. Z. Sluch).

> approach to international relations in favour of 'spheres of influence' (a euphemism for military and ideological domination).[82]

On August 23 the Soviet-German non-aggression pact and secret protocol were duly signed. The protocol declared that 'in the event of a territorial and political transformation', in the Baltic states, the northern frontier of Lithuania would be the dividing line between the spheres of influence of Germany and the USSR. It set out the division of Poland between Germany and the USSR, while leaving the question of the continuing existence of Poland for future decision. It also stated that the USSR was interested in Bessarabia (at present, part of Romania), and that Germany was not interested in South-East Europe, generally.[83] The German side made clear that Finland, although not mentioned in the protocol, would come under the influence of the USSR.

Germany soon resolved the fate of Poland. It invaded Poland on September 1, and in consequence, Britain and France declared war on Germany on September 3. The Soviet Union waited until it was clear that Poland had been defeated, and on September 17 it seized those parts of Poland which were allocated to it in the secret protocol. On September 28, the secret protocols of the pact were revised to give Lithuania to the Soviet Union; in return, Germany took a larger share of Polish territory. In September and October, the Soviet Union forced non-aggression treaties on Lithuania as well as on Estonia and Latvia, which allowed for Soviet troops to be stationed on their soil.[84]

Stalin soon presented himself as adhering to the German camp in the war between Western Europe and Germany. On November 30, 1939, he published in *Pravda* a bitter riposte to the French news agency Havas:

> (a) It was not Germany which attacked France and England, but France and England which attacked Germany. taking on themselves the responsibility for the present war.

[82] Gorodetsky, ed. (1994): 58 (J. Haslam).

[83] *Documents on German Foreign Policy*, D-7 (1956): 245–246 (Treaty of Non-aggression between Germany and the Union of Soviet Socialist Republics, August 23, 1939) and 246–247 (Secret Additional Protocol, the same day).

[84] On the implementation and revision of the secret protocols, see Kasekamp (2010).

(b) After the start of hostilities Germany offered peace proposals to France and England. The Soviet Union openly supported the peaceful proposals of Germany, as it considered and still considers that the rapid end to the war would fundamentally assist the situation of all countries and peoples.
(c) The ruling circles of France and England rejected both the peaceful proposals of Germany and the attempts of the Soviet Union to bring about the most rapid end to the war.[85]

By this time the Soviet Union had already embarked on negotiations with Finland with the aim of weakening Finland's strong defences on its Eastern border. The negotiations broke down, and on the same day as Stalin's pro-German statement, the Soviet Union invaded Finland. Finnish resistance proved strong. Agreement on Soviet terms was signed between the two powers only on March 12, 1940. In between, there was much bloody fighting and hundreds of thousands of casualties, predominantly on the Soviet side. The performance of the Red Army was so poor that in the middle of the campaign, on January 7, Stalin dismissed Voroshilov as head of the armed forces and replaced him with Timoshenko.

Alongside the implementation of the Molotov-Ribbentrop Pact, the Soviet Union and Germany embarked on a new phase of economic cooperation. The two countries concluded a credit agreement (for 200 million Reichsmarks) just before the pact on August 19, 1939. The pact was followed by bilateral agreements of February 11, 1940, and January 10, 1941 for trade valued in total at up to 1.3 billion Reichsmarks on each side over two and a half years.[86] By the time of the trade agreements, Germany was at war in the West, and its economy was blockaded at sea so that its import requirements were correspondingly urgent. On March 30, 1940, Hermann Göring instructed his economic officials that Soviet raw materials were now so vital that German exports to the Soviet Union must be given priority over deliveries to the Wehrmacht.[87]

[85]This declaration greatly upset Western sympathisers with the Soviet Union, including one of the present authors, then a strongly antifascist and pro-Soviet fourteen-year old …

[86]For the texts of these agreements see Ericson (1999): 227–240.

[87]Ericson (1999): 112–113.

The result was to open the Soviet economy, all but closed in the years before 1939, to a sudden rush of trade with Germany (see Table 10; for the situation before 1939, see Sect. 9 in Chapter 4). In the eighteen months from the beginning of 1940 through the first half of 1941, the Soviet Union supplied Germany with 1.6 million tons of grain, 1.2 million tons of timber, and nearly one million tons of oil. At an annual rate, these deliveries placed burdens on total Soviet availability that were modest (if non-trivial): 0.9, 3.8, and 1.7% respectively. These three commodities made up 83% of Soviet exports to Germany by volume (but not necessarily by value). In addition, the Soviet Union also delivered substantial quantities of chemicals and rare metals including manganese, chromium, asbestos, phosphates, and glycerine.

The two sides that made the Soviet-German accord shared certain values: in domestic politics, authoritarianism; in economics, mercantilism in economics; in international relations, self-aggrandisement. But these values did not bring their leaders into sympathy or common purpose. To that extent, the treaty was (in modern terms) 'transactional', so that each side was in it for what it could get. The same applied to the economic agreements that accompanied the re-division of Eastern Europe.

There is no doubt that, by opening up the trade with Germany, Soviet leaders aimed for a two-sided gain: by exporting the goods that were relatively abundant in the Soviet economy, while importing those that were relatively scarce, to reduce the overall tensions on the Soviet side while allowing the German side to profit by just enough to bind the potential enemy into the alliance, at least for a time. In the moment, the German economy gained a significant boost to its war potential. The historian Stephen Kotkin notes,

> Stalin had staked Soviet security on France's fighting capabilities, then contributed mightily to France's defeat ... in 1940, the Soviets would supply 34 percent of German oil, 40 percent of its nickel, 74 percent of phosphates, 55 percent of manganese ore, 65 percent of chromium ore, 67 percent of asbestos, and more than 1 million tons of timber and grain.[88]

But in the long term this was not enough to keep Germany in the partnership, which Hitler broke within less than two years, at a time when the Soviet side was still working hard at its economic treaty obligations.

[88] Kotkin, *Stalin*, 1 (2017): 768.

Table 10 Soviet trade with Germany in selected commodities, September 1939 to June 1941, compared with Soviet output in 1940 (thousand tons and per cent)

	Total trade, Sept. 1939 to June 1940	*Trade at annual rate*	*Soviet annual output, 1940*	*Trade, per cent of Soviet output at annual rate*
Soviet exports to Germany, total	4,541.2	–	–	–
Of which, matched goods				
—Grains	1,611.1	878.8	95,496	0.9
—Timber	1,227.6	669.6	17,400	3.8
—Oil	941.7	513.7	31,121	1.7
—Meats	5.5	3.0	1,501	0.2
—Vegetable oil	9.4	5.1	798	0.6
Unmatched goods	745.9	–	–	–
Soviet imports from Germany, total	5,421.1	–	–	–
Of which, matched goods				
—Coal	5,119.5	2,792.5	165,923	1.7
—Tubular steel	175.8	95.9	966.1	9.9
Unmatched goods	125.8	–	–	–

Note Unmatched exports are those that cannot be matched to reported Soviet output in 1940, because of either nomenclature or the unit of measurement: textiles, rags, animal skins, pulses, oilseed cake, manganese, chromium, asbestos, phosphates, and glycerine. The unmatched exports amounted to 16.4% of Soviet exports to Germany by weight, and probably more by value. Unmatched imports are machinery, iron and steel tools, motor vehicles and aircraft, raw chemicals, electrical goods, optical equipment, metals, and naval equipment. The unmatched imports accounted for 2.3% of Soviet imports by weight, and again probably more by value. Various difficulties with the source material hinder systematic evaluation of the unmatched exports and imports in the currencies of either country.

Source Ericson (1999): 198–199, gives major Soviet exports to Germany from September 1939 to June 1941 (22 months) and major German exports to the USSR year by year from 1938 to June 1941. Total trade is calculated from the source; Soviet imports therefore include those delivered between January and August 1939, but the difference is not significant because so little trade took place in that period. Trade at the annual rate is then calculated as total trade divided by 22 months (disregarding the extra months included in the import totals) and multiplied by 12 months in the year. Where the product nomenclature can be matched, annual Soviet output in 1940 is taken from archival sources cited by Harrison (1996): 195–199, except grain for which we use the barn yield figure shown in Table 7 in Chapter 7. The Soviet figure for timber output, given in cubic metres, is converted to tons at the rate of 500 kilograms per cubic metre. Annual output is divided into trade at annual rate for the percentages in the right-hand column.

What was gained from the 22 months of trade with Germany? Whether the Soviet Union benefited economically from the 22 months of trade with Germany is an open question. While we know roughly the commodities that were traded, we lack the scarcity prices at which they should be valued. Indeed, the Soviet decision makers themselves lacked the scarcity prices that would have allowed them to judge the profitability of the trade. Not surprisingly, the currency in which the bilateral agreements valued the Soviet-German trade was the German Reichsmark; no one thought of the Soviet ruble, a currency that was both inconvertible and of arbitrary value, as a useable yardstick.

Given the urgency of German war requirements, the Soviet side should have been able to secure favourable terms. By volume, the imports that the Soviet Union received from Germany were made up almost entirely by 5.1 million tons of coal, and this added 1.7% to the total of coal available in the Soviet economy (Table 10). But in the late 1930s Soviet official transfer prices valued black coal at 36.25 rubles per ton, making the entire coal import quota worth less than 200 million rubles to the domestic economy. In contrast, the domestic grain price of 225 rubles per ton made the Soviet export of grain alone worth more than 350 million rubles.[89] Thus, if the trade with Germany is to be counted as 'profitable' in the sense of yielding a net surplus to the Soviet side at domestic prices, all the gain must be found in the relatively small-scale exchanges of Soviet chemicals and rare metals for German machinery and equipment. Based on present knowledge, the best summary remains that of Edward Ericson: 'gas and grain for coal and cruisers', understanding gas (in the American sense of motor fuel) as the end-product of Soviet oil, and that there was only one German cruiser, the *Lützow*, supplied without guns.[90]

During 1940 enormous changes took place in the map of Europe. German forces invaded Norway and Denmark in April, and France and the Low Countries in May. Western Europe was now under the control of the Nazis.

In Eastern Europe, the spheres of influence envisaged in the secret protocols of the Molotov-Ribbentrop pact were revised and finalised

[89] Harrison (1996): 199 (black coal), 264 (grain).

[90] Ericson (1999): 109.

in June 1940, when Stalin ordered the annexation of the three Baltic republics. At the same time, the Soviet Union annexed the Romanian territories of Bessarabia and Northern Bukovina, which were reconstituted as the Soviet Republic of Moldavia. With the exception of Northern Bukovina, all these territories had once been parts of the Russian Empire, and the Soviet Union now got them back.

At the time of these events in Europe, the Soviet Union also secured its Far Eastern flank against Japan. Since the Japanese annexation of Manchuria in 1931, the Soviet Union and the Japanese Empire had shared a common border. This border was a focus of continuous tension, while the Japanese leaders considered the 'northern' option of expansion into Siberia (Vol. 4: 80–81, 166–167, 278–279, 332–333, 358–360) and probed Soviet defences from time to time.

For Soviet-Japanese relations, 1939 saw two decisive events, both in August, one military and the other diplomatic. The military event was the culminating battle of Khalkhin Gol (termed the 'Nomonhan incident' in Japanese history), an engagement on the Mongolian border with Japanese-controlled Manchuria that involved tens of thousands of troops and hundreds of tanks and airplanes. In August, while Molotov and Ribbentrop negotiated their agreement, a Soviet army led by Georgii Zhukov, then an army corps commander (lieutenant-general) crushed the attacking Japanese force. Zhukov's victory changed history as much as any of his later triumphs: after it, Japan's leaders no longer hoped to expand their empire into Siberia at the expense of the Soviet Union. The diplomatic event was the Soviet-German accord itself, by which Germany violated the terms of its existing alliance with Japan. The Japanese understood from it that they could not count on German cooperation if they pursued the border conflict with the Soviet Union. The Soviet Union's military and diplomatic successes, which occurred simultaneously, precipitated the resignation of the Japanese cabinet. Its successor transferred Japan's diplomatic efforts to restoring relations with both Germany and the Soviet Union. Meanwhile, its military efforts shifted away from the 'northern' route of expansion into Siberia to the 'southern' option: the softer targets presented by the weakly defended British, French, and Dutch colonies in South East Asia.[91]

[91] Paine (2012): 146–148.

As the risk of outright war receded, Soviet-Japanese relations were normalised to the point where, in April 1941, Molotov received the foreign minister of Japan in Moscow and the two signed a Soviet-Japanese pact of neutrality. Unlike the accord with Germany, the agreement with Japan would last until the closing days of the Second World War.

CHAPTER 10

The Soviet Economy: The Late 1930s in Historical Perspective

In eight volumes and a million words, we have narrated the development of the Soviet economy since 1928. The first of these volumes was the concluding instalment of the *History of Soviet Russia*, the great project begun by E. H. Carr after the Second World War.[1] That volume fixed the starting point for the industrialisation of the Soviet Union, at that time a country of thousands of factories and millions of farms, barely recovered from seven years of foreign and civil war, its economy strained between plan and market, pushed and pulled by a autocratic, modernising regime with shallow roots and vaulting ambitions.

In the present series, *The Industrialisation of Soviet Russia*, Volumes 1–3 narrated the dramatic transformations that Stalin set in motion in 1929 and 1930: the collectivisation of 25 million peasant farms, and the centralisation of the entire economy under a hierarchy of plans and quantitative controls. These changes were aimed at securing the basis of a vast effort to industrialise the country and modernise its economic and military power. While great steps were now taken towards these goals, the immediate result was a crisis of vast dimensions that spread across both town and countryside. In the context of unexpected harvest shortfalls in 1931 and 1932, Stalin's policies brought about a famine

[1] Carr and Davies, *Foundations*, 1 (1969).

R. W. Davies et al., *The Industrialisation of Soviet Russia Volume 7: The Soviet Economy and the Approach of War, 1937–1939*,
https://doi.org/10.1057/978-1-137-36238-4_10

that carried away up to six million lives. The evolution of the crisis was recounted in Volumes 4 and 5.

In the middle years of the decade—that is, from 1934 to 1936—the crisis receded. The harvest returned to a more normal level in 1933, and this was followed by a more general recovery. The recovery was promoted by a turn away from the extremes of 1929 and 1930. The more moderate policies of the mid-1930s included greater toleration of private farming and food markets, the limitation of repression and violence directed at managers and industrial specialists, and a more stable, predictable policy framework. This allowed not only the recovery of agriculture and food distribution but also the belated completion of many projects begun in earlier years. There was an upsurge of industrial production and productivity. The progress of this period, described in Volume 6, was remarkable.

On Western and post-Soviet measures of the Soviet Union's real national income, by 1939 the aggregate real output of the Soviet economy was twice that of the same territory in 1913. The natural increase of the Soviet population would no doubt have been slowed over the same period by the decline of fertility that normally accompanies economic growth, but wars, famine, and terror held it back additionally. By 1939 real output per person was 60% greater than in 1913 (Table 1). But the comparison of two years separated by a quarter century does not reveal the pattern of growth, which was extremely unsteady. The figures for output per person show no growth from 1913 to 1932 and almost no growth from 1937 to 1939. The entire increase of output per person recorded between 1913 and 1939 was squeezed into the five years that began from the low point of 1932, after the failed harvest of that year, and ended in 1937 as the circle of repressions widened. Without those five years, there would have been no growth for a quarter of a century.

In 1937, as narrated in the present volume, the upsurge was suddenly halted, and progress was barely resumed by the outbreak of the Second World War. Certainly, economic expansion could not have been sustained for long at the pace of the mid-1930s. Not only was it vulnerable to the weather, as the harvest failure of 1936 demonstrated; it was now disrupted by the things that we have described: terror, mass killings, and accelerated mobilisation for war.

What did it all mean? This chapter reflects on the wider significance of these events. We will consider and briefly evaluate the pattern of Soviet industrialisation, the measures of its progress that were made available at

Table 1 Soviet real GDP and mid-year population, 1913 and 1928–1940

	1913	*1928*	*1929*	*1930*	*1931*	*1932*	*1933*	*1934*	*1935*	*1936*	*1937*	*1938*	*1939*
Population, million	134.8	153.2	156.1	158.6	160.8	162.4	159.8	157.5	159.2	161.3	164.0	167.0	170.2
Gross domestic product at 1937 factor cost													
Billion rubles	112.9	123.7	127.0	134.5	137.2	135.7	141.3	155.2	178.6	192.8	212.3	216.1	229.5
Rubles per head	837.6	807.7	813.8	847.9	853.0	835.7	884.0	985.5	1,122.2	1,195.2	1,294.5	1,293.9	1,348.2

Source Population is from Andreev, Darskii, and Khar'kova (1993): 118, who give totals for January 1 each year, here converted to mid-year; the figure for 1939 is based on the January 1 figure extrapolated to mid-year based on the population movement from 1939 to 1940 within post-war frontiers. GDP for 1928 to 1939 is from Moorsteen and Powell (1966): 623, extrapolated back to 1913 on the basis of figures for 1913 and 1928 given in the *Journal of Economic History*, 71(3) (2011), 672–703 (A. Markevich and M. Harrison). Finally, GDP per head is GDP divided by population.

the time and subsequently, the extraordinary militarisation of a mobilised society and economy, the emergence of the Soviet Union as a global military power, and the reformability of the economic system that Stalin created. Concluding, we will ask what kind of economic development this was.

1 Forced Industrialisation

In the late nineteenth and early twentieth centuries, the Russian Empire experienced rapid industrial growth. For the quarter-century from 1883/87 to 1909/13, industrial production expanded at 4.5% annually, compared with 3.3% for national income over the same period.[2] Despite the pace of industrial expansion, in 1913 only 15% of the population of the empire lived in towns, and less than 9% of the working population (within interwar Soviet frontiers) was employed in industry.[3] Thus, imperial Russia's market economy continued to retain a very large share of labour resources in agriculture. A sign of disproportion was that value added by Russian industry in 1913, expressed as a share of national income, was 21.4%, more than twice industry's employment share.[4] Under the standard assumption of diminishing returns to labour, a considerable gain could have been made by accelerating the movement of workers into industry, but this gain was not realised.

Several hypotheses have been identified to account for Russia's relatively low level of industrialisation prior to the First World War. Alexander Baykov argued that industrialisation was delayed by the distances separating Russia's mineral resources from markets and labour and by poor internal communications.[5] According to Alexander Gerschenkron, the rigidity of rural institutions such as the peasant commune endowed peasants with inalienable land rights, and with collective responsibility for the obligations arising, and so created an incentive to retain labour in agriculture.[6] Subsequent scholarship suggested that

[2] Gregory (1982): 133.

[3] Urban population: *Rossiya 1913 god* (1995): 23 and industrial employment: based on numbers given in Davies, ed. (1990): 251.

[4] Gregory (1982): 73.

[5] *Economic History Review*, 7(2), (1954): 137–149 (A. Baykov).

[6] Postan and Habakkuk, eds., 6(2) (1966), 706–799 (A. Gerschenkron). Gerschenkron wrongly maintained that (for this reason) the labour productivity of Russian agriculture

the restrictions on peasant movement may not have been as binding as Gerschenkron supposed. Peasants were more than capable of working around the limits of the law, and were able to exchange land rights, engage in both local and distant markets for hired labour, and ultimately, leave the land altogether.[7] It could not be assumed, however, that the peasants could do these things freely or that the workarounds did not come at a cost.

Other evidence suggests that agrarian markets were not fully efficient. The serf emancipation of 1861 raised agricultural productivity everywhere, but by a smaller margin where the repartitional land commune was entrenched. The Stolypin land reforms of 1906 were followed by sharp increases of both peasant migration and agricultural productivity, further evidence that the supplies of both food and labour from agriculture were previously limited by the communal land tenure that Stolypin aimed to undermine.[8] At the same time, the experience of the First World War indicates that, as labour was mobilised from agriculture, peasants tended to reallocate effort in favour of land that was held communally, despite its lower productivity there, for the sake of the associated land rights and social insurance.[9] For these reasons it remains plausible to think of Russian agrarian institutions as a brake on industrialisation.

Other limitations on industrialisation before the Bolshevik Revolution have been identified on the side of industry. Various mechanisms gave incumbent firms the power to raise profits by restricting output and raising prices, and also by restricting employment and reducing wages. These included legal obstacles to incorporation, the lack of legal obstacles to the formation of cartels that restricted competition at home, and tariff barriers that limited foreign competition.[10] Thus, Russia's

stagnated over the last quarter of the nineteenth century; for discussion see Kingston-Mann and Mixter, eds. (1991): 131 (Wheatcroft).

[7] Gregory (1994): 49–52; *Explorations in Economic History*, 47(4) (2010): 381–402 (S. Nafziger).

[8] The serf emancipation: *American Economic Review* 2018, 108 (4–5): 1074–1117 (A. Markevich and E. Zhuravskaya). The Stolypin reforms and migration: *Journal of Development Economics* 2014, 110: 191–215 (E. Chernina, P. Castañeda Dower, and A. Markevich); and productivity: Castañeda Dower and Markevich (2018), working paper.

[9] *Review of Economics and Statistics* (forthcoming) (Castañeda Dower and Markevich).

[10] Barriers to incorporation: Gregg and Nafziger (2016), working paper. Cartels: Mathias and Postan, eds. (1978); 477–482 (M. C. Kaser). Tariffs: *Journal of Economic History*, 27(4) (1967): 460–477 (A. Kahan). See also discussion of obstacles to Russian industrialisation before 1913 in the *Review of Economic Studies*, 84(2) (2017): 613–649 (A. Cheremukhin, M. Golosov, S. Guriev, and A. Tsyvinski).

business institutions are also a plausible source of frictions impeding industrialisation.

These findings suggest Russia's industrialisation could have been accelerated by policy reforms aimed at both industry and agriculture. Consolidation of the Stolypin land reforms could have encouraged a land market and easier migration from the countryside. Legal reforms could have given private businesses easier access to the benefits of incorporation, making the capital market more competitive. In product markets, a competition policy could have discouraged collusive price setting. The reform of commercial policy could have liberalised foreign trade. With an easier supply of labour, subject to fiercer competition, Russia's industries would have grown more rapidly still, despite making lower profits, and would have employed more workers, despite paying higher wages.

In the outcome, the Soviet economy achieved its industrial breakthrough by other means. All obstacles to the the supply of labour to industry disappeared in the early 1930s, when millions of peasants were driven from the countryside by famine. The mechanism and the extent of its success were unintended, and the famine was accompanied by a return to restrictions on agrarian labour mobility (Vol. 4: 290–291). As for the obstacles on the side of industry, these too were overcome by compulsion. The state imposed compulsory quotas on producers and overrode cost constraints on output by guaranteeing financial losses, and the quotas forced output to higher levels.[11] Industrialisation was violently accelerated. Between 1928 and 1940, the real growth of Soviet civilian industry was around 10% per year, and that of the defence industries was much higher than that.[12] By the time of the 1939 census, 33% of the population lived in towns (up from 15% in 1913), and 19% of the employed population (up from 9%) worked in industry.[13]

The forced industrialisation of the 1930s achieved a 'Great Breakthrough'. It changed the structure of the economy abruptly, pushing up the shares of industry in output and employment. The rush of labour up the productivity gradient from agriculture to industry should

[11] As argued by Allen (2003): 91–94.

[12] Civilian industry: various Western estimates, summarised by Davies, Harrison, and Wheatcroft (1994): 292. Defence industry: *Europe-Asia Studies*, 49(3) (1997): 374 (Davies and Harrison).

[13] *Vsesoyuznaya perepis' naseleniya 1939 goda* (1992): 22 (urban population share), 96 (industrial share).

have improved allocation in the economy as a whole; it should have raised output per head across the economy, more rapidly in agriculture than in industry. But the outcome was different: it reduced productivity in both agriculture and industry, so that the overall results fell far short of expectations.[14] In the period of the first five-year plan, there was industrialisation without growth (Table 1).

Taking a longer view, the damage to productivity is not hard to understand. The working arrangements of all economic systems rely on incentives and norms of behaviour. The Bolshevik Revolution destroyed the old incentives and norms and struggled to replace them with new ones. Private property was confiscated in successive waves from the Revolution of 1917 to the collectivisation of peasant farms, launched at the end of 1929. The waves of confiscation destroyed incentives to work, to save, and to innovate. The famine of the early 1930s arose from the interplay of unexpectedly poor weather with the confiscation of grain stocks to meet the needs of industrialisation. Famine and the repression that accompanied it, destroyed millions of lives. Later in the 1930s, the purges arose from the party leaders' need to secure their regime and from Stalin's calculation that the greatest danger to the regime arose from the 'potential' and even 'unconscious' enemies that were hiding around him and more widely in society. The purges also destroyed millions of lives by mass killing and ruined further millions by condemning the victims not killed at once to forced resettlement and slave labour. Their legacy, like that of collectivisation, was a demoralised society characterised by mistrust and alienation from regime objectives and social norms.

An economy without incentives and without norms of behaviour to which most people are willing to conform soon collapses. Russia's economic history provides the clearest evidence for this in two episodes: one, the meltdown of the economy of Soviet Russia immediately after the Revolution, and the other, the collapse of Russia's economy at the end of Communism.

It is reasonable to interpret the Soviet institutions built under Stalin in the 1930s as improvised to replace the market incentives to work, save, and innovate by substituting artificial incentives to do the same things. These institutions were those described in our previous volumes:

[14] *Review of Economic Studies*, 84(2) (2017): 617–619 (Cheremukhin et al.).

the compulsion to work, the wage and salary structures that established managers' and officials' promotion pathways, the bonuses for meeting quotas, the payments to collective farms for food surpluses, the charges levied on farms for state machinery services, the penalties for shirking and disloyalty, the systems for forced resettlement and forced labour by detainees, and the spectrum of real, artificial, and illegal markets for goods and labour services, including the calculation of collective farm labour contributions and their reimbursement. In their time, these institutions worked, even if they did not work optimally or efficiently. That they worked is shown by their resilience: the Soviet economy did not collapse in the face of famines (in 1933 and 1947) or of deep invasion (in 1941 and 1942). It collapsed only when the central political institutions fell to pieces (after 1987).

Despite this judgement, which some might interpret as favourable, it remains the case that the incentives provided by the Soviet economic system were always impaired and often perverse. The satisfaction of bureaucrats took precedence over the satisfaction of final consumers living in households and of intermediate consumers running businesses. High performance was rewarded at first, and then penalised by the burden of higher expectations. The value of rewards was uncertain; simulated effort was more likely to be rewarded than disruptive innovation.

The UK and US economies would share many of these features in the coming World War, when government priorities replaced market prices and administrative success indicators replaced profits.[15] The British and American war economies were distinguished from the Soviet economy, however, by the fact that their decision makers remained accountable to the rule of law and public opinion, with some limitations that, although important, were temporary, being limited to the war period. The absence of all such restraints in the Soviet economy permitted not only costly excesses of radicalism but also the mass incarceration and killing of people in very large numbers, including many who were only suspected of some potential disloyalty and many just to fill the quota. At work this was reflected in harsh penalisation of workers and managers, supposedly for mistakes or low effort, but there was a large random factor in the distribution of punishments, which encouraged everyone to shift their

[15] Described in Harrison, ed. (1996), 43–80 (S. N. Broadberry and W. P. Howlett); 81–121 (H. Rockoff).

efforts from production to self-protection.[16] Thus, brakes on growth arose from everyday disincentives that were felt by many millions of people. The frictions could be overcome only by the still greater countervailing force of the state, expressed in a limited range of policies that relied on still more coercion.

Under Stalin the Soviet state became a near monopolist of land, productive capital, and housing, and a near monopolist of labour. Used to the full, these powers were used to dramatic effect. Within 12 years, nearly one in five workers was shifted from lower-value jobs in agriculture to higher-value jobs in industry, transport, and construction. Over a similar period, nearly one-third of GDP was taken out of private hands into the hands of the state.[17] The state used the extra one-third in its hands to build national capacities of all kinds: productive capital in state-owned industry and transport, human capital through education, the intangible capital of shared knowledge arising from scientific and technological research, the state capacity necessary to mobilise society and direct efforts, and the military power embodied in a mass army equipped with large quantities of modernised weaponry.

To summarise, Russia began to industrialise before the First World War, and the economy expanded both in the aggregate and in output and consumption per head. By 1913, however, Russia's industrialisation was still quite limited. The sources of its limitation have been identified in both agriculture and industry. Agrarian property rights restricted the supply of resources from agriculture, and the structure of markets and corporate ownership limited the demand for them from industry. While policy reforms could have surmounted those obstacles within the framework of a market economy, the Bolsheviks chose an alternative path to industrialisation. Sweeping acts of confiscation and coercion broke through the limits. The pace of industrialisation that followed was without precedent in Russian history. But the industrialisation of the Soviet economy did not bring rapid or stable economic growth. Economic

[16] *Journal of Economic Literature*, 43(3) (2005): 721–761 (P. R. Gregory and M. Harrison).

[17] One in five workers: the change in the share of the employed population between the census of December 1926 (using data adjusted for comparability) and January 1939, from Davies, Harrison, and Wheatcroft (1994): 277. Nearly one-third of GDP: the change in the GDP shares of government consumption and domestic investment between 1928 and 1940 (ibid., 272).

growth was limited, was not reflected in higher living standards, and was continually interrupted by periodic disasters that were either self-inflicted or, if they had some other origin, were made worse by the policy response.

2 The Measurement of Economic Performance

In its appearance, the pyramid structure of the Soviet planned economy was arranged so that orders could flow down from the Politburo to the productive units, becoming more detailed and more disaggregated at each level of the cascade. At the same time, information on the capacities and the performance of the productive units would flow upwards to the Politburo, providing it with the evidence base for the next round of orders.

The reality was somewhat different. The production of knowledge was highly politicised, and information flows were contaminated by political pressures at every level. From the Politburo, Stalin and other leaders set limits on what could be known, and on what facts would be politically acceptable. At every level, managers and others responsible for reporting primary data used their initiative to shape the flows of facts to the criteria of success and acceptability that were fixed from above.

In the present volume, we have described in detail two focal points for statistical manipulation. One was the grain harvest. Here the pattern was longstanding, being established in the 1920s. At that time the party leaders sought and approved optimistic predictions of the availability of grain to support their ambitious plans for forced industrialisation, so that contemporary harvest estimates became inflated in comparison to pre-war measures (Vol. 1: 63–66). When the harvest then fell short, they wished not to admit to the failure of an important precondition for the success of their plans, and to press forward regardless. As a result, in the decade covered by our seven volumes, there was not one year in which the harvest was reported honestly to the public.

In our work we have identified successive moments in the development of the statistical methodology for harvest evaluation from the situation that prevailed in the 1920s. One moment came in 1933, when a harvest measure based on the 'biological' yield (of the crop standing in the field, after allowance for harvesting and storage losses) replaced the concept of the 'barn yield' (of the crop after reaping and threshing (Vol. 5: 442–447). A second moment came in 1939 when, encouraged by Stalin and Molotov, Voznesenskii recommended a more encompassing concept of the biological yield, making no allowance for harvesting and storage losses and even adding supposed pre-harvest losses and a factor for under-reporting (Chapter 4). In practice, both these moments proved to be steps on a path towards increasing exaggeration of the harvest.

We have found that statisticians who were professionally responsible for harvest measurement pushed back against manipulation from time to time. In 1933, for example, Osinskii, the incoming head of the newly formed TsGK, presented the biological yield as a more evidence-based harvest measure which, done carefully and after time for due consideration of the aggregated yield data, would correct the subjectively inflated barn-yield estimates of preceding years (Vol. 5: 246–247). But things did not work out in the way he evidently hoped. The underlying reason was that the political leaders could never admit the failure of their plans.

In a highly centralised and closed political system, most professional statisticians (like other 'experts') lacked the independence to 'speak truth to power'. When the political system was also highly mobilised to search for enemies and eliminate them, to speak out was not only difficult but dangerous. Those responsible for reporting from lower levels were at least as vulnerable to the pressures of triumphalism as higher officials. Nonetheless, evidence of continuing resistance to exaggeration can found in the pattern of harvest reports over time. When the harvest was in progress, preliminary harvest claims were most responsive to the spirit of victory. When the harvest was in and the flag waving was over, it was easier for realism to prevail, and so final harvest reports were generally more sober than the preliminary reports submitted within the harvest period (Table B.37). Even so, the final harvest measures based on the biological yield continued to be substantially overstated through the 1930s. As for the more encompassing harvest concept introduced by Voznesenskii in 1939, the change was then imposed retrospectively to the harvest reports of 1936 to 1938 (Chapter 7), but not to previous years. The results softened the appearance of harvest failure of 1936, overstated the success of 1937, and supported a false impression of an upward long-term trend.

A second focus of statistical manipulation was the size and growth of the population, which Stalin considered to be an indicator of national power and prosperity. On that basis, the five-year plans made optimistic projections of the population, which did not live up to the expectations placed upon it. Among the reasons was the substantial mortality arising from food shortages and repressions. It damaged the party leaders' authority if its projections were known to be wrong, and it damaged their legitimacy if the population shortfall was attributed (at least in part) to their own policy failures.

In both the censuses of the late 1930s, as far as we can tell, the census workers did a professional job, a surprise, perhaps, given the circumstances. But the fate of their findings (and in some cases their personal fates) was entirely dependent on the leaders' overriding objective, which was to support Stalin's authority and cover up all evidence of mistakes (Chapter 5). In 1937 the census findings were buried; in 1939, they were manipulated before publication. The effect of the manipulation was to make the Soviet population appear to be larger and more rapidly growing than was the case, and to suppress evidence of millions of missing people, the casualties of the 1933 famine, especially among the male populations of Ukraine and Kazakhstan.

It is true that the officially accepted outcome of the 1939 census also represented a major concession to reality. At the risk of their lives, the professional statisticians persuaded Stalin and Molotov to accept a population figure of around 170 million. This was two to three million more than the census findings justified. Perhaps more significantly, it was also 13 million less than the 183 million that any moderately numerate reader of *Pravda* could have inferred from Stalin's projections. A possible explanation is that following the conclusion of the Great Terror, Stalin was confident that not a single person would point this out.

The boosting of claimed results that we have described in demography and agriculture exemplifies practices that affected most if not all aspects of Soviet economic measurement. A third focal point of manipulation was the system of accounting for planned production and prices.

The presence of manipulation in Soviet measures of real output has been long established. In 1939 the real volume of Soviet economic activity was twice that of 1913 (on the same territory), and also of 1928 (Table 1). This was based on the reconstruction of the Soviet production accounts from the bottom up on the basis of admittedly incomplete published data by independent Western scholars. It was not the picture presented by Soviet official statistics of output and productivity. According to an official measure, based on the plan prices of 1926/27, real

Table 2 The Soviet economy, 1940 compared with 1937: Soviet official and Western estimates (per cent of 1937)

	A Soviet official measure	*A Western estimate*
At current prices		
National income	151	155
At fixed prices		
National income	133	118–121
Industrial production	145	119
Munitions output	283	272–282

Source National income: net material product in current prices and in plan prices of 1926/27 from Table B.57; gross national product at current prices and factor costs of 1937 from Table B.58, the upper limit being taken from Bergson and the lower limit from Moorsteen and Powell. Industrial production: Table B.60. Munitions output: Table B.61, the upper limit being taken from Moorsteen and Powell and the lower limit from *Europe-Asia Studies*, 49(3) (1997): 374 (Davies and Harrison).

Soviet material production in 1940 exceeded that of 1928 by a factor not of two but of more than five.[18]

Over the shorter period covered by the present volume, we can contrast Soviet official and Western measures of the real growth of industry and of the economy as a whole from 1937 to 1940 (Table 2).[19] As the figures show, Soviet reports and Western estimates agree that the nominal value of national income in rubles and the prices prevailing at the time increased from 1937 to 1940 by about one-half. A gap emerges only when correction is made for inflation. The Soviet statistics, which again used the plan prices of 1926/27, claimed that the real national income increased by one-third in just three years, and real industrial production by 45%. The Western estimates also show real growth, but of no more than one-fifth, whether our focus is on industry or on the economy as a whole.

How did these gaps arise? Soviet measures of the real volume of output relied on the fixed prices used to plan the economy, that is, to set production quotas in rubles that could be devolved to ministries and their enterprises at the beginning of the plan period and used afterwards to evaluate their performance against the plan. This required a fixed

[18] *Narodnoe khozyaistvo* (1955): 16.

[19] Vol. 6: xvi reports similar (but smaller) discrepancies over the period of our previous volume.

standard of value, in order to prevent managers from fulfilling the quota by the simple expedient of raising prices. The standard of value chosen for the first five-year plan was the 'unchanged prices of 1926/27'. In the 1930s (and in fact up to 1950) the plans handed down to Soviet managers at every level were usually denominated in these prices (In this respect the plans for the harvest and the population, which were set out in unambiguous physical units, were untypical. The problem for the accountable officials was the same, however: how to manipulate the performance indicator to show success).

The underlying sources of bias in Soviet accounting for planned production are now well known.[20] Overstated claims did not arise from any high-level authority for managers to lie about achievements. Managers were caught lying from time to time, but they took great risks when they did so because to hoodwink the authorities by fabricating results was a serious crime. Rather, higher officials imposed continuous pressure on managers to meet performance indicators and to demonstrate outstanding results, and managers responded by finding less risky ways to satisfy appearances without undue effort. While there were many such stratagems, those that were quantitatively important exploited an intrinsic weakness in the plan's standard of value, the 'unchanged' prices of 1926/27. The weakness arose because, as 1926/27 receded into the past, the scope increased to vary the qualities of products that had been produced and priced in 1926/27, and also to introduce entirely new products. From this there followed the opportunity to set new 'unchanged' plan prices for the upgraded and new products, which were generally based on unit costs at the time the changes were made. Because this was an era of high inflation, and inflation was particularly rapid in the early 1930s, such new 'unchanged' plan prices were always higher than the old ones. As a result, it was generally easier to show real growth and to satisfy the plan with newer products than with older ones, the plan prices of which remained anchored in 1926/27.

As the product profile of the Soviet economy lengthened, so did the lists of 'unchanged' plan prices, and the new additions were always tilted towards the higher price level current at the time of each successive innovation. The outcome was a bias that was particularly favourable

[20] Davies, Harrison, and Wheatcroft (1994): 30–32 (Davies and Wheatcroft) and 138–141 (Davies); *Journal of Economic History*, 58(4) (1998): 1032–1062 (Harrison) and *Journal of Comparative Economics*, 28(1) (2000): 134–155 (Harrison).

to those branches of industry where product changes were particularly rapid, such as the machine-building and metalworking industries and especially military machine building. The manager of a bakery producing a standard Soviet loaf of bread year after year had little opportunity to make the changes that would allow the production assortment to be re-priced favourably. In the aircraft industry, in contrast, the aeroplane of 1939 was unrecognisable by the standards of the 1920s. The entire production profile of an aircraft factory changed from year to year with extreme rapidity, and each successive design was radically different from its predecessor. It is not surprising to find, therefore, that measures of the real growth of heavy industry over time in plan prices and in current prices were virtually identical. It was only in the consumer industries, where product improvements and new products were less encouraged, that measured growth in the plan prices of 1926/27 lagged substantially behind.

As in accounting for grain and for birth and deaths, the professional statisticians responsible for planned production were aware of the biases in the system they operated, discussed them in private, and devised schemes to try to limit them. The most obvious solution lay in frequent updating of the base year. In the period of our volumes there was one attempt at such a reform, which was ordered in September 1933 by Sovnarkom and implemented in February 1935 for the compilation of the 1936 plan. But the reform encountered strong resistance and, while some minor rationalisation was achieved, 1926/27 was retained as the base year. The most important source of conservatism was evidently the desire of the authorities not to have the statisticians revalue the sectors of the economy in such a way that its most rapidly growing branches would have less weight in the aggregate growth rate that would be claimed in public.[21] In this sense, the party leaders expressed a clear preference for exaggeration.

The Soviet accounts did not only systematically overstate the dynamism of the economy. They also understated the burdens of accumulation and defence. We see this when we turn to shares of income denominated in current prices—that is, in the ruble prices used for transactions in the Soviet economy at the time. The main issue was the subsidy of prices of products used for accumulation and defence, which was

[21] *Journal of Economic History*, 58(4) (1998): 1048 (Harrison).

Table 3 The uses of Soviet national income, 1937 and 1940 (per cent of national income)

	1937	*1938*	*1939*	*1940*
A Soviet official measure				
Investment	11.4	11.4	9.3	–
Defence	7.2	9.0	11.9	–
A Western estimate				
Investment	25.9	–	–	19.1
Defence	8.8	–	–	18.7

Source Soviet official measure: Table B.61. Western estimate (by Bergson): Table B.62.

partly paid out of the taxation of consumer goods and services. Because of this, the prices of consumer goods were raised above their 'factor costs', while the prices of industrial materials and civilian and military equipment were held down. When measured in these prices, the shares of national income allocated to investment were systematically lower in Soviet measures than in Western estimates, which attempted to identify the 'factor costs' of Soviet activities by removing taxes and subsidies. The same was true, although to a lesser extent, for defence (Table 3). The subsidies of accumulation and defence persisted through the the lifetime of the Soviet system, serving the same function that is sometimes found behind wartime controls in market economies: to 'suppress one of the indicators that the government is involved in an expensive enterprise'.[22]

An effect of the manipulations and biases in Soviet economic statistics was that the Politburo was misinformed almost as frequently as the public. Occasions when the party leaders ordered the publication of one set of facts, knowing them to be fabricated, and having access to another set that it believed to be the unvarnished truth, were rare. One such example was the decision to falsify the defence line in the Soviet state budget from 1931 to 1935 in order to conceal the rapid growth of defence outlays at the time of the World Disarmament Conference in Geneva (Vol. 4: 117–118). In that case, the leaders knew the truth, and those responsible for funding defence were in no doubt that they should supply funds in line with the secret budget line, not the published one. Stalin's decision to declare a larger population than that found by the census takers

[22]The words are by Rockoff (2012): 11, writing about price controls as a way of suppressing wartime inflation.

in 1939, leading to fabrication of the published results of the census, discussed in the present volume (Chapter 5), has some similarities. Even if the published results of the census falsified the numbers and whereabouts of the 'special contingents' of the armed forces and the forced labour system, Stalin knew what the preliminary results of the census had revealed, and those in charge of the Defence Commissariat and the NKVD knew perfectly well who was under their control and where they were. But in the general run of Soviet statistical practices, the instances where the Politburo knew the truth and ordered the public to be told a lie were somewhat unusual. More commonly, if the truth could not be revealed, the public was told nothing at all.

Also common, however, was the statistical exaggeration that arose spontaneously from the universal pressure to declare victory in the struggle to implement the party's directives. This tendency was felt at every level, high and low, and in every locality from the field and factory to the ministerial boardroom. There were periodic attempts to check it, made visible by the efforts of statisticians to exercise the critical, sceptical function that is essential to their profession. But such efforts were too feeble, too infrequent, and too threatening to powerful interests to be effective. One result was that, on such basic matters as the rate of growth of planned production, the Politburo was as likely to be misinformed as the public. Unlike the public, Stalin and Molotov had the chance from time to time to authorise improvements of the statistical system, or to prevent deteriorations, or to scale down the public boasting that encouraged everyone below them to overstate their achievements and, when they were offered the opportunity, they typically chose not to. In that sense we can say that they preferred to be fooled by their own propaganda, but it is important to understand that this was not unwilling or unwitting on their part.

3 Militarisation: A War Economy in Peacetime

The economic system that Stalin built in the 1930s persisted, with remarkable continuity, to the end of the Soviet Union. The way of life that the Soviet Union imposed on its citizens would be utterly unfamiliar to Western readers of the millennial generation. But their grandparents and great-grandparents, who lived through the world wars of the twentieth century, even if they saw only the external appearance of the Soviet neighbourhood or workplace, would quickly have recognised it.

This was the atmosphere of a country at war and under siege. At work, long hours of effort were motivated by patriotic appeals and managed by regimentation. Household goods and service were often unavailable. There were shortages in the stores and queues in the streets. At home there was austerity, leavened by occasional pleasures, sometimes forbidden. Slackers and speculators lurked in the shadows, to be tolerated or exposed and eliminated depending on the period and season.

No one expressed this more pointedly than the Polish economist, Oskar Lange. In a lecture that he delivered in Belgrade in 1957, not long after Khrushchev's denunciation of Stalin, he described the generic features of a war economy, pointing out how closely they resembled those of the Stalinist command system:

> Concentration of all resources towards one basic objective …, centralisation of disposal of resources in order to avoid leakages of resources to everything that was considered non-essential … Allocation of resources by administrative decision according to administratively established priorities and large-scale use of political incentives to maintain the productivity and discipline of labour through patriotic appeals.[23]

If one were to ask how the Bolsheviks came upon this model, the answer would be that they found it not in the economic ideas of Marx and Engels, but in the lived experience of the First World War, the first interstate conflict of modern times that was fought by mass armies equipped by mass industrial production. The Bolsheviks observed closely how the capitalist countries managed their resources for this conflict, and they watched and admired, in particular, the experience of Germany, mobilised for total war by Walther Rathenau and Erich Ludendorff. On taking power in their own country, they set about implementing this model with enthusiasm. Unencumbered by private property rights and constitutional restraints, they expected that they would do a better job than the Germans. But the Bolsheviks also quickly forgot where they found their inspiration, as Lange himself acknowledged:

[23]Lange (1962): 18. On the misperception of the Soviet economy as an economic development project with primarily civilian goals, see also Samuelson (2000); Stone (2000); *Europe-Asia Studies*, 61(9) (2009): 1579–1601 (V. Kontorovich and A. Wein) and *Comparative Economic Studies*, 57(4) (2015): 669–692 (Kontorovich).

> One of the methods of war economy, which most of the socialist countries have resorted to at one stage or another, is the compulsory delivery by peasants of part of their product. Many Communists in Poland feel rather upset by the present programme of our government of abolishing such deliveries. I usually answer them by asking if they remember who first introduced compulsory deliveries in Poland. For, the fact is that such deliveries were first introduced during the First World War by the occupation army of Kaiser Wilhelm the Second, whom I do not think anybody regards as a champion of socialism.[24]

The transformation of the economy under Soviet rule was dramatic in all its branches, but the changes were less striking in some than in others. To most appearances, a great motor factory was organised on similar lines whether in Moscow or in Detroit. Likewise, a great steel mill was recognisably similar in Magnitogorsk and in Gary, Indiana. Such similarities should not be surprising, because the Bolsheviks also admired American mass production and the scale and centralisation of production that it fostered.

The transformation was at its most extreme in farming. Russia was a country where, for a thousand years, without instruction, farmers had followed the rhythm of the seasons, planting and sowing in autumn and spring, enduring the winter reaping and threshing in summer. No one from that background can have imagined that in the fourth decade of the twentieth century, on orders from Moscow, tens of millions of farmers would have been regimented in battle formation to rise up and occupy a million square kilometres of land to be ploughed, sown, reaped, and threshed on a weekly schedule in militarised struggles marked by victories, setbacks, campaign medals for heroes, and exemplary punishment for deserters.

Most strikingly, all this was brought about in time of peace, for the Soviet Union was not at war when it collectivised agriculture, any more than when it built Magnitorgorsk. It is true that in the period between the two world wars, 'peacetime' was often a relative concept. Soviet borders were continually disputed, and these disputes sometimes erupted into open conflict. But while Soviet military planning continually envisaged existential threats and drew up plans to deal with them, the Soviet Union did not face any real and present danger from 1920, when the

[24] Lange (1962): 19.

Red Army withdrew from Poland, to 1937, the year in which Japanese leaders began to push the 'northern' strategy of expansion into Siberia, and Hitler began to turn war on the Eastern Front from a contingency to a plan.[25]

If the Soviet regimentation of industry and the industrial worker showed how far the centralisation of mass production could proceed, the militarisation of agriculture showed its limits. In Moscow, the centralised state placed great stress upon its detailed plans for agricultural operations. The truth, however, seems to be that this merely imposed the appearance of order on tasks that would be performed anyway, as and when the rural cadres would get around to them. In practice, the harvest was much less responsive to centralised plans than to the weather. This could be observed from year to year. But in 1937, specifically, something more could be observed. In that year the nomenklatura purge wreaked havoc among the officials responsible for both managing and coordinating all branches of the economy. But the results were not the same in all branches. In industry and transport, production was visibly disorganised, and productivity declined sharply. In agricultural production, in contrast, there was no particular effect. The weather was better than average, and so the harvest was better than average, regardless of the chaos in the bureaucracy. What was affected by the disorganisation at the centre was not agricultural production but distribution: the state failed to capture the gains from the good harvest (Sect. 7 in Chapter 4). In 1938 and 1939 that capacity had to be rebuilt (Chapter 7). This confirms that Soviet state capacity for agriculture was focused on extraction; it played little or no productive role.

Long before 1939, the Soviet Union looked like a country at war. For the sake of national targets for production and for economic and military construction, all of society was mobilised in military-style campaigns that celebrated heroism and penalised shirking and desertion. We see the same in other countries in the twentieth century, but only when total war was being waged or actively prepared. The militarisation of the Soviet economy was facilitated by the industrial technologies of the time, which promoted mass production and made centralised coordination relatively effective. But militarisation was also applied to Soviet agriculture, where

[25] Soviet military planning: Samuelson (2000). Japanese leaders: Paine (2012): 146–148; Hitler: Adamthwaite (1992): 71.

the productive returns to standardisation and coordination were low or negative. While the militarisation of agriculture was damaging to production, however, it still benefited the state by enhancing controls over the distribution of agricultural produce.

4 The Emergence of the Soviet Union as a World Power

By 1939 the Soviet Union ranked alongside Germany as one of the world's two leading producers of weapons. Globally, aviation was the branch of military of technology that advanced most rapidly during the interwar period. Aviation was also the technology on which the great powers placed their greatest hopes. Fighters and bombers, it was widely believed, would enable a country to attack its adversaries from a distance. The same fighters and bombers would provide the means of defence and deterrence. Some of these hopes were exaggerated or premature, but the fact remains: air power, or the lack of it, was decisive in every theatre in the Second World War. Every major power committed at least one-quarter of its wartime budget for military equipment to aviation and air forces.[26] It is notable, therefore, that, as the war broke out in 1939, the Soviet Union produced more than one-quarter of the world's military aircraft, and was the second largest producer of military aircraft in the world, lagging Germany by a barely perceptible margin (Table 4).

A broader comparison of the Soviet Union's military production with Germany's in 1939 is also instructive. We find that the two countries' profiles were broadly matched (Table 5). The Soviet Union gave first place to Germany in aircraft and naval shipbuilding, but by small margins. The Soviet Union was ahead across a wide range of armaments and munitions and was seriously deficient only in the production of automatic infantry weapons.

Legitimate questions might be raised concerning the relative quality of Soviet military power, including weaponry. Such defects certainly existed and would be exposed by the experience of the battlefield; this happened in the winter war of 1939/40 with Finland and, on a much larger scale, in the first period of the Soviet-German war that began in

[26] O'Brien (2015): 23, 38–39, 53, 60; *Journal of Strategic Studies*, 39(4) (2016): 592–598 (M. Harrison).

Table 4 Combat aircraft produced, 1939: the great powers (units and per cent)

	Units	*Per cent of total*
Germany	8,295	29
Soviet Union	7,480	26
United Kingdom	3,731	13
France (estimated)	3,564	12
United States	2,141	7
Japan (estimated)	2,100	7
Italy	1,750	6
Total	29,061	100

Source Germany, from US Strategic Bombing Survey (1945): 6; USSR, from *Europe-Asia Studies*, 49(3) (1997): 405 (Davies and Harrison), counting fighters, bombers, and reconnaissance aircraft only. UK, from *Statistical Digest* (1951): 152, counting fighters, bombers, reconnaissance, and naval aircraft. France: aircraft produced, September to December 1939, from Higham (2012): 169, multiplied by three for an upper bound on production at yearly rate. United States, from Modley (1945): 8. Japan: combat aircraft produced, September to December 1939, from Grechko, ed., *Istoriya*, 12 (1982): 201, multiplied by three for an upper bound on production at yearly rate. Italy, from Harrison, ed. (1998): 196 (V. Zamagni). Where possible, training aircraft (relatively cheap, and often produced in large numbers) are excluded; these contributed to air force capacity building, but not to immediate combat strength.

Table 5 War production, 1939: Soviet Union versus Germany (units and per cent)

	Germany	*Soviet Union*	*Soviet Union, per cent of Germany*
Rifles and carbines, thou.	1,352	1,497	111
Automatic pistols, thou.	120	0	0
Machine guns, all types	59,100	96,400	163
Guns, all types and calibres	6,300	16,459	261
Mortars	4,200	4,457	106
Tanks and self-propelled guns	2,100	2,986	142
Combat aircraft	8,295	7,480	90
Warships, main types	30	28	93

Source Germany, from US Strategic Bombing Survey (1945): 6; USSR: *Europe-Asia Studies*, 49(3) (1997): 403–406 (Davies and Harrison).

Table 6 Research, design, and production facilities of the Soviet defence industry by specialisation, selected years (number of establishments)

	1917	*1928*	*1935*	*1940*
Munitions	98	143	268	506
Aviation	38	75	154	391
Electronics	35	101	188	296
Armament	27	71	121	221
Shipbuilding	28	55	100	149
Armoured vehicles	4	16	44	96
Atomic research	0	1	13	21
All facilities	230	460	886	1,679

Source Table B.25.

June 1941. When war transpired, however, and the qualitative defects of Soviet armaments were exposed in combat, Soviet industry would prove fully capable of forcing the necessary technological improvements to the extent that Soviet armaments would eventually prevail.

The pre-war position of the Soviet economy as a world-class supplier of military equipment had broad foundations. It was the goal to which vast efforts had been directed since the mid-1920s, when the political leaders began to receive increasingly precise formulations of the problem of 'future war' from the Red Army.[27] In aviation, armour, armament, and ammunition, the later Soviet military-industrial complex was largely created in the 1930s. Measured by the number of research, design, and production facilities (in other words, counting one for each factory and institute, regardless of size), the size of the Soviet military industry accelerated steadily from 1917, when the war effort of the Russian Empire reached its peak. On that measure, the Soviet defence industry doubled in size by 1928, and this first doubling took 11 years. The second doubling was achieved by 1935, which was just seven years. From 1935, only five more years were required for a third doubling, which was achieved by 1940, when the number of defence industry facilities reached more than 1600 (Table 6). The largest element of the defence industry in 1940 was the traditional branch of munitions, but this was closely followed by two branches that barely existed in 1917: aviation and electronics. A sign of things to come, atomic research was already under way.

[27] 'Future War' was the title of an influential report by the Red Army intelligence directorate in 1928, discussed by Samuelson (2000): 22–28.

Underlying the growth of the defence industry was the propagation of all branches of modern heavy industry and engineering, which supported rearmament by supplying industry and the armed forces with metals and metal goods, fuels, and chemicals. Many of these goods were 'dual-purpose', that is, they could be applied equally to civilian and military uses. Everyday examples ranged from engines and motor vehicles to nitrates, which held chemical energy in unstable compounds that were applicable both for plant fertilisation and for explosives. As rearmament was pursued with increasing urgency, these goods were directed increasingly towards the defence sector at the expense of civilian production and household consumption.

The emergence of the Soviet Union as a world-class military power might be thought surprising when viewed from some angles, though not others. The element of surprise arises partly from the Bolshevik narrative, which repeatedly emphasised Russia's historic backwardness, its lack of modern industries and technologies, its vulnerability to penetration and aggression by hostile forces, the likelihood that external enemies would victimise it for these weaknesses, and the reactive, defensive character of its war preparations. From that perspective, it is disconcerting to find that, by the end of our period, the Soviet Union disposed of as many weapons in a year as another great power, Germany, that was to a considerable extent already mobilised for a war with other great powers, a war that its leaders had long planned and now initiated.

From another perspective, the Soviet position as a world leader in military production is less surprising. The Soviet Union was one of a handful of countries with enough size in population and natural resources to contend for global leadership. Imperial Russia, the predecessor of the Soviet state, had participated willingly in the great-power rivalry of the nineteenth and early twentieth centuries. Even if, in other aspects, the Bolsheviks emphasised their break with Russia's past, in the aspect of international affairs they declared from the outset the necessity of restoring Russia as a great power. This was expressed, above all, by Lenin when he put forward the goal to 'catch up and overtake' the imperialist powers in economic and military capabilities, and by Stalin when he deliberately echoed this goal.

Preparation for 'future war' was an explicit motivation behind all the most consequential decisions of Soviet economic policy in the 1920s and 1930s. A great obstacle that confronted the decision makers was that, in Russia after the end of the Civil War (as in every other European country after the Great War), a longing for peace was widespread, so that many citizens were unwilling to be further regimented and forced to make further sacrifices.[28] The Stalinist command system could emerge only by censoring this longing and overwhelming it by ceaseless propaganda of the external threat and the dangers posed by the enemy within.

Concluding the present volume (Sect. 5 in Chapter 9), we sought to understand the Soviet-German rapprochement of the last summer before the Second World War. The sudden warming of relations between the two powers at that time helps to clarify the long-standing character of Soviet great-power ambitions. In August 1939 Stalin's Russia and Hitler's Germany displayed both commonalities and differences. The two leaders had in common their opposition to the existing boundaries of the European states and the balance of power that went with it. The goals of Stalin's foreign and military policies, like Hitler's, went beyond 'defence' in the narrow, literal sense of passive response to immediate threat. Defence under Stalin was forward looking, calibrated to a wide range of future threats and future opportunities. It was also active, and actively revisionist, in seeking opportunities for advantage over his country's neighbours at the cost of their integrity and sovereignty.

The comparison has its limits. The foreign and military policies of Stalin's Russia and Hitler's Germany were not the same. While Hitler actively planned to secure world domination for Germany within his own lifetime, the Bolsheviks had shelved the prospect of world revolution, at least for a time. When the opportunities arose, Stalin was pleased to restore Soviet control of neighbouring territories in 1939–1940, and he would make and take opportunities to do so in 1944–1945. But he was no more than an opportunist, when compared with Hitler as a strategist. This gave Hitler the advantage in the Soviet-German friendship of 1939; both sides sought to use each other for short-term gain, but it was Germany that held the initiative, making the alliance in the first place, then breaking it by war in 1941.

The Soviet pursuit of great-power status was a long-term project, finally realised after the Second World War, but already a considerable success before the war broke out. If there should be an element of surprise, it is because great-power status was achieved without 'catching up and overtaking' the Soviet Union's rivals in productivity and mass

[28] Harrison, ed. (2008): 34 (A. K. Sokolov); Velikanova (2013): 33–36.

prosperity. In the Second World War the Soviet Union was able to rival Germany, a country of similar economic size, measured by its real GDP, but with a longer and deeper history of industrial revolution, skills, and education, and higher overall living standards and productivity. After the war, the Soviet Union became a global nuclear superpower to rival the United States, although the American economy was much larger and more productive than even Germany's. The combined experience of many countries in two world wars shows that, as a rule, countries of lower pre-war productivity were much less able to mobilise their economies for total war in all respects that we can easily measure. But the rule is proved by one clear exception. The Soviet Union, a relatively poor country, should have failed the test of the Second World War, much as imperial Russia failed in the First World War. The fact that the Soviet Union did not fail is testimony to the mobilisation capacity of the economic system that Lenin and Stalin built, and to the ruthlessness with which they exploited its properties.[29]

Measured against civilian criteria of productivity and prosperity, the Soviet economy of the 1930s failed. Measured against benchmarks of national capability, such as military power, it looks far more successful. A distinctive and enduring feature of the Soviet economy was its capacity to support military power out of proportion to its level of development. By the end of our story in 1939, the Soviet economy was one of the first producers of military hardware in the world, equalled only by Germany under national socialism. This is remarkable, given that by the end of 1939 Germany was fully engaged in the first of a series of wars that was intended to end in victory over all the other great powers.

5 The Reformability of the Soviet Economy

Soon after Stalin's death, reform-minded economists, among them Oskar Lange in Poland, began to discuss openly whether it was possible to reform the Soviet-type economy. The root cause of their dissatisfaction was the position of the government as the compulsory purchaser of nearly everything. The government dictated what was to be produced, paid for it, and then sold it to the eventual users: the industrial and military users of equipment and materials, and the household users of food,

[29] Harrison (2015): 67–98.

clothing, and consumer services. This system gave the party leaders in the Politburo immense discretion over immediate allocations, but it also broke the link between the seller and the final user; it built neglect of public assets, disdain for the consumer, and resistance to innovation into the Soviet economy. The reformers of the post-Stalin period sought, therefore, to restore the direct link between buyer and seller by widening the sphere of market exchange while retaining the property framework of state-owned enterprises and offices and collective farms.

It is correctly supposed that Stalin resisted such reforms. It is widely believed that the search for solutions therefore began only after Stalin's death, but this is wrong. Our research in the archives has shown, in contrast, that those who operated the system from day to day became aware of its adverse consequences and began to look for solutions almost immediately, although much of their search remained hidden from the public. In other words, the case for reform became evident to insiders from the very beginning; it did not wait to arise until the Soviet economy had become industrially more developed.

Early attempts at reform were aimed at both industry and agriculture (Vol. 4: 11–18, 201–228, 265–270, 345–346). In 1931 and the first months of 1932, measures were adopted to reduce the pressure on agriculture, to improve incentives for the peasants to participate in the collective farms, and to give urban consumers access to the kolkhoz households' private produce through the 'kolkhoz markets'. These measures were soon overwhelmed by the onset of famine following the failed harvest of 1932 (Vol. 5). Nonetheless, some aspects of these reforms, such as the kolkhoz markets, became permanent.

At the same time, attempts were made to reform industrial planning. Early experiences quickly convinced Sergo Ordzhonikidze, the chief of Vesenkha (the industrial ministry of the time), that detailed inter-plant transactions should be decentralised. By 1931 he had become a keen advocate of cost accounting and the idea that if placed under stricter financial discipline, industrial enterprises could be relied on to make contracts for material supplies in a decentralised way, without guidance from a central plan (Vol. 4: 12).

This idea became a project that Orzhonikidze shared with his subordinates, some of whom went further, advocating the liberalisation of credit and prices. It was eventually blocked, however, by Stalin and Molotov, who considered quantitative controls of outputs and inputs to be the only reliable way to get desired results. Moreover, Ordzhonikidze's own experimentation appeared to prove them right. At the end of 1932 Ordzhonikidze unexpectedly cancelled centralised equipment supply plans for the iron, steel, coal, and oil industries for 1933. The buyers and sellers of the equipment were instructed to contract with each other independently of the plan. The buyers, disbelieving that they would be held to account for financial losses, tried to place orders that were vastly inflated. The sellers, who were criminally liable if they refused an order, did not know whom to refuse. The market was frozen by indecision and mistrust (Vol. 4: 269). Still committed to a reform, Ordzhonikidze turned the problem over to a conference of industry representatives in Moscow. In the spring of 1933, the Politburo stepped in, ordering the dismissal of the more radical reformists. Ordzhonikidze was isolated and humiliated.

Given their objectives, Stalin and Molotov made the right choice. They aimed for a highly mobilised economy, able to deliver surplus resources for economic and military capacity building. If that was the primary goal, it did not make sense to give broad discretion over detailed implementation to middle managers, let alone to consumers. For these would only use their control of day-to-day transactions to divert resources away from the government's 'one basic objective' (to use Lange's phrase) to 'non-essential' uses.

In the mid-1930s there was some softening of the Soviet economic system. After the worst of the famine, food products were taken off the ration (Vol. 6: 121–129, 173–176). There were attempts at financial reform (Vol. 6: 248–252) and a more conciliatory approach to 'elements' formerly regarded as hostile, such as former kulaks and their children (Vol. 6: 282–284). But no further substantial moves were made towards economic decentralisation before the war.

In the present volume, considering the late 1930s, we describe conditions that were perhaps uniquely unfavourable to the consideration of further reforms: a hunt for traitors, widespread arrests and executions amongst the party elite, and mass killings and mass incarcerations in society as a whole. A series of measures increased the centralisation of the economy: the expanding scope of forced labour (Chapters 4, 6, and 9), the growing pressure on the peasantry and the private sector (Chapter 7), and the harsher regimentation of waged non-agricultural employment (Chapter 8). Other changes in the system at this time were also designed to protect the authority of the centre as the economy expanded and its supply chains became increasingly complex. These included breaking up the empires of the industrial commissariats and giving Gosplan more authority to coordinate the supply chains that linked them (Chapter 2).

Was the Soviet economy reformable? At its most general, this question cannot be answered on the evidence of the Soviet Union in the 1930s. The examples of Russia, China, Vietnam, North Korea, and Cuba since the 1950s show many transitions away from economic institutions of the Soviet type. The Soviet experience of the 1930s does show us two things. First, the post-war stalemate of reformers versus conservatives was rooted in the system from its first years. It is wrong to suppose that pressure for economic reforms began only when reformist opinions first found a public voice in the 1950s. Such pressures appeared almost as soon as the command system was instituted, and they were felt at every level of the system from bottom to top, although they remained secret for the time being. Second, the stalemate would not be resolved while Soviet leaders were committed to uphold the party's absolute monopoly of power. The Soviet economy was certainly not reformable while Stalin lived, and the reason is that Stalin and Molotov immediately headed off any and all attempts at reform. In other words, whenever the top leaders were offered the chance to trade a little power for more productivity or more efficiency in the economy, they chose power.

6 The Nature of Soviet Economic Development

One of the chief claims of Stalin and other Soviet leaders for their right to preside over an authoritarian system was that the system they had built gave superior outcomes for peaceful economic and social development, as in time of war.[30]

What is economic development? Economic development has many dimensions. Most commonly acknowledged have been the various aspects of 'structural change': the widening of markets, the division of labour and specialisation, the diversification of production from agriculture to industrialisation and the emergence of modern services, the rise of towns, the movement of workers into factories and offices, the increase of living standards and longevity, the transition to a low-mortality, low-fertility society including the advancement of women and the protection of children, the creation of a skilled and literate workforce

[30] Stalin, *Sochineniya*, 15 (1997): 169; (1997), 16: 10–11.

through education and training, the rise of entrepreneurs and corporations that sponsor systematic productivity growth by linking science to production, and the trading and borrowing of goods, services, ideas, and cultures across the world. While all these aspects are logically connected, economists and economic historians have found many varied patterns in their ordering and rates of change across countries and over time.[31]

During the Cold War, the discipline of economics as it was practised in the West gave rise to several new fields, including development economics, the study of Soviet-type economies as a specialism in its own right, and 'comparative economics': the comparison of all types of economic systems, including capitalism and socialism. The economic history of the Soviet Union was a unifying thread, binding these fields together. The scholars involved gave much attention to the advantages and limitations of various historical paths of economic development, including that of the Soviet Union. They often described Soviet economic policies as one possible 'strategy for growth' or 'model of development'.[32] It was common to engage in some form of cost-benefit analysis. The Soviet pattern of economic development was held to confer benefits, such as accelerated industrialisation and the building of infrastructural capital. There were also costs, such as inefficiencies and forms of wastage associated with the heavy hand of authoritarian rule. Among these were the destruction of raw labour and human capital by mass killing and their misallocation by mass imprisonment and negative selection, although orders of magnitude were unknown and unknowable at that time. Whether the costs were avoidable and whether the achievements could be thought of as worthwhile were debated.

The mobilised character of Soviet society was one factor that gave the Soviet pattern of economic development undeniable appeal among contemporary observers. In the 1930s, the Soviet mobilisation for labour suggested a contrast to the conditions of depression and widespread unemployment in the much wealthier market economies of Western Europe and North America. In the 1940s the Soviet mobilisation for war inspired admiration for the unexpected resilience shown in the face of overwhelming military attack and a cruel war of annihilation. In the 1950s the Soviet mobilisation for post-war reconstruction and the Cold

[31] Gerschenkron (1962); Kuznets (1971).

[32] *International Affairs*, 37(1): 29–38 (A. Nove); Spulber (1964); Wilber (1967).

War suggested a model to the new leaders of much poorer countries, such as China and India, which wished to build national identity and national capabilities after military occupation or colonial rule.

How should we evaluate the Soviet pattern of economic development? The record of the Soviet economy of the 1930s shows plenty of structural change. This evidence is stronger in some aspects than in others. Most obvious was the rise of modern industries and cities. Linked to these were other structural changes, such as a phase of the Soviet demographic transition (described in Chapter 5). The position of women in society also changed radically. As millions of new jobs were created in factories and offices, and as thousands of new schools and colleges raised their literacy and numeracy, millions of young women were beneficiaries. From the beginning of Soviet rule, the Bolsheviks saw a wasted asset in Russia's illiterate women and worked to retrieve their efforts and talents through literacy campaigns and education. In 1926, 57% of Soviet women aged 9 to 49 could not read or write; by 1939 that proportion had fallen to 18% (the comparable rates for men were 28 and 6%).[33] Until this time, Russian women of humble origin generally had no better options than drudgery in the household or the field or factory. Illiteracy trapped them in these roles. With mass schooling, women could aspire to skilled work and to vocational and professional employment. The industrialisation of the Soviet economy created these roles in vast numbers. By 1940 women made the majority of employees in health, education, and culture, and one–third of employees in government administration.[34] It is true that a glass ceiling continued to restrict women's promotion, and the urban family maintained the traditional division of domestic labour between the sexes found in the countryside. Still, many women experienced a dramatic widening of opportunities.

The young women who benefited so much from access to education and office work also found they had much to lose. The state that provided their education and employment demanded absolute loyalty in return. The same state not infrequently rewarded that loyalty by breaking careers, friendships, and family bonds, imprisoning and killing loved ones and, as often as not, their family members.[35]

[33] *Narodnoe khozyaistvo* (1972): 35.

[34] *Narodnoe khozyaistvo* (1972): 348.

[35] A fictional account is the story of *Sofia Petrova* by Chukovskaya (1967).

While opportunities were widened for many, for many others they narrowed or became entirely closed. As millions of young people moved upward towards the light, they were passed in the opposite direction by significant numbers of their own cohorts, as well as of older and young people who, having begun to rise, and meeting with some political or social difficulty, were caught up in one of the periodic famines or mass operations and were thrown back down into darkness. Thus, from farm to factory and office was not the only direction of movement in society. There was a counter-movement from farms, factories, and offices to resettlement, to the labour camp, and to the mass grave.

In the outcome, the Soviet society of the 1930s shows a paradox. As new jobs were created in factories and offices, and as new schools and colleges raised their literacy and numeracy, millions experienced a widening of opportunties. But this was brought about without their agency; it was done to them by a coercive state in the name of a party that cast down as many as it raised up, while denying nearly all of them any significant voice in the process.

For Joseph Schumpeter, the agent of economic development was the entrepreneur, without whom there was no innovation.[36] In this aspect the Soviet economy of the 1930s suggests backward movement. Collectivisation reduced millions of independent farmers to servants of the collective (Vols. 1 and 2). As things turned out, the Soviet state could not manage agriculture and urban food supplies without leaving a role for decentralised household economic activities (Vol. 5). Within the period of the present volume, as we have seen (Chapter 7), the state acted repeatedly to restrict their scope and penalise their successes. In Soviet industry, construction, transport, and distribution, entrepreneurial functions were reserved entirely for the closed circle of party leaders who determined the plan and the party directives that implemented and supplemented the plan; no one could start up a new project or venture without their approval.

Schumpeter associated innovation with independent entrepreneurship. The Soviet economy of the 1930s showed that centralised policy initiatives could force new products and processes in limited fields such as machine building and the defence industry. But centralised decision

[36] Schumpeter (1934); for extension of this idea to the relationship of economic development to human agency in a more general sense, see Sen (1999).

making also made mistakes for which there was no market-economy corrective, such as in the selection of agricultural seed varieties (Chapter 7). As for the incentives faced by Soviet managers in their daily routines, these either discouraged innovation or channelled it into the simulated improvement of the production profile (see Sect. 2 in Chapter 10 above). Thus, the economic system failed to foster innovation. At the same time Soviet society was deliberately closed off from the fertilising influence of foreign ideas and examples, except to buy Western technologies and designs when terms were acceptable and steal them otherwise. The Russian demographer Anatolii Vishnevskii has characterised the outcome as 'conservative' modernisation, a style of economic development that aimed first to copy and then to rival the West, but that lacked the capability to succeed.[37]

Under Stalin's rule, Soviet Russia made a giant leap towards industrialisation. The radicalism and sweep of the economic policies that brought industrialisation about distributed large gains and large losses amongst the population. It is a mistake, however, to think that these gains and losses were the point, to suppose that the primary goal of Soviet economic policies was to promote the welfare of some groups in society or to enserf or exterminate others. The changes of this nature that came about were typically improvised in support of a greater goal. The greater goal was to build the military and industrial capabilities of the Soviet state, making it secure and powerful at home and abroad. This was the objective that Stalin and his colleagues pursued at all costs. While doing so, they made many miscalculations. Every mistake distributed additional losses across society, and the losses were magnified by Stalin's reluctance to recognise or adapt his policies to them. Despite this, hindsight leaves us with a measure of success: by 1939 Stalin had built an economy able to supply enough of the means of national power that the Soviet state would survive the coming war and be in position to compete for global influence in the decades that followed.

[37] Vishnevskii (2010); Ellman (2014): 363–365.

Afterword: The History of the Soviet Union

Credit: Nicky Vinti

I began my studies of the history of the Soviet Union in the early 1950s by writing a PhD thesis on the Soviet budgetary system. My thesis surveyed the whole period of Soviet development up to that time. In 1958 it was published as *The Development of the Soviet Budgetary System* by Cambridge University Press. In this book I already assumed that what had been emerging in the Soviet Union was a new civilisation.

I continued this work in the next half century by embarking on a quite detailed examination of Soviet history, concentrating on the economy. I began by working jointly with E. H. Carr on two of the volumes of his *Foundations of a Planned Economy, 1926–1929*. My own study began from 1930 and covered the period to the eve of the Second World War. In 1930 the Soviet planned economy (as I characterised it then) began to emerge, and to develop an increasingly large and elaborate industry. By 1940 Soviet industry, while much weaker than United States industry, was the second largest in the world, and it was powerful enough to play a major part in the defeat of the Axis powers in the Second World War.

R. W. Davies et al., *The Industrialisation of Soviet Russia Volume 7: The Soviet Economy and the Approach of War, 1937–1939*,
https://doi.org/10.1057/978-1-137-36238-4

But the Soviet system which emerged by 1940 was fundamentally different from the new civilisation which I had envisaged when I began this work. I continued to hold my original conception when I was writing about the early 1930s. But as my work continued, and my knowledge of the later 1930s became more detailed and more reliable, it became clear that the Soviet system, despite playing a major role in the defeat of Nazism, was no longer any kind of 'new civilisation' or socialist society, but a repressive regime in which violence and tyranny played a major part. My earlier conception of the course of Soviet history was fundamentally mistaken.

While my view of Soviet history has changed, two things have remained the same. One constant factor in my work has been the idea that when the details of history are in conflict with preconceived ideas, the latter should give way. Another is that I remain on the Left, believing today, as before, that a better organisation of society is possible.

R. W. Davies

Appendix A: All-Union People's Commissariats and Other Agencies of the USSR, 1937–1939

This appendix lists the nomenclature and reorganisations of the principal people's commissariats and state committees of the Soviet Union that existed on or between January 1, 1937 and December 31, 1939.[1] Note that a 'people's commissariat' was just a ministry by another name. In 1946, all people's commissariats were renamed ministries.

The order in which agencies are listed reflects function and importance mixed with chronology. The acronyms that are in use in the present and previous volumes are also provided in brackets, together with dates of original formation and final dissolution.

Our list illustrates a variety of processes. All organisations are shown with the dates of their creation and eventual disappearance. Some organisations continued without change of name, or they were re-graded up or down, and this involved a change of name, but no substantial change of function. Examples are the elevation of the bodies responsible for construction and procurements from government committees to people's commissariats in 1938.

Many new organisations were created by the subdivision of existing bodies, which disappeared; or by being spun off from parent organisations that persisted alongside. In industry, for example, there were just four people's commissariats on the first day of 1937, and this number

[1] Based on *Gosudarstvennaya vlast'* (1999) and *Sovet narodnykh komissarov* (1999).

R. W. Davies et al., *The Industrialisation of Soviet Russia Volume 7: The Soviet Economy and the Approach of War, 1937–1939*,
https://doi.org/10.1057/978-1-137-36238-4

increased to 20 by the first of 1940. Subdivisions and spin-offs are shown by a right ⇒arrow. Whether or not the original body continued to exist can be inferred from the dates of formation dissolution that are given.

Occasionally, a new body was created by amalgamating old ones, which disappeared, and this is shown by a left⇐arrow. This was how a people's commissariat with combined responsibility for both domestic and foreign trade was created in 1938.

Finally, the entries of those organisations for which the terminal date fell before the end of our three years are distinguished by a close ⊣ sign to the right.

The Central Government and Its Subcommittees

Council of People's Commissars (Sovnarkom: July 6, 1923–March 20, 1991)
Council of Labour and Defence (STO: July 17, 1923–November 23, 1937) ⊣
⟹ Economic Council (Ekonomsovet: November 23, 1937–March 21, 1941)

Note: Below this point, bodies listed were generally All-Union people's commissariats unless some other sufficient designation is given, so 'Finance' refers to the People's Commissariat of Finance of the USSR.

Other Central Regulatory Bodies

State Planning Commission (Gosplan: August 21, 1923–January 9, 1948)

Note: In many countries the statistical agency would have been an independent body, but in our period the Central Administration for National Economic Accounts (TsUNKhU: February 7, 1933–January 9, 1948) was a subordinate department of Gosplan.

Finance (Narkomfin: July 6, 1923–November 28, 1991)
State Bank (Gosbank: July 6, 1923–December 12, 1991)
Internal Affairs (NKVD: July 10, 1934–January 13, 1960)

Note: Although listed here as a regulator, the NKVD also had service and supply functions. While its administrations for state security (GUGB) and the police (GURKM) acted as regulators, the internal and border troops (GUPVO) provided services, and the labour camps (GULAG) functioned as a supply department for industry, agriculture, and construction.

Labour (Narkomtrud: July 6, 1923–December 31, 1991)
Commission for Soviet Control (KSK: February 11, 1934–September 6, 1940)

Note: Parallel to the KSK and with the same date of original formation was a party body, the Commission of Party Control (KPK).

The Service Commissariats

Defence (Narkomoborony: June 20, 1934–February 25, 1946)
⟹ Navy (December 30, 1937–February 25, 1946)
Communications (Narkomsvyaz: January 17, 1932–November 28, 1991)
Foreign Trade (Narkomvneshtorg: July 29, 1934–January 19, 1938) ⊣
Domestic Trade (Narkomvnutorg: July 29, 1934–January 19, 1938) ⊣
⟸ Trade (Narkomtorg: January 19, 1938–March 5, 1953)
Procurements, People's Commissariat of (Narkomzag: January 15, 1938–March 15, 1953)

Note: Narkomzag was formed on the basis of the previously existing Committee for Procurements (Komzag) of Sovnarkom.

Health (Narkomzdrav: July 20, 1936–November 30, 1991)

Note: Throughout this period, responsibility for education was devolved to the Union Republics, exercised in the RSFSR by a republican People's Commissariat of Education (Narkompros).

The Supply Commissariats (Industry, Transport, Agriculture and Construction)

Heavy Industry (Narkomtyazhprom: January 5, 1932–January 24, 1939) ⊣
⟹ Defence Industry (8 December 1936–January 11, 1939) ⊣
⟹ Aircraft Industry (January 11, 1939–March 15, 1953)

⟹ Ammunition (January 11, 1939–January 7, 1946)
⟹ Armament (January 11, 1939–March 15, 1953)
⟹ Shipbuilding Industry (January 11, 1939–March 5, 1953)
⟹ Machine Building (Engineering) (August 22, 1937–February 5, 1939) ⊣
⟹ General Machine Building (February 5, 1939–November 26, 1941)
⟹ Medium Machine Building (February 5, 1939–February 17, 1946)
⟹ Heavy Machine Building (February 5, 1939–March 5, 1953)
⟹ Construction Materials (January 24, 1939–May 10, 1957)
⟹ Fuel Industry (January 24, 1939–October 12, 1939) ⊣
⟹ Oil Industry (October 12, 1939–March 4, 1946)
⟹ Coal Industry (October 12, 1939–January 19, 1946)
⟹ Chemical Industry (January 24, 1939–June 7, 1958)
⟹ Nonferrous Metallurgy (January 24, 1939–July 29, 1948)
⟹ Ferrous Metallurgy (January 24, 1939–July 29, 1948)
⟹ Electrical Industry (January 24, 1939–April 17, 1940)
Timber Industry (Narkomles: January 5, 1932–July 29, 1948)
Light Industry (Narkomlegprom: January 5, 1932–March 15, 1953)
⟹ Textile Industry (January 2, 1939–December 28, 1948)
Food Industry (Narkompishcheprom: July 29, 1934–March 15, 1953)
⟹ Fishing Industry (January 19, 1939–May 8, 1946)
⟹ Meat and Dairy Industry (January 19, 1939–March 15, 1953)

Note: In addition to the industrial supply departments shown above, each Union-Republic had its own People's Commissariat of Local Industry through this period.

Transport (Railways) (Narkomput': July 6, 1923–January 20, 1992)
Water Transport (Narkomvod: January 30, 1931–April 9, 1939) ⊣
⟹ Maritime Fleet (April 9, 1939–March 15, 1953)
⟹ River Fleet (April 9, 1939–March 15, 1953)
Agriculture (Narkomzem: December 7, 1929–February 4, 1947)
State Farms (Narkomsovkhozov: October 1, 1932–March 26, 1946)
Construction, People's Commissariat of (Narkomstroi: May 29, 1939–January 19, 1946)

Note: Narkomstroi was formed on the basis of the previously existing Committee for Construction of Sovnarkom.

Appendix B: Tables

Repression and Forced Labour

See Tables B.1 to B.4.

R. W. Davies et al., *The Industrialisation of Soviet Russia Volume 7: The Soviet Economy and the Approach of War, 1937–1939*,
https://doi.org/10.1057/978-1-137-36238-4

Table B.1 Persons arrested by the NKVD, 1936–1940, by social background (numbers and per cent)

		(A)		*(B)*			
	1936	*1937*	*1938*	*1937*	*1938 (Jan.–July)*	*1939*	*1940*
Persons investigated, total	175,752	945,268	641,762			149,426	203,806
Persons under arrest and investigation, total	131,168	936,750	638,509	914,542	473,637	145,407	132,958
Persons newly arrested and under investigation, total	–	–	–	–	–	44,731	–
Total for which further detail is available	131,168	936,750	–	914,542	473,637	44,731	132,958
Of which, subtotals							
Socially alien elements	35,229	615,053	–	608,316	264,424	13,478	21,516
Religious servitors	–	33,382	–	33,191	11,186	414	–
Farmers and rural artisans	21,294	76,163	–	73,094	50,369	8,928	27,400
Manual workers	22,973	45,706	–	42,563	39,464	5,351	19,560
Office workers	41,009	134,989	–	129,250	90,440	8,513	18,381
Military personnel	2,840	14,339	–	11,406	6,300	2,418	5,431
Security personnel	1,945	3,837	–	3,679	3,113	1,546	280
Other and unspecified	5,878	13,281	–	13,043	8,341	5,629	31,616
Unexplained residual	–	–	–	–	–	–1,546	8,774
Subtotals, per cent of all arrests							
Socially alien elements	26.9	65.7	–	66.5	55.8	30.1	16.2
Priests and religious servitors	–	3.6	–	3.6	2.4	0.9	–
Farmers and rural artisans	16.2	8.1	–	8.0	10.6	20.0	20.6
Manual workers	17.5	4.9	–	4.7	8.3	12.0	14.7
Office workers	31.3	14.4	–	14.1	19.1	19.0	13.8
Military personnel	2.2	1.5	–	1.2	1.3	5.4	4.1
Security personnel	1.5	0.4	–	0.4	0.7	3.5	0.2

Source 1936, 1937 (A), 1938 (A), 1939, and 1940 from Mozokhin (2011): 450–480; 1937 (B) and 1938 (January–July) (B) from *Tragediya*, 5(2) (2006): 156, 158–159. For 1938, further detail is available only for January–July. For 1939, further detail is available only for persons newly arrested. Subtotals are calculated from data in the sources, as shown in Table B.2.

Table B.2 Persons arrested by the NKVD, 1936–1940, by social background: the composition of subtotals (numbers)

		(A)	(B)			
	1936	*1937*	*1937*	*1938 (Jan.–July)*	*1939*	*1940*
Socially alien elements						
'Former kulaks'	–	370,422	367,530	151,894	–	–
'Former people' (landowners, gentry, traders, gendarmes, etc.)	–	114,674	113,739	74,519	–	–
All 'former' elements	–	485,096	481,269	226,413	11,358	20,606
Persons without identified employment and déclassé elements	–	129,957	127,047	38,011	2,120	910
All socially alien elements, subtotal	35,229	615,053	608,316	264,424	13,478	21,516
Priests and religious servitors						
Servitors of religious cults	–	33,382	33,191	11,186	414	–
Farm workers and rural artisans						
Artisans	–	7,337	7,221	8,543	1,253	5,012
Individual peasants	8,425	27,209	25,731	13,443	4,603	16,121
Collective farmers	12,869	41,617	40,142	28,383	3,072	6,267
Farm workers and rural artisans, subtotal	21,294	76,163	73,094	50,369	8,928	27,400
Manual workers						
Industrial and transport workers	–	–	–	–	3,364	9,120
Seasonal agricultural and other workers	–	–	–	–	1,987	10,440
All manual workers, subtotal	22,973	45,706	42,563	39,464	5,351	19,560
Office workers				–		
Engineering and technical staff	2,087	–	–	–	362	702
Scientists	438	–	–	–	81	117

(continued)

Table B.2 (continued)

		(A)	*(B)*			
	1936	*1937*	*1937*	*1938 (Jan.–July)*	*1939*	*1940*
Teachers	1,549	–	–	–	381	1,449
Doctors	208	–	–	–	107	413
Workers in literature and the arts	359	–	–	–	121	352
Agricultural technicians	261	–	–	–	65	154
Leaders of organisations and institutions	–	–	–	–	971	1,123
All office workers listed above	4,902	–	–	–	2,088	4,310
Other office workers	36,107	–	–	–	6,425	14,071
All office workers, subtotal	41,009	134,989	129,250	90,440	8,513	18,381
Military personnel						
Senior Red Army commanders and political commissars	–	7,650	5,927	4,375	135	194
Red Army soldiers, junior officers, and trainees	–	6,689	5,479	1,925	611	4,483
Administrative Red Army staff	–	–	–	–	126	348
All military personnel, subtotal	2,840	14,339	11,406	6,300	2,418	5,431
Security personnel	–	–	–	–		
NKVD operative staff	–	–	–	–	1,362	123
Militia operative staff	–	–	–	–	184	157
All security personnel, subtotal	1,945	3,837	3,679	3,113	1,546	280
Others and unspecified						
Others (housewives, pensioners, etc.)	3,449	13,281	13,043	8,341	5,629	31,616
No information	2,429	–	–	–	–	–
Others and unspecified, subtotal	5,878	13,281	13,043	8,341	5,629	31,616

Source 1936, 1937 (A), 1939, and 1940 from Mozokhin (2011): 450–480; 1937 (B) and 1938 (January–July) (B) from *Tragediya*, 5(2) (2006): 156, 158–159.

Table B.3 Numbers held by the NKVD in GULAG labour camps and colonies and in prisons, January 1, 1936–1940 (thousands)

	1936	*1937*	*1938*	*1939*	*1940*
In labour camps	839	821	996	1317	1344
Of which, sentenced for counter-revolutionary crimes	106	105	185	454	445
In labour colonies and prisons					
In labour colonies	–	–	–	355	316
In prisons	–	–	–	350	190
In labour colonies and prisons, subtotal	457	375	885	705	506
Total	1,296	1,196	1,882	2,022	1,850

Source: *Sotsiologicheskie issledovaniya* (1991), no. 6: 10–27 (V. N. Zemskov), except that the numbers given there by Zemskov for labour colonies (only) include numbers in prisons up to 1938, and not thereafter. To compare 1939 and 1940 with earlier years, therefore, numbers in prisons are added from other sources. See GARF, 9413/1/11: 1–10, 9414/1/330, 55, and 9414/1/1156: 1–20.

Table B.4 Accounting for the GULAG camp population, 1937–1941 (thousands)

	1936	*1937*	*1938*	*1939*	*1940*
Present on January 1	839	821	996	1,317	1,344
Inflows, total	626	885	1,036	750	1,158
Of which, from					
NKVD camps	157	211	203	348	498
Other places of detention	431	637	803	384	645
Escapes	36	35	23	10	9
Other	1	1	8	7	6
Outflows, total	645	709	715	722	1,002
Of which, to					
NKVD camps	170	215	240	347	563
Other places of detention	24	44	56	75	57
Released	370	364	280	224	317
Died	21	25	91	51	47
Escaped	58	58	32	12	12
Other	2	3	17	14	6
Present on December 31	821	996	1,317	1,344	1,501

Source As Table B.3. *Note* In each year, numbers present on December 31 are made up of numbers present on January 1, plus inflows during the year, less outflows; numbers present on January 1 equal numbers present on December 31 of the previous year. Since the publication of these figures, the numbers of releases have been widely discussed. The evidence is convincing that many prisoners on the point of death were 'released to die', so that their deaths, expected to be imminent, would be accounted for outside the totals for which the GULAG might be held responsible (Nakonechnyi 2017; see especially *Europe-Asia Studies* 54(7), 1151–1172 (M. Ellman); Alexopoulos (2017); Nakonechnyi (2017), working paper.

Capital Investment

See Tables B.5 to B.10.

Table B.5 Capital investment plans, 1937 (million rubles and estimate prices)

		Targets for 1937, dated			
	Targets for 1936, dated May 29, 1936	*July 19, 1936*	*Dec. 7, 1936 (in estimate prices of 1935)*	*Dec. 27, 1936 (in prices of Dec. 1, 1936)*	*Mar. 29, 1937*
Heavy industry (inc. defence industry)	10,005	7,200	8,440	8,667	8,667
Light industry	1,372	1,250	1,400	1,406	1,406
Food industry	1,178	770	970	970	970
Timber industry	899	800	900	1,010	1,010
Local industries	1,078	770	770	770	770
Agriculture	2,192	2,300	2,300	2,301	2,314
Railways	5,487	4,200	4,200	5,541	5,553
Education	1,100	1,100	1,100	1,100	1,100
Health	–	1,000	1,000	1,000	–
Defence	2,400	2,250	2,450	2,450	–
NKVD	–	1,805	1,971	2,031	–
Other items	9,342	5,155	5,169	5,291	10,803
Total	35,053	28,600	30,670	32,537	32,593

Note Rows omit minor items, defined as not more than 100 mi.llion rubles at any point, or not more than 500 million and with no more than two points observed. Figures for 'Other items' are calculated as the difference between the total below and the rows above.

Source 1936 (dated May 29, 1936), from Vol. 6: 414; figures given here for Defence and Education, although not included in the May 29 plan, were fixed on December 19, 1935 and were not subsequently changed. Targets for 1937 (dated July 19, 1936), from RGASPI, 17/3/979: 56–59; GARF, 5446/1/487: 114–122 (art. 1282/236s). Targets for 1937 (dated December 7, 1936): RGASPI, 17/3/982: 67–69 (the document, dated December 6, was approved by Sovnarkom on the following day); GARF, 5446/57/43: 168–201 (art. 2075/413s). 1937 (dated December 27, 1936), from RGASPI, 17/3/982: 1–2. 99–100. 1937 (dated March 29, 1937) from *Narodno-khozyastvennyi plan na 1937g.* (1937).

Table B.6 Capital investment plans, 1938–1940 (million rubles and estimate prices)

	Targets for 1938			*Targets for 1939*		
	Dated Feb. 23, 1938		*No date, but 1939 or 1940*	*Dated Nov. 22, 1938*	*Added on Mar. 2, 1939*	*No date, but 1939 or 1940*
	In prices of Dec. 1, 1937	*In prices of 1938*				
Defence industry	5,000	4,650	–	4,900	+1,050	5,142
Machine building	2,000	1,850	–	1,800	–	1,682
Other heavy industry	6,032	5,610	–	6,700	–	8,688
All heavy industry, subtotal	13,032	12,110	14,821	13,400	–	15,512
Light industry	1,265	1,176	1,296	1,050	–	1,048
Food industry	990	921	1,029	900	–	987
Timber industry	850	791	773	500	–	447
Local industries	500	465	485	300	–	440
Agriculture (collective farms)	2,100	2,050	2,010	1,350	–	1,408
State farms	340	326	362	250	–	323
Railways	5,030	4,728	4,665	4,200	–	3,388
Water transport	710	678	773	600	–	601
Education	807	738	785	480	–	491
Health	790	727	737	450	–	435
Defence	2,147	1,997	–	0	+1,776	
NKVD	2,970	2,732	–	3,150	+803	
Urban services (narkomkhozy)			1,987	500	–	1,376
Not included in above	4,847	4,500	9,884	6,259	–	11,608
Total	36,378	33,939	39,606	33,389	37,018	38,063

Note The row classification of spending departments aims at broad consistency with that of Table B.5; but note that by 1939 the main industrial commissariats had been greatly reorganised, as described in Appendix A. Rows omit minor items, defined as not more than 100 million rubles in any year, or not more than 500 million and with no more than two years observed. Figures 'Not included in above' are calculated as the difference between the total and the rows above.

Source 1938 (dated February 23, 1938), from RGASPI, 17/3/996: 1, 44–46. 1938 (no date, but 1939 or 1940), RGAE, 1562/10/710a: 1–2. 1939 (dated November 22, 1938), from RGASPI, 17/3/1003: 49–50. 1939 (added, March 2, 1939): these supplementary allocations are from RGASPI, 17/162/24: 113. 1939 (no date, but 1940), from RGAE, 1562/10/991a: 3–5.

Table B.7 Capital investment, 1936–1939 (million rubles and current or estimate prices)

	1936	1937			1938	1939
		(A)	(B)	(C)		
	(current prices)	*(current prices)*	*(estimate prices)*	*(estimate prices)*	*(estimate prices)*	*(estimate prices)*
Defence industry	–	–	–	–	–	4,457
Machine building	–	–	–	–	–	1,339
Other heavy industry	–	–	–	–	–	6,759
All heavy industry, subtotal	10,099	9,266	8,609	8,794	10,471	12,555
Light industry	1,133	1,233	1,003	1,044	1,038	931
Food industry	1,546	1,368	789	798	884	870
Timber industry	790	786	680	669	559	401
Local industries	830	552	419	362	355	340
Domestic trade	350	363	–	166	171	155
Food procurements	369	255	–	192	326	380
Agriculture (collective farms)	3,050	2,209	1,964	2,007	1,683	1,250
State farms	579	535	–	273	258	260
Railways	4,602	4,217	3,957	4,007	3,642	2,800
Water transport	1,249	982	–	550	656	507
NKVD (highway construction only)	575	595	–	517		
Communications	330	263	–	202	202	152
Education	896	746	649	799	596	393
Health	525	805	–	630	458	297

(continued)

Table B.7 (continued)

		1937				
	1936 *(current prices)*	*(A)* *(current prices)*	*(B)* *(estimate prices)*	*(C)* *(estimate prices)*	*1938* *(estimate prices)*	*1939* *(estimate prices)*
Urban services (*narkomkhozy*)	1,585	–	–	–	1,489	1,045
Not included in above	6,803	7,854	9,449	6,649	6,526	8,061
Total	35,311	32,029	27,519	27,659	29,314	30,710
Investments not included in total						
'Above the limit'	–	–	684	–	–	–
'Outside the plan'	–	–	3,826	–	–	–

Note The row classification of spending departments aims at broad consistency with that of Table B.5, but note that by 1939 the main industrial commissariats had been greatly reorganised, as described in Appendix A. Rows omit minor items, defined as not more than 100 million rubles in any year, or not more than 500 million and with no more than two years observed. Figures 'Not included in above' are calculated as the difference between the total and the rows above.

Source 1936: Vol. 6: 406. 1937 (A): RGAE,1562/10/502a: 27 (no date, but 1938). These figures include not only capital investment which formed part of the main state plan, but also earmarked (*tselevye*), 'outside-the-limit' (*vnelimitnye*) and 'above-the-plan' (*vneplanovye*) outlays. Such outlays, which did not form part of the main state plan, increased sharply in 1936 and 1937. The figures for 1937 (B) and (C), 1938, and 1939 exclude these items, and also most of the capital repair figures previously included in capital investment. 1937 (B): RGAE, 4372/35/255, 48–49. In addition to the state plan total of 27,519 million rubles, and not counted here, above-plan (*vneplanovye*) outlays amounted to 684 million rubles, and extra-limit (*vnelimitnye*) outlays to 3826 million rubles. 1937 (C), GARF, 5446/22a/1441, 33 (September 20, 1938): 1938, RGAE, 1562/10/710a, 1–2 (no date, but 1939 or 1940). 1939, RGAE, 1562/10/991a, 3–5 (no date, but 1940).

Table B.8 Capital investment in defence and the NKVD, 1936–1939 (million rubles and per cent)

		1937		*1938*		*1939*	
	1936 outcome	*Plan*	*Outcome*	*Plan*	*Outcome*	*Plan*	*Outcome*
Defence industry	1,467	3,380	2,200	5,000	3,708	5,950	5,142
Defence (army and navy)	2,518	2,450	1,936	2,147	–	1,776	–
NKVD	2,694	2,047	2,643	2,970	–	3,953	–
Defence subtotal	6,679	7,877	6,779	10,117	–	11,679	–
All capital investment	35,311	32,593	32,029	36,378	29,314	37,018	30,710
Defence, per cent of total	18.9	24.2	21.2	27.8	–	31.5	–

Note In Tables B.5 and B.6, capital investment in defence industry would have been counted under heavy industry; capital investment in defence (army and navy) and by the NKVD would have been counted under 'other investment'.

Source 1936 (outcome), defence industry and defence (army and navy) from *Europe-Asia Studies*, 49(3) (1997): 380, 384 (Davies and Harrison); NKVD from GARF, 1562/10/582a: 6; all capital investment is from Table B.7. 1937 (plan), defence industry from RGASPI, 17/162/20: 191–192 (January 17, 1937); defence (army and navy); NKVD from GARF, 5446/1/490: 2 (January 5, 1937); all capital investment is from Table B.5 (March 29, 1937). 1937 (outcome), defence industry from RGAE, 4372/91/218: 7 (February 5, 1939) but an alternative figure of 2473 (in 'estimate prices') is given in GARF, 5446/22a/1441: 33 (the head of TsUNKhU to Molotov, September 20, 1938; it is not clear whether the latter figure includes investment in the residual defence production facilities of the Commissariat of Heavy Industry); defence (army and navy) from *Europe-Asia Studies*, 49(3) (1997): 380 (Davies and Harrison); NKVD from GARF, 1562/10/582a: 6; all capital investment is from Table B.7 (1937 (A)). 1938 (plan): RGASPI, 17/3/996: 44–45 (February 23, 1938); all capital investment is from Table B.6 (1938, in prices of December 1, 1937). 1939 (plan): Table B.6. 1939 (outcome): Table B.7.

Table B.9 Capital investment in the defence industries, 1937–1939: plans and outcomes (million rubles)

	1937	*1938*	*1939*
Outcomes			
—Aviation Industry	722	1,493	–
—Armament	360	491	–
—Ammunition	536	779	–
—Shipbuilding	421	680	–
—Sixth administration	–	265	–
Total	2,200	3,708	4,457
Targets			
Plan dated February 23, 1938, total	–	4,650	–
Plan dated January 4, 1939			
—Aviation Industry	–	–	1,427
—Armament	–	–	575
—Ammunition	–	–	1,525
—Shipbuilding	–	–	945
Total	–	–	4,900
Plan dated February 5, 1939			
—Aviation Industry	–	–	1,853
—Armament	–	–	1,050
—Ammunition	–	–	1,636
—Shipbuilding	–	–	1,181
—Sixth administration	–	–	255
Total	–	–	5,975
Plan dated March 2, 1939, total	–	–	5,950

Note The sixth administration of the Commissariat of the Defence Industry was responsible for the supply of chemical weapons.

Source Outcomes for 1937 and 1938, from Samuelson (2000): 193; for 1939, from GARF, 1562/10/991a: 4 (not dated but 1940). Targets: until 1938, the Commissariat of the Defence Industry was not planned separately from its parent ministry, the Commissariat of Heavy Industry. Plan of 1938 (February 23, 1938): as Table B.6 (in 1938 estimate prices). Plan of 1939 (January 4, 1939): Stepanov (2006): 492; these figures break down the total given in Table B.6 as approved on November 22, 1938. Plan of February 5, 1939: Samuelson (2000): 193. Plan of March 2, 1939: Table B.6, combining the additional allocation of that date with the sum previously approved on November 22, 1938.

Table B.10 NKVD capital construction, billion rubles: plans and outcomes, 1937–1940 (million rubles)

	1936	*1937*	*1938*	*1939*	*1940*
Initial target	–	2,060	2,970	3,150	3,400
Final target	–	2,500	–	4,300	4,500
Outcome	2,490	1,786	3,073	3,600	4,400

Note Figures shown are capital works 'within the [budgetary] limits' of the NKVD. They exclude capital projects subcontracted to NKVD by other agencies and paid for by them, except as noted below. For this reason, they fall short of the numbers shown under NKVD capital investment in Table 3 in Chapter 4.
Source 1936 (outcome) and 1937 (initial target of March 10, 1937), from GARF, R-5446/20/461: 1; R5446/1v/491: 119–121; see also RGASPI, 17/3/979: 61. 1937 (final plan): calculated as outcome divided by 71.6% (plan fulfilment) from GARF, R-9414/4/3: 19. 1937 (outcome) and 1938 (initial plan of 27 April 38), from GARF, R-6757/1/7, 13–56. In addition to the sum shown, the 1938 plan also obligated NKVD to undertake capital work for other agencies to the value of 566 million rubles. 1938 (outcome), from GARF, R-5446/24a/2332: 59. 1939 (initial plan), from RGASPI, 17/3/1003: 49. 1939 (final plan and outcome), from GARF, R-5446/24a/18: 68–74. 1940 (initial plan), from GARF, R-5446/25a/18: 90–93, 134. 1940 (final plan), from GARF, R-5446/24a/4: 59. 1940 (outcome), from GARF, R-5446/25a/7181: 17. The NKVD also completed capital work for other agencies in 1940 to the value of 375 million rubles.

INDUSTRY

See Tables B.11 to B.25.

Table B.11 Industrial production, 1935–1940

	1935	*1936*	*1937*	*1938*	*1939*	*1940*
Gross value of output in million rubles at plan prices of 1926/27						
All industry	66,782	85,929	95,532	106,834	123,915	138,479
Of which (1)						
Large-scale	62,137	80,929	90,166	100,602	116,128	129,460
Small-scale	4,645	5,000	5,366	6,232	7,787	9,019
Of which (2)						
Producer goods	38,898	50,915	55,254	62,087	73,793	84,774
Consumer goods	27,884	35,014	40,273	44,747	50,122	53,705
Change over previous year, per cent						
All industry	–	28.7	11.2	11.8	16.0	11.8
Of which (1)						
Large-scale	–	30.2	11.4	11.6	15.4	11.5
Small-scale	–	7.6	7.3	16.1	25.0	15.8
Of which (2)						
Producer goods	–	30.9	8.5	12.4	18.9	14.9
Consumer goods	–	25.6	15.0	11.1	12.0	7.1

Source RGAE, 1562/329/4145: 3–4 (not dated but 1951). Growth rates are calculated from the source.

Table B.12 Industrial employment, 1936–1940: alternative estimates (thousands and annual average)

	1936	*1937*	*1938*	*1939*	*1940*
Thousands					
The 1938 industrial census					
Industrial-production employees	9,466	10,112	10,357	–	–
Of which, manual employees	7,447	7,924	8,031	–	–
Post-war revisions					
Manual employees, all industry	–	10,563	10,736	10,992	11,567
Of which, large-scale industry	8,872	9,079	9,150	9,284	9,787
Change over previous year, per cent					
The 1938 industrial census					
Industrial-production employees	7.7	6.8	2.4	–	–
Of which, manual employees	7.1	6.4	1.4	–	–
Post-war revisions					
Manual employees, all industry	–	–	1.6	2.4	5.2
Of which, large-scale industry	7.2	2.3	0.8	1.5	5.4

Note and Source The 1938 industrial census, from RGAE, 4372/36/871: 34ob, 35 (not dated but 1939). Industrial production employees comprised manual workers, engineers and technicians, staff (i.e. management personnel), junior service personnel, and apprentices. Numbers excluded cooperative artels and collective farmers working in kolkhoz industrial enterprises, and auxiliary industrial enterprises in non-industrial commissariats. Workers in auxiliary industrial enterprises in 1938 would bring the overall total in that year to 11,001 thousand, and the manual total to 8474 thousand.

Post-war revisions, from RGAE, 1562/329/4145: 10 (not dated but 1951). Numbers included cooperative artels and collective farmers working in kolkhoz industrial enterprises. The large increases shown for 1940 are to be explained partly by the border changes of 1939.

Table B.13 Gross value of production of the defence industry by commissariat, 1937–1940 (million rubles at plan prices of 1926/27 and per cent)

	1937	*1938*	*1939*	*1940*
Million rubles				
Aviation	2,345	3,238	4,883	6,310
Shipbuilding	1,726	2,011	2,866	4,448
Armaments	2,127	3,001	4,432	5,500
Ammunition	1,561	2,424	3,719	5,710
Total	7,759	10,673	15,900	21,968
Change over previous year, per cent				
Aviation	–	38.1	50.8	29.2
Shipbuilding	–	16.5	42.5	55.2
Armaments	–	41.1	47.7	24.1
Ammunition	–	55.3	53.4	53.5
Total	–	37.6	49.0	38.2

Source Samuelson (2000): 194.

Table B.14 Defence-related industrial products, 1937–1940 (physical units)

	1937	*1938*	*1939*	*1940*
Aircraft (all types)	6,033	7,690	10,336	9,776
Tanks	1,610	2,386	3,107	2,793
Artillery units	5,443	12,687	16,459	13,724
Machine guns (thousands)	75	112	96	–
Cartridges (millions)	1,015	1,848	2,194	2,820
Shells (thousands)	4,924	12,426	18,099	14,921
Aviation bombs (thousands)	795	1,728	2,834	2,194
Rifles (thousands)	567	1,171	1,497	1,461
Motor vehicles (all types and thousands)	200	211	202	145

Source Aircraft, as Table B.19; tanks, as Table B.20; motor vehicles, from Zaleski (1980): 553, 580; all other items from *Europe-Asia Studies*, 49(3) (1997): 403–406 (Davies and Harrison), correcting thousands of cartridges to millions.

Table B.15 Civilian industrial products, 1937–1940 (physical units)

	1937	*1938*	*1939*	*1940 (expected)*
Oil and gas, mn tons	21.5	30.2	30.3	34.7
Ferrous metallurgy				
Iron, mn tons	14.5	14.7	14.5	15.0
Steel, mn tons	17.7	18.1	17.6	18.5
Rolled steel, mn tons	13.0	13.3	12.7	13.2
Of which, high-grade	2.5	2.7	3.0	3.3
Iron ore, mn tons	27.8	26.6	26.9	29.9
Coking coal, mn tons	19.8	19.4	19.9	20.9
Timber industry				
Unprocessed timber and firewood, mn cu. metres	201.5	212.7	252.6	244.0
Unprocessed timber, mn cu. metres	111.3	110.8	122.2	119.0
Sawn timber, mn cu. metres	28.8	28.1	28.7	28.8
Paper, thou. tons	831.6	832.8	799.8	786.0
Building materials				
Cement, thou. tons	5,454	5,688	5,197	5,400
Structural timber, thou. cu. metres	3,998	4,190	5,951	6,500
Ferroconcrete, thou. cu. metres	135.4	141.0	163.2	210.0
Textiles				
Cotton cloth, mn metres	3,360	3,510	3,665	3,730
Linen cloth, mn metres	252.8	–	255.4	263.0
Food industry				
Fish catch, mn centners	16.1	–	15.7	14.1
Meat, thou. tons	797.2	986.5	1,221	1,135
Lump sugar, thou. tons	2,421	–	1,826	2,250
Conserves, mn cans equivalent	872.4	926.0	1,032	1,095
Raw spirit, mn dekalitres	76.1	84.6	93.7	83.0

Note Figures under textiles are for products of enterprises of the People's Commissariat of the Textile Industry and, under meat, of the People's Commissariat of the Meat and Dairy Industry; both departments were formed in 1939. The 1938 figures for cotton cloth, meat, conserves, and raw spirit, not given in the source, are interpolated on the given 1939 figures and ratios of 1939–1938.
Source Industrializatsiya, 1938–1941 (1973): 127–145.

Table B.16 Coal, 1936–1939: average daily production by year and month (thousand tons)

	1936	*1937*	*1938*	*1939*
January	358	351	366	379
February	356	351	361	381
March	346	337	357	371
April	343	329	351	353
May	330	326	341	349
June	320	341	345	353
July	310	327	338	359
August	324	333	336	359
September	328	330	333	363
October	349	343	343	376
November	356	359	354	386
December	355	375	342	399
Annual average	339.6	341.8	347.3	369.0

Source Osnovnye pokazateli (December 1936): xv–xix; 11 (1940): 7–13.

Table B.17 Crude oil and gas, 1936–1939: average daily production by year and month (thousand tons)

	1936	*1937*	*1938*	*1939*
January	78.4	76.4	84.6	83.2
February	79.8	72.1	84.8	85.0
March	79.6	75.2	84.5	85.7
April	78.9	79.8	87.7	87.7
May	81.1	85.0	90.4	92.2
June	81.2	87.7	94.6	93.9
July	79.9	88.0	92.9	93.8
August	78.3	89.2	91.1	91.9
September	76.3	91.0	88.8	92.0
October	80.0	89.5	88.6	89.1
November	82.4	86.8	87.5	89.7
December	80.3	85.2	84.7	86.2
Average for year	79.7	83.8	88.4	89.2

Source as Table B.16.

Table B.18 Rolled steel, 1936–1939: average daily production by year and month (thousand tons)

	1936	*1937*	*1938*	*1939*
January	34.1	37.3	34.3	32.2
February	33.2	35.7	39.5	40.1
March	33.3	36.8	39.2	40.6
April	35.3	36.7	40.8	39.9
May	33.5	35.4	36.6	36.0
June	33.0	34.3	38.6	35.2
July	29.6	32.1	32.4	30.8
August	31.2	33.3	33.9	30.6
September	33.3	34.5	34.6	30.9
October	37.2	38.1	39.1	31.9
November	36.9	35.5	38.2	32.5
December	39.5	38.9	31.0	35.3
Average for year	34.2	35.7	36.5	34.7

Source as Table B.16.

Table B.19 Aircraft produced by type and model, 1936–1940 (units)

	1936	*1937*	*1938*	*1939*	*1940*
Fighters					
I-15bis	–	–	1,104	1,304	–
DI-6	10	112	100	–	–
I-16	906	1,887	1,175	1,835	2,710
I-153	–	–	–	1,011	2,362
Other models	41	73	–	–	–
Fighters, total	957	2,072	2,379	4,150	5,072
Bombers					
TB-3	115	23	1	–	–
SB	268	926	1,427	1,778	2,195
DB-3		12	204	555	808
DB-3F		33	195	404	298
Yak-4 (BB-22)	–	–	–	–	138
Other models	31	2	–	–	–
Bombers, total	414	996	1,827	2,737	3,439
Reconnaisance					
R-5 SSS	129	270	–	–	–
RZet	885	135	–	–	–
R-10 (KhAI-5)	11	43	115	331	18
MBR-2	109	360	364	192	38

(continued)

Table B.19 (continued)

	1936	*1937*	*1938*	*1939*	*1940*
Other models	5	10	–	–	13
Recon., total	1,139	818	479	523	69
Trainers					
U-2	968	1,782	2,016	1,584	522
UT-1	–	155	534	551	1
UT-2	–	–	145	540	548
Trainers, total	968	1,937	2,695	2,675	1,071
Passenger and other					
VS	298	–	–	–	–
AP	270	50	100	125	125
SP	118	160	210	126	–
Other models	110	–	–	–	–
P&O, total	796	210	310	251	125
All aircraft, total	4,274	6,033	7,690	10,336	9,776

Source Byushgens, ed. (1992), 1: 432–435 (G. S. Kostyrchenko). 'Other models' are those models of which less than 100 units were produced over the five years shown.

Table B.20 Tanks produced by type and model, 1936–1940 (units)

	1936	*1937*	*1938*	*1939*	*1940*
Small tanks					
T38	1,046	216	–	158	–
T-40	–	–	–	–	41
Light tanks					
T-26	1,313	550	1,054	1,399	1,601
BT-7/7M	1,063	788	1,221	1,402	780
Medium tanks					
T-28	101	46	100	140	13
T-34	–	–	–	2	115
Heavy tanks					
T-35	15	10	11	6	–
KV	–	–	–	–	243
Total	3,948	1,610	2,386	3,107	2,793

Source Mel'tyukhov (2002): 511–516.

Table B.21 Tractors and combine harvesters produced, 1936–1940 (units and horsepower)

	1936	*1937*	*1938*	*1939*	*1940*
Production					
Tractors					
—In thousand units	112.9	50.1	49.2	48.1	31.6
—In thou. 15 hp equivalents	173.2	66.5	93.4	88.8	66.2
Grain combines (thou. units)	42.6	43.9	22.9	14.8	12.8
Plan targets					
Tractors					
—In thousand units	96.2	79.0	56.0	–	–
—In thou. 15 hp equivalents	154.3	172.7	–	–	–
Grain combines (thou. units)	61.0	55.0	30.0	–	–
Production, per cent of target					
Tractors					
—In thousand units	117	65	88	–	–
—In thou. 15 hp equivalents	112	39	–	–	–
Grain combines (thou. units)	70	80	76	–	–

Note In the mid-1930s the tractor production plan was regularly over-fulfilled. This reflected, among other factors, the urgency of mechanising agriculture to replace the horses lost during collectivisation. The last year in which this happened was 1936.

The table, which is based on published data, suggests that the supply of tractors collapsed in 1937, the number of units by 56%, and the number of horsepower by 62%. It might be asked whether this reflects the chaos in production or the chaos in statistical reporting. A partial check on the figures is provided by the secret *Pokazateli vypolneniya*, which report the aggregate capacity of tractors produced in 1937 as 1,240,000 horsepower compared with 2,616,000 in 1936, a decline of 53%. This is in proportion to the published decline in the number of tractors produced. It implies that average horsepower per tractor produced was 23.2 in 1936 and 24.3 in 1937, which is plausible. The figures suggest that the collapse of tractor production was real, although not perhaps as large as implied by the published figures on horsepower.

The figures in the table generally support the idea that the tractors supplied to Soviet agriculture were becoming more powerful over the period. On the published figures, horsepower per tractor rose from 23.0 in 1936 to 28.5 in 138, 27.7 in 1939, and 31.4 in 1940.

Source Production and plan targets: Zaleski (1980): 552–553, 580–581, except 1938 plan figures from *Pokazateli vypolneniya* (1938): 37.

Table B.22 Agricultural fertiliser produced, 1936–1940 (thousand tons)

	1936	*1937*	*1938*	*1939*	*1940*
Production					
Mineral fertiliser	2,839	3,240	3,413	3,562	3,238
Phosphoric fertiliser 14%	1,671	1,963	2,070	2,380	1,810
Phosphoric fertiliser 18.7%	1,257	1,472	1,596	1,638	1,352
Ground natural phosphate	623	650	632	582	382
Potash fertiliser	407	356	358	383	532
Ammonium sulphate	523	762	828	959	972
Target					
Mineral fertiliser	–	–	–	–	–
Phosphoric fertiliser 14%	1,680	2,500	–	–	–
Phosphoric fertiliser 18.7%	1,258	1,872	1,767	–	–
Ground natural phosphate	720	884	–	–	–
Potash fertiliser	514	–	–	–	–
Ammonium sulphate	–	–	937	–	–
Production, per cent of target					
Mineral fertiliser	–	–	–	–	–
Phosphoric fertiliser 14%	99.5	78.5	–	–	–
Phosphoric fertiliser 18.7%	99.9	78.6	90.3	–	–
Ground natural phosphate	86.5	73.5	–	–	–
Potash fertiliser	79.0	–	–	–	–
Ammonium sulphate	–	–	88.4	–	–

Source Zaleski (1980): 550–553, 580–581.

Table B.23 Gross value of industrial production of Union and Union-Republic commissariats, 1937–1939 (million rubles at 1926/27 prices and per cent)

	Report of Jan. 1939			*Report of Jan. 1940*		
	1937	*1938*	*Change, per cent*	*1938*	*1939*	*Change, per cent*
Industrial production, total	69,189	77,520	12.0	78,854	90,686	15.0
Of which						
Heavy and defence industry	36,924	42,517	15.1	42,799	51,186	19.6
Timber industry	3,006	2,891	−3.8	2,848	2,999	5.3
Light industry	14,508	15,301	5.5	16,146	17,519	8.5
Food industry	12,803	14,747	15.2	14,987	16,536	10.3
Procurements	1,948	2,065	6.0	2,073	2,446	18.0

Source Report of January 1939, from ***Pravda***, January 17, 1939. Report of January 1940: comparable row totals are calculated from the more detailed data reported in Table B.24. 'Heavy and defence industry' is the total of the defence industries, machine building, and 'other' heavy industries, except the timber industry, which is counted separately. 'Light industry' is the light and textile industries. 'Food industry' is the meat, fish, and food industries.

Table B.24 Gross value of industrial production of Union and Union-Republic People's Commissariats in 1939 compared with 1938 (million rubles at 1926/27 prices and per cent)

	1938	*1939*	*Change, per cent*
Union and Union-Republic commissariats, total	84,104	96,462	14.7
Of which			
Union and Union-Republic industrial commissariats			
Defence industry and machine building			
Defence Industry	11,556	16,935	46.5
Medium Machine Building	6,078	6,998	15.1
Heavy Machine Building	2,393	2,720	13.7
General Machine Building	2,102	2,257	7.4
Other heavy industry			
Non-ferrous Metallurgy	1,419	1,619	14.1
Chemical Industry	3,860	4,347	12.6
Coal Industry	1,888	2,063	9.2
Electrical Industry	3,838	4,117	7.3
Construction Materials	1,550	1,633	5.3
Timber Industry	2,848	2,999	5.3
Oil Industry	2,836	2,974	4.8
Ferrous Metallurgy	5,279	5,525	4.7
Procurements and food and light industry			
Procurements	2,073	2,446	18.0
Meat Industry	3,791	4,330	14.2
Fish Industry	847	943	11.4
Food Industry	10,350	11,264	8.8
Textile Industry	9,055	9,851	8.8
Light Industry	7,092	7,668	8.1
Union and Union-Republic non-industrial commissariats			
Maritime Fleet	119	144	20.6
River Fleet	208	250	20.2
Film Industry	300	355	18.3
Health	267	311	16.5
Communications	230	263	14.5
Finance	179	188	5.3
Transport	1,265	1,269	0.4
Union Republic commissariats			
Local industry	2,413	2,703	12.0
Local fuel industry	270	293	8.4

Source: *Pravda*, January 15, 1940.

Table B.25 Research, design, and production facilities of the Soviet defence industry by production specialisation, 1917–1940 (number of establishments and selected years)

	1917	*1928*	*1935*	*1936*	*1937*	*1938*	*1939*	*1940*
Munitions	98	143	268	306	326	359	444	506
Aviation	38	75	154	182	199	215	287	391
Electronics	35	101	188	207	216	235	267	296
Armament	27	71	121	159	166	176	208	221
Shipbuilding	28	55	100	112	115	126	140	149
Armoured vehicles	4	16	44	49	50	58	83	96
Atomic research	0	1	13	15	15	17	20	21
All defence facilities	230	460	886	1,028	1,085	1,184	1,449	1,679

Source Dexter and Rodionov (2017) at http://warwick.ac.uk/vpk/. There is some rounding in the totals, because not all enterprises were uniquely identified with one specialisation, and a few are distributed fractionally.

Transport

Table B.26 Railway freight, 1928 and 1936–1939 (standard two-axle daily goods wagons loaded per day in thousands and monthly and annual averages)

	1936	*1937*	*1938*	*1939*
January	77.6	79.3	75.2	81.3
February	76.4	78.1	79.8	89.5
March	86.7	81.2	80.0	89.9
April	89.0	89.7	85.3	92.3
May	92.4	95.9	92.6	95.2
June	89.9	98.0	96.7	100.2
July	90.5	98.7	96.3	102.0
August	92.2	97.6	94.8	100.3
September	92.0	96.9	94.6	92.2
October	86.5	94.1	93.9	96.8
November	84.0	89.7	90.9	94.9
December	80.4	78.0	76.0	85.6
Full year	86.5	89.8	88.0	93.4

Source: *Zheleznodorozhnyi transport (1926–1941)* (1970).

Agriculture

See Tables B.27 to B.41.

Table B.27 The stock of draft power in Soviet agriculture, 1929 and 1936–1940 (units and horse-equivalents)

		1929	*1936*	*1937*	*1938*	*1939*	*1940*
Thousand units							
Horses		34,638	15,514	15,884	16,220	17,200	17,700
Tractors		391	6,134	7,672	8,385	9,256	9,937
Thousand horse-equivalents							
Tractors	(A) at 2:1	783	12,268	15,344	16,770	18,512	19,874
	(B) at 3:1	1,174	18,402	23,016	25,155	27,769	29,811
Million horse-equivalents							
Draft power, total	(A) at 2:1	35,421	27,782	31,228	32,990	35,712	37,574
	(B) at 3:1	1,566	24,536	30,688	33,540	37,025	39,748

Note Tractors are converted into horse-equivalents at the rate of two horses (lower limit) or three horses (upper limit) to one tractor. It is reasonable to conclude that the total of draft power in Soviet agriculture returned to the previous peak of 1929 no earlier than 1937 and no later than 1939.
Source For 1929, from *Sel'skoe khozyaistvo* (1936): 513–519. For 1936–1938, from *Pokazateli vypolneniya* (1938): 90. For 1939–1940, from RGAE, 1562/33/118: 31–32.

Table B.28 Predicted weather effects on grain yields across producer regions, 1936–1940 (per cent and percentile over 1883–1992)

	1936	*1937*	*1938*	*1939*	*1940*
Central Blacksoil	−9.2	6.9	−3.0	−7.9	−4.7
Ukraine	−2.4	−8.0	−1.1	−8.1	3.3
Volga	−46.6	23.6	−11.1	−34.2	−17.5
Urals	−48.2	−1.8	13.6	−42.1	−0.4
North Caucasus	31.3	54.1	15.7	−16.6	23.1
Siberia	−18.2	−0.3	32.8	3.7	−2.2
All producer regions, average	−12.7	9.8	6.5	−16.4	1.4
Percentile over 1883–1992	20	78	71	13	50

Note As described in the source, estimates are based on the impact of weather conditions on annual grain yields observed in two sample periods, from 1883 to 1913, and from 1953 to 1992. During the sample periods, the yield data are considered to be more reliable than in the Stalin years. The sample periods are used to estimate the net impact on grain yields in the given year predicted by weather conditions through the growing season, and the estimators can then be applied to out-of-sample weather observations. The unit of measurement is per cent of the yield under average weather conditions. In the Central Blacksoil region in 1936, for example, weather conditions during the growing season are estimated to have reduced grain yields by 9.2% and across all the producer regions by an average of 12.7%.
Percentile over 1883–1992: the methodology estimates the impact of weather, averaged over all producer regions, in each year from 1883 to 1992. (The North Caucasus and Siberia are not counted until 1914, however, when they are added to the average.) This gives 110 annual observations, which can be ranked from best to worst, and the rank of each observation can be represented as a percentile, meaning the percent of years with worse weather than in the given year. In 1936, for example, the poor weather was worse in just 20% of years over the long century, and in 1939 it was even less favourable: only 13% of years had worse weather than in that year. In 1937 and 1938 it was the converse: the weather was worse in 78% and 71% of all the years respectively. The weather in 1940 was exactly at the median for the century. The extremes of the distribution are found at −45.8 in 1921 (the worst year of the century) and at +30.0 in 1941 (the best year).
Source Bishop and Wheatcroft (2018), working paper.

Table B.29 Sowing plans, all crops, 1934/35 to 1938/39 (million hectares)

			1936/37			
	1934/35	*1935/36*	*Initial*	*Revised*	*1937/38*	*1938/39*
Autumn sowing target						
Approved by Sovnarkom	37.8	37.8	38.4	–	36.5	36.8
Implied by *Izvestiya* reports	38.0	37.7	38.2	38.2	36.5	36.0
Proposed by Gosplan	–	37.6	38.6	–	37.0	–
Proposed by Narkomzem (exc. many state farms)	–	34.5	35.6	–	36.9	–
Spring sowing target						
Approved by Sovnarkom	93.8	96.3	99.4	–	98.2	93.7
—Exc. previously sown perennial grass	90.9	92.2	94.5	–	90.8	84.2
Implied by *Izvestiya* reports	90.9	92.2	93.4	84.7	84.3	–
Proposed by Gosplan	–	97.4	100.7	–	–	–
Proposed by Narkomzem (exc. previously sown perennial grass, exc. many state farms	–	83.3	88.1	–	–	–
Sowing target, total						
Approved by Sovnarkom	131.6	134.1	137.8	–	134.7	130.5
—Exc. previously sown perennial grass	128.7	130.0	132.9	–	127.3	121.0
Implied by *Izvestiya* reports	128.9	129.9	131.6	122.9	120.8	–
Proposed by Gosplan		135.0	139.3	–	–	–
Proposed by Narkomzem (exc. previously sown perennial grass, exc. many state farms		117.8	123.7	–	–	–

Note 1934/35, etc.: The years shown run from autumn sowing in one calendar year (1934, say) through the spring sowing of the following year (1935). Grass: Unless otherwise stated, all figures include land sown to perennial grass in previous years. These figures gave the measure of land under crops at the time of the harvest, but overstated the scale of sowing work planned for the spring of the current crop year. To gauge the latter, it was necessary to deduct the land under previously sown perennial grass from the land scheduled to be under crops at the time of the harvest.

Narkomzem figures: the Commissariat of Agriculture (Narkomzem) was responsible for some state farms, but most were subordinated to the Commissariat of State Farms and other commissariats. The spring sowing target proposed by Narkomzem was a plan of work to be undertaken (therefore, excluding land previously sown to perennial grass) on the land for which the commissariat was accountable (therefore, excluding the large number of state farms not subordinated to Narkomzem).

Source Targets approved by Sovnarkom: Autumn 1934, from SZ (1934) no. 39: art. 310 (July 29, 1934). Spring 1935, from SZ (1935) no. 10: art. 74 (February 15, 1935). Autumn 1935, from SZ (1935) no. 41: art. 346 (July 28, 1935). Spring 1936, from SZ (1936) no. 10: art. 74 (February 10, 1936). Autumn 1936, from SZ (1936) no. 44: art. 376 (July 28, 1936). Spring 1937, from SZ (1937) no. 10: art. 34 (February 2, 1937). Autumn 1937 and spring 1938, from RGAE 7486/4/557 ('O gosudarstvennom plane sel'sko-khozyaistvennykh rabot na 1938 g.,' sent for printing on February 1, 1938). Autumn 1938 and spring 1939, from RGAE, 7486/4/588: 11–13 (February 8, 1939). Targets implied by *Izvestiya* reports, as Table B.31. Targets proposed by Gosplan and Narkomzem: 1935/36 and 1936/37, from RGAE, 4372/35/452: 20, 52 (December 23, 1936). The allowance for grass in the Gosplan proposal for spring sowing in 1936/37 was 1.2 million hectares; for 1937/38, proposed by Gosplan for autumn and spring sowing, from RGAE, 4372/35/473: 24–39; proposed by Narkomzem, RGAE 7486/4/557 ('O gosudarstvennom plane sel'sko-khozyaistvennykh rabot na 1938 g.,' sent for printing on February 1, 1938).

Table B.30 The sown area of Soviet agriculture, 1912/13 and 1934/35–1938/39 (million hectares)

	1912/13	*1934/35*	*1935/36*	*1936/37*	*1937/38*	*1938/39*
All grains	94.4	103.4	102.4	104.4	102.4	99.9
Of which						
—Autumn sown	32.9	36.0	35.0	37.6	36.5	–
—Spring sown	61.5	67.4	67.4	66.8	65.9	–
Technical crops	4.6	10.6	10.8	11.2	11.0	11.1
Vegetables and potatoes	3.8	9.9	9.8	9.0	9.4	9.2
Feed crops	2.1	8.6	10.6	10.6	14.1	13.5
Sown area, total	105.0	132.8	133.8	135.3	136.9	133.7

Note 1934/35, etc.: The years shown run from autumn sowing in one calendar year (1934, say) through the spring sowing of the following year (1935). The figures in this table should be considered more final than the 'completed' sowings reported in Table B.31, which were operational figures reported contemporaneously from day to day. The figures for 1913 and 1939 raise two issues of consistency. First, Soviet statistics for sown area were inflated in the mid-1920s and for consistency an upward correction of 9% was applied to data of the pre-revolutionary years. In the 1930s this correction was removed; see *Soviet Studies* 26 (1974): 157–180 (Wheatcroft). On that basis, the figures for 1913 given by the Soviet handbooks cited for this table understate sown area in 1913 relative to the later years. Second, the data for 1939, published in 1960, are consistent with those published in 1939, except that autumn and spring sowings are not distinguished.
Source All years from *Posevnye ploshchady* (1939): 5, except 1938/39 from *Posevnye ploshchady* (1960): 127.

Table B.31 The progress of sowing, 1934/35–1938/39 (thousand hectares)

			1936/37			
	1934/35	*1935/36*	*Initial*	*Revised*	*1937/38*	*1938/39*
Autumn sowing						
August 15	1,614	1,497	–	–	–	–
September 1	15,518	14,967	–	–	–	15,189
September 15	26,143	27,689	28,469	–	28,480	24,633
October 1	31,884	33,301	34,178	–	32,515	31,037
October 15	34,553	35,546	35,714	–	34,261	33,332
November 1	35,611	36,409	36,779	–	34,441	–
November 15	–	–	–	–	36,119	35,299
Completed	36,986	37,417	37,675	37,675	36,495	35,299
Target	37,756	37,786	38,244	38,244	36,484	36,019
Spring sowing						
March 15	2,310	4,008	734	734	779	–
April 1	6,646	9,639	5,766	5,766	5,825	4,200
April 15	22,278	13,927	19,711	19,711	14,352	17,869

(continued)

Table B.31 (continued)

	1934/35	1935/36	1936/37		1937/38	1938/39
			Initial	*Revised*		
May 1	50,079	34,711	49,670	47,848	44,113	42,522
May 15	76,330	73,002	72,797	68,719	71,185	67,158
June 1	89,404	88,216	87,645	81,612	81,897	81,950
June 15	91,459	91,075	90,361	83,888	83,895	84,128
Completed	94,700	91,700	–	83,900	83,895	84,128
Target	90,864	92,215	93,374	84,735	84,317	–

Note 1934/35, etc.: The years shown run from autumn sowing in one calendar year (1934, say) through the spring sowing of the following year (1935).

Source Area sown: the progress of sowing in hectares was published by *Izvestiya* every five days through the sowing season. In 1938 the coverage was revised to exclude sowing by individual farmers, by kolkhoz farmers on individual allotments, and by minor state farm trusts, and this revision was extended retrospectively to the spring 1937 figures.

Sowing targets: these were printed in regular government bulletins until the spring of 1936. The last autumn sowing target that we have found appeared in *Kratkie itogi* (1935): 14. For spring sowing, the last target available to us was published in *Osnovnye pokazateli* (March 1936): 126. These reports gave the area sown in hectares and also as per cent of the plan target. While the target was not stated, the figures allow us to compute the target implied. For 1936/37 onward, we rely on the regular five-daily reports that appeared in *Izvestiya*. Where comparison is possible, the results generally coincide with the targets formally adopted by Sovnarkom. No spring sowing plan fulfilment percentage was published in 1939, however.

Table B.32 The progress of harvesting, 1935–1939 (thousand hectares)

	1935	1936	1937	1938	1939
Reaping					
July 15	–	13,836	12,524	13,587	12,399
August 1	31,466	43,414	37,165	40,893	35,040
August 15	57,126	62,818	57,846	60,078	57,379
September 1	73,428	75,522	74,133	73,769	72,233
September 15	80,831	82,023	84,521	81,068	80,205
October 1	83,263	85,041	89,000	85,667	83,938
Final	83,834	85,680	89,816	86,768	84,530
Threshing					
July 15	–	3,618	5,372	7,323	7,070
August 1	8,939	18,340	17,351	21,995	21,090
August 15	23,603	37,512	29,041	37,455	37,270
September 1	41,563	54,844	44,344	51,788	53,150
September 15	54,673	65,788	56,388	62,646	64,093
October 1	63,514	73,490	64,850	70,859	71,029

(continued)

Table B.32 (continued)

	1935	*1936*	*1937*	*1938*	*1939*
October 15	69,591	77,301	69,979	74,813	74,114
November 1	73,173	–	74,007	–	–
Threshing lag					
July 15	–	−10,218	−7,152	−6,264	−5,329
August 1	−22,527	−25,074	−19,814	−18,898	−13,950
August 15	−33,523	−25,306	−28,805	−22,623	−20,109
September 1	−31,865	−20,678	−29,789	−21,981	−19,083
September 15	−26,158	−16,235	−28,133	−18,422	−16,112
October 1	−19,749	−11,551	−24,150	−14,808	−12,909
October 15	−14,243	−8379	−19,837	−11,955	−10,416

Source Calculated from reports published by *Izvestiya* every five days through the sowing season. The threshing lag is the area threshed at each time, less the area reaped.

Table B.33 The grain harvest, 1935–1940: plans and outcomes (million tons)

	1935	*1936*	*1937*	*1938*	*1939*	*1940*
Harvest targets						
Second five-year plan (1934)	–	–	110.6	–	–	–
Stalin's aspirational target (1935)	–	–	——115–131——			–
Third five-year plan						
—Preliminary directives (1937)	–	–	107.0	(115.6)	(124.2)	(132.8)
—Final targets (1939)	–	–	120.0	(122.6)	(125.2)	(127.8)
Annual plans	94.9	104.8	108.3	–	106.5	–

(continued)

Table B.33 (continued)

	1935	*1936*	*1937*	*1938*	*1939*	*1940*
Harvest outcomes						
Biological yield, 1933 basis						
—Preliminary evaluation (during harvest)	–	84.8	120.1	95.1	–	–
—Final evaluation (after harvest)	90.1	77.4	114.0	88.9	–	–
Biological yield, 1939 basis	–	82.7	120.3	95.0	100.9	108.2
Barn yield estimated by Wheatcroft and Davies (1994)	75	56	97	74	73	87

Source and Note Harvest targets in second five-year plan (1934), from *Vtoroi pyatiletnii plan*, 1 (1934): 462. Stalin's aspirational target (1935), from Vol. 6: 23. Targets in third five-year plan directives (1937), from RGAE, 4372/26/1415: 13 (May 1937); the source gives 107 million tons as the target for 1937, and 150 million tons for 1942, and we fill in the years up to 1940 by linear interpolation (we ignore the still higher target of 156 million tons in 1942 given on page 2 of the same document). Targets in final text of third five-year plan (1939), from *Tretii pyatiletnii plan* (1939): 72, 218; the source gives 120 million tons (in puds) as the harvest achieved in 1937, and 133 million tons as the target for 1942, and again we fill in the years up to 1940 by linear interpolation. Annual plans for 1935, in *Narodno-khozyaistvennyi plan na 1935 god* (1935): 586; for 1936, in *Narodno-khozyaistvennyi plan na 1936 god* (1936): 435; for 1937, in *Narodno-khozyaistvennyi plan na 1937 god* (1937): 25 (in puds); for 1939, in *Gosudarstvennyi plan v 1939 god* (1939): 5, 67 (in puds).

Harvest outcomes, 1933 basis (biological yield, excluding normed storage, harvesting, and pre-harvest losses): figures to 1936 are based on annual reports of the TsGK, which was then dissolved, and after that of TsUNKhU, to which its functions were transferred. Preliminary evaluations (during the harvest) are calculated from data in RGAE, 1562/1/982: 158–168. Final evaluations (after the harvest) for 1935, from RGAE 1562/3/363: 2; for 1936, from RGAE 1562/3/434:2; for 1937, from RGAE 1562/84/21: 15–17; for 1938, from RGAE 1562/84/21:43–46. Harvest outcomes, 1939 basis (biological yield, including harvest and pre-harvest losses, as recommended by Voznesenskii), in 1936, 1937, and 1938, from RGAE, 4372/36/1407: 1–6 (Voznesenskii to Stalin and Molotov, not dated but before February 19; 1939 and 1940 from RGAE, 1562/3/739: 10 (A. Pavlov, July 14, 1941), which also reproduces Voznesenskii's figures for 1936 to 1938. Barn yield: Wheatcroft and Davies (1994) is the 'low' estimate given in Davies, Harrison, and Wheatcroft (1994): 286. All the estimates available point to the same ranking of harvests in our period: the harvest of 1937 was the best of the period; that of 1940 was the second best; and the harvests of 1938 and 1939 were substantially worse, but still better than the failed harvest of 1936.

Table B.34 Grain available for use, 1935–1940 (million tons)

	1935	*1936*	*1937*	*1938*	*1939*	*1940*
Annual grain-forage balances						
Gross harvest: final official evaluation	90.1	77.4	120.3	95.0	100.9	108.2
less Harvest losses (previously *nevyazka*)	−10.9	−11.9	−13.5	−12.4	−17.4	−14.5
less Storage losses	−2.6	−2.6	−1.8	−2.0	−1.5	−1.6
Implied balance of grain available for use	76.6	62.9	105.0	80.6	82.0	92.1
Grain-forage balances, revised retrospectively by Pavlov (1941)						
Gross harvest: final official evaluation (as above)	90.1	77.4	120.3	95.0	100.9	108.2
less Pre-harvest unregistered expenditures in field	–	–	−2.0	−1.9	−2.4	−1.9
less Pre-harvest under-reporting	–	–	−4.5	−4.9	−5.7	−3.8
less Harvesting and milling losses	–	–	−15.4	−14.3	−19.3	−17.8
Implied balance of grain available for use	–	–	98.4	73.9	73.5	84.7

Source Annual grain-forage balances of the TsUNKhU sector of balances for 1935/36, from RGAE, 1562/3/363: 2 (November 16, 1936); for 1936/37, from RGAE, 1562/3/434: 2; for 1937/38, from RGAE, 1562/329/3110: 29; for 1938/39, from RGAE, 1562/329/3110: 26; for 1939/40, from RGAE, 1562/329/3110: 21. The 1935/36 balance is the only one that was dated. The 1936/37 balance, although undated, was likely drawn up at the same time in the following year. The 1937/38 and subsequent balances were drawn up on a model that differed by incorporating Voznesenskii revisions; by adding pre-harvest and other losses to the declared harvest, these allowed the latter to be further inflated above any measure of grain available for use. Because Voznesenskii completed his work on the revisions only in early 1939, the original 1937/38 balance must have been withdrawn and replaced afterwards by one that conformed to Voznesenskii's recommendations. Harvest and storage losses: from 1933/34 through 1936/37, grain-forage balances reported two items under post-harvest deductions: storage losses and the discrepancy (*nevyazka*). The discrepancy accounted for the fact that the grain available for use, although itself overstated, consistently fell far short of the reported harvest after accounting for storage losses. From 1937/38, harvest and post-harvest deductions continued to be reported as the sum of two items: storage losses (as before), and harvesting losses, which replaced what was previously reported as the *nevyazka*, but had the same accounting function, that is, to 'explain' the remaining gap between the declared harvest and the grain available for use. The implied balances of grain available for use each year are calculated by us.

Table B.35 Grain collections: plans, 1935/36–1939/40 (million tons)

	1935/36 annual plan	*1936/37 annual plan*	*1937/38 target in second five-year plan*	*1937/38 annual plan*	*1938/39 annual plan*		*1939/40 annual plan*
					ver. 1	*ver. 2*	
Compulsory deliveries (postavki)							
By collective farms	13.1	12.0	–	9.6	10.1	9.7	10.3
By collective-farm and individual peasant households	0.8	0.3	–	0.1	0.1	0.1	–
All compulsory deliveries (postavki), subtotal	13.9	12.3	12.5	9.7	10.3	9.8	10.6
Payments in kind to MTS (naturoplata)	5.3	7.8	12.0	9.1	12.5	11.5	13.4
Milling levy (garntsevyi sbor)	1.6	1.4		0.5	1.7	1.7	2.0
Returned seed loans	1.7	2.7		1.2	1.6	1.5	3.0
Deliveries by state farms	2.6	3.2	3.0	3.2	4.4	3.3	4.2
Rescheduled debt repayments	–	–	–	0.6	1.0	–	–
All collections, exc. purchases, subtotal	25.1	27.5	30.0	24.3	31.4	27.9	34.6
State purchases (zakupki)	3.5	1.3–2.4	3.0	4.0	1.8	–	–
All collections, total	28.6	28.8–29.9	33.0	28.3	33.2	–	–

Note 1935/36 annual plan, etc.: unless stated otherwise, in this table the years shown run from the start of the harvest in one calendar year (1934, say) through to the end of harvest preparations in the following year (1935). Most collections took place in the first months of the harvest year; these collections determined how much was available for utilisation through the harvest preparations of the next year.

Source 1935/36, from RGAE, 4372/35/548: 11–21. The 1937/38 target in second five-year plan, from *Narodno-khozyaistvennyi plan na 1936 god* (1936): 336. Foe 1936/37 and 1937/38: RGAE, 8040/8/360, 65–69. For 1936/37, the lower target for state purchases is that of September 9, 1936; the higher target is that of October 5, 1936. 1938/39 (version 1), from RGASPI, 17/3/2115: 50–55 (targets for kolkhoz peasants and state farms, and joint Sovnarkom and Central Committee decree of August 28, 1938); see also *Tragediya*, 5(2) (2006): 210–219. For 1938/39 (version 2) and 1939/40, from RGAE, 8040/3/36: 96–98. For 1939/40 the figure given for all planned collections (34.6 million tons, excluding purchases), exceeds the sum of the rows above by 1.4 million. The source of this discrepancy is not known, but may reflect rescheduled debt repayments, as in 1937/38 and 1938/39 (version 1).

Table B.36 Grain collections: outcomes, 1935/36–1939/40 (million tons)

	1935/36	1936/37	1937/38	*1938/39* ver. 1	*1938/39* ver. 2	1939/40
All compulsory deliveries (postavki)	14.2	11.0	10.3	9.8	9.7	9.1
Payments in kind to MTS (naturoplata)	6.0	6.5	11.3	10.1	10.1	12.1
Milling levy (garntsevyi sbor)	1.4	1.1	1.7	1.5	1.5	1.3
Returned seed loans	1.7	1.8	1.2	1.2	1.2	2.6
Deliveries by state farms	2.8	3.1	3.9	3.4	3.4	3.1
Collections, exc. purchases, subtotal	26.0	23.5	28.3	26.1	25.9	28.3
Subtotal, per cent of annual plan	104	85	116	83	93	82
State purchases (zakupki)	3.6	2.0	3.6	3.0	–	2.7
Total of collections	29.6	25.5	31.9	29.1	–	31.0

Note and Source As Table B.35. Fulfilment of annual plan is based on comparison with the equivalent row in Table B.35.

Table B.37 Grain stocks held by producers, 1935–1940 (million tons on July 1)

	1935	*1936*	*1937*	*1938*	*1939*	*1940*
State farms	0.6	0.9	0.1	0.2	0.2	0.2
Collective farm sector	7.1	7.0	2.9	15.9	10.5	4.8
Of which						
—Farm stocks	–	3.6	0.9	3.3	2.3	1.2
—Household stocks	–	3.4	2.0	12.6	7.2	3.6
Individual peasant households	0.8	0.3	0.1	0.1	0.1	0.0
Grain stocks, total	8.5	8.2	3.1	16.2	9.8	5.0

Source RGAE 1562/3/383: 2; 1562/3/434: 2; and 1562/329/3110: 29, 26, 23, 21 (estimates of the TsSUNKhU Department of Balance of the National Economy).

Table B.38 Planned livestock herds by sector on January 1, 1937–1940 (thousands)

	1937	*1938*		*1939*	*1940*
	In annual plan for 1936	*In second five-year plan*	*In annual plan for 1937*	*In annual plan for 1938*	*In annual plan for 1939*
Horses					
In collective farms	12,828	21,000	14,095	13,974	14,512
In collective farm households	648	–	703	799	–
In individual households	895	–	580	385	–
Peasant sector, subtotal	14,371	–	15,378	15,158	–
Other horses	2,649	–	2,534	2,540	–
Horses, total	17,020	–	17,912	17,698	18,400
Large horned cattle					
In collective farms	14,850	–	16,836	18,050	17,250
In collective farm households	26,240	–	31,434	30,743	–
In individual households	2660	–	1,950	1,477	–
Peasant sector, subtotal	43,750	–	50,220	50,270	–
Other large horned cattle	2,731	–	9,202	11,850	–
Large horned cattle, total	46,481	60,300	59,422	62,120	57,000
Cows					
In collective farms	4,010	–	4,880	5,160	5,130
In collective farm households	12,032	–	13,550	14,130	–
In individual households	1,094	–	790	610	–
Peasant sector, subtotal	17,136	–	19,220	19,900	–
Other cows	4,752	–	4,460	5,200	–
Cows, total	21,888	26,200	23,680	25,100	26,000
Sheep and goats					
In collective farms	17,395	–	20,887	24,670	32,500

(continued)

Table B.38 (continued)

	1937	*1938*		*1939*	*1940*
	In annual plan for 1936	*In second five-year plan*	*In annual plan for 1937*	*In annual plan for 1938*	*In annual plan for 1939*
In collective farm households	29,066	–	38,963	41,112	–
In individual households	4,050	–	3,604	2,440	–
Peasant sector, subtotal	50,511	–	63,454	68,222	–
Other sheep and goats	10,538	–	10,346	11,818	–
Sheep and goats, total	61,049	–	73,800	80,040	92,500
Pigs					
In collective farms	7,250	–	9,000	9,512	8,200
In collective farm households	16,961	–	22,140	19,912	–
In individual households	989	–	710	444	–
Peasant sector, subtotal	25,200	–	31,850	29,868	–
Other pigs	9,962	–	7,825	7,432	–
Pigs, total	35,162	–	39,675	37,300	31,000

Source 1937, from ***Narodno-khozyaistvennyi plan na 1936 god*** (1936): 440–441. For 1938 and 1939, from RGAE, 4372/36/1513: 7–9, 21–22. For 1940, from *Gosudarstvennyi plan v 1939 g.* (1939): 105.

Table B.39 Livestock herds by sector, 1936–1940 (thousands and January 1)

			1938		
	1936	*1937*	*(A)*	*(B)*	*1939*
Horses					
In collective farms	11,592	12,267	12,732	–	–
In collective farm households	593	665	722	–	–
In individual households	800	425	388	–	–
Peasant sector, subtotal	12,985	13,357	13,842	–	–
Other horses	2,529	2,522	2,540	–	–
Horses, total	15,514	15,879	16,382	16,200	17,200
Large horned cattle					
In collective farms	13,442	14,404	15,400	–	–
In collective farm households	21,238	22,190	25,550	–	–
In individual households	2,537	1,433	1,477	–	–
Peasant sector, subtotal	37,217	38,027	42,427	–	–
Other large horned cattle	8,744	9,518	10,093	–	–
Large horned cattle, total	45,961	47,545	52,520	50,900	53,500
Of which, cows					
In collective farms	3,420	3,829	4,300	–	–
In collective farm households	11,096	11,634	12,540	–	–
In individual households	1,054	584	604	–	–
Peasant sector, subtotal	15,570	16,047	17,444	–	–
Other cows	4,381	4,921	5,236	–	–
Cows, total	19,951	20,968	22,680	22,700	24,000
Sheep and goats					
In collective farms	16,120	18,692	21,238	–	–
In collective farm households	20,688	22,808	30,664	–	–
In individual households	3,580	2,232	2,439	–	–
Peasant sector, subtotal	40,388	43,732	54,341	–	–
Other sheep and goats	9,509	9,984	10,708	–	–
Sheep and goats, total	49,897	53,716	65,049	66,600	80,900
Pigs					
In collective farms	5,102	5,307	6,793	–	–
In collective farm households	12,215	8,621	12,784	–	–
In individual households	876	404	444	–	–
Peasant sector, subtotal	18,193	14,332	20,021	–	–
Other pigs	7,711	5,909	6,430	–	–
Pigs, total	25,904	20,241	26,451	25,700	25,200

Source 1936, 1937, and 1938 (A), from RGAE 4372/36/151: 4,18,39. For 1938 (B), 1939, and 1940, from *Sel'skoe khozyaistvo* (1960): 263. Cows were a subset of large horned cattle, which included bulls, oxen, and calves.

Table B.40 Meat and dairy produce, 1936–1939, by supplier category (million rubles and plan prices of 1926/27)

	1936	*1937*	*1938*	*1939*
Meat				
State farms	211.3	176.6	175.5	166.8
Collective farms	240.5	257.9	351.4	3,67.8
Collective farmer households	809.4	578.8	987.1	1177.8
Worker and staff households	172.8	115.7	191.3	207.6
Independent farmers	68.0	32.3	47.2	66.5
All output	1,502.0	1,161.3	1,752.5	1,986.5
Milk				
State farms	163	146	138	126
Collective farms	276	300	344	352
Collective farmer households	912	1,021	1,125	1,066
Worker and staff households	218	282	340	297
Independent farmers	44	44	46	30
All output	1,613	1,793	1,992	1,872

Source RGAE 1562/83/38: 1–2.

Table B.41 Gross value of agricultural production by type of produce (million rubles and plan prices of 1926/27)

	1937	*1938*	*1939*	*1940*
Grains	7,779	6,466	6,719	7,190
Technical crops	1,746	1,719	1,934	1,919
Potatoes and vegetables	2,949	1,782	2,076	2,939
Livestock	5,054	6,061	6,001	5,580
All agriculture	20,123	18,603	19,194	20,484

Source As Table B.40.

Public Finance and Private Consumption

See Tables B.42 to B.50.

Table B.42 USSR state budget outlays and revenues in standardised classification, 1936–1940 (million rubles)

	1936	*1937*	*1938*	*1939*	*1940*
Outlays					
Defence	14,883	17,481	23,200	39,200	56,800
National economy, all items	41,931	43,412	51,724	60,416	58,264
Of which					
—Industry	14,929	16,743	23,617	31,112	28,576
—Agriculture	9,158	9,506	11,409	13,334	12,204
—Transport and communications	8943	8,101	7,413	6,587	6,818
—Municipal economy and housing	2,307	2,760	2,891	2,513	2,525
—Other outlays on national economy	6,595	6,303	6,394	6,871	8,141
Social and cultural services, all items	24,990	30,897	35,256	37,429	40,903
Of which					
—Education	13,905	16,455	18,739	20,314	22,489
—Health and physical culture	5,699	7,027	7,590	8,249	8,955
—Social security and insurance	5,235	6,460	8,006	7,760	8,230
—Grants to mothers	150	956	922	1,106	1,229
Administration	–	–	5,307	6,122	6,752
State loans	–	3,458	1,955	1,855	2,785
Other outlays	10,677	10,991	6,597	8,277	8,847
Outlays, total	92,480	106,238	124,039	153,299	174,350
Revenues					
Current revenues					
Turnover tax	65,673	75,911	80,411	96,869	105,881
Deductions from profits	5,269	9,294	10,466	15,838	21,719
Social insurance	8,890	6,610	7,167	7,606	8,518
Income tax	1,205	1,497	1,952	2,537	3,677
Cultural and housing levies	1,785	1,876	2,327	2,829	3,546
Customs revenues	820	8,60	2,350	3,210	2,500
Agricultural tax and single tax	628	509	665	1,515	2,095
MTS income	–	–	1,391	1,782	2,007
Other current revenues	5,238	6,907	13,156	15,463	18,848
Capital revenues					
State loans	4,892	5,866	7,596	8,365	11,450
Revenues, total	94,399	109,329	127,481	156,014	180,241

Note For simplicity, on the expenditure side, some items have been amalgamated or omitted. Transport and communications (given separately only in 1937) are amalgamated, as are social security and social insurance; trade, supply, and procurements (given only in 1937) is omitted, and therefore counted under 'other' outlays. On the revenue side, items collecting less than one billion rubles in any year have been omitted: the tax on 'non-commodity operations', the income tax on socialised enterprise, and the income tax on collective farms.

Source Adapted from Davies (1958): 295–296.

Table B.43 Soviet household money incomes, 1936–1940 (billion rubles)

	1936	*1937*	*1938*	*1939*	*1940*
A. Proceeds from state and cooperative enterprises and organisations	116.1	135.3	155.8	187.7	208.2
Of which					
Wages	86.2	93.0	112.5	138.3	161.9
—Less unpaid wages	-0.1	–	–	–	–
Travel allowances	–	2.0	1.8	2.1	–
Pensions and benefits	4.4	6.2	6.9	6.8	7.9
Grants	–	2.2	2.2	2.4	–
Artisan cooperative incomes	–	4.4	5.2	6.7	–
Collective farmers' monetary compensation	6.5	8.3	8.7	8.7	9.2
—For labour days	–	6.9	7.7	8.0	8.6
—Other incomes from collective farms	–	1.4	1.0	0.7	0.6
Proceeds from sales	5.0	4.0	4.7	5.0	8.6
Of which					
—Agricultural	4.7	–	4.2	4.7	8.6
—Non-agricultural	0.3	–	0.5	0.3	–
Proceeds from shipment of freights	–	1.8	1.7	2.5	–
Receipts from the financial system	1.9	3.5	1.8	2.1	3.0
Other incomes	12.2	9.9	10.3	13.1	17.6
B. Proceeds from sale of goods and services to the population	9.9	14.7	16.3	20.1	20.1
Of which					
Proceeds from the kolkhoz market	7.2	12.2	11.8	15.7	18.7
—Of which, agricultural	6.4	–	10.8	14.7	18.7
—Non-agricultural	0.8	–	1.0	1.0	–
Other proceeds	2.7	2.5	4.5	4.4	1.4
All household money incomes	126.0	150.0	172.1	207.8	228.3

Source: *Po stranitsam*, 1 (2006): 22–24.

Note The arrangement of figures in this table is somewhat complicated by changes in classification and valuation from year to year. Most changes are minor and can be inferred from the discontinuities that are visible. For 1940 the figures in the source are expressed in rubles as revalued in 1961; in the table they are restored to a contemporary basis (i.e. multiplied by 10).

A significant anomaly in the table is the reported decline in kolkhoz market trade in 1938. From other reports, kolkhoz market trade increased by as much as 6052 million rubles in 1938 (RGAE, 1562/12/2322: 77); this was accompanied by a considerable rise in kolkhoz market prices (RGAE, 1562/12/2122: 29). Finance Commissariat data (Table B.46) suggest that the volume of kolkhoz trade increased by 15%, and prices by 14%. A Trade Commissariat report prepared towards the end of 1938 (*Istoriya tsenoobrazovaniya* (1973): 565–566) shows a slower increase, by 8.2%. In the first half of the year, according to the latter, grain supplies remaining from the 1937 harvest were still abundant, and in June 1938 kolkhoz market prices were lower than in June 1937. But from July onwards they steadily increased until, by November, they were 19.4% higher than in November 1937. The change between the first and second half of the year was particularly marked for grain, potatoes and vegetables. In March 1938 volume of sales was 22% higher and prices were 22% lower than in March 1937, but by November sales of vegetables were 11% less and prices 76% higher than in November 1937 (the sale of grain products on the kolkhoz market was illegal during the grain delivery period).

Table B.44 Soviet household money outlays, 1936–1940 (billion rubles)

	1936	*1937*	*1938*	*1939*	*1940*
A. Outlays with state and cooperative enterprises and organisations and savings	114.9	133.2	152.3	182.9	208.9
Of which					
Purchases of goods (inc. public catering)	95.7	111.9	124.1	148.0	165.0
—Of which, in state and cooperative trade	92.8	108.0	120.4	143.7	159.6
—From state and collective farms	2.9	3.9	3.7	4.3	5.4
Payment for services	8.5	10.0	12.5	16.2	19.3
Subscriptions to public organisations	0.9	0.7	1.3	1.7	2.5
Taxes and other payments	5.1	5.1	7.4	9.5	12.9
Formal saving	4.7	5.5	7.0	7.5	9.2
—Of which, acquisition of state loans	3.6	4.4	5.4	6.1	9.2
—Increase of savings bank deposits	1.1	1.0	1.5	1.0	0.0
—Share subscriptions to cooperatives	–	0.1	0.1	0.4	–
B. Outlays on goods and services from the population	9.9	14.7	16.3	20.1	20.1
Of which					
Purchases of goods in the kolkhoz market	7.2	12.2	11.8	15.7	18.7
—Of which, agricultural	6.4	–	10.8	14.7	18.7
—Non-agricultural	0.8	–	1.0	1.0	–
Payment for services and other outlays	2.7	2.5	4.5	4.4	–
Payment for other goods and services	–	–	–	–	1.4
All household money outlays	124.8	147.9	168.6	203.0	229.0
Excess of incomes over outlays	1.2	2.1	3.5	4.8	−0.7

Note The definition of 'Taxes and other payments' changes from year to year. In 1938 these are 'Taxes, levies, and insurance payments'; in 1937–1939, 'Taxes and payments to the financial system'; in 1940, 'Taxes, levies, insurance and other payments.' The subtotal of 'Formal saving' is introduced by us. The 'Excess of incomes over outlays' is based on the total of household money incomes shown in Table B.43; in the absence of errors and omissions, this row implies households' net accumulation of unspent cash during the year.

Source As Table B.43.

Table B.45 Retail trade turnover, 1935–1938 (million rubles and current prices)

	1935	*1936*	*1937*	*1938*
Urban socialised trade				
Retail trade	52,381	67,568	78,155	87,123
Public catering	6,381	7,050	8,453	11,088
Urban, total	58,762	74,618	86,607	98,210
Rural socialised trade				
Retail trade	22,125	31,169	37,631	40,199
Public catering	825	974	1,705	1,582
Rural, total	22,950	32,143	39,336	41,781
All socialised trade				
Retail trade	74,506	98,737	115,785	127,322
Public catering	7,206	8,024	10,158	12,670
All socialised trade, total	81,712	106,761	125,943	139,991
Kolkhoz market trade	14,500	15,607	17,800	–
All retail trade, total	96,212	122,368	143,293	–

Source Socialised trade, from *Torgovlya za 1938* (1939): 9. Kolkhoz trade, from RGAE, 4372/92/101: 230 (May 11, 1938). Public catering covers restaurants, cafès, and canteens.

Table B.46 Kolkhoz market trade, 1938–1940: volumes and prices of selected commodities (per cent of previous year)

	1938		*1939*		*1940*	
	Volume	*Prices*	*Volume*	*Prices*	*Volume*	*Prices*
All commodities	115.0	113.7	105.6	125.2	80.1	162.0
Livestock	96.2	117.2	93.8	109.6	69.7	158.1
Grain	238.2	81.7	69.7	135.8	89.8	202.0
Potatoes	148.2	97.5	83.2	190.8	122.4	148.4
Vegetables	95.9	129.7	105.6	145.9	113.4	136.7
Fruit	87.0	138.9	126.6	131.4	77.2	148.2
Cucurbits	134.8	103.2	102.5	124.7	93.1	122.3
Vegetable oil	289.7	93.6	86.8	125.5	89.5	167.3
Concentrated fodder	98.5	97.8	74.8	177.9	72.2	174.7
Meat products	130.5	114.6	118.9	114.7	67.8	174.3
Poultry and game	110.1	120.0	108.6	131.5	100.0	148.0
Dairy products	101.9	112.7	91.6	132.5	97.9	168.3
Eggs	87.6	87.6	115.0	128.1	91.2	160.3
Fish	101.2	114.5	93.7	144.0	89.7	155.3
Honey	98.0	118.5	118.8	128.4	154.9	231.6
Wood fuel	83.5	133.7	94.5	130.2	74.6	149.5

Source RGAE, 7733/36/1576: 52–52a (not dated but 1943). The number of towns where transactions were sampled was 67 in 1938, 142 in 1939, and 74 in 1940.

Table B.47 Currency in circulation, 1936–1940 (million rubles)

	1936	*1937*	*1938*	*1939*	*1940*
January 1	9,710	11,256	13,582	17,216	22,214
April 1	9,397	11,267	13,978	16,572	–
July 1	9,994	11,964	15,477	18,176	–
October 1	10,490	12,909	16,319	20,548	–
Change over calendar year, per cent	15.9	20.7	26.8	29.0	–

Source: *Po stranitsam*, 2 (2007): 40–42. The final row is calculated from figures for January 1 of the given and following years.

Table B.48 Real consumption per head: estimates for 1928 and 1937–1940 (1937 prices and per cent of 1937)

	1928	*1937*	*1938*	*1939*	*1940*
Chapman (1963), all households					
Consumer purchases	103	100	–	–	96
Consumption inc. communal services	91	100	–	–	96
Allen (2003), consumption of					
Farm households	81	100	86	84	–
Non-farm households	84	100	101	99	–
All households, average	78	100	95	94	–

Source Bergson and Kuznets, eds. (1963): 238 (Chapman), and calculated from Allen (2003): 147. Communal services are represented by education and health care provision.

Table B.49 Energy consumption from food: survey-based estimates for the mid-1920s and late 1930s (calories per person per day)

	1925/26–1926/27 average	*1937*	*1938*	*1939*	*1940*
Wheatcroft (2009)					
Peasant households	3,039	2,175	2,311	2,360	2,182
Manual worker households	3,792	2,637	2,679	2,696	2,633
Office worker households	3,815	–	–	2,911	2,894
Nefedov (2012)					
Peasant households (February)	2,981	2,373	2,682	2,614	2,514
Manual worker households (October or November)	2,626	–	2,756	2,764	–

Note 'Peasant households' refers to individual family farm households in the 1920s, and to collective farm households in the late 1930s—in both cases, the overwhelming majority of the farm population. Estimates are based on households' reported food consumption in contemporary surveys. Wheatcroft converts foodstuffs into calorie equivalents using coefficients approved by TsSU (the Soviet statistical administration); Nefedov uses those of the UN Food and Agriculture Organisation. Wheatcroft's data are year-round; Nefedov provides some year-round estimates, but these are less complete, so for present purposes we use his estimates based on surveys of peasant households carried out in February, and of worker households in October (in the 1920s) or November (in the 1930s). In the table above, for comparability, results for February 1926 are allocated to 1925/26, and those for October 1926 to the next year, 1926/27, and so on.
Source Wheatcroft (2009) from *Explorations in Economic History*, 46(1) (2009): 47. Nefedov (2012) from *Voprosy istorii* (2012), no. 12: 75–76.

Table B.50 Urban household income and expenditure, 1934 and 1937–1940, by occupational status of principal earner (rubles per person)

	1934	*1937*	*1938*	*1939*	*1940*
Manual workers					
Household income	923.47	1,525.16	1,734.27	2,058.59	2,386.85
Taxes	21.04	40.30	53.33	64.69	78.31
State loan obligations	50.68	57.67	58.47	64.38	90.94
Membership dues of social organisations	8.00	15.02	17.33	17.48	30.70
Disposable income	843.75	1,412.17	1,605.14	1,912.04	2,186.90
Outlays on food and dining	509.93	834.65	947.87	1,132.84	1,273.05
Office workers					
Household income	1,276.02	–	–	2,979.83	3,268.59
Taxes	31.54	–	–	105.26	131.15
State loan obligations	75.27	–	–	123.92	164.20
Membership dues of social organisations	10.83	–	–	29.77	32.46
Disposable income	1,158.38	–	–	2,720.88	2,940.78
Outlays on food and dining	706.02	–	–	1,437.88	1,671.01
Engineering and technical workers					
Household income	1,685.38	2,358.32	2,547.85	2,870.41	3,272.65
Taxes	63.43	93.07	103.67	115.99	150.75
State loan obligations	112.08	120.72	122.33	124.43	167.58
Membership dues of social organisations	22.68	39.90	44.08	42.83	52.96
Disposable income	1,487.19	2,104.63	2,277.77	2,587.16	2,901.36
Outlays on food and dining	818.52	1,134.58	1,215.63	1,434.63	1,638.50

Note Disposable income is calculated from the source data as household income, less outlays that could be classified as compulsory or semi-compulsory: taxes, state loan obligations, and membership dues of social organisations. Figures are based on samples the size of which increased over the period: for manual workers, from approximately 10,000 to 12,000; for staff workers, from less than 1500 to more than 5000; and for engineering and technical workers, from around 700 to 1600.
Source RGAE, 1562/15/1119: 17–22 (June 7, 1941).

FOREIGN TRADE

See Tables B.51 and B.52.

Table B.51 Exports, 1936–1940 (thousand tons)

	1936	*1937*	*1938*	*1939*	*1940*
I. From farming, etc.					
1. Products for food					
—Grain	321	1,277	2,054	277	1,155
—Other	27	47	5	4	5
Total products for food	348	1,326	2,059	281	1,160
2. Products not for food					
—Timber	6,042	5,106	3,232	1,724	1,020
—Fur	3	2	2	1	1
—Other	257	182	251	155	329
Total products not for food	6,302	5,290	3,485	1,880	1,350
Total from farming etc.	6,650	6,616	5,544	2,161	2,510
II. Consumer goods					
3. Food, drink and tobacco	501	444	538	311	262
4. Industrial consumer goods	40	42	35	17	22
Total consumer goods	541	490	573	328	284
III. Producer goods					
5. Machinery and equipment	17	29	34	13	16
6. Mining and products					
—Oil	2,666	1,930	1,388	474	874
—Coal and anthracite	1,876	1,314	428	182	31
—Ores and concentrates	764	1,352	453	467	330
—Iron and steel	784	246	74	14	60
—Nonferrous metals	0	0	0	0	0
—Other	178	204	148	47	110
Total mining and metals	6,268	5,046	2,492	1,184	1,405
7. Chemicals, fertilisers and rubber	622	722	853	626	357
8. Building materials and components	106	90	49	10	52
Total producer goods	7,013	5,887	3,428	1,833	1,830
Total exports	14,204	12,989	9,545	4,327	4,625

Source: *Vneshnyaya torgovlya* (1960).

Table B.52 Imports, 1936–1940 (thousand tons)

	1936	*1937*	*1938*	*1939*	*1940*
I. From farming, etc.					
1. Products for food	146	118	265	292	222
2. Products not for food	147	154	139	95	200
Total from farming, etc.	293	272	404	387	422
II. Consumer goods					
3. Food, drink and tobacco	126	106	126	38	89
4. Industrial consumer goods	2	1	1	1	3
Total consumer goods	128	107	127	39	92
III. Producer goods					
5. Machinery and equipment					
—Of which, for:					
Metalworking	51	41	50	51	32
Power, electrical engineering	17	11	11	10	14
Mining, iron and steel, oil	10	4	5	6	8
Lifting and handling	1	3	0	0	1
Food and light industry	8	5	0	0	0
Chemicals, timber and other	22	28	11	6	11
—Instruments, ball bearings, etc.	6	5	6	2	2
—Tractors, agricultural machines	0	0	0	0	0
—Ships	23	27	35	35	34
—Other means of transport	1	0	1	0	0
Total machinery and equipment	139	113	120	112	102
6. Mining and metals					
—Iron and steel	285	221	146	60	126
—Nonferrous metals	96	138	160	75	113
—Other	64	176	160	93	3,496
Total mining and metals	445	535	466	228	3,735
7. Chemicals, fertilisers and rubber	41	39	37	34	24
8. Building materials and components	108	238	1	0	11
Total producer goods	733	925	624	374	3,872
Total imports	1,155	1,304	1,155	800	4,387

Source As Table B.51.

Population

See Tables B.53 to B.56.

Table B.53 The size of the Soviet population, 1927 and 1933–1939: reports and estimates (millions and January each year)

	1927	*1933*	*1934*	*1935*	*1936*	*1937*	*1938*	*1939*
Five-year plans								
First (1927)	147.9	169.2	–	–	–	–	–	–
Second (1934)	–	165.7	168.7	171.7	174.7	177.7	–	–
Stalin (1934–35)	–	–	168	171	174	177	180	183
Censuses								
December 1926	147	–	–	–	–	–	–	–
January 1937	–	–	–	–	–	162	–	–
January 1939	–	–	–	–	–	–	–	167
Extrapolated from the December 1926 census on estimated or reported natural increase								
ZAGS (1937)	147.0	164.9	163.7	164.8	167.1	169.3	–	–
Kurman (1937)	145.5	160.6	157.2	158.0	160.0	161.2	–	–
Popov (1937)	147.0	162.0	160.5	161.3	163.5	166.9	169.3	–
Pisarev (1940)	147.0	159.1	159.8	160.5	162.1	164.1	167.3	–
Lorimer (1948)	147.1	158.2	159.2	160.0	161.3	163.4	166.9	170.5
ADK (1993)	148.7	162.9	156.8	158.2	160.1	162.5	165.5	168.7

Source Five-year plans, from *Pyatiletnii plan*, 1 (1929): 129; *Vtoroi pyatiletnii plan*, 1 (1934): 501. Stalin (1934/5): his claim of January 1934 made to the Seventeenth Party Congress, in Stalin, *Sochineniya*, 13 (1951): 336, which we extrapolate to 1939 based on his claim in December 1935 that the population was growing by three million per year, in *Soveshchanie peredovykh kombainerov* (1935): 118. Censuses, of 1926 (17 December), from *Golod v SSSR*, 3 (2013): 730 (Wheatcroft); of 1937 (January 6) and 1939 (January 17) from the text. Census totals are reported as the civil registered population plus special contingents of NKVD and NKO, excluding other adjustments. Extrapolated from 1926 census plus estimated natural increase: ZAGS (1937) and Popov (1937), from RGAE, 105/1/10: 201. Kurman (1937): these figures are imputed from Kurman's assumptions as explained in Davies, Harrison, Wheatcroft, eds. (1994): 75. Popov (1939), from RGAE, 1562/329/279: 114; Pisarev (1940). from RGAE, 1562/20/195: 13; Lorimer (1948), as listed in the bibliography, and ADK (1993) from Andreev et al. (1993): 118.

Table B.54 The natural increase of the Soviet population, 1933–1939: reports and retrospective estimates (thousands)

	1933	*1934*	*1935*	*1936*	*1937*	*1938*	*1939*
Births							
Reports							
Kraval' (January 5, 1937), annualised	–	–	4,598	4,995	–	–	–
Bel'skii (January 27, 1937), annualised	–	–	4,667	5,329	–	–	–
Sautin (February 1938)	–	–	4,742	5,350	6,291	–	–
Popov (February 2, 1939)	4,155	3,393	4,742	5,350	6,405	–	–
Sautin (March 1940)	–	–	–	–	–	–	6,203
TsUNKhU final tables	–	–	4,919	5,460	6,405	6,323	6,286
Retrospective estimates							
Bekunov and Rodnoi (1964)	4,435	4,229	4,888	5,350	6,405	6,323	–
ADK (1990)	5,545	4,780	5,249	5,589	6,549	6,516	–
Deaths							
Reports							
Kraval' (January 5, 1937), annualised	–	–	2,493	2,899	–	–	–
Bel'skii (January 27, 1937), annualised	–	–	2,527	3,070	–	–	–
Sautin (February 1938)	–	–	2,501	2,994	2,916	–	–
Popov (February 2, 1939)	4,999	2,536	2,501	2,994	2,978	–	–
Sautin (March 1940)	–	–	–	–	–	–	2,935
TsUNKhU final tables	–	–	2,630	3,120	2,977	2,961	2,974
Retrospective estimates							
Bekunov and Rodnoi (1964)	6,885	3,782	3,118	3,144	3,126	2,961	–
ADK (1990)	11,450	3,410	3,282	3,223	3,557	3,483	–
Natural increase							
Reports							
Kraval' (January 5, 1937), annualised	–	–	2,105	2,096	–	–	–

(continued)

Table B.54 (continued)

	1933	*1934*	*1935*	*1936*	*1937*	*1938*	*1939*
Bel'skii (January 27, 1937), annualised	–	–	2,140	2,259	–	–	–
Sautin (February 1938)	–	–	2,241	2,356	3,375	–	–
Popov (February 2, 1939)	–844	857	2,241	2,356	3,427	–	–
Sautin (March 1940)	–	–	–	–	–	–	3,268
TsUNKhU final tables	–	–	2,289	2,340	3,428	3,362	3,312
Retrospective estimates							
Bekunov and Rodnoi (1964)	–2,450	447	1,770	2,206	3,279	3,362	–
ADK (1990)	–5,905	1,370	1,967	2,366	2,992	3,033	–

Note Contemporary ZAGS (civil registration) reports of births and deaths covered only the civil population, excluding personnel of the armed forces and NKVD and the detainees of the latter. Just as the 'special contingents' of these two agencies were enumerated separately in population censuses, deaths in the special contingents were also registered separately. As for deaths in the NKVD system, there were approximately 682,000 executions in 1937–1938 (Table 3 in Chapter 1) and 167,000 deaths in camps and colonies in 1937–1939, not counting those 'released to die' (see the note to Table B.4); the latter ought to have been included in ZAGS reports but possibly were not. Finally, the growth of the population should fall below its natural increase by the size of net emigration, which is set at 200,000 in 1933 by Andreev et al. (1993): 118, and zero in all other years.

Source Reports: Kraval' (January 5, 1937), from RGAE,1562/329/107: 101–104. Kraval' reported figures for January through October each year; the figures in the table area adjusted to an annual rate pro rata. Bel'skii (January 27, 1937), from RGASPI, 82/2/538:5–17. For the sake of direct comparison with Kraval', Bel'skii also reported figures for January through October each year, and the figures in the table are adjusted to an annual rate pro rata. Sautin (February 1938), from RGAE, 1562/20/195: 29–33. Figures for 1935 and 1936 are listed as final, and for 1937 as preliminary. Popov (February 2, 1939) from RGAE, 1562/329/279: 113–115 (evidence to the Voznesenskii commission on the 1939 census). Sautin (March 1940). RGAE, 1562/329/402: 20. TsUNKhU final tables are figures taken from Table 1a ('Natural movement of the population') found in undated annual reports as follows: 1935, from RGAE 1562/329/83: 48 (the USSR population is given as 153.7 million); 1936, from RGAE, 1562/329/109: 62 (no population figure is given); 1937, from RGAE, 1562/329/790: 246; 1938, from RGAE, 1562/329/790: 30; 1939, from RGAE 1562/329/790:214 (the USSR population is given as 170 million). Retrospective estimates (i.e. births and deaths adjusted for consistency with the 1959 census): Bekunov and Rodnoi (1964), from an internal TsSU evaluation cited by Andreev et al. (1990): 56. ADK (1990) adjusted, from Andreev et al. (1990): 54–56 (a TsSU re-evaluation, commissioned in the time of Gorbachev's ***perestroika*** by party secretary for ideology A. N. Yakovlev).

Table B.55 Life expectancy and infant mortality, 1927 and 1933–1939

	1927	*1933*	*1934*	*1935*	*1936*	*1937*	*1938*	*1939*
Life expectancy at birth, years								
Total population	37.5	11.6	38.2	39.6	41.1	39.9	41.4	43.6
Of which								
—Men	35.5	10.3	35.6	36.9	37.7	35.2	37.2	40.5
—Women	39.7	13.0	41.0	42.4	44.7	44.8	45.7	46.8
Infant mortality, per thousand								
—Deaths in first year of life	182	317	204	198	186	184	174	168

Source Andreev et al. (1993): 58. Figures for 1938 and 1939 are within post-war frontiers.

Table B.56 Age-specific fertility, 1927 and 1933–1939 (births per thousand women, by age)

Age, years	*1927*	*1933*	*1934*	*1935*	*1936*	*1937*	*1938*	*1939*
20–24	232.7	165.9	153.8	170.1	191.5	217.6	210.8	217.8
25–29	274.7	197.9	165.7	188.3	189.9	231.1	228.9	237.6
30–34	259.9	180.6	146.6	155.0	155.8	188.5	188.8	189.0

Source Andreev et al. (1993): 136. Figures for 1938 and 1939 are within post-war frontiers.

Soviet and Western Estimates Compared

See Tables B.57 to B.62.

Table B.57 Soviet net material product, 1937–1940: official estimates (billion rubles and per cent)

	1937	*1938*	*1939*	*1940*
Billion rubles				
—At current prices	243.8	257.4	328.8	368.2
—At plan prices of 1926/27	96.3	105.0	117.2	128.3
Per cent of 1937				
—At current prices	100	106	135	151
—At plan prices of 1926/27	100	109	122	133

Source Simonov (2015): 240–241. Figures in per cent of 1937 are calculated from the ruble figures given in the source. Part of the expansion from 1939 to 1940 is attributable to border changes.

Table B.58 Soviet gross national product, 1937–1940: Western estimates (billion rubles and per cent)

	1937	*1938*	*1939*	*1940*
Billion rubles				
—Expenditure in current prices	280.7	–	–	435.2
—Expenditure in adjusted factor costs of 1937	215.6	–	–	261.9
—Value added at adjusted factor costs of 1937	212.3	216.3	229.5	251.1
Per cent of 1937				
—Expenditure in current prices	100	–	–	155
—Expenditure in adjusted factor costs of 1937	100	–	–	121
—Value added at adjusted factor costs of 1937	100	102	108	118

Source GNP (expenditure) from Bergson (1961): 128; GNP (value added) from Moorsteen and Powell (1966): 622–623. Figures in per cent of 1937 are calculated from the ruble figures in the sources. Part of the expansion from 1939 to 1940 is attributable to border changes.

Table B.59 Real industrial production, 1937–1940: official measures versus Western estimates (billion rubles at plan prices of 1926/27 and per cent)

	1937	*1938*	*1939*	*1940*
Billion rubles				
—Official: gross value at plan prices of 1926/27	95.5	106.8	123.9	138.5
—Western: value added at 1937 factor costs	65.4	68.6	73.7	77.8
Per cent of 1937				
—Official	100	112	130	145
—Western	100	105	113	119

Source Official: from Table B.11, all industry. Western: from Moorsteen and Powell (1966): 622–623; index numbers reported as per cent of 1937 are multiplied by the values of income originating in 1937, and civilian and munitions industries are summed for industry as a whole. Figures in per cent of 1937 are calculated from the data in the sources. The territories annexed between 1939 and 1940 were mainly agricultural, so only a small part of the expansion between the two years is attributable to border changes.

Table B.60 The gross output of the munitions industries, 1938–1940: official measures versus Western estimates (per cent of 1937)

	1937 (%)	*1938 (%)*	*1939 (%)*	*1940 (%)*
Official measure	100	138	205	283
Western estimates:				
Moorsteen and Powell (1996)	100	135	200	282
Davies and Harrison (1997)	100	171	246	288

Source The official measure is gross value of output at plan prices of 1926/27, from Table B.13, calculated as per cent of 1937. Moorsteen and Powell (1966): 622, show a procurement-based index of munitions production at 1937 prices, as described on pp. 628–629. *Europe-Asia Studies*, 49(3) (1997): 374 (Davies and Harrison), shows production-based index of the output of munitions, relying primarily on numbers of units produced, incompletely weighted by changes in quality and costs. The borders of the Soviet Union expanded between 1939 and 1940, but no defence output was located on the annexed territories.

Table B.61 The uses of Soviet national income, 1937–1939: official estimates (billion rubles at current prices and per cent)

	1937	*1938*	*1939*
Net material production	243.8	257.4	328.8
Capital investments	27.7	29.3	30.7
Defence outlays in budget	17.5	23.2	39.2
Per cent of NMP			
Capital investments	11.4	11.4	9.3
Defence outlays in budget	7.2	9.0	11.9

Source Net material product, from Table B.57; capital investments from Table B.7; defence outlays in budget from Table B.42.

Table B.62 The uses of Soviet national income, 1937 and 1940: Western estimates (billion rubles at factor costs of 1937 and per cent)

	1937	*1940*
Gross national product	215.6	261.9
Gross investment	55.9	50.1
Defence:		
—Defence outlays in budget	17.0	45.2
—Military subsistence	1.9	3.8
Defence, total	18.9	49.0
Per cent of GNP		
Gross investment	25.9	19.1
Defence, total	8.8	18.7

Source Bergson (1961): 128.

Abbreviations, Acronyms, and Technical Terms

art.	article (*stat'ya*) of a law, decree, or list of decisions
artel	the traditional term for a workers' cooperative, adopted as the legal form of the *kolkhoz* (collective farm)
cde	comrade (used to translate '*tov.*', the written abbreviation of the Russian word tovarishch)
centner	100 kilogrammes or 0.1 metric tons
Cheka	the Soviet acronym for the *Chrezvychainaya komissiya po bor'be s kontrrevolyutsiei i sabotazhem* (Extraordinary Commission for Struggle against Counterrevolution and Sabotage, the original designation of the Soviet secret police, established in December 1917)
cooperative	if not further qualified, usually applied to non-agricultural artisan and timber cooperatives and cooperatives of disabled workers
Dal'stroi	the Soviet acronym for the *Gosudarstvennyi trest po dorozhnomu i pro-myshlennomu stroitel'stvu v raione verkhnei Kolymy* (State Trust for Road and Industrial Construction in the region of the Upper Kolyma, a subsidiary unit of the GULAG)

R. W. Davies et al., *The Industrialisation of Soviet Russia Volume 7: The Soviet Economy and the Approach of War, 1937–1939*,
https://doi.org/10.1057/978-1-137-36238-4

Donbass	*Donetskii ugol'nyi bassein* (the Donetsk coal-mining basin)
element, elementy	Russian word for element(s), also signifying a social group, often pejoratively ('socially-alien elements')
garntesevyi sbor	Milling levy (paid by collective farms to state millers for the milling of grain)
Glavsevmorput'	*Glavnoe upravlenie Severnogo morskogo puti* (Chief Administration of the Northern Sea Route, attached to the USSR Sovnarkom)
Glavspetsstal'	*Glavnoe upravlenie kachestvennoi metallurgii i ferrosplavov* (Chief Administration of High-Grade Metallurgy and Steel Alloys of the People's Commissariat of Heavy Industry)
Gosplan	*Gosudarstvennaya planovaya komissiya* (State Planning Commission)
Gossortfond	*Gosudarstvennyi fond sortovykh semyan sel'skokhozyaistvennykh kul'tur* (State reserve of selected seeds of agricultural crops)
'Group A' industries	Industries producing producer goods (capital goods and intermediate goods)
'Group B' industries	Industries producing consumer goods
GULAG	*Glavnoe upravlenie lagerei* (Chief Administration of Camps of the NKVD)
GUSHOSDOR	*Glavnoe upravlenie shosseinykh dorog* (Chief administration of Highways, i.e. of highway construction, of the NKVD)
GVS	*Glavnyi voennyi sovet* (Chief Military Council of the People's Commissariat of Defence)
hectare	10,000 square metres or 100×100 metres
Ispolkom	*Ispolnotel'nyi komitet* (Executive Committee of Local and National Soviets)
ITR	*inzhenerno-tekhnicheskie rabotniki* (office workers employed as qualified technical specialists rather than as managers or clerical workers)
Izvestiya	*The News*, the daily newspaper of the government, issued until the end of 1937 in the name of the TsIK, and thereafter of the 'Soviets of working people'

kolkhoz	*kollektivnoe khozyaistvo* (collective farm)
kolkhoz market	Collective-farm market, where collective farmers sold private produce to private buyers at unregulated prices
Komsomol	*Kommunisticheskii soyuz molodezhi* (Communist League of Youth)
Komzag	*Komitet po zagotovkam sel'skokhozyais-tvennykh produktov* (Committee for the Procurement of Agricultural Products under STO and later under Sovnarkom)
kopek	One-hundredth of a ruble
Kuzbass	*Kuznetskii ugol'nyi bassein* (Kuznetsk coal-mining basin)
-lag	The Soviet abbreviation for *lager*, or camp, so Volzhlag was the Volga Labour Camp.
Limit, limity	Russian word for upper limit(s) or ceiling(s)
Mobfond	*mobilizatsionnyi fond* (reserve of commodities for war-mobilisation)
MTS	*Mashino-traktornaya stantsiya* (Machine-Tractor Station, owned by the Commissariat of Agriculture, supplying machinery services such as ploughing, reaping, and transport to local collective farms in return for the *naturoplata*, a share of the harvest)
Narkomfin	*Narodnyi komissariat finansov* (Peoples' Commissariat of Finance)
Narkomkhozy	*Narodnye komissariaty kommunal' noi ekonomiki* (People's Commissariats of Municipal Economy of the Republics)
Narkomlegprom	*Narodnyi komissariat legkoi promyshlennosti* (People's Commissariat of Light Industry)
Narkomles	*Narodnyi komissariat lesnoi promyshlennosti* (People's Commissariat of Timber Industry)
Narkomoboronprom	*Narodnyi komissariat oboronnoi promyshlennosti* (People's Commissariat of Defence Industry)
Narkompishcheprom	*Narodnyi komissariat pishchevoi promyshlennosti* (People's Commissariat of Food Industry)
Narkomput'	*Narodnyi komissariat putei soobsheniya* (People's Commissariat of Transport, mainly railways)

Narkomtorg	*Narodnyi komissariat torgovli* (People's Commissariat of Trade)
Narkomtyazhprom	*Narodnyi komissariat tyazheloi promyshlennosti* (People's Commissariat of Heavy Industry)
Narkomzem	*Narodnyi komissariat zemledeliya* (People's Commissariat of Agriculture)
naturoplata	payment in kind (by collective farms for machinery services to the MTS)
Nepfond	*neprikosnovennyi fond* (untouchable fund, or reserve stocks of food and other commodities)
nevyazka	discrepancy (between the official estimate of the grain harvest and the estimated total of uses of harvested grain)
NKVD	*Narodnyi komissariat vnutrennikhh del* (People's Commissariat of Internal Affairs)
OGPU	*Ob"edinennoe gosudarstvennoe politicheskoe upravlenie* (Unified State Political Administration, the security police until its absorption by the NKVD in 1934)
orgnabor	*organizovannyi nabor* (organised recruitment of peasants for work in construction and industry)
ORSy	*Otdely rabochego snabzheniya* (departments of workers' supply, i.e. shops selling consumer goods to employees at work)
plan prices of 1926/27	the 'unchanged prices of 1926/27', the unit of value used in Soviet production plans from the first five-year plan to 1950
Politburo	*Politicheskii byuro* (Political Bureau, the executive subcommittee of the Central Committee of the Communist Party)
postavka	delivery (in an agricultural context, compulsory delivery of produce by collective farms to the state)
Pravda	*The Truth*, the daily newspaper of the Central Committee of the Communist Party
pud	16.38 kilogrammes or 0.01638 metric tons
Rabkrin	*Narodnyi komissariat raboche-krest'yanskoi inspektsii* (People's Commissariat of Workers' and Peasants' Inspectorate)

sovkhoz	*sovetskoe khozyaistvo* (literally, Soviet farm, a state-owned enterprise, or 'state farm')
Sovnarkom	*Sovet narodnykh komissarov* (Council of People's Commissars of the USSR, or if so indicated, of one of the Union Republics)
SP	*Sobranie postanovlenii* (Compendium of Decrees, an official serial publication from 1938)
STO	*Sovet Truda i Oborony* (Council of Labour and Defence, the economic sub-committee of Sovnarkom)
SZ	*Sobranie zakonov* (Compendium of Laws, an official serial publication until 1938)
troika	committee or group of three persons empowered to try and sentence accused persons in a simplified manner that dispensed with most aspects of due process, including presumption of innocence
TsGK	*Tsentral'naya gosudarstvennaya komissiya po opredeleniyu urozhainosti i razmerov valovogo sbora zernovykh kul'tur* (Central State Commission for Determining Yields and the Size of the Gross Harvest of Grain Crops of Sovnarkom, 1933 to 1936)
TsIK	*Tsentral'nyi Ispolnitel'nyi Komitet* (Central Executive Committee of the USSR)
TsK	*Tsentral'nyi Komitet* (the Central Committee of the Communist Party)
TsSU	*Tsentral'noe statisticheskoe upravlenie* (Central Statistical Administration, the Soviet national statistical agency until 1931 and from 1948)
TsUNKhU	*Tsentral'noe upravlenie narodno-khozyaistvennogo ucheta* (Central Administration of National-Economic Accounts of Gosplan, the national statistical agency during the period of this volume)
UNKhU	*Upravlenie narodno-khozyaistvennogo ucheta* (administration of national-economic accounts (1) of Gosplan of the USSR, subsequently renamed TsUNKhu; (2) local units of TsUNKhU)

Vesenkha	*Vysshii sovet narodnogo khozyaistva* (Supreme Council of National Economy, the unified ministry of industry in the early years of Soviet industrialisation)
VK	*Valyutnaya komissiya* (Foreign-Currency Commission, a joint sub-committee of the Politburo and Sovnarkom)
VKP(b)	*Vsesoyuznaya Kommunisticheskaya Partiya (bol'shevikov)* (All-Union Communist Party (of Bolsheviks), the Communist Party)
VTsSPS	*Vsesoyuznyi Tsentral'nyi Sovet Professional'nykh soyuzov* (All-Union Central Council of Trade Unions)
zagotovka	procurement (in an agricultural context, of produce from collective farms by the state)
Zagotzerno	*Vsesoyuznoe ob"edinenie po zagotovke zernovykh, bobovykh, krupyanykh, maslichnykh i furazhnykh kul'tur* (All-Union Corporation for the Collection of Grain, Beans, Groats, Oil Seeds and Fodder Crops)
zakupka	purchase (in an agricultural context, of produce by the state from collective farms on a supposedly voluntary basis)

Bibliography

Archives

Documents from Russian archives are generally cited in footnotes by the abbreviated name of archive, followed by the numbers of the *fond* (collection), *opis'* (catalogue), *delo* (file), and *list* (folio or page numbers). In those infrequent cases where the archivist numbered the folios from the back of the file, the folio numbers are declining rather than increasing.

APRF: *Arkhivy prezidenta Rossiiskoi Federatsii* (Archives of the President of the Russian Federation), Moscow, Russian Federation.

GARF: *Gosudarstvennyi arkhiv Rossiiskoi Federatsii* (The State Archive of the Russian Federation), Moscow, Russian Federation.

NA: National Archives (The), Richmond, United Kingdom.

RGAE: *Rossiiskii Gosudarstvennyi arkhiv ekonimiki* (The Russian State Economic Archive), Moscow, Russian Federation.

RGASPI: *Rossiiskii Gosudarstvennyi arkhiv sotsial'noi-politicheskoi istorii* (The Russian State Archive of Social and Political History), Moscow, Russian Federation.

Official Publications

Official publications are cited in footnotes by an abbreviated title (always including the first word or syllable, except SZ for the *Sobranie zakonov* and SP fot the *Sobranie postanovlenii*). The place of publication is always Moscow.

Gosudarstvennyi plan razvitiya narodnogo khozyaistva SSSR v 1939 god (1939).

R. W. Davies et al., *The Industrialisation of Soviet Russia Volume 7: The Soviet Economy and the Approach of War, 1937–1939*,
https://doi.org/10.1057/978-1-137-36238-4

Kratkie itogi vypolneniye narodno-khozyaistvennogo plana za noyabr' 1935 g. (1935).
Narodnoe khozyaistvo SSSR. 1922–1972. Yubileinyi statisticheskii sbornik (1972).
Narodnoe khozyaistvo SSSR. Statisticheskii spravochnik. 1932 (1932).
Narodno-khozyaistvennyi plan na 1935 god, 2/e (1935).
Narodno-khozyaistvennyi plan na 1936 god (in 2 vols?), 2/e? (1936).
Narodno-khozyaistvennyi plan Soyuza SSSR na 1937 g. (1937).
Pokazateli vypolneniya narodnokhozyaistvennogo plana 1938 goda (1938).
Posevnye ploshchady SSSR (1960).
Posevnye ploshchady SSSR (dinamika za 1928, 1932–1938 gg. v sopostavlenii s 1913 g.) (1939).
Promyshlennost' SSSR. Statisticheskii sbornik (1957).
Pyatiletnii plan narodno-khozyaistvennogo stroitel'stva SSSR (in 2 vols) (1929).
Report of Court Proceedings in the Case of the Anti-Soviet Trotskyite Centre (1937).
Sbornik zakonodatel'nykh aktov o trude (1956).
Sel'skoe khozaistvo SSSR. Ezhegodnik. 1935 (1936).
Sel'skoe khozaistvo SSSR. Statisticheskii sbornik (1960).
Sobranie postanovlenii pravitel'stva SSSR (from 1938).
Sobranie zakonov i rasporyazhenii raboche-krest'yanskogo pravitel'stva SSSR (to 1937) (note that the *Sobranie zakonov* was issued in two sections, separately numbered; section 1 is always cited unless section 2 is specified).
Soveshchanie peredovykh kombainerov i kombainerok SSSR i chlenami TsK VKP(b) i pravitel'stva 1 dekabrya 1935 g. (1935).
Statistical Digest of the War (1951).
Torgovlya Soyuza SSSR za 1938 g. Statisticheskii ezhegodnik (1939).
Tretii pyatiletnii plan razvitiya narodnogo khozyaistva Soyuza SSSR (1938–1942 gg.) (1939).
Vneshnyaya torgovlya SSSR. Statisticheskii sbornik, 1918–1940 (1960).
Vtoroi pyatiletnii plan razvitiya narodnogo khozyaistva SSSR 1933–1937 (in 2 vols) (1934).
XVIII [Vosemnadtsatyi] s"ezd vsesoyuznoi kommunistickeskoi partii (bol'shevikov) 10–21 marta 1939 g. Stenograficheskii otchet (1939).

Collections of Documents and Works of Reference

Collections of documents and works of reference are cited in footnotes by an abbreviated title (always including the first word or syllable). The place of publication is Moscow or Moscow-Leningrad (for books in Russian), or London or New York (for books in English), unless otherwise stated.

Bol'shaya tsenzura. Pisateli i zhurnalisty v Strane Sovetov, 1917–1956, compiled by L. Maksimenkov (2005).

Documents on German foreign policy, 1918–1945, Series D *(1949–1964)* (in 14 vols), 1 (1949), 2 (1950), 7 (1956).

Dokumenty vneshnei politiki SSSR (in 24 vols), 21 (1977).

Glavnoe upravlenie lagerei 1918–1960: Dokumenty, compiled by A.I. Kokurin and N.V. Petrov (2000).

Glavnyi voennyi sovet RKKA 13 mart 1938g.—20 iyun' 1941g. Dokumenty i materialy (2004).

Golod v SSSR, 1929–34 (in 3 vols), compiled by V. Kondrashin et al. (2011–2013).

Gosudarstvennaya vlast' SSSR. Vyshhie organy vlasti i upravleniya i ikh rukovoditeli, 1923–1991: istoriko-biograficheskii spravochnik, compiled by V. I. Ivkin (1999).

I. V. Stalin: istoricheskaya ideologiya v SSSR v 1920–1950-e gody: sbornik dokumentov i materialov (in 2 vols), 1, 1920–1930-e gody, compiled by M. V. Zelenov (2006).

Industrializatsiya SSSR. Dokumenty i materialy, 1933–1937 (1971).

Industrializatsiya SSSR. Dokumenty i materialy, 1938–1941 (1973).

Istoriya sozdaniya i razvitiya oboronno-promyshlennogo kompleksa Rossii i SSSR, 1900–1963, 4, *Oboronno-promyshlennyi kompleks SSSR nakanune Velikoi Otechestvennoi voiny (1938-iyun' 1941)*, compiled by A. K. Sokolov et al. (2015).

Istoriya Stalinskogo Gulaga. Konets 1920-kh—pervaya polovina 1950-kh gg. (in 7 vols), 1, *Massovye repressii v SSSR*, compiled by I. A. Ziuzina; 3, *Ekonomika Gulaga*, compiled bya O. V. Khlevniuk (2004).

Istoriya tsenoobrazovaniya 1929-iyun' 1941 (1973).

Kratkii kurs istorii VKP(b). Tekst i ego istorii (in two vols.), 1, *Istoriya teksta Kratkogo kursa istorii VKP(b). 1931–1956*, compiled by M. V. Zelenov and D. Brandenburger (2014).

Leningradskii martirolog, 1937–1938, 5 (2002).

Lubyanka. Stalin i Glavnoe upravlenie gosbezopasnosti NKVD. Arkhiv Stalina. Dokumenty vysshikh organov partiinoi i gosudarstvennoi vlasti. 1937–1938, compiled by V. N. Khaustov, V. P. Naumov, and N. S. Plotnikova (2004).

Moskva-Berlin. Politika i diplomatiya Kremlya. 1920–1941 (in 3 vols) (2011).

Na prieme u Stalina. Tetradi (zhurnali) zapisei lits, prinyatykh I. V. Stalinym (1924–1953gg.) (2008).

Po stranitsam arkhivnykh fondov Tsentral'nogo Banka Rossiiskoi Federatsii (in 17 vols), 1, *Denezhnye dokhody i raskhody naseleniya. 1924–1990 gg.* (2006); 2, *Oborot nalichnykh deneg v SSSR. 1922–1990 gg.* (2007); 4, *Opyt issledovanii v oblasti deneg i kredita v Narkomfine i Gosbanke SSSR v 1920–3 gody. O podgotovke plana denezhnogo obrashcheniya na tret'yu pyatiletku (1928–1942 gody)* (2007).

Politbyuro i krest'yanstvo. Vysylka, spetsposelenie, 1930–1940 (in 2 vols) (2006).

Rossiya. 1913 god. Statistiko-dokumental'nyi spravochnik, compiled by A. M. Anfimov and A. P. Korelin (1995).

Schast'e literatury': gosudarstvo i pisateli, 1925–1938. Dokumenty, compiled by D. L. Babichenko (1997).

Sovet narodnykh komissarov SSSR, Sovet ministrov SSSR, Kabinet ministrov SSSR, 1923–1991, compiled by Garnyuk, S. D. (1999).

Sovetskoe rukovodstvo. Perepiska. 1928–1941 gg., compiled by A. B. Kvashonkin, L. P. Kosheleva, L. A. Rogovaya, and O. V. Khlevniuk (1999).

Soviet government officials, 1922–1941: a Handlist, compiled by, R.W. Davies, M.J. Ilič, and, H.P. Jenkins (Univesity of Birmingham, 1989).

Stalin i Kaganovich: perepiska, 1931–1936 gg., compiled by O. V. Khlevniuk, R. U. Devis (R. W. Davies), A. P. Kosheleva, E. A. Ris (E. A. Rees) and L. A. Rogovaya (2001).

Stenogrammy zasedanii Politbyuro TsK RKP(b)—VKP(b) 1923–1938 gg. (in 3 volumes), 3 (1928–1938 gg.), compiled by L. P. Kosheleva, L. A. Rogovaya and O. V. Khlevniuk (2007).

Tragediya sovetskoi derevni. Kollektivizatsiya i raskulachivanie. Dokumenty i materialy, 1927–1939 (in 5 volumes), compiled by V. Danilov et al., 5(1) *1937* (2004), 5(2) *1938–1939* (2006).

Tsentral'nyi komitet KPSS, VKP(b), RKP(b), RSDRP(b): istoriko-biograficheskii spravochnik, compiled by Yu. V. Goryachev (2005).

VKP(b), Komintern, i Kitai. Dokumenty (in 5 vols), 5. *VKP(b), Komintern, i KPK v period antiyaponskoi voiny. 1937-mai 1943* (2007).

Voennyi sovet pri narodnom komissare oborony SSSR. 1-4 iyun' 1937. Dokumenty i materialy (2008).

Vsesoyuznaya pepepis' naseleniya 1939 g. Osnovniye itogi, compiled by Yu. A. Polyakov, V. B. Zhiromskaya, A. A Isupov, and I. N. Kiselev (1992).

Vsesoyuznaya perepis' naseleniya 1937 g. Kratkie itogi, compiled by V. B. Zhiromskaya and Yu. A. Polyakov, 1/e (1991); 2/e (2007).

Zaklyuchennye na stroikakh kommunizma. Gulag i ob"ekty energetiki v SSSR, compiled by O. V. Khlevniuk, V. A. Kozlov, S. V. Mironenko, and Yu. G. Orlova (2008).

Zastol'nye rechi Stalina. Dokumenty i materialy, compiled by V. A. Nevezhin (2003).

Zheleznodorozhnyi transport v gody industrializatsii SSSR (1926–1941) (1970).

Monographs and Other Books

All books are cited in footnotes by their author or editor, followed by the year of publication. Multi-volume works may also have a short title. The place of publication is Moscow or St Petersburg (Leningrad) (for titles in Russian), or London or New York (for titles in English), unless otherwise stated.

Adamthwaite, A. P., *The making of the Second World War* (1992).
Alexopoulos, G., *Illness and inhumanity in Stalin's Gulag* (New Haven, CT, 2017).
Allen, R. C., *Farm to factory: A reinterpretation of the Soviet industrial revolution* (Princeton and Oxford, 2003).
Andreev, E. M., Darskii, L. E., and Khar'kova, T. L., *Istoriya naseleniya SSSR. 1920–1959 gg.* (1990).
Andreev, E. M., Darskii, L. E., and Khar'kova, T. L., *Naseleniya Sovetskogo Soyuza, 1922–1991* (1993).
Barber, J., and Harrison, M., eds., *The Soviet defence-industry complex from Lenin to Khrushchev* (Basingstoke, 2000).
Baron, N. P., *Soviet Karelia: Politics, planning and terror in Stalin's Russia, 1920–1939* (2007).
Baryatinskii, M., *Sovetskie tanki v boyu ot T-26 do IS-2* (2007).
Bergson, A., *The real national income of Soviet Russia since 1928* (Cambridge, MA, 1961).
Bergson, A., and Kuznets, S., *Economic trends in the Soviet Union* (Cambridge, MA, 1963).
Biskupski, M., ed., *Ideology, politics, and diplomacy in East Central Europe* (2003).
Biushgens, G. S., et al., ed., *Samoletostroenie v SSSR, 1917–1945 gg.* (in 2 vols), 1 (1992).
Blum, A., and Mespoulet, M., *L'anarchie bureaucratique: pouvoir et statistique sous Staline* (Paris, 2003).
Brandenburger, D., *Propaganda state in crisis: Soviet ideology, indoctrination, and terror under Stalin, 1927–1941* (New Haven, CT, 2011).
Carley, M. J., *1939: The alliance that never was and the coming of World War II* (Chicago, 2000).
Carr, E. H., and Davies, R. W., *Foundations of a planned economy, 1926–1929*, 1 (in two parts) (1969).
Chapman, J. G., *Real wages in Soviet Russia since 1928* (Cambridge, MA, 1963).
Chuev, F., *Sto sorok besed s Molotovym* (1998).
Chukovskaya, L., *Sofia Petrovna* (Evanston, IL, 1967).
Clark, M. G., *The economics of Soviet steel* (Cambridge, MA, 1956).
Conquest, R., *The Great Terror: Stalin's purge of the thirties* (1968).
Cooper, J., Perrie, M., and Rees, E. A., eds., *Soviet history, 1917–1953* (Basingstoke, 1995).
Davies, R. W., *The development of the Soviet budgetary system* (Cambridge, 1958).
Davies, R. W., ed., *From Tsarism to the New Economic Policy: Continuity and change* (1990).
Davies, R. W., Harrison, M., and Wheatcroft, S. G., eds., *The economic transformation of the Soviet Union, 1913–1945* (Cambridge, 1994).

Dimitrov, G., *The diary of Georgi Dimitrov, 1933–1949*, edited by I. Banac (New Haven, 2003).

Dudintsev, V., *Ne khlebom odnym* (1957).

Elantseva, O., *Stroitel'stvo no. 500 NKVD SSSR: zheleznaya doroga Komsomol'sk-Sovetskaya Gavan', 1930–1940-e gody* (Vladivostok, 1995).

Ellman, M., *Socialist planning*, 3/e (Cambridge, 2014).

Ericson, E. E., *Feeding the German eagle: Soviet economic aid to Nazi Germany, 1933–1941* (Westport, CT, 1999).

Filtzer, D., *Soviet workers and Stalinist industrialization: The formation of modern Soviet production relations, 1928–1941* (1986).

Filtzer, D., *The hazards of urban life in late Stalinist Russia: Health, hygiene, and living standards, 1943–1953* (Cambridge, 2010).

Garros, V., et al., eds., *Intimacy and terror: Soviet diaries of the 1930s* (1995).

Gerschenkron, A., *Economic backwardness in historical perspective: A book of essays* (Cambridge, MA, 1962).

Getty, J. A. and Manning, R. T., eds., *Stalinist terror: New perspectives* (Cambridge, 1993).

Getty, J. A. and Naumov, O. V., *The road to terror: Stalin and the self-destruction of the Bolsheviks, 1932–1939* (New Haven, CT, 1999).

Gorodetsky, G., *Grand delusion: Stalin and the German invasion of Russia* (New Haven, CT, 1999).

Gorodetsky, G., ed., *Soviet foreign policy, 1917–1991: A retrospective* (1994).

Graham, L., *Science in Russia and the Soviet Union* (Cambridge, 1993).

Grechko, A. A., et al., eds., *Istoriya Vtoroi Mirovoi voiny. 1939–1945* (in 12 vols) (1973–1982).

Gregory, P. R., *Before command: An economic history of Russia from emancipation to the first five-year plan* (Princeton, NJ, 1994).

Gregory, P. R., *Russian national income, 1885–1913* (Cambridge, 1982).

Gregory, P. R., *Terror by quota: State security from Lenin to Stalin (an archival study)* (New Haven, CT, 2009).

Gregory, P. R., and Lazarev, V. (ed.) *The economics of forced labor: The Soviet gulag* (Stanford, CA, 2003).

Hagenloh, P., *Stalin's police: Public order and mass repression in the USSR, 1926–1941* (Washington and Baltimore, 2009).

Harris, J., ed. *The anatomy of terror: Political violence under Stalin* (Oxford, 2013).

Harrison, M., *Accounting for war: Soviet production, employment, and the defence burden, 1940–1945* (Cambridge, 1996).

Harrison, M., *Soviet planning in peace and war, 1938–1945* (Cambridge, 1985).

Harrison, M., *The economics of coercion and conflict* (2015).

Harrison, M., ed., *Guns and rubles: The defense industry in the Stalinist state* (New Haven, CT, 2008).

Harrison, M., ed., *The economics of World War II: six great powers in international comparison* (Cambridge, 1998).
Haslam, J., *The Soviet Union and the struggle for collective security in Europe, 1933–39* (Basingstoke and New York, 1984).
Haslam, J., *The Soviet Union and the threat from the East, 1933–41* (Basingstoke and New York, 1992).
Hessler, J., *A social history of Soviet trade: Policy, retail practice, and consumption* (Princeton, NJ, 2004).
Higham, R., *Two roads to war: The French and British air arms from Versailles to Dunkirk* (Annapolis, MD, 2012).
Hill, C., Cab*inet decisions on foreign policy: The British experience, October 1938–June 1941* (Cambridge, 2010).
Ilič, M., ed., *Stalin's terror revisited* (Basingstoke and New York, 2006).
Jansen, M., and Petrov, N. V., *Stalin's loyal executioner: people's commissar Nikolai Ezhov, 1895–1940* (Stanford, CA, 2002).
Joravsky, D., *The Lysenko affair* (Chicago, 1986).
Kasekamp, A., *A history of the Baltic states* (2010).
Khaustov, V., and Samuel'son (Samuelson), L., *Stalin, NKVD i repressii 1936–1938 gg.* (2009).
Khlevniuk, O. V., *Master of the house: Stalin and his inner circle* (New Haven, CT, 2009).
Khlevniuk, O. V., *Politbyuro: mekhanizm politicheskoi vlasti v 1930-e gody* (1996).
Khlevniuk, O. V., *The history of the Gulag: From collectivization to the Great Terror* (New Haven, CT, 2004).
Khrushchev, S., ed., *Memoirs of Nikita Khrushchev* (in 2 vols), 1, *Commissar, 1918–1945* (2004).
Kingston-Mann, E., and Mixter, T., eds., *Peasant economy, culture, and politics of European Russia, 1800–1921* (Princeton, NJ, 1991). 128–172 (S. G. Wheatcroft).
Kojevnikov, A. B., *Stalin's great science: The times and adventures of Soviet physicists* (2004).
Kondrashev, D. D., *Tsenoobrazovanie v promyshlennosti SSSR* (1956).
Kornev, V. P., *Vidnye deyateli otechestvennoi statistiki, 1686–1990: biograficheskii slovar'* (1993).
Kotkin, S., *Magnetic mountain: Stalinism as a civilization* (Berkeley and Los Angeles, 1995).
Kotkin, S., *Stalin* (in 3 vols), 2. *Waiting for Hitler, 1928–1941* (2017).
Kuznets, S., *Economic growth of nations: Total output and production structure* (Cambridge, MA, 1971).
Lange, O., *Problems of political economy of socialism* (Delhi, 1962).
Lar'kov, S., and Romanenko, F., *'Vragi naroda' za polyarnym krugom*, 2/e (2010).

Litvinov M., *Against aggression* (1939).

Lorimer F., *The population of the USSR* (Geneva, 1948).

Maiolo, J. A., *The Royal Navy and Nazi Germany, 1933–1939: A study in appeasement and the origins of the Second World War* (1998).

Maksimenkov, L., *Sumbur vmesto muzyki. Sovetskaya kul'turnaya revolyutsiya 1936–1938* (1997).

Malafeev, A. N., *Istoriya tsenoobrazovaniya v SSSR, 1917–1963 gg.* (1964).

Man'kov, A. G., *Dnevniki tridtsatykh godov* (2001).

Mathias P., and Postan, M. M., eds., *Cambridge economic history of Europe,* 7(2) (Cambridge, 1978).

Mel'tyukhov, M. I., *Upushchennyi shans Stalina: Sovetskii Soyuz i bor'ba za Evropu 1939–1941 gg. (dokumenty, fakty, suzhdeniya)* (2002).

Mikoyan, A. A., *Tak bylo. Rasmyshleniya o minuvshem* (1999).

Modley, R., *Aviation facts and figures* (1945).

Moorsteen, R., and Powell, R. P., *The Soviet capital stock, 1928–1962* (Homewood, IL, 1966).

Mozokhin O. B., *Pravo na repressii. Vnesudebnye polnomochiya organov gosudarstevennoi bezopasnosti (1918–1953)* (2011).

Neiman, G. Ya., *Vnutrennyaya torgovlya SSSR* (1935).

O'Brien, P. P., *How the war was won: Air-sea power and Allied victory in World War II* (Cambridge, 2015).

Okhotin, N. G., and Roginskii, A. B., eds., *Zven'ya: istoricheskii al'manakh* (in 2 vols), 1 (1991).

Osinskii, N., *Chto znachit uchet?* (1932a).

Osinskii, N., *Polozhenie narodnokhozyaistvennogo ucheta* (1932b).

Osokina, E. A., *Za fasadom 'Stalinskogo izobiliya'. Raspredelenie i rynok v snabzhenii naseleniya v gody industrializatsii, 1927–1941* (1998).

Ozerov, G., *Tupolevskaia sharaga*, 2/e (Frankfurt am Main, 1973).

Paine, S. C. M, *The wars for Asia, 1911–1949* (Cambridge, 2012).

Petrov, N. V., and Roginskii, A. B., *Pol'skaya operatsiia NKVD 1937–1938. Repressii protiv polyakov i pol'skikh grazhdan* (1997).

Platt, K. M. F., and Brandenberger, D., eds., *Epic revisionism: Russian history and literature as Stalinist propaganda* (Madison, WI, 2006).

Polyakov, Yu. A., ed., *Naselenie Rossii v XX veke* (in 2 vols), 1, *1900–1939* (2000).

Pons, S., *Stalin and the inevitable war, 1936–1941* (2002).

Popov, P. I., *Organizatsiya gosudarstvennoi statistiki* (1918).

Postan, M., and Habakkuk, H. J., eds., *Cambridge economic history of Europe,* 6(2) (Cambridge, 1966).

Rees, E. A., ed., *Centre–local relations in the Stalinist state, 1928–1941* (Basingstoke, 2002).

Rees, E. A., ed., *Decision-making in the Stalinist command economy, 1932–37* (Basingstoke, 1997).

Rockoff, H., *America's economic way of war: War and the US economy from the Spanish-American War to the Persian Gulf War* (Cambridge, 2012).

Rosenberg W. G. and Siegelbaum L. H., eds., *Social dimensions of Soviet industrialization* (Bloomington, IN, 1993).

Safronov, V. P., *SSSR, SShA i Yaponskaya agressiya na Dal'nem Vostoke i Tikhom Okeane, 1931–1945 gg.* (2001).

Samuelson, L., *Plans for Stalin's war machine: Tukhachevskii and military-economic planning, 1925–1941* (Basingstoke, 2000).

Schlögel K., *Moscow 1937* (2012).

Schumpeter, J. A., *The theory of economic development: An inquiry into profits, capital, credit, interest, and the business cycle* (Cambridge, MA, 1934).

Sedik, D., Sotnikov. S., and Wiesmann, D., *Food security in the Russian Federation*, FAO Economic and Social Development Paper no. 153 (Rome, 2003).

Sen, A., *Development as freedom* (Oxford, 1999).

Shearer, D. R., *Policing Stalin's socialism: Repression and social order in the Soviet Union, 1924–1953* (New Haven, 2009).

Shestakov, A. V., *Kratkaya istoriya SSSR* (1937).

Shikheeva-Gaister, I., *Deti vragov naroda. Semeinaya khronika vremen kul'ta lichnosti. 1925–1953* (2012).

Shirokov, A. I., *Dal'stroi v sotsial'no ekonomicheskokm razvitii Severo-Vostoka SSSR* (2014).

Shirokov, A. I., *Dal'stroi: predistoriya i pervoe desyatiletie* (Magadan, 2000).

Siegelbaum, L. H., *Stakhanovism and the politics of productivity in the USSR, 1935–1941* (Cambridge, 1988).

Simonov, N. S., *Voenno-promyshlennyi kompleks v 1920–1930-e gody: tempy ekonomicheskogo rosta. struktura, organizatsiya proizvodstva i upravlenie*, 1/e (1996); 2/e (2015).

Sladkovskii, M.I., *Istoriya torgovo-ekonomicheskikh otnoshenii SSSR s Kitaem (1917–1974)* (1977).

Slavin, S. N., *Oruzhie pobedy* (2005).

Smirnov, M. B., *Sistema ispravitel'no-trudovykh lagerei v SSSR, 1923–1960. Spravochnik* (1998).

Spulber, N., *Soviet strategy for economic growth* (Bloomington, IN, 1964).

Stalin, I. V., *Sochineniya* (in 18 vols), 1–13 (1946–1951), 14–18 (1997–2006),

Stepanov, A. S., *Razvitie sovetskoi aviatsii v predvoennyi period (1938 god—pervaya polovina 1941 god* (2006).

Stites, R., *Russian popular culture: Entertainment and society since 1900* (Cambridge, 1992).

Stone, D. R., *Hammer and rifle: The militarization of the Soviet Union, 1926–1933* (Lawrence, KS, 2000).

Striliver, I. L., Khazanov, S.A., and Yampol'skii, L. S., *Khlebooborot i standarty* (1935).

Svirin, M., *Bronevoi shchit Stalina: istoriya sovetskogo tanka 1937–1943* (2006).

Svirin, M., *Bronya krepka: istoriya sovetskogo tanka 1919–1937* (2005).

United States Strategic Bombing Survey, *Report no. 3. Effects of strategic bombing on the German war economy* (Cambridge, MA, 1945).

Upadyshev, N. V., *GULAG na Evropeiskom Severe Rossii: genesis, evolyutsiya, raspad* (Arkhangel'sk, 2007).

Velikanova, O., *Popular perceptions of Soviet politics in the 1920s: Disenchantment of the dreamers* (Basingstoke, 2013).

Vinogradov, N. A., *Rukovodstvo po sotsial'noi gigiene i organizatsiya zdravookhraneniya* (in 2 vols), 1 (1974).

Vishnevskii, A., *Serp i rubl'. Konservativnaya modernizatsiya Rossii*, 2/e (2010).

Viola, L., *Stalinist perpetrators on trial: Scenes from the Great Terror in Soviet Ukraine* (Oxford, 2017).

Volkov A. G., *Izbranniye demograficheskiye trudy* (2014).

Weinberg, G. L., *A world at arms: a global history of World War II* (Cambridge, 1994).

Weinberg, G. L., *The foreign policy of Hitler's Germany* (in 2 vols), 2. *Starting World War II, 1937–1939* (Chicago, 1980).

Wheatcroft, S. G., ed., *Challenging traditional views of Russian history* (Basingstoke, 2002).

Wilber, C. K., *The Soviet model and underdeveloped countries* (Chapel Hill, NC, 1969).

Yunge (Junge), M., Bordyugov, G., and Binner, R., *Stalinizm v sovetskoi provintsii: 1937–1938 gg. Massovaya operatsiya na osnove prikaza No 00447* (2009).

Yunge (Junge), M., Bordyugov, G. and Binner, R., *Vertikal' bol'shogo terrora: istoriya operatsii po prikazu No 00447* (2008).

Zaleski, E., *Stalinist planning for economic growth, 1933–1952* (Basingstoke, 1980).

Zelenin, I.E., *Stalinskaya 'revolyutsiya sverkhu' posle 'Velikogo pereloma'* (2006).

Zhigulin, A. V., *Chernye kamni* (1989).

Periodical and Serial Publications

Articles in serial publications are cited in footnotes by the publication title, followed by some combination of serial identifiers (for newspapers the date; for Russian journals the year and issue number; for Western journals the volume and issue numbers and the year), then page references if required, and the names of authors if known and appropriate.

American Economic Review (journal).
Australian Journal of Politics and History (journal).
Bulletins on Soviet Economic Development (occasional papers of the University of Birmingham).
Cahiers du Monde russe (journal).
Demoscope Weekly (internet journal, available at http://demoscope.ru/weekly/).
Economic History Review (journal).
Economist (The) (newspaper).
Ekonomicheskaya zhizn' (newspaper).
Europe Asia Studies (journal, formerly *Soviet Studies*).
Explorations in Economic History (journal).
Finansovo-khozyaistvennoe zakonodatel'stvo (journal).
Industriya (newspaper).
International Affairs (journal).
Istoricheskii arkhiv (journal).
Izvestiya (newspaper).
Journal of Comparative Economics.
Journal of Development Economics.
Journal of Economic History.
Journal of Economic Literature.
Journal of Strategic Studies.
Molodaya gvardiya (journal).
Osnovnye pokazateli vypolneniya narodno-khozyaistvennogo plana za... (monthly journal of TsUNKhU SSSR, circulated for official use only).
Otechestvennaya istoriya (journal).
Plan (journal).
Planovoe khozyaistvo (journal).
Pravda (newspaper).
Review of Economic Studies (journal).
Review of Economics and Statistics (journal).
Rossiskaya istoriya (journal).
Slavic Review (journal).
Sotsiologicheskie issledovaniya (journal).
Soviet Studies (journal, now *Europe-Asia Studies*).
Studies in East European and Soviet Planning, Development, and Trade (occasional papers of the University of Indiana).
Vestnik statistiki (journal).
Vestnik Tambovskogo universiteta (journal).
Voprosy istorii (journal).
Voprosy istorii KPSS (journal).
Za industrializatsiyu (newspaper).

Internet Sources

Internet sources are cited in footnotes by the author and date of publication, or by the title of the document or website, followed by the uniform resource locator.

Bogoyavlenskii D. D., 'O pripiskakh v perepisi 1939 g.' Demoscope Weekly (14 October 2013), at http://demoscope.ru/weekly/2013/0571/arxiv01.php (accessed April 11, 2017).

Davies, R. W., review of R. C. Allen, *Farm to factory: A reinterpretation of the Soviet industrial revolution* on EH.net (June 2004), at http://eh.net/book_reviews/farm-to-factory-a-reinterpretation-of-the-soviet-industrial-revolution/ (accessed November 17, 2017).

Dexter, K., and Rodionov, I., 'The factories, research and design establishments of the Soviet defence industry: a guide: ver. 18,' University of Warwick, Department of Economics (2017), at http://warwick.ac.uk/vpk/ (accessed September 3, 2017).

'Eikhe, Robert Indrikovich,' on Wikpedia at https://ru.wikipedia.org/wiki/Эйхе,_Роберт_Индрикович (accessed December 8, 2017).

Maddison, A., 'Statistics on world population, GDP, and per capita GDP' (2010), at http://www.ggdc.net/maddison/oriindex.htm (accessed December 1, 2010).

Melbourne gateway to research on Soviet history (Stalin's meetings day by day), at http://www.melgrosh.unimelb.edu.au/php/pol_meeting.php (accessed May 5, 2017).

Muralova, Yu., 'O tom, chto nikogda ne zabudetsya' (1990), at http://scepsis.net/library/id_3568.html (accessed October 25, 2018).

Narodnoe khozyaistvo SSSR za 1913–1955 gg. (1955), available at http://istmat.info/files/uploads/36699/narodnoe_hozyaystvo_sssr_za_1913-1955_gg.pdf (accessed December 17, 2017).

'Proekt obvinitel'nogo zaklyucheniya po delu "Antisovetskogo parvo-trotskistskogo bloka." 21 yanvarya 1938 g.' (1938), at http://istmat.info/node/40171 (accessed October 25, 2018).

Rodionov, I., 'Chronology of the aviation and aircraft industry of Russia and the Soviet Union, 1916 to 1946, Version 11' (2016), at http://warwick.ac.uk/aviaprom/ (accessed September 3, 2017).

Unpublished Working Papers

Unpublished papers are cited in footnotes by the author and date of draft, followed by 'working paper'.

Allen, R. C., and Khaustova, E., 'Russian real wages before and after 1917 in global perspective,' Discussion Papers in Economic and Social History no. 158, University of Oxford (2017).

Bishop, I., and Wheatcroft, S. G., 'Modelling the influence of weather conditions on historical grain yields in the Soviet Union,' Working Paper, University of Melbourne (in preparation).

Castañeda Dower, P., and Markevich, A., 'The Stolypin reform and agricultural productivity in late imperial Russia,' SSRN Working Paper (2018) at https://papers.ssrn.com/sol3/papers.cfm?abstract_id=2361860 (accessed January 16, 2018). Forthcoming in the European Review of Economic History.

Gregg A., and Nafziger, S., 'Capital structure and corporate performance in late imperial Russia,' Department of Economics Working Papers 2016–2012, Williams College (2016).

Nakonechnyi, M. 'Factory of invalids: Mortality, disability and early release on medical grounds in GULAG, 1930–1955: A historiographic essay,' Working Paper, University of Oxford (2017).

Pollock, E., 'Conversations with Stalin on questions of political economy,' Working Paper No. 33, International Cold War History Project, Washington, DC (2001).

Index of Names

R. W. Davies et al., *The Industrialisation of Soviet Russia Volume 7: The Soviet Economy and the Approach of War, 1937–1939*,
https://doi.org/10.1057/978-1-137-36238-4

Index of Subjects

R. W. Davies et al., *The Industrialisation of Soviet Russia Volume 7: The Soviet Economy and the Approach of War, 1937–1939*,
https://doi.org/10.1057/978-1-137-36238-4

D

E

F

GPSR Compliance
The European Union's (EU) General Product Safety Regulation (GPSR) is a set of rules that requires consumer products to be safe and our obligations to ensure this.

If you have any concerns about our products, you can contact us on

ProductSafety@springernature.com

In case Publisher is established outside the EU, the EU authorized representative is:

Springer Nature Customer Service Center GmbH
Europaplatz 3
69115 Heidelberg, Germany

www.ingramcontent.com/pod-product-compliance
Lightning Source LLC
Chambersburg PA
CBHW071639030826
49219CB00005B/271
9781137362377